THE GIRL IN THE K.

THE GIRL IN THE KINGS ARMS

YVONNE MANDEVILLE

© Yvonne Mandeville, 2018

Published by Crowning Glory Publishing Ltd

All rights reserved. No part of this book may be reproduced, adapted, stored in a retrieval system or transmitted by any means, electronic, mechanical, photocopying, or otherwise without the prior written permission of the author.

The rights of Yvonne Mandeville to be identified as the author of this work have been asserted in accordance with the Copyright, Designs and Patents Act 1988.

A CIP catalogue record for this book is available from the British Library.

ISBN 978-1-9996863-0-7

Book layout and cover design by Clare Brayshaw

Prepared and printed by:

York Publishing Services Ltd
64 Hallfield Road
Layerthorpe
York YO31 7ZQ

Tel: 01904 431213

Website: www.yps-publishing.co.uk

I have written this book from my own memory, prompted a few times by old photos, school reports etc., and also from the recollections of people who knew me as a child. Everything I have said is totally true, although some names and events have been changed to protect the privacy of persons still alive.

"Memory is the diary that we all carry about with us."
Oscar Wilde

ACKNOWLEDGEMENTS

I might not have had the confidence to go forward to publication of this book without the backing of the following people who believe in me...

First and foremost my thanks go to Flora, who has confided in me, and given me her love and her blessing to write about her experiences as a child at the Kings Arms.

Aunty Hilda, who has given me her love and support in writing my story.

My childhood friends, Georgie, Emma and Alison, who unbeknown to them, gave me the solace that I needed, and who have now given me their permission to write about our lifelong friendships.

Margaret Smillie at BKF, my literary solicitor, for her excellent advice and for legalising my book.

Sarah Goodwin, my proof reader, and for her positive comments.

Nico Evans at MCPS, Leah Mack at Sony/ATV, Ebony Reid at Peermusic, Jenifer Baptiste at Carlin Music and Tim Hayes at Warner/ Chappell for their help in getting permission to use the various lines of songs I have quoted - with special thanks to Donovan.

Kevin Pearson - 21st Century Internet - for his website design.

Duncan, David, Clare and Cathi at York Publishing Services - for their help, advice, and for bringing my book to fruition.

Last, but not least, my husband Michael, for believing in me and encouraging me to continue with my writing when it all got too much for me, and I felt that I could no longer carry on...

Thank you all so much.

CREDITS

PREFACE

Essex these days is portrayed by the media as a land made of brass, where the women have big hair and big lips, and the men have big wallets, the houses huge and made of steel and glass, and there is an awful lot of kitsch.

Not so. Essex is wonderful, and so are the people. To the visitor, who these days is usually only passing through, Essex may seem flat and boring, but it has the longest coastline of any English county covering nearly 400 miles, and also more acres of agricultural land than any other county in Britain. Yes, towns are now bigger and greyer, motorways are now longer and wider, but still the fields and meadows stretch to the horizon, with little villages dating back hundreds of years, nestling amongst those green and corn yellow expanses.

This was the Essex in which I grew up, in the fifties and early sixties. This was the countryside that I knew and loved. The fields that were my escape... To anyone else, my world – the village – my life growing up in my grandparents' pub, may have seemed privileged. But my home life was one of silent sadness and despair.

Those were the days that may have scarred me for life.

This is my story...

PART 1

THE INFANT AND PRIMARY YEARS

The Birth Of Spring

The fresh green leaves shimmered on the newly clothed trees in the spring sunshine. It was unusual to have such a warm and sunny day in March, but this day was bathed in a bright midday warmth that made people smile in anticipation of better things to come. Things had been hard during the war, and in the years following, but now, with the joy of being reunited with loved ones, and many babies being born, the feeling of post-war euphoria was still in everyone's hearts.

Dogs yapped behind garden fences to no avail at the odd passer-by, and cats lounged on front garden paths, luxuriating in the warmth of the spring sunshine. Band music was dancing through open windows from wirelesses that sometimes crackled and sometimes resonated with the deep tones of King's English accents.

Sweetly scented violets were shyly showing their faces in the woods, pale yellow primroses adorned the hedgerows and golden daffodils nodded in unison in the village's front gardens, welcoming the spring – and the new baby girl that was about to enter this new world.

"Now push – push..." the stern midwife instructed the young mother giving birth in the village hospital. She didn't see the sunshine streaming through the third window on the left of the maternity wing. She was only aware of the intensive and overwhelming pain of giving birth.

"Mrs. Mandeville – you have a baby girl", the midwife informed as the new mother gave one last agonising push. She turned her head to one side, not looking at the new life held firmly in the midwife's stout hands. The baby took her first breath and let out a weak cry.

"Do you want to see your baby?" the midwife asked, wrapping the tiny pink baby in a white towel.

But my mother didn't answer.

An Appropriate Name

"She's ginger!" my father exclaimed later that Saturday in the pub, as he wetted my blonde haired head with a substantial toast.

"Of course she's not ginger" my grandmother scolded, informing him that a baby's red head can make fine blonde hair look that colour.

"I tell you she's ginger!" my father laughed, jokingly looking around the smoke filled bar for a suitable culprit.

"It's not me!" joked ginger-haired Jim when my father spotted him, and whose wife was five months pregnant. "I haven't been *that* busy..."

"And what are you going to name her?" people were asking, as pints were pulled and glasses chinked.

My father paused. "I don't know" he pondered. "Joan didn't say..."

~

It was my maternal grandmother, Nanny Felstead, who suggested Yvonne. My mother agreed, and I don't think my father would have been afforded any opinion in the matter...

The name originally came to Britain with the Norman invasion. It seems strange to me that all those years ago there were women in Britain called Yvonne. However, the name soon went out of usage. Probably something to do with King Harold being defeated! Who would want to give their child a French name then? At the beginning of the 20th Century, Yvonne was the seventh most popular name in France.

The name means "Yew", the sacred tree with so many mystical connotations. But these days it has come to be associated with a much darker meaning... "Operation Yew Tree..." Little did I know when I first looked into the history of my name, how apt the meaning was to me...

It is only in recent years that I have found out more about the dark and sinister things that went on at the pub. From what I have been told, it seems that the Kings Arms was even worse than what I had known about when I lived there.

I was sworn to secrecy by my mother, who threatened me that if ever I "told" anyone *anything* about what went on I would be taken away to the children's home in Essex. It was run by nuns, and as unfair as it may sound, we children in Orsett feared the nuns. I don't know why it was, but we were told to stay well away from them. Even when walking along Grays High Street, if any were coming towards us – we would cross over the road to avoid them. Hence it was a great fear of mine to be sent there. And so – I always kept quiet.

Looking back, I am now so angry that my parents put me into such a dangerous situation, and at such an early age.

"Give her here" Nell had said, as she kindly took me from my parents' cottage up the road to live with my grandparents at the pub. Nell was my grandfather's live-in mistress – and housekeeper – who slept with him in his dark and foreboding bedroom.

He had met Nell at his sister's pub in Kent and had brought her over to the Kings Arms to live with him – as well as *her sister* Lil. Lil had left when her husband came home from the war, but Nell stayed, as somehow she suited him – she must have been a perfect match. My parents knew all that went on in that pub, with my mother being very aware of what my grandfather and Nell were like. And yet – they let me go there to live without a care for my welfare.

"Your mother couldn't cope with your crying all the time" my father told me once, and even though gin was put in my milk to make me sleep, I still cried. Maybe it was something to do with the fact that the inside of my mouth was often covered with ulcers. Maybe though that could have had something to do with the gin!

Now all babies cry, but I think that although my mother was in her early twenties when I was born, she may have been rather too immature to have a child. Or it could be the fact that being a misogynist, she was rather disappointed at giving birth to a baby girl? She did make that clear to me on many occasions throughout my childhood.

"Girls are horrible" she would say, "boys are so much nicer..." which didn't help me at all when I spent my life trying to please everyone...

A Little Cinderella

Some years ago a friend sent me a greetings card which featured meanings for the name Yvonne. Amongst yew tree and archer meanings, it suggested that my name can also mean a "Cinderella" type, which considering I was born a Saturday Child who "works hard for a living", as the old rhyme goes, is very apt.

Even though I was so young, I should have realised what was in store for me when I was a little girl, pre-school age. My parents suddenly disappeared without telling me anything, but my grandmother told me they had gone on holiday. I think they had gone to Wales.

I clearly remember the day they came back though – I was sitting on the little stool in the kitchen and they came through the kitchen door. Although they weren't the archetypal parents, sending me to live at the pub with my grandparents when I was just a baby, I was aware of a sense of "connection" to them and hated the fact that they had just disappeared.

I didn't smile when they came into the kitchen, even though they had brought me back a present – and my face dropped even more when I saw what it was... It wasn't a normal holiday memento for a little girl, like a little Welsh girl doll or something similar, nor anything to do with their holiday at all – it was a red dustpan and brush! Was that a precursor to what my life was going to be from then onwards? It was telling me so much...

~

Even as a very young girl this little Cinderella had to work hard doing domestic chores and helping in the pub. With no domestic machines, I had to do dish washing and wiping up, using only soda crystals for the dish washing, or sometimes Tide laundry powder – and with no rubber gloves. Nell even used to use Brillo pads just using her bare hands – it used to make me cringe! I had to help with the laundry, polishing, clearing and cleaning tables, help with the cooking, picking up litter, stacking bottles on shelves, all those sort of things.

Washing the glasses and crockery for the pub had to be done particularly meticulously, and we had two sinks – one for washing and the other for rinsing. It was as late as 1960 when Fairy Liquid was first introduced, that we had something available that was more effective than the soda crystals or Tide to use. Even so, my grandfather was reluctant to have such a luxury. He didn't have to do any washing-up...

I also had to learn how to iron, using an old black iron that was heated up on the fire. The only protection for my little hands was a piece of old cloth wrapped around the handle. That iron was so heavy to lift all the time, and my right arm would ache so much. I would use a rectangular shaped bottle filled with water that had a blue sprinkler on the top for dampening the laundry for easier ironing, but it was still such a chore.

Nell did the laundry – sometimes with my help – by boiling cotton items in what was known as a large "copper", which resided in the "cook house", and took ages to heat up to boiling point. Then, amidst all the steam, one or the other of us would pummel the laundry with something that resembled a baseball bat. Other washing was done in an old tin bath using a washboard to help get things clean. Emptying this could be a problem, so it would be used by the drain outside the cook house next to the cellar flap. No matter how cold it might be, Nell would kneel down on the ground, sleeves rolled up, and with bare hands pummelling away at the washing and rubbing it against the washboard.

All washing was then rinsed in the tin bath – by hand of course – using a Reckitts "Blue bag", to brighten the whites with a blue hue. But why would people want their whites to have a blue hue? This little muslin bag of blue brightener was then dissolved in the water by swishing it around with your hand. Hmm – a blue-hued hand is *not* a good look... But that was not the *end* of the washing procedure...

Then came the final rinse in starch water, using Robin powdered starch, which again had to be carefully mixed with water so as not to have any lumps. After the washing was all swished around in that, it was then put through a mangle a few times before being pegged on to the washing line, using wooden, hand-carved "dolly" pegs that we had bought from the gypsies who lived down on the fen. That mangle though – it looked rather like a torture implement! I used to be terrified that one day my little fingers might be caught in that green iron monster as I helped to push the washing through!

I can't help but wonder whether anyone was actually bothered that the disgusting animal intestines – or "lights" – were cooked in the copper too!

~

The "cook house" was an old stone building attached to the pub, with a rickety ladder going up to the loft above it, where my grandfather kept all manner of strange things, including dark blue coloured bottles with stoppers marked with "skulls and crossbones". Those bottles used to worry me, because I guessed that they contained something rather ominous, and I knew I must never touch them. Little did I know then just what the contents of those sinister bottles may have been used for...

One day I must have been very adventurous and had climbed up the ladder to the musty-smelling loft on my own. It was a home-made ladder and the steps slanted downwards so I had to be very careful, but it felt quite an achievement climbing that ladder all by myself.

In the loft there was a bag of women's clothing – and I was curious – so I looked inside. Some items had been shredded by mice, but there was something else in there – it was a pair of women's knickers – totally blood-stained all over.

This was long before I knew anything about periods, but thinking back, this was no menstrual blood – it was more than that. Besides, if it had been, then the knickers would have either been washed or thrown away. They wouldn't have been just put in a bag with other women's clothing – and it certainly wasn't a bag for the rag and bone man.

~

The cook house was so named because that was where the "lights" were cooked for the animals. How I hated going in there when *they* were cooking! The smell was atrocious – absolutely sickening. I also hated seeing them hanging up waiting to be cooked. I soon got to know what internal organs looked like!

I have a memory of being very small and being shut in there. I don't know how that happened, but I remember being in that awful dark place, looking around and feeling bewildered. I felt cold, and I went over to the small window on the roadside, but it was covered with mud, splashed from the road, so I couldn't see out.

I feel sure my arms were bare because I can feel myself now, hugging myself, trying to get warm. I looked up at the partly whitewashed walls that were flaking and showing bare patches of grey. There was greeny-grey mould growing in the corners. I didn't know it was mould at the time, but I remember the dank smell that it exuded, and the shocking pink colour of the lights that hung on the wall.

I was also afraid of the mice that lived in there – at that age, I didn't know that they were timid, and were probably hiding from me. One of our cats had recently caught one in there. He had very proudly looked at me, with the mouse's wriggling tail hanging out of his mouth, and then he crunched – and swallowed. Seeing that was so horrible, but a cat's digestive system is designed to eat mice whole.

When I was eventually let out, it was dusk. The door was opened and I walked up the steps, and all the lights were on in the pub. To this day I can't remember how I got shut in there, nor who let me out. All I can remember is the pervading smell of the mould and cow's innards – and most of all – the fear. It was really frightening being shut in there...

It was also to the cook house that my grandfather would take me to pull out my milk teeth when they became loose. I used to be terrified when he took me in there to, quite unnecessarily, yank out a tooth. No-one ever stopped him, even though everyone knew how frightening it was for me to be held still by this huge man to have that done. Subsequently, if ever I felt a tooth coming loose, I would keep biting into an apple to try to loosen it more myself.

It wasn't just me who experienced pain in the cook house. I was just a little girl when I saw my grandfather give Nell an almighty punch into the pit of her stomach in there. I will never forget the look on her face.

Her eyes and mouth were contorted into an excruciating agony that at that young age I had never seen before. She looked straight ahead at me as she fell down onto the cold stone floor. He didn't care that I was in the doorway, having just appeared looking for Nell. Maybe he wanted me to see what punishment naughty girls who didn't do as they were told could expect.

My grandmother was also a victim of his sadistic violent abuse. In later years my mother told me that at some time my grandmother had been pregnant with her second child. My grandfather had punched her so hard into the pit of her stomach too, so that she lost the baby.

One day I was unwell with flu and was home from school. There was a lot of noise coming from the kitchen at the opposite end of the landing, then hurried footsteps, and my mother burst into the bedroom ordering me to stay in there until I was told I could come out. Nanny was screaming.

According to my mother, my grandmother had boiled a large fatty bacon joint on top of the stove – it had been cooling down and was covered in grease. It was just as well that it had cooled somewhat, because my grandfather had tipped it all over her head – just after he had wrapped a wet tea towel around her neck, and pulled it tight. My mother told me that this is what had happened, but she had obviously not tried to stop him. To her mind it seemed that if her father wanted to do something bad – *anything* – then no-one should try to stop him...

When I was eventually let out of the bedroom, Nell was still washing my grandmother's hair over the kitchen sink, trying to get rid of all the grease. Nanny looked in a terrible state of shock. She was still crying and had raw red marks around her neck. Why hadn't my mother done anything about it? Why had she not called the police? Should she have at least called a doctor? No, nothing was ever reported, and as always, I was told – *not to say a word...*

~

And so I lived in fear. Always trying to please my mother and my grandfather. Together they ruled the pub. I wasn't allowed to express my dislike and fear of doing things that I really didn't want to do. Neither could I tell anyone outside of the pub what was going on. There was always that threat of the children's home, the possibility of physical punishment, and of course, my mother's wrath...

I tried to run away a few times. Even though I was probably only around seven years old, I would get out of bed, go outside in my nightdress, then walk up Baker Street in the dark. It was quite a long road, and most of the way being without a path.

It was also so dark. We only had gas lights along Baker Street to the end of the houses, which were lit in the evenings by the gas lighter man who wore a bowler-type hat. So stepping out of the somewhat dimly-lit road at the end of the houses and into the very black darkness that might possibly lead me somewhere was very daunting. But I just wanted to get away from the pub – no matter where the path might lead me.

Then the A13 would come into sight and I would walk up to the edge of the road. Whenever I reached that road though, I was afraid to cross it, because I didn't really know where to go and I had never crossed a main road before. The roads then were fairly quiet, although I can't help but wonder how many people in cars might have seen me – a little girl in her nightdress walking at the side of the road – in the dark...

So then I would turn around and walk back down to the pub again. I would go upstairs, and back to bed, and no-one ever knew I had been gone...

~

Even as young as the tender age of just nine, I was made to serve behind the bar sometimes. As unbelievable as it may sound, my mother put make-up on me to make me look older – a little bit of pale pink powder on my face, bright pink rouge on my cheeks, and her cherry red lipstick – goodness knows what I looked like! Being so young, I can't imagine that it really made me look old enough to be serving behind the bar. I don't think any of the customers were bothered about that though.

"Now just get behind that bar – and put a smile on your face" my mother would command if ever I tried to express my feelings about it.

Sometimes she would say "now get into that bar – and show yourself off". Show myself off? What was there to show off? That I was a little girl, being made to do things far beyond my years? A little girl being made to be a barmaid, someone to joke with – and leer at?

I hated being behind the bar so much. I was very shy, and it was so embarrassing pulling pints when I could hardly reach the pumps – but I soon learned to pull a perfect pint! My mother also told me to never take any notice of what men said to me. "You may not understand some of the things they say to you" she said, "but *just smile...*" As it happened, most of the customers were locals, well, in the public bar – or as we knew it, the taproom – they were. There were sometimes people that I didn't know in the saloon bar, and I wasn't terribly keen to be in there. Some men would look over the bar at me in a strange sort of way, but it was probably because such a little girl had such pink cheeks and red lips! Maybe though that could be very appealing to some men...

~

Sometimes I had to stay up until late at night after the pub had closed. Nell would bring my nightdress down to me, and then I would have to undress and put it on in front of the fire in the saloon bar. I hadn't started to develop, but I still found it embarrassing. I really didn't like it, but I had to do as I was told. There were usually a few men sitting around after time, and they would watch me. They weren't locals, and normally I didn't know any of them, apart from one who was Fred Sawger, my grandmother's boyfriend, who stayed and slept with her on Saturday nights. Apart from Fred, my only recollection of what the other men looked like were of them wearing dark clothes, possibly suits. Looking back now, I can't help but wonder whether there was more to it.

~

One afternoon when I was ten years old, I can't remember what had happened, but something must have been just too much for me – and I walked out. It wasn't just going out to play, for my heart was drawing me somewhere else... I walked up to the top of Baker Street and stood at the edge of the A13. Then for the first time ever, I crossed over to what I saw as sanctuary on the other side.

I walked all the way through Orsett Heath until I reached Chadwell St. Mary. Then I kept walking until I somehow found my Auntie Hilda's house – nearly two miles in all. Goodness knows how I found it – all I knew was what the house looked like, the name of the road, and that it was opposite the cemetery.

She was naturally very surprised to see me, and asked me in.

"Have you eaten dear?" she asked, with a concerned expression on her face.

Well no, I hadn't. I hadn't even thought about eating before I went on the long walk finding my way over to her house.

"Er no", I answered shyly.

"Well you must have something to eat dear" she said kindly, going to the kitchen. She made me some strawberry jam sandwiches, which were the best strawberry jam sandwiches I had ever eaten! Of course they were, having been made by Auntie Hilda. She watched me quietly as I enjoyed them, sitting on her soft settee. She sat upright on the armchair opposite, with her hands folded sedately in her lap, and smiling gently. Goodness knows what had led me off in her direction that day, but I loved every minute I spent with her.

She telephoned the pub and said I was there with her. I don't think anyone was bothered really. I stayed the afternoon with Auntie Hilda, and then my father picked me up once he was home from work in the evening. Nobody asked me why I had gone to see her, or even how I had found my way. Nobody was interested.

~

As well as being my grandfather's mistress, Nell was also general dogsbody for my grandmother. She cleaned the pub too, rising at six in the morning to clean the floors dirty from the night before, etc. We didn't exactly have spittoons or sawdust on the floor, but sometimes the morning after a raucous night in the taproom could seem like a scene from a Western bar.

Nell also cooked the breakfasts, got me ready for school when the time came, and took me to school, all before working in our shop all day. The shop was next door to my grandfather's cottages at the end of our garden, in one of which my parents lived at the time.

Sometimes, early on autumn mornings, Nell and I would go across the damp, mist-laden fields, looking for cowpats to gather mushrooms for my grandfather's breakfast, which he always preferred to be cooked without being washed! It was a long, long time before I was brave enough to try a mushroom myself...

I remember the chill of those mornings, and how the mist hung low over the fields. But I learned to know the difference between mushrooms and toadstools. Just as well I did really. Hmm...

I also had to help Nell in the shop, which was much nicer than working in the pub. The "Trailer Man" would arrive every Thursday. He was the bringer of all kinds of sweets in large jars that stood on the shelves and were weighed out in ounces into little brown paper bags. I used to love going into his trailer and helping Nell choose which sweets to sell.

Then there were the large tea chests delivered that contained bananas and grapes from far-away places. When we unpacked them I had to wipe them because they were sticky, and the tiny cork pieces that they were packed in used to stick to them. That was quite a job, especially as I was always worried that there might be a foreign spider in there! I enjoyed helping Nell though, and at least it was usually women who came to the shop.

A lot of the items for sale were in dark blue plain packets, with just a small label saying what it was. Things like flour, sugar, and sanitary towels. I didn't know what they were, because they were deemed to be "secret" things that I shouldn't ask about. "You will find out one day" Nell said mysteriously. I soon learned not to ask questions about the unknown contents of some of the packets...

The women who lived in Baker Street and who were her main customers, would come over to the shop all looking basically the same. They wore wraparound floral patterned overalls, had scarves in a "turban" over their hair, with metal curlers sticking out at the front, and had their Lisle stockings rolled down to their ankles above their fur-trimmed slippers. It was a sort of uniform in a way.

Nell had a chair in the corner on the customer side of the shop, where these women would sit and chat. It must have been the highlight of their day. Oh the gossip that went on – no-one escaped! I gleaned lots of little snippets about life from those women gossiping behind their hands. One woman told Nell one day that she had something growing between her legs that wobbled as she walked – goodness knows what *that* might have been... I wasn't there at the time, but I was there when Nell was telling my mother and grandmother about it! Did they really think that I wasn't hearing what they were talking about? Did they even care? Well I did hear these things that were being talked about – and I haven't forgotten them. That poor unfortunate woman, along with others, didn't know that what she confided to Nell, would later that day be related to my mother and grandmother.

~

No-one ever spoke about goings-on at the pub though. I could have told them a few tales if I'd had a mind to... But I didn't of course – I always kept quiet.

That little shop, with its high wooden shutters that closed off the window for the night, was also where I learned to iron in the back room, with the old black iron that had to be heated on the fire in the corner. I began by ironing my grandfather's handkerchiefs, with their bold monogrammed *"A"* in the corner, always having to make sure that it stood out in the corner of the final fold. Then I went on to tea towels, pillowcases and sheets. All the time I had to keep re-heating the iron on the fire.

Curiously, there was a bed in that back room too. I don't remember Nell ever sleeping there, but it must have been there for a reason...

~

As well as running the shop and cleaning the pub, Nell also served in the bar in the evenings, and then made supper for us all at eleven o'clock after the pub closed. One might wonder why she stayed there, but she had this strange attraction to my grandfather – she was besotted with him and, as I have since found out, shared his warped sense of sexual pleasures, which held her to him, no matter what he did.

Nell had left her husband, her daughter Flora, and her two little sons when Flora was only nine years old – six years before I was born – so as her father was in the Navy, Flora too spent her childhood living with her grandparents. As I have said before, my grandfather had previously taken Nell's sister Lil home to live at the pub as his mistress, and then once he met Nell, she also took a place in his bed. He wanted her too – and just *had* to have her...

Somehow though, Flora never seemed to mind that as well as being her mother's charge, I had also become Nell's surrogate daughter. I loved Flora – I always have done. I still do. She was pretty, with brown wavy hair, and twinkling blue eyes that always smiled at me, and she was also very kind. No-one would have ever guessed what secrets she held about her times spent at the pub, secrets that she *too* had to keep to herself...

~

Although Nell had left her three children, she kept everything from her past with her, literally all the time – in her soft cream leather handbag. These keepsakes consisted of a photo of her children, with Flora as a young girl about nine years old, looking very pretty with her hair in plaits, sitting with her two younger brothers, and one of a young man wearing an army uniform. It wasn't the normal British army uniform, he was wearing a brimmed hat with one side of the brim turned up.

There were also some strange cards that she liked showing me sometimes. A picture of conjoined twins that, although intriguing, disturbed me, and made me wonder about all sorts of things regarding two people being joined together physically forever. It wasn't something I needed to think about at such a young age. There was also a picture of a bearded lady, who I later found out that, along with the conjoined twins, would be displayed at Victorian fairs and circuses as curios that people would pay to see. I would ponder upon these strange images, and worry about them sometimes.

There was also a joke postcard of a little girl looking up a woman's skirt saying "Oh Auntie – so that's where you keep the hairbrush!"

Such peculiar things for her to keep with her photos, and which I didn't understand at the time. Whenever Nell got them out of her handbag to show me, I was always intrigued by that handsome young man in the army uniform. At least I know now, after all these years, who he was... He was Nell's brother Jack, which makes it even more sad that her handbag was stolen, especially as they were the only two photos she had – and they were both family.

Another one of her cards that stays in my mind is of a young woman clad in a long skirt and shawl trudging away from a cottage, holding a baby wrapped in a blanket. Snow is everywhere and still falling. Her father is standing in the doorway of the cottage looking very mean, with his arm outstretched and pointing to the snow-laden horizon – shouting "GO!"... I didn't know what that card was all about at the time. I just guessed that the poor young woman had done something very wrong, and was cast out of the family to fend for herself in the depths of winter...

That particular card was one that really struck me; there was an emotion about it, and something so very disturbing. That image and its connotation have stayed with me all my life...

~

The customers at the pub were mainly the locals, the domino players, the darts team, and anyone who just wanted to sit either alone or chatting, whilst enjoying a pint or two in the taproom. They would either walk or cycle there, and the cycle rack was always full up on Sunday mornings. My grandfather would play dominoes with all the old boys every evening, as always wearing his yellow check waistcoat. The, let's just say snottier, customers who frequented the saloon bar on a Sunday morning, would usually arrive by car – or on horse! – but it's fair to say that we normally knew most of the people who came to the pub.

One day though, when I was at school, I came home to find Nell very distressed. She told me that there had been two tall black men in the saloon bar, wearing white or light coloured suits – it was unusual to see strangers at the time, especially as they were wearing such striking clothes. There was nothing untoward about them, and they seemed very friendly and polite.

Nell was serving in the bar that lunchtime and, as always, she kept her handbag under the bar counter. At one point, she had gone round to the taproom to get something, and when she went back to the saloon bar the two men had gone – along with her handbag.

For days we all searched and searched the lanes, and the ditches, thinking that they might have just taken the little money she had in her bag, and then thrown the handbag away. But it was all in vain. Everything from her past had gone. All she had had was a photo of her children, and one very special man. But now those images were gone...

Forever.

Living The Fairy Tale

Once upon a time (or rather once a month on a Wednesday if I was not at school)... I was able to escape into another world. A fairy tale world where everything was good, and people were loving and nice. Nell, who I saw as my fairy godmother at the time, and who *was* literally my godmother, would magic me away to the land the other side of the Thames, the land called Kent. That is when I would spend delightful times with her daughter Flora and her family.

As far back as I can remember we did this.

~

In a state of melancholy, my grandmother once told me that she had urged Nell to "go back to see her poor three children". I knew that she was purely thinking of Flora and her two little brothers – and not of Nell's relationship with my grandfather. I think my grandmother had accepted this – there was nothing else she could do.

So Nell *did* go back to her mother's house to see the three children that she had abandoned when Flora was nine years old, and continued to do so – but sometimes in the school holidays, she also took Flora back to the pub with her... What happened then is something I will address later...

~

At five years old I had been Flora's bridesmaid when, at the age of twenty she married Bernard, a much older man with two sons, one a year older than me, and the other two years older.

I was the youngest bridesmaid, and I wore an eau-de-nil coloured bridesmaid's dress, which had large hoops stitched into the skirt, like a crinoline dress straight out of the 1840's. With my little white patent shoes with their large oversized silver buckles, and the flower basket, I must have looked very much the part. The other two bridesmaids wore soft flowing dresses in shades of lilac and yellow. It wasn't unusual in those days to have bridesmaids' dresses that didn't match – unlike today, when everything has to be matched to perfection, thus creating what can sometimes be a rather stilted formality.

Flora's wedding was very pretty, the other two bridesmaids were directly behind Flora as she walked up the aisle to meet her husband-to-be, and I was behind them. People were turning round and smiling, and I remember people looking at me, that little girl with the crinoline dress and basket of flowers and going "ahh..." as I slowly walked by. I was very shy, but it was nice being smiled at with genuinely kind pleasure.

~

With an early morning start Nell and I would embark on that long journey, taking our fairy coach, i.e. the green No.53 country bus, from our village to the local town, and then another bus to the Tilbury ferry. This took us over the Hair Pin Bridge – so named because of its shape! To the right of the bridge was a block of sombre looking flats called "The Dwellings" and I was told that this was where the "poor people" lived. That instilled a fear in me of never wanting to be a "poor person".

I can't help but think though, that those children who lived in The Dwellings may have had a happier home life than me.

I loved it on the ferry boat. It was somewhat romantic knowing that King Henry VIII had started it with a small rowing boat, and later decreed that there would always be a ferry at Tilbury. And so to this day, despite the Dartford Crossing, the Tilbury ferry still runs.

We would sit on the deck on those large, slatted wood, chest-like seats, and the adventure would begin all over again. But oh how I hated those steep open steps over the water to the landing stage at Gravesend. I always felt that I would fall through, straight down into that murky brown water that swished around with the roll of the boat, threatening to drag me under. I always felt sure that I was so thin that I would easily slip through those awful steps...

Then it was a quick jaunt up the lovely old Gravesend High Street to the Chatham bus stop, where we took the bus to Chatham, going past the farmers' market, where they sold sheep and cows, then changing there for yet another bus journey through the countryside, passing through Borstal, where we would see the Borstal boys working in the fields. Then finally to Flora's village.

Nell and I would call in at the little shop next to the bus stop and buy some of their delicious freshly cooked ham, sliced off the bone, some for Flora, and some to take home, back to the pub. That little shop is now a house, as I suppose there's not much call for shops like that now, what with people having cars. Somehow, the ham in supermarkets has never tasted as good as the ham from that little shop though.

Flora would always cook chipolatas and home-made chips. Those chipolatas were so much better than the coarse home-made sausages with their tough, chewy sheep's intestine coverings that we would get from Mr. Dodd's, the local village butcher at home. We never had chipolatas at the pub, just those big fat sausages.

Flora always called her chipolatas "chips", so it could be somewhat confusing when being asked how many I would like!

Sometimes we would all go to another village, to see Nell's mother, sister and brothers. Nell's mother lived in a small terraced house in a small narrow street, where she had brought up not only Nell and her brothers, but also Flora and her brothers, and other children at times. There was a sweet shop along the road on the corner, where she would take me to buy me some treat. As an adult I have been back to the village and tried to find that little sweet shop – but it is no longer there. Another house I imagine.

"Nanny" as I called Nell's mother, for I really believed that she was another grandmother, was such a lovely, kindly sort of woman, with a round smiling face, permed grey hair, and she always wore an apron. She had brought up Flora and her brothers, when Nell had abandoned them, but there was never any animosity shown towards her daughter, nor indeed to me, who she treated as though I was another granddaughter.

Flora has told me a little tale about how her grandmother would make food stretch... For instance if she was making cheese sandwiches and, as would normally be the case, didn't have enough cheese to stretch to everyone, she would say "before you bite into the sandwich – sniff the cheese – and that will make it seem that there's more in it." Flora said that really did work!

Not far from the house, there were some allotments. Strangely, I can only picture them at twilight – they seemed to have some sort of eeriness to them, and an unexplainable chill pervading over them.

What I never knew then though – was what grave secrets the dark earth of those misty allotments held...

~

During the spring and summer months Flora, Nell and I would go for long walks up on the downs. It always intrigued me why the hills were called downs, but never mind, it was a lovely place to go.

We would walk for hours, picking small posies of primroses in the spring, and in the summer sitting on the soft grass just looking at the vast rural view over the Kent countryside. I loved being in this other land, the land that the ferryboat took us to – the other side of the rainbow. For this little Cinderella, there really was a pot of gold there – the precious gold that was Flora and her family...

This is an extract from a letter that Flora sent to me a few years ago, along with a photo of me with her other bridesmaids. The warmth and affection for me within its words is tangible...

"I used to enjoy walking on the downs, it brings back happy memories especially when you have got a small child (you) to point different things out. The lovely summer sunshine, the wild flowers, different little paths to wander, nut picking (hazelnuts), blackberries, seeing the wild roses. Sometimes walking down to the village brings back memories long gone. I wish we could go back in time. Did we ever walk along to the pub and have any lunch or crisps and lemonade do you remember? It is such a long time ago."

Yes, we did have crisps and lemonade – and it was a very good lunch!

I love the way that when Flora mentions that small child who pointed different things out – she said it was *me*...

~

Sometimes we would walk to Kit's Coty, and the nearby group of stones known as Little Kit's Coty or "The Countless Stones", which we would walk round and round, counting the stones. Of course, true to the legend, we never arrived at the same number twice. What magical days they always were.

Then, having had our "chips" and chips, it would be back on the long journey homewards and to catch the very last ferry. It was always dark by then, and Bernard would take us in his little car. He never used to hurry, but there was always time though for a drink in the stark, children's room of the little pub at the ferry.

I would have a bottle of Vimto, a burgundy coloured fruit flavoured fizzy drink, which I drank through a paper straw. I would suck and suck on that straw until it turned a strange shade of mauve, and Nell would have a glass of dark brown stout. Then it would be on to the pumpkin that took us back to the other side of the river.

On this trip back though, being dark and chilly on the river, we would go below deck, and stand and watch the rugged and dirty stokers down below at the furnaces, stoking the pungent-smelling coal for the journey. What a job they had in all that heat, and covered in black soot.

Then, after each long and weary, but very happy trip, Cinderella would be on her way back to the pub – for more work and heartache...

Earliest Memories

Over the years, whenever I have heard the instrumental version of Mario Lanza's "Loveliest Night of the Year" I have been transported directly back to being three years old, especially if it is played on a Wurlitzer organ. It is very rare to hear such a song these days, but sometimes I find I have it on my mind, and there I am – my first evening outside in the dark – and my parents taking me to the fairground.

It was a little unnerving going outside in the dark for the first time. How strange it was, breathing in the crisp evening air, and seeing the stars in the sky and the man in the moon for real, and not just through a window. I climbed into the back of my father's old black Morris, stepping onto the running board, then sitting on the brown leather seat. It felt cold on my legs, and I sat there looking at my shoes and wondering what was going to happen next.

It was only a short journey, so I imagine it wasn't far from the village. My father parked the car near some trees, and I could see the bright lights of the fairground. I had both arms up, holding my parents' hands as we walked along a rough pathway, the grass felt wet against my little legs in the evening air. There was a distinctive smell wafting from the fairground, which I have since realised was the smell of the raw steam, which powered the merry-go-rounds and other fairground rides. I was overawed by all the noise and the bright lights which reached up to the sky, and the various stalls where stall holders shouted out, inviting passers-by to "have a go". But above everything was the sound of the barrel organ, playing what I later found out to be "The Loveliest Night of the Year". They must have played that song over and over again, and that is the very first music I remember.

The olfactory sense is remarkable at transporting us back to certain situations regarding smell, but music also has the same effect on me. In fact a lot of my childhood memories are based on music, whether they are good or bad... The friendly sound of that barrel organ though, is one of the most evocative.

~

Something that was never music to my ears though was the sound of loud male guffaws, and the trundling of army trucks, which still disturb me even now. If ever I am out and I see army trucks coming along the road, I feel that same uneasiness as I did all those years ago...

Even in the very early fifties, there were still soldiers down at the army camp on the fens. They would come up to the pub in their khaki uniforms, and would get very drunk and loud – I was always frightened by them. Being so young I wanted to hide from them, and would cry if they spoke to me. I am sure they didn't mean any harm, because they would bend down to talk to me with big smiles, even if I was hiding behind the bar, but I was always so frightened of them. My mother and grandmother liked the soldiers though, and would often talk about them, especially the "Sergeant Major", with smiles on their faces too, and lots of giggles. I just wish they had realised how frightened I was of them, and would not take me into the bar when they came in.

~

These earliest memories go back to "before the pub was altered" in 1952, a milestone which my family referred to quite a lot. I remember this all going on when I was three years old. There was a plank I had to walk along upstairs, whilst holding on tightly to the banisters, in order to get to the bathroom. I expect Nell must have been with me at such a young age to guide me along, but it terrified me, looking down through the large gap at the bar below. Health and Safety rules were obviously not the same in those days. Then again, when did my grandfather ever adhere to any rules – health, safety, or otherwise! Meanwhile, my parents were living up the road in the cottage away from it all – I really think they should have taken me back for a while to get me away from such potential danger.

~

Before the pub was altered though, there was a sitting room on the ground floor facing the car park. This was later turned into a small bar coming off the taproom, which became known as The Snug.

I was two years old at the time, and I have a photo of me wearing a puffed sleeve dress and a frilly bonnet standing in what looks like a rather wild part of the pub garden, although there is a rambling rose behind. I am with our little white Pekinese dog called Bimbo. She is sitting on the grass next to me and looking so sweet – she was such a pretty little dog, with long soft white fur, and I loved her.

Looking towards the sitting room, there was a window that overlooked the car park, and a door, which led straight inside.

Forsythia grew around the door, which had bright yellow blooms in spring that glowed in the sunshine. Its natural, unruly shape must have been kept in check by my grandfather, for it formed a perfect arch over the door.

Beneath it on the left-hand side grew a patch of clover. I once pulled a few pieces out – and ate them. I've never eaten it since – I didn't like it – maybe one of the dogs had cocked its leg over it...

It's funny how children do these things – wanting to taste things that they've never tasted before. I remember a friend telling me once how she had tried to eat a worm when she was little. Her mother was horrified as she pulled the still wriggling creature out of her mouth!

Well having eaten the clover, I then went into the sitting room. My mother and grandmother were in the room, and Bimbo sat on the brown leather settee, looking at me intently. Behind the settee was a sideboard on which stood three rather fine cut glass decanters, with heavy cut glass stoppers, and filled with various colours of liquid, probably port, sherry and whisky. It's funny how one remembers such things, even though it goes so far back in the memory.

One day though, I was in the sitting room, and Bimbo was sitting on the settee, looking a picture, with her white paws hanging over the edge. I crouched down next to the settee where Bimbo was sitting, and I then knelt on the floor talking to her, while she was looking intently at me. I leant over to kiss her little face and, suddenly – she snapped and went for me – and bit my nose...

Well I've never wanted to kiss a dog since – not even one as pretty as Bimbo! It was the first time any animal had drawn blood on me. The pain was awful, but what hurt even more though, especially for a little three year old, was the sting of the iodine that was put on my nose to heal the wound. This made my nose turn a bright shade of yellow – as bright as the forsythia that grew around the door.

~

Above the sitting room was my grandfather's bedroom, which was later changed into the kitchen. And this brings me onto my absolute first ever memory...

I recall Nell carrying me into his bedroom one morning... I was around two or three years old. Nell put me on his bed, and then she left the room. My grandfather would sit me across his tummy, and bounce me up and down a few times saying he was giving me a "gee-gee" ride. I am not sure how many times I was taken into his room and he did that, but I think it was a fairly frequent thing. This time though, he turned me round, facing the bottom of the bed – then he pulled the sheet down...

I remember wondering what these strange looking things were growing out of his tummy. I didn't have things growing out of *my* tummy, and they looked a bit scary. That is all I recall, apart from him putting my hands on them...

I do not remember anything else from that incident, but this is something that has haunted me all my life. I didn't know what he was doing at the time, and I don't know whether I actually told anyone. I probably didn't, as I didn't understand what he was doing, but if I had done, I don't think there would have been any reaction.

My grandfather could do whatever he wanted – whenever he wanted. No-one would ever challenge him or stop him. He was Lord and Master of the household, and was treated as such.

~

Sometime later, I don't know how old I was, it may have been months, or even a couple of years or so afterwards, I was in bed in the little box room at the front of the pub, which had become my bedroom. It was furnished with just a single bed and a dressing table – with no back. This was riddled with woodworm, which were still active, scattering wood dust, and slowly but surely, gradually munching their way into the drawers as well. How could I have been put to bed every night with a room infested with such destructive creatures? As well as that, I worried whether they might come out of their expansive larder during the night to find *me* and turn me into another nocturnal feast...

Lying awake one particular Saturday night, I got out of bed and went out of the door to go to the toilet. I don't even know if I was big enough to turn on a light, but the landing light was on. At that moment Fred Sawger came out of the bathroom, looked straight at me, then went back across to my grandmother's bedroom. He was completely naked, but in no way did he seem concerned or even surprised that I had seen him. I remember seeing that he had got things growing out of his tummy too...

A Girl Called Bill

December 1953

"Boys are so much better than girls", my mother had a penchant for saying to me, even though, as young as I was, I was always trying to please her. Nothing ever worked though. She wouldn't even allow me to wear pink, like other little girls. It was always blue or green, or sometimes the most unflattering neutral colours for a child, like beige and fawn.

One day, she decided that I was even going to be *dressed* as a boy, and bought me a pair of grey flannel trousers. No other girls in the village wore trousers in those days, but that was what I was made to wear.

I would have been four years old at the time, because I have a photo of me meeting "Father Christmas" in December 1953. It should have been a wondrous and magical moment for me, but I am looking very unhappy. For there I am – dressed as a boy... It is a black and white photo, but I can tell that the trousers are the grey ones I had to wear. My coat is shapeless and looks more like a boy's, my lovely blonde hair was cut short, and I remember the little brown cap I was wearing – it was a very displeasing shade of brown. Father Christmas is handing me a gift, which looks the shape of a book – I just hope it wasn't about trains...

There was a man who lived over the road in a house on the corner – he was Mr. Marvin, a nice man, and not at all scary. What I remember most about him was that for a while he was the only person in the area who had a television – a little six-inch black and white one. He kindly invited us all to his house to watch the Coronation on that tiny screen. I remember us all huddled around that little television, in darkness, for even though it was a grey and drizzly day, the curtains were closed to give a clearer picture. I was only four then, but I remember so well watching the procession making its way through the streets of London, and seeing this wonderful looking woman becoming our dear Queen.

One morning Mr. Marvin came over to the pub for his usual pint – I was in the bar as normal – and wearing the grey trousers... A man had sat me on his lap, as customers were wont to do sometimes, and he was tickling me, which was something that I hated. I still do – I have never found it amusing. These days I think a parent would be very wary of strange men sitting their little girl on their laps and tickling them. Maybe they weren't strangers to my family – but they were to *me*...

"Ah – a little boy!" Mr. Marvin exclaimed, seeing how I was dressed, and to the amusement of everyone in the room. From then on he called me Bill.

Bill sort of stuck to me, and soon other customers were calling me Bill too. I wouldn't say it was confusing, but my name was Yvonne.

When I first started school, my mother said to me, "now if anyone calls you anything other than 'Y-*vonne*' – don't answer. Some people might call you '*Eee*-von' or even Eve – don't answer." That wasn't the best way to make friends, when so many people in the area would only call me '*Eee*-von' and there was no way I wasn't going to answer them.

But now I was being called Bill.

That was in the pub though, by the customers. School was another matter, and when I started school I was still of course me – *Yvonne*.

One day though, my mother showed me another pair of trousers she had bought for me. These ones were brown corduroy, and she decided that she was now going to send me to school wearing them. I really don't remember much about that day, because I think I must have erased it from my memory, but I do remember being sent home with a note telling my mother to send me to school appropriately dressed – i.e. as a girl.

And so, I was back wearing my navy blue gymslip, with a little blue jumper. As far as I can recall, that was the only girls' clothing my mother bought me around that time. The only other girls' clothes I had were hand-me-downs from my cousin Lyn. Her mum, my Auntie Audrey, would bring her old clothes over to the pub in a large plastic bag, and it was always so exciting. My mother used to give her a pound for the clothes, which I suppose was quite a lot at the time, but they were all good quality, and I didn't mind wearing hand-me-downs. At least I had some girls' clothes.

Thank goodness the school had taken a hand, and stopped my mother sending me to school in trousers. Thank goodness also that I could now definitely be called Yvonne.

~

It was many years before I actually wore trousers again. I was fifteen, they were a very chic French style, and what's more – they were *pink!*

My First Day At School

It was September 1954, and although the days were still warm and sunny, the early mornings were just beginning to feel a bit chilly. I was sitting on the old well-scrubbed wooden table in the kitchen, and Nell was tying a pale blue satin ribbon into my blonde hair, which she had just lovingly combed. Although at that time I was still mainly being dressed as a boy at home, for this huge milestone in my life, I was thankfully dressed appropriately for my first day at school.

I felt proud of that navy blue gymslip, which I was wearing over a pale blue woollen jumper that did up with three little pearly buttons at the back of the neck. I remember the wool feeling a bit scratchy on my back, but never mind, I would get used to it. Underneath my school clothes I wore a natural-coloured woollen vest, which was not the most comfortable of underwear. On top of that was a cream liberty bodice, which was done up with buttons down the front, and on top of that a white cotton petticoat, which did up with buttons down the back. So many buttons – and navy blue knickers with elasticated legs that stretched almost down to my knees – were the order of the day!

"Come on, lift your feet up" Nell said, sitting me on the table as she put on my new brown leather shoes. "You are going to have to start to do these up yourself" she said, as she fastened the instep straps with the little round buttons.

A very strange feeling came over me as I got down from the table. The room started going round and round, and then the next thing I knew I was waking up, with Nell looking very concerned. "You have just fainted" she told me.

I don't know why fainting then has stayed in my memory so much, I had never fainted before. I expect it was just nerves – or it might have been some cocktail I had been given to calm my nerves. There seemed to be a different alcoholic solution for anything that I might be suffering from.

But this was no time for me to be feeling nervous; my first day at school beckoned, and I was on my way.

It was a twenty minute walk to Orsett School from the pub, down High Road, and past the Brickfield on the left in the dip. It had nothing to do with bricks at all, so I don't know why it was called that. It was an area of long grass, brambles, and subtly-scented pink and white dog rose bushes that had been left to grow wild, a place in which a few of the local children would go to play.

Then it was up the hill and past the lizard nest in the sandy bank of the hedgerow. I soon found out that some of the local boys would try to catch the lizards and hold them by their tails. The defence mechanism for the creatures was that they would leap from their prey, leaving their tails, still wriggling in their prey's mouths, or in this case, the boys' fingers. Thankfully, I never witnessed any of this. Just being told about it was enough, and anyway, if I had been around at the time, then I feel sure I would have been chased with those wriggling tails!

But this was my first day at school, and I didn't as yet know about the cruel behaviour to the lizards. So onward we went, up the hill, past Dr. Bull's house that laid back on the right, with its sombre black-painted doors and window frames. Not a good colour for a doctor's house! Then we crossed the road to the cornfield opposite the appropriately named Hill Farm at the top. To everyone in the village though it was known as Reynolds Farm, because it was owned by the Reynolds family. It was the same with other farms and some properties in the area. So many properties were handed down to their children and grandchildren – who were in turn happy to have them, and enjoy their history, no matter what state of disrepair they may have been in.

Reynolds Farm, or rather Hill Farm, was a beautiful old farmhouse. I have been in there, well, in the kitchen. I was walking back from Orsett village one day with Roger Reynolds. As we got to the farmhouse he asked me if I would like to go in and see his mother – she was really nice, and was sorting eggs on the kitchen table. It was a typical old farmhouse kitchen, with a huge wooden table in the middle, and an old dresser, things like that.

Opposite Hill Farm there was a rickety stile to get over into the cornfield, which for the little legs of a five-year-old was something to accomplish every school day morning and afternoon. I can picture myself now, climbing precariously over that wobbly stile, holding on to Nell's hand as she helped me down to the other side.

It was always a pleasure for me though, walking through that field, no matter how rough the narrow footpath was that led to the lane at the other end. At that time of year, occasional poppies and cornflowers peeped up through the gently swaying spears of corn, their vibrant scarlet and blue flowers accentuated against the gold. These were the sights and feelings of nature that I was already loving and attuned to, even at such a young age.

Taking the path through the cornfield though was a short cut and saved us from going past the spinney, where adders lived in the long grass beneath the trees. I saw one once, squashed on the road. The skin remained there for quite a long time, being a reminder to me not to venture into the spinney. Not even the crows fancied eating it! It was a zigzag shape, and that is how for a long while I pictured adders to be – it was, of course, like that because it was run over as it was wriggling...

Eventually, at the end of the cornfield we turned right into the lane. Where the lane met School Lane, there was a house nestling back on the corner, and as we passed by, two black Scottie dogs came scampering out yapping at us. I had never seen a Scottie dog before, and they looked so funny with their square chiselled jaws. But I knew I was not going to like going past that house one little bit!

The Scottie dogs were the least of my worries though, as I clung onto Nell's hand. I had been worrying all the time about something in particular...

"Are they the toilets?" I asked her, as we neared the electricity sub-station next to the school playground. Nell laughed, and told me that no, the toilets were in the field behind the playground.

In the field? Oh dear. Well, I was soon to find out...

Mrs. Ridgewell, the kindly playground lady, greeted us at the school gate and she took my hand and led me over to a group of children who were playing "Ring a Ring o' Roses". A few of them had already been at school for a year, and they were asked to look after the newcomers. A girl with wavy dark hair was assigned to me, although I think her interest in looking after a new girl soon wore thin.

Mrs. Ridgewell was a lovely lady, and wore a long, brown tweed coat with a brown brimmed hat. She had a very kind face, and lived in a large and very old house next to Mr. Dodd's the butcher at the beginning of High Road. She obviously loved her job, being with the children and organising singing games, like "Oranges and Lemons", which actually used to worry me – "Here is a candle to light you to bed – here is a chopper..." Ugh! I hated that bit!

Well, on this first day at school I noticed a boy who lived over the road from the pub. He was a very small boy with sandy coloured hair. His name was Georgie, and he had had polio when he was younger. I had seen him walk along High Road, struggling with leg irons, and had always felt so sorry for him. He also spent time in the isolation hospital in Long Lane, which for a child of that age must have been very difficult.

Like me, he also lived with his grandparents, and his teenage aunties. Unlike my life at the pub though, he had a very happy home life, enveloped by love, warmth, and laughter. Well for Georgie, being just a few months younger than me, it was also *his* first day at school too.

Before going into school, we all had to form a double line, holding the hand of the person next to us – girl with girl, and boy with boy, and then we were led across the playground and into the field at the back. Standing there were two air raid shelters – the boys were led into one, and the girls into the other. It was very dark and dank in there – but that was where the toilets were. They were non-flushing Elsan ones. Yuk! It was horrible in there!

The toilets at the pub could be rather awful too though. My grandfather had a rule that the one upstairs, which was our private one, was not to be flushed until it was brown. Well that was when he was at home – luckily he went out a lot. I hated sitting on a toilet when the contents were the colour of a peat bog. So I would sneak downstairs to the Ladies whenever I could. Even in there the only toilet paper was the torn up pages of the News of the World and the Morning Advertiser, which hung from a meat hook on the overhead cistern – somehow the Morning Advertiser seemed softer! Looking back, the Elsan toilets at school would have been far more hygienic than what we had at home.

~

Mr. Paterson was Headmaster at that time, and he had taken over from Mr. Fox, who was Headmaster in the days when the only school to go on to from there was Palmers Grammar School – if you were intelligent enough... Other than that, you stayed at Orsett School until you were fourteen, and I can only guess that from there – you went to work...

Mr. Paterson lived in one of the lovely little Victorian terraced cottages in Rowley Road, which was very close to the school. I don't remember much about him, except that he was a small and very nice man.

My first teacher was Mrs. Anderson, another lovely and very kindly lady with grey hair, and she always smelled nice. The nearest I can get to her scent is that of a soft powdery pink rose. If ever I happen to smell a scent anything like that, I am immediately back there, in that little classroom. She taught us how to count using an abacus, and how to write using a wooden-framed slate and chalk. She also read us stories about Milly Molly Mandy and her mongoose, and other children's' stories, but Milly Molly Mandy was my favourite.

~

At the first playtime, Mrs. Ridgewell organised a game of "The Farmer's in his Den". I held back as everyone formed a circle.

"Come on Yvonne", Mrs. Ridgewell said smiling, beckoning me to join in. I still stood back, as I was very shy and didn't really want to take part in something that I didn't know what to do. She came over to me and took my hand, and gently guided me into the circle between two of the girls.

"Now Georgie" she said, "you come into the middle and be the farmer". Then we all had to hold hands and dance around him singing -

"The farmer's in his den – the farmer's in his den – ee-ay ee-ay – the farmer's in his den."

Then came the next verse –

"The farmer wants a wife – the farmer wants a wife – ee-ay ee-ay – the farmer wants a wife."

"Come on Georgie", Mrs. Ridgewell said, "you have to choose a wife."

Georgie looked around the circle at all the girls, and then he stopped, looked and pointed – to *me...*

I didn't know what I had to do, but Mrs. Ridgewell told me that I had to get into the middle of the circle – because Georgie had chosen *me...*

~

By the time the very first Christmas at Orsett School came around, we were all well versed with the Christmas story. I didn't know what a virgin was of course at that time, and I certainly didn't know where babies came from, but I was intrigued by the magic of it all, and had also been very worried about whether or not Mary and Joseph would find somewhere to spend the night. Knowing that the Three Wise Men were on their way, following that glowing star that led them to the stable, made me feel a little less anxious about Mary and Joseph's plight!

Then came the day of the nativity play... This took place in the Infants School, and there was a lot of hay around, and a crib with a baby doll in it, wrapped in a shawl, that I took to be the swaddling clothes. I was overjoyed to be chosen to play Mary! I was clothed in a dark blue swathe of cotton, that wrapped around me like a cloak, covering my hair, just as Mary is depicted in biblical paintings. I didn't have to say anything, all I had to do was to gaze down lovingly at the baby doll in the crib – baby Jesus.

Guess who was Joseph? The teachers had chosen Georgie to be my husband! It's as though they saw some kind of connection between us.

Well that year was the beginning of a very innocent six year friendship with Georgie. We met up again for the first time since we left Orsett School about forty years later – and since then we have stayed in touch – friends from afar...

Cabbage And Custard

September 1954

During that first week at school, we were all taken into the hall each day to learn hymns. The first hymn I ever remember singing at school is "Gentle Jesus Meek and Mild", which was a lovely little hymn, but I don't think I really got the words "pity my simplicity" right at the time. We couldn't read, so we were learning the words by ear, and I was singing something like "piddy-my-sim-piddy-tee", so didn't really know what it was all about!

We also learned a grace that we sang every day before going to lunch...

Thank you for the world so sweet
Thank you for the food we eat
Thank you for the birds that sing
Thank you God for everything
Amen

Then we were led, in a double line, holding hands, across the road to the Nissen hut that served as the school canteen. Refectory tables were lined up one after the other down each side, with the kitchen and servery at the very end. Once we were all standing at our seats, we then had to say proper Grace, with our eyes closed and our hands together in prayer -

For what we are about to receive, may the Lord make us truly thankful
Amen

~

During one of those early days at school, I had got my meal and had taken it to one of the refectory tables. I was seated on the end next to the queue of children who were gradually walking by. At the tail end of the queue was a boy called Jimmy. He was from one of the families who had been squatting at the army camp down on the fen once the soldiers had left – gypsies as they were called then. He was very dirty and smelly, with a permanently runny nose, something that my mother always referred to as "candles". Sometimes he would wipe his arm across his nose, leaving the shiny green mess across his sleeve. Usually though the candles remained there, from his nose down to his mouth. Whenever the school nurse came, it was always Jimmy and another gypsy boy called Freddie who had nits. I don't suppose they passed them on to any of the other children though, because no-one would get that close to them!

Well Jimmy certainly came close to *me*... As he came alongside my table, he turned and spat – right in my dinner. I hope I told Mrs. Ridgewell and that she took it away from me and brought me a replacement. All I remember though is sitting looking at the globule of spittle in my gravy.

I think Jimmy and Freddie must have been in the juniors, and thankfully, they had a different playground to the infants. I don't remember how long they were at the school for, but what I do know is that he never came near me again. Maybe I did tell someone what he had done.

At first school dinners were 9d, although by the time I was in the juniors, they had gone up to a shilling a week, which is 1p a day in today's money. They were nice meals though, mainly based on meat, potatoes, greens and gravy. One day a week we had a cheese and potato pie with salad, but I wasn't terribly keen on this, because we had to eat diced beetroot with it, and the beetroot always bled into the mashed potatoes, turning them into a soggy purple mess.

Although it was a Church of England school, we always had fish on Fridays. It wasn't a nice piece of fried cod or haddock with chips though, but boiled cod or plaice in parsley sauce which, again, mixed into the mashed potatoes, and I didn't like the messy mixture – at all! On the whole though, I did like the school dinners, and would eat my greens as well as my meat and potatoes. Well I wanted what was coming next...

Afters, as we called desserts then, were always something hot and substantial. Rice or semolina served with jam, which we would stir around to make the milk pudding go pink and more palatable. I really disliked tapioca though, it reminded me of the frog spawn that Georgie and I would find in the puddles and ditches down the lane. In fact, we all called the tapioca frog spawn!

There was treacle tart and Bakewell tart, and then there were the lovely steamed puddings – chocolate pudding with chocolate custard or that also lovely sweet hot white sauce; ginger pudding served with golden syrup, and of course, the old favourite, "Spotty Dick" – as we called it – full of dried fruit and served with vanilla custard. We had to eat all our dinner though if we wanted to have "afters".

One of the school cooks was a plump lady who lived in Baker Street. She was nice, but didn't always *think*... Being a little slapdash with her serving, she would dollop food onto the plates and splash it onto the server. One day she used the same ladle for the custard as she had for serving the cabbage. So my custard had little bits of green in it – a bit like the parsley sauce really!

All Creatures Great And Small

Another hymn that we learned in those early days at primary school was "All Things Bright and Beautiful", which I loved, because I did love all things bright and beautiful, and all creatures great and small. Well those of the furred and feathered kind – I wasn't keen on the mice that ran around in the pub! They used to be everywhere, and I was always worried that one might come up one of the legs of the bedstead and onto the bed.

I remember my grandfather taking me into the back room in our shop when I was only eye height to the table in there. "I have something to show you", he said, as he led me into the room. There, laid out along the table was a row of dead mice in traps, all facing towards me – with their eyes popping out. It was horrific. I think it might have been that experience that set me off on some sort of eye phobia, never being to look at images of eyes close-up.

We had cats at the pub to keep down the mouse population, but that was a never ending job for them. The mice would obviously play while the cats were away, and continue to breed. Grandpop – as I always called him – told me one day that he had got up out of bed, went to pull on his trousers, which he always had laying on the floor next to the bed (in readiness for any burglars), and found a nest of new born baby mice – pinkies, as they are known these days – in the crotch of his trousers. I remember him chuckling about this, but he never said what he did with them. Maybe he fed them to the cats? That very thought makes me shudder!

We always had a menagerie of animals at the pub, but at least we didn't have any pet snakes to feed the pinkies to!

Grass snakes and adders though were sometimes found in the garden. However Grandpop was good at catching them and killing them with a stick. Then he would carry them on the stick to the dustbin – and just put them in there! Oh, it was horrible. Goodness knows what the dustmen thought!

The first pet at the pub I knew about, was a monkey that my grandfather had around 1945, which was before I was born – fortunately! He was a brown monkey with a white face and front, and actually quite big. In fact, in a photo I have of him, he is the same size as a pet mongrel dog, Peggy, my grandfather had. I have been told that he would sit on the counter of the taproom and amuse – or annoy – the customers, rather like the jackdaw that became somewhat of a pet to my grandfather. He would appear in the pub in the evenings, and also sit on the counter – sipping out of pints of beer and, even more annoyingly – taking people's change! Grandpop always said that he knew he flew off to Kent every day, because he was covered in chalk from the cliffs of Dover. I suspect he may have just flown to the local chalk pits though. I really don't know what happened to the monkey, but I have a photo of Grandpop cradling him like a baby, with my mother standing beside him looking very glum indeed!

That photo had been taken in part of the pub garden behind the garages, which were built between the car park and the lawned garden where there were picnic tables for customers and their children. The garages were part of the outbuildings that had been built by the German prisoners of war, who were kept in the army camp down on the fen. They were still there after the war, waiting to go home, but with it being such a long wait, they needed something to keep them occupied. That is where my grandfather stepped in. He arranged for them to build the garages, and also later to build a row of arbours with tables and chairs, where customers' children could sit outside, no matter what the weather. These arbours were covered with Virginia creeper, which would glow in all colours of red and purple, and they were very attractive little places in which to sit, especially in the early evening at sunset.

The prisoners of war were rewarded with beer and cigarettes, and I remember my mother and grandmother saying what lovely young men they were. I don't remember any of the German soldiers though, because they had probably been sent home by the time I was old enough to remember people, but I do remember the English soldiers who were still down at the camp, being around when I was a little girl. As I have already mentioned earlier, they used to worry me when they came to the pub, and I was always frightened when they got drunk and laughed so loud. My mother and grandmother liked them though, and later told me how when the American soldiers had been there during the war they had given them gifts of nylon stockings and expensive French perfume.

On the back of the garages that the German soldiers had built, my father had built a large aviary which housed well over forty budgerigars, in pretty shades of blue and lime green. I have never liked the thought of birds of any kind being caged, but they seemed happy, flying around amongst the decorative branches chirruping.

Next to the aviary was a conservatory that my father had also built onto the back of the garages. I used to be put in there in my pram to sleep, and I actually have another very early memory of being in there in the pram. It was a large black Silver Cross coach pram, and I can remember lying in there looking up at the flaking whitewashed walls, and across to a hammock that was strung between two walls. I could hear the budgerigars singing to each other next door. I also remember it being very hot in there...

One day, when I was still small enough to be in the pram, but big enough to move, I actually managed to get over the side of the pram. I don't remember actually doing that, but what I do remember is the look of horror on Nell's face when she found me, hanging over the side on my reins. I was very lucky not to have been strangled by those reins, and that Nell found me when she did.

In front of the conservatory was a rockery, over which mauve aubretia, blue lobelia, and honey-scented alyssum scrambled. There were also clumps of London pride, with its pink fronds and thick glossy leaves – these, I imagine, held any number of small creatures! When I was still small enough to be not much taller than the rockery itself, I would go round there every morning to see one of these creatures – one I couldn't even bear to look at now – it was a large *toad* and he would be there every morning, at the same time, sitting on the same rock. I would bend down and look at him, and he would sit there staring back at me. It never bothered me though, well not then! Many years ago a toad jumped on my foot, and ever since then I have not been able to even look at pictures of frogs or toads, let alone get anywhere near one. I dread to think how I would have felt if, being such a little girl, that toad had jumped off the rock towards me. It doesn't bear thinking about...

~

The very first pet that I actually remember was Bimbo, the little Pekinese dog that bit my nose when I was three years old. I don't know where my mother got the name from, but maybe it was after the very old song which goes back to the twenties, and which Jim Reeves later recorded in 1953, but at least it was the dog that she named Bimbo and not me!

Somehow, Bimbo became very attached to me, and I have photos taken with her in front of a pink rose bush in 1952 when I was three years old. The original photo was black and white, but the larger one I have in a frame was expertly, and probably expensively, coloured by hand.

Although Nell always took me to school in the mornings – when I was in the infants that is – my mother would sometimes pick me up in the afternoons because Nell had to look after the shop. Mummy had a seat on the back of her bike, and I would sit on that with my legs stretched out to the sides so as not to get caught in the spokes of the wheels. One day when my mother picked me up from school, we had got as far along High Road for the pub to be in sight, and she suddenly told me that little Bimbo had died. I was so upset, especially still sitting there, on the back of the bike. It really wasn't the best place to tell me such devastating news. My mother could have told me in a much gentler way. She could have sat me down and told me very kindly what had happened, and maybe even given me a hug. But that was not the sort of thing she did. In fact, I don't recall there ever being a time when she gave me a hug, or even a kiss. Maybe she didn't even want to see my face when she told me, so told me just so matter of factly when I was sitting behind her.

I couldn't understand why Bimbo had died so young, when Peggy, who was a far older dog, was still alive. Also poor Peggy was blind. But Bimbo? She was that lovely little girl, who despite biting my nose so painfully a couple of years earlier, would follow me around everywhere. This was my logic though at that tender age. Older animals died, but young ones didn't. It was years later that I found out how Bimbo had died. A large dog had got to her, and it was the resulting puppies that had killed her. Something I would never have understood though when I was just five years old.

~

My parents lived in one of my grandfather's 16th Century cottages, which were along the road in Baker Street, situated between the end of the extensive pub garden and our shop. Ivy Cottage had originally been one cottage that also incorporated the baker's shop, after which the street was named.

My father worked all day of course, and my mother spent a lot of time at the pub with my grandmother. For a while, I didn't even know that my father was actually my father, and I even used to refer to him as "the man who lives up the cottage"! When I was first told that he was my father, I thought that it was Bert Jobson who at the time lived in the other cottage. It was all very confusing! I did come to realise who he was though, and I would walk up the road to see my parents, even before I was school age. Sometimes I would sit with my mother in the early evenings while she waited for my father to come home from work. Things were somewhat different in those early days. But even so, I still had to go back to the pub to sleep – I was only allowed a short time at the cottage.

I remember sitting on the floor by the fire, while she knitted little squares out of oddments of wool, of varying colours. She subsequently sewed them all together, backed them with cotton, and edged the result with blue satin ribbon. I later found out that this was to be a blanket for a doll's pram that they had secretly bought me for my birthday. It was very unusual for her to make something like that. Maybe that was her only way of showing me any affection. That was the only thing she ever made for me, but that, along with my doll's pram, soon disappeared – the beginning of a continuous thread throughout my childhood.

I remember so well being sent up to the cottage to see my parents on my birthday. I am not sure how old I was, but I think I was five. I was told to close my eyes, and hold my hands over my eyes, and then I was led into a downstairs room that was pretty much empty. That was when I saw my birthday surprise – my doll's pram...

It was dark shiny blue, and inside – there was the patchwork knitted blanket that my mother had made for me.

I was allowed to take it down to the pub with me, but the only memory I have of doing anything at all with it, was that walk down Baker Street back to the pub. I loved that pram – I *really* loved it!

So where did it disappear to? As with all the other things that I loved over the years – it had probably also found its way into some other little girl's home...

~

One summer evening I went up to the cottage to see my parents, and my father told me to look under the sideboard. Peeping out from there was a fluffy little black kitten, with a white neck and paws. The first thing he did was hiss at me, and refused to come out. That was understandable though, having being brought to this alien world. This little kitten had been born at Tileman and Company in Grays, where my father was a foreman steel bender and fixer, and he had brought the little mite home in his jacket pocket.

I didn't really know at the time what his work involved, but a few times he took me to his office, of which he seemed very proud. I used to sit at his desk, and he would give me a sheaf of paper and a pencil, and I would sit there and draw.

He would cycle there and back, and sometimes, I would walk up Baker Street to meet him on his way home from work, and would ride on his crossbar back down to the pub again. I used to like that – it was a chance for me to talk to him on his own, albeit briefly.

"What do you do at work Daddy?" I asked him one day, while I was riding on the crossbar.

"Earn money!" he said.

"How much money do you earn Daddy?" I asked innocently.

He didn't answer. So later on I asked my mother. "You must never ask questions like that!" she scolded. So money went on the list of all the questions I should never ask.

~

Tileman and Company was part of the Tunnel Portland Cement works in the vast chalk quarry that later became the site of what was once the largest shopping centre in the South East – Lakeside. No-one knew at the time how the cement dust would get into the workers' lungs, and cause problems in later years, even though the cement seemed to colour the whole of Grays – well, grey...

It seemed appropriate to name this little kitten Sooty, which was due to his colouring of course (rather than the cement dust in which he was born!). Well Sooty turned into a loving little cat, and I have one photo of him. I remember my father taking it with his box Brownie camera, where everything was seen upside down, and I am holding little Sooty in my hands. I was around four years old, so Bimbo was still alive then, along with Peggy and the pub cats. Now, we had this latest little addition. Unfortunately though, I am wearing a most awful hat. It looks like a large sunflower sitting on my head, decorated with two quite large hearts, and tied under the chin – to make it stay on! I remember my mother buying it for me on Southend seafront where they sold "Kiss me quick" hats. I didn't like it – nor want it – and certainly didn't want to wear it. But my mother, being as she was, made me wear it, and even at that early age I felt very, very stupid. Actually, I look like the "Little Weed" in "Bill and Ben the Flower Pot Men".

~

Going to Southend was always a welcome treat, well in the summer that is. It was the tradition to go there on an August evening and go to Never Never Land. First of all though we would walk along the sea front, eating hot chips out of newspaper, and buying cockles and whelks from the cockle stall to take home for supper – not that I would ever even try one though! Women would stagger along the seafront, giggling, wearing those "Kiss me Quick" hats, and then we would make our way to Never Never Land. When dusk fell, it was dark enough to see all the joys that that wonderful fairyland offered. Subtly-lit paths wound their way upwards and round, with little fairy enclaves around each corner. There we would stop awhile, and I would wonder about the fairies that lived there. Of course, I didn't realise at such a young age that they were just little figures. But even when I got a little older, I still enjoyed the wonder of it all.

Summer evenings in Essex always seemed warm in my childhood, even when darkness fell. It wasn't only enjoying the family trip in August to Never Never Land, but also, sometimes my grandmother would take me there on our own. It must have been such a long bus journey from Orsett. This outing wasn't to see the fairies though, this was to walk along the seafront and then take me to a pub called "The Hole in the Wall". I don't know why, but she loved that pub, even though it was very stark with its bare brick walls. Even more, I don't know how I was allowed in – but I always was, and I have a photo of me taken with Nanny sitting at a bare wooden table, with me drinking from a straw out of a bottle of fizzy orange. I look about four at the time.

~

Some years later, the Kursaal was on the agenda. The Kursaal was one of the world's first amusement parks, and was also in Southend – it was more for grown-ups though, especially the Wall of Death. I found that very scary, as Tornado Smith would ride his motorbike around the wall, getting higher and higher with each circle. It was at its most scariest when he would come right up to the top, especially if it was where I was standing – I was afraid he might knock my head off! His girlfriend Yvonne Stagg used to do it too. Rather more dangerous than my earlier pleasures of the Big Wheel, the Crooked House, and the Laughing Policeman! Ha-ha-ha-ha-ha – ho-ho-ho-ho-ho... We never ever knew what he was supposed to be laughing about – but people used to put money into the slot just to hear him laugh!

~

"How much is that doggie in the window..."

One of my favourite early childhood songs was "How Much is that Doggie in the Window?" by Lita Roza, way back in 1953. Years later this actually rang true in our household.

My mother had been to Romford with my grandfather, and he dropped her off at Romford Market while he went to one of his meetings at Ind Coope, the brewery. There was some kind of arcade next to the market. Not like the rather grand Victorian arcade in Brighton, where my grandmother would buy her hats, but a covered walkway with a few crummy-looking shops on each side.

That day I came home from school, and as so often was the case, something had happened. Usually, one or more of my possessions had gone missing, but this day wasn't negative, it was actually very positive – we had a new puppy at the pub.

My mother had been browsing through that rather unkempt arcade, and had seen a little puppy sitting in the window of a pet shop on some rather over used straw. It was a little grey, curly haired, Cairn Terrier, and my mother said that he was sitting there looking so sad, and when he saw her, he looked at her with pleading eyes. Considering how harsh she could be with me, her heart had apparently gone out to this little puppy – and she had bought it and brought it home...

Goodness knows how he behaved in the car, I never found that out. Well maybe he was in a box, because there was no such thing as a pet carrier in those days in which to transport him.

Susan Maughan's "Bobby's Girl" had been in the UK charts for many months and was still being played on the wireless. My mother and grandmother liked that song, and I liked it too. It was one of those uplifting songs that made you want to sing and dance – although not my mother and grandmother that is! I never knew my mother to sing, and certainly never saw her dance, which is a little sad, as my father was a good ballroom dancer. I remember my grandmother though singing and dancing with a saucepan on her head to amuse me when I was very little – some visions stay in your memory forever!

"Who's that old woman singing about Bobby?" my grandmother would ask – but she liked it, and smiled whenever she heard it. My mother would actually raise a smile too. And so this new little puppy was named Bobby.

My mother decided that Bobby was going to live at home with her, although she did used to bring him along to the pub. He was a sweet little chap, and I enjoyed taking him for walks around the lanes.

One day – yet another day when I came home from school – Bobby was gone. What I didn't know was that he had a problem. He would eat – then vomit – then eat the vomit – and then eat whatever came out his other end...

"What comes out of his mouth is like afterbirth" I remember my mother saying. I didn't know what afterbirth was though at the time, and I didn't feel I could ask.

My parents took him to the vet thinking there was something physically wrong with him. But no, it wasn't that, even though all this cycle of eating, vomiting, defecating, eating, vomiting, defecating, seemed like something physical. The vet said he was *traumatised* from having been very ill treated before being put up for sale in that shop window in Romford Market.

It wasn't his fault. But the poor little soul had to be put down...

Thank goodness puppies aren't sold by looking sad in a dirty window any more...

~

The main cat at the pub was called "Old Woman", so named by my grandmother – because she was. The cat that is. She was a sharp-looking tabby/tortoiseshell cross, and was half wild as the result of the male feral cats that would hang around the pub sometimes. She did enjoy home comforts though, just like any true domestic cat, and particularly liked to sleep in the kitchen on the pile of daily newspapers that were always on top of one of the cupboards. This is where she would sleep most of the day.

One day, my grandfather had gone to take a newspaper from underneath her and she had flown at him. He told me that she had bitten his finger so hard that her teeth had gone through to the bone.

"So where is she?" I asked him, seeing that she was not in her usual, er, daily place.

"She's gone", he said – "I punched her straight in the face..."

Poor Old Woman. She didn't deserve that. But she came back, as loyal as ever. Just like my grandmother and Nell, whenever he punched them.

My grandfather kept Old Woman "intact", maintaining that an intact feline was a good mouser. True, but most cats instinctively, and especially those with a free reign, are good mousers anyway. Grandpop also believed that feeding a cat raw blood kept their taste for blood going. So Old Woman had a steady supply of raw blood that oozed from any meat joint or game bird that we were given, and also waddled around carrying various unborn kitten litters at frequent intervals each year.

Although the odd kitten was either kept to keep up the cat supply, or given away as a pet to someone my grandfather might fancy, most of the kittens were straight away put in a sack and drowned in the water butt by my father. I never actually saw a drowning, and certainly did not want to, but whenever I asked where the kittens were, this was what I was told had happened to them, and I have actually seen my father walking off to the water butt with a sack of tiny squealing kittens. The dartboard in the taproom had to be kept in water sometimes when not in use, in order to keep the cork in shape, and so that would sit on top of the water butt. This was then used to hold the sack of kittens down until they drowned. Or so I was told.

One winter's day, Old Woman was waddling around as usual, with little bodies pushing out against her fur at various times, and my mother said "she's going to drop those kittens any time now". Of course, although I knew she had kittens in her tummy and that was what made her waddle, I didn't exactly know how she was going to "drop" them though.

She had a favourite place for giving birth, and that was in one of the kitchen cupboards. I don't know how she got in there to make her bed, but she did, and I suspect that the door would be left ajar for her to go in there so it was known where her newly born kittens were.

Well, Old Woman disappeared for a few days, and in the mornings she wasn't at the door as usual waiting to come in – with five dead mice lined up on the doorstep. Oh those mice! I had to step over them to get out of the door to go to school. But there they were, every morning, five of them. I suppose Old Woman thought that five was enough to get her supply of food and comfort for the day.

Nell and I searched for Old Woman everywhere, but to no avail – she had just disappeared. A week passed by, and one night we had a heavy snowfall, and everywhere was white as far as we could see. Then – to our great delight – Old Woman appeared! She was waiting on the doorstep, but this time, not with yet another dead mouse – but a tiny kitten in her mouth, alive and well.

She brought it indoors and took it up to the kitchen and into the cupboard where she would have given birth, and then went back outside into the snow again. She then did the same thing all over again, with another tiny kitten in her mouth – then again, and again – until she had five little kittens safely in the cupboard.

Then it occurred to Nell and me – there were her footprints in the snow. So we wrapped ourselves up, put on our wellingtons, and followed them. They went across the car park, across the garden, through the fence into the field and then straight up and alongside the field to where there was a little burrow, deep in the snow. That was where Old Woman had made a safe place to have her kittens. I so much wanted her to be able to keep her kittens. She had gone to so much trouble to find and make a safe place to give birth to them, to tend to them, keep them warm with her body, and then bring them home – one by one.

Like that deep cold snow, my grandfather's and father's hearts melted, and this time Old Woman was allowed to keep her kittens.

More Creatures Great – But Not So Small!

Butch

The most memorable pet that my grandfather had, was a rather handsome Boxer dog, called Butch. A very appropriate name for such a dog! His fur was dark tan, almost chestnut in colour, with a white blaze on his rather lovely face, and he had dark brown, soulful eyes – I could almost be describing a fine stallion. Butch must have surely been sent to us by some noble angel, who deemed that all pets should look like their owners. Well indeed, Butch certainly did!

My grandfather was not, of course, of chestnut colour with a white blaze, but he did have dark brown eyes, and there was a very great likeness between him and his number one pet. Butch's jowls perfectly matched my grandfather's, and when Grandpop took him out for car rides, the resemblance was intrinsically clear. If my grandmother was lucky enough to be invited along for the ride too, she would be ushered to the back seat of the car. Meanwhile Butch would take pride of place on the front passenger seat, alongside my grandfather.

To see the two of them sitting side by side was a very strange and amusing sight to behold, as they were so alike, and sat at exactly the same height. Butch would sit on his haunches, as pleased as Punch. Later they would arrive home, Butch still sitting there, enjoying every moment, with my grandmother cowering on the floor behind the front seats, terrified of Grandpop's erratic driving. He had learned to drive during the First World War, driving army trucks, and his first job after the war was driving lorries for Harland & Wollf, so he was actually a well-experienced driver, although he never actually took a driving test as they were not brought in until 1934.

The first time I ever met Butch, he was a playful puppy living in a hotel in Grays, so he was well used to the hustle and bustle of pub life. It was one of my grandfathers "landlady" visits, and this time it was a certain Mrs. Binns. My grandfather made it his business to get to know all the landladies in the area, from South to North Essex, and into Kent. He made every one of them feel special, and he didn't seem to have a care for the women who really shared his life.

The hotel had a huge ballroom upstairs, and Butch was taking little runs then sliding backwards and forwards from each side of the wooden floor, along the whole length of the ballroom. Backwards and forwards – backwards and forwards – oh how he was loving it! My grandfather took him to his heart straight away, and before long he came to live at the pub with us. Crikey, wasn't he a handful – absolutely into everything! I must say though, he was a very loveable puppy, and it wasn't long before Grandpop had him under his total control. In fact, my grandfather was the only person that Butch would ever answer to and obey.

I loved Butch. My grandmother could never take to him though. No, of course not – Butch had put her even further down the pecking order of my grandfather's affections. "I can't *stand* that hound!" she used to say.

Feeding time was quite an event – every day. The day's scraps from all the family meals, and those from the bar, were all put into one very large baking dish, and Butch would relish this each evening – no matter what would be in there, the whole contents would be gone in an instant.

"Have a lick of this" Grandpop would say to Butch, as he sat at the dining table having his dinner, with Butch sitting by his side, his jowls dripping with anticipation. Butch would lick at the pork chop, or whatever else was offered, his long tongue going round and round the piece of meat – and then Grandpop would put it, covered in saliva, back to his own mouth to finish it off. Mealtimes were very often extremely stomach churning!

As Butch quickly grew into adulthood, he became huge, so much larger than the smaller bred Boxers these days. He was a one man dog, and no-one, but no-one, could command him other than his master.

Grandpop had quite a collection of walking sticks, one in particular was what he used for training Butch. It had a gnarled, twisted top and he would use that top to hit Butch on his forehead to make him obey. *Clunk!* it used to go as Grandpop reprimanded him. Poor Butch. His dark, expressive eyes would look up at my grandfather as if to say "I'm so sorry". He knew he had to obey his master.

I would often accompany Grandpop on his long walks down the lane that led down to the fen and then curled its way around back to High Road, making it a very pleasant route to take. Butch would lead the way, and our little Jack Russell, white with a patch over one eye, and called – Patch – would follow along beside us. I learned so much about nature during these walks down the lane with Grandpop. He would point out things to me all the time. The flowers in the hedgerow, and the birds. He knew the name of every bird, and their habits.

Butch knew our route very well. He knew exactly where he was going, where he was allowed to go, and how to get back home. I tried taking him for a walk on my own once, on the lead of course, as he never took any notice of *me*. But the moment we got a little way down the lane, and out of sight of the pub, and therefore my grandfather, Butch jumped the lead. He was such a heavy dog that I just couldn't hold on, and in a second he was off. I was so worried. I thought he might run away, and although I ran as fast as I could to catch him, he still raced onwards. There was no way he was going to stop and just enjoy the walk, he just ran and ran.

And so I followed him, still running around the lane. He knew exactly where he was going though, and found his way to the top of the lane, back onto High Road, then all the way along the pavement, back to the pub. Well I never tried to take him for a walk on my own again!

In the evenings Grandpop would take the animals for a walk up Baker Street, and I still get told to this day what he used to do by people who remember this at the time. It was always the same routine, and the same formation. Grandpop would be in the front, always wearing his old brown felt, brimmed hat with a bullet hole in it, which he shot himself with a gun – to give it character, he told me! He seemed to like the idea that people might think someone had taken a shot at him!

So, Grandpop would lead the way, with his walking stick, Butch by his side, Patch behind, Old Woman behind him, her daughters Sue and Florrie (I had had the privilege of naming Florrie myself – well *I* thought it was a good name for a cat!), and hopping along behind – a pigeon, that Grandpop had taken under his wing.

I really don't know how or why that pigeon had taken to Grandpop, but as I say, all creatures great and small – they all loved him. As always though, Butch was number one pet – and he knew it!

This walk up Baker Street and back though wasn't enough for Butch. He loved to go for an evening walk on his own. And so, late in the evening, before the pub was closed, and therefore while the customers were still there (Butch had it all worked out), he would go down the lane on his own. This time though, he was on a mission. The mission was to find a hedgehog – and he always did. He would come back into the pub, always the taproom, and present Grandpop with the poor creature. Butch's mouth and jowls would be dripping with blood as he would gently put the hedgehog down on the floor for Grandpop, and all the customers, to see. I suppose he thought he was going to get another arrowroot biscuit as a treat. I think really though, he just enjoyed the attention.

Oh those arrowroot biscuits – Butch loved them, they were a form of praise for him. But so did Grandpop. We sold them in the pub for one old penny each, and they were very large and very dry. It was a real challenge to eat one without a drink – but Grandpop could. They were larger than a digestive biscuit, and yet Grandpop loved to demonstrate how he could put one in his mouth – whole. As I said, he and Butch were *very* much alike!

Those walks with my grandfather and Butch were all so idyllic, and Butch's little sojourns down the lane at night – until someone who lived in a house a little way down the lane got a Doberman. I absolutely hated walking past that house. The owners had built a large wire fence in the front garden, but that dog was absolutely ferocious and would bark so aggressively as we walked past. He was the most violent-looking dog I had ever seen, and I feel sure his mouth would foam with hatred as we walked past with Butch. I was so afraid that one day that awful dog would get out and attack us.

One day, the Doberman's owner came up to the pub, ranting and raving at Grandpop.

"Your dog has broken my dog's leg" he fumed.

"Well you shouldn't have let your dog get out" Grandpop replied, totally composed.

Obviously Butch was totally fearless, and Grandpop seemed very pleased with him.

~

Winter would come and fires would be lit in the bars. We had three open fires, one in the saloon bar, one in the taproom and one in the snug at the back of the taproom. My grandmother didn't serve behind the bar, but she liked to sit by one of the fires in the evenings chatting to customers, especially one called Doob, who used to make her chuckle. What he used to say to make her smile so much, I do not know, but I know she loved him coming to the pub and sitting with her.

Well Nanny always chose to sit by the fire in the taproom, for they were the customers she preferred. But so did Butch. He would sit in front of the fire on winter evenings, taking all the warmth away from my grandmother.

"Arthur – can you get that hound away from this fire? I can't feel any heat" she would ask my grandfather, as no-one else could move him.

"NO", he would answer – "he's enjoying it!". Such was their relationship.

And so my grandmother would pull her cardigan a little further over her chest, and make the most of whatever heat she could get.

At the end of each evening when the embers would die down in the fire in the taproom, Butch always knew that the fire in the saloon bar would be stoked up. Grandpop loved doing this and seemed to take great satisfaction in making a perfect fire. He would stand there for some time, prodding the fire with the long, black, iron poker.

Butch would slowly raise himself from his spot in front of the fireplace in the taproom, and with his blanket still on his back, he would walk round to the saloon bar, where he would settle down again in his prime position, right in front of the fire. His blanket never moved.

I remember one evening when my grandmother was sitting in the saloon bar in front of the fire, and my grandfather was leaning over the fireplace with his legs apart stoking the fire.

"Look at that scropulous old man", she said in disgust. A bit like Butch really.

Scropulous. What a word – it could only be one of Nanny's rather unique inventions that described exactly what she meant to anyone who understood her sense of humour... *"Scropulous"* Yes, that summed up rather succinctly an elderly man's testicles being rather too large, and hanging heavily... To this day, I can still hear Nanny saying it, and it still brings a little smile to my face.

Nanny was particularly disgusted by Butch's nether regions. "Look at them hanging down – those black things, banging together", she said. Why she wanted me to look at them, I do not know, but maybe it was to share her disgust. Yes, Butch did have big black balls that banged as he walked. What I disliked most of all though, was the red pencil that stuck out from between his legs sometimes. He would sit on his docked tail, with hind legs apart, and his dark brown eyes looking rather human... Then the pencil would come out. I really didn't like him when that happened – I didn't like him *at all!*

One day, Butch's nether regions were particularly disgusting. Something was hanging out. "I think old Butch has eaten that ball of string", my grandfather informed me. Each day, that string got longer – and longer – until one day, it was hanging down to the ground and trailing behind him. Why Grandpop didn't just cut it off, I do not know. Maybe he wanted to see just how long that string was, and how long it would take for it to come out completely. I think that sort of thing would have interested him.

As time went by, we all found this string rather off-putting. It was awful seeing Butch walking around like that, particularly when he was indoors. So one day Grandpop decided to take action. But did he take a pair of scissors to the offending string? No...

"I just gave it one big yank" he said – "and didn't he yelp!" I asked Grandpop where Butch was.

"I don't know", he said, "he's gone off somewhere... But he'll be back..."

Of course, the ever faithful dog did come back – but he never ate another ball of string!

~

Butch lived to a good age; in dog years he probably lived to over ninety, just like my grandfather. During his latter years though, he lost his zest for life, no longer hunted for hedgehogs, and was a bit doddery walking alongside my grandfather. This was all due to something that happened at the pub one night.

Luckily, for me that is, I wasn't there that night. Luckily also, for my grandfather this time, he didn't wake up while it was all going on. The gun that he kept by the side of his bed was for burglars, and he always said that he would shoot at their ankles first before calling the police. It never occurred to him that those burglars just might get to him first.

And so it happened. The thieves broke in one night, timing it to perfection. It was the day that cigarettes were delivered, so there was a good haul to be had, along with the alcohol that they took. They were cheeky whatsits too, apparently drinking out of the liqueur bottles whilst carrying out their heist. They had cut the telephone wires too. Stocks of spirits and cigarettes were cleared from the shelves and taken, along with the television that we had in the snug for the customers. The value of the haul was £225 which, in today's money, some forty-odd years later, would amount to thousands.

Luckily, no-one was hurt. But poor old Butch – the burglars had thrown him a poisoned bone, and although he recovered from the physical problems that caused, mentally, he was never the same again.

Adventures With Georgie

1950s

Over the Farm

Georgie and I became very good playmates during those early years at Orsett School. If ever the teachers paired children off, it was always Georgie who was paired with me. When we weren't at school we would tend to go roaming together over the fields, exploring. Every time we went on these adventures, we would venture a little further – there were no boundaries as far as we were concerned. No field gate that couldn't be climbed over, and no hedge that couldn't be crawled under. Just endless fields that went on forever – and that had to be explored. However, we always kept away from the gypsy camp down on the fen. We really did know that, as the poem says, we "should never play with the gypsies in the wood".

Mr. Watt, the farmer, owned Whitfield's Farm over the road from the pub. As with Reynolds Farm (Hill Farm), everyone knew the farm as Watt's Farm, because the local farms were all known by the farmer's name. He would allow Georgie and me to play in the farmyard. It was always a good source of adventure – we would climb up the wall of the bull's compound and look over the top at him. He seemed to be a happy bull – perhaps it was because we never bothered him! We would run up and down the trailer parked there, using it like a see-saw; that was so much fun, and we never got hurt. Our summer days were always filled with so much fun...

On summer evenings, Georgie and I sometimes went into the barn and climbed up the hay bales, which was really quite daring, especially for me being a girl. Then we would sit right at the top, and as it got dusk the bats would be flying around. They would come over and have a little nose at us, then get on with their business. I wasn't afraid of bats then. It was only later when my older friend Valerie, who was Georgie's aunt, told me that if they got into my hair I would have to have it all cut off, that they worried me. One day something actually did happen though regarding a bat – that put me off those strange creatures forever – but I will talk about that another time...

Considering Georgie and I were still at primary school, nobody seemed to worry about where we were or what we were doing. Somehow we always seemed to know what the time was anyway, even though we didn't have watches. Maybe it was our body clocks telling us when it was time to go home to eat!

Sometimes I would go over to the farm on my own. I knew when it was time for the cows to be milked because they all started walking in single file across the field to the milking shed. They had their hierarchy, with the head cow leading the way, and they all followed in line according to their status. Mr. Jennings, the cow hand, knew them all by name as well – and they really were called Daisy, Buttercup, Bluebell – names like that.

I would go to the cow shed and watch the cows being milked while talking to Mr. Jennings. It was interesting, and you could sense the cows' relief as their udders got lighter and lighter. The milk would go straight into metal urns and be left at the side of the road opposite the pub to be collected. No-one ever thought that anyone would take any. It wasn't as though people wouldn't drink unpasteurised milk, because Mr. Jennings always took some home straight from the cow's udder!

It was always lovely when the calves were born. Mr. Watt would let me know when I could go and see them, and then when they were in the little calves' byre, he would let me feed them with grass cuttings. They were so sweet. They seemed to know me, and that I would be there with these very fresh and fragrant grass cuttings for them.

~

In front of Mr. Watt's farm was a lovely grassed area called "the lea" – that word that is so often a clue in crosswords meaning meadow! The lea would be covered in buttercups and daisies in the summer, and Georgie and I would go over there sometimes, sitting in the grass amongst the wild flowers, and drinking ginger beer. We knew it wasn't *real beer,* but I remember another boy coming along at some time to join us, and when I offered him some – he said they weren't allowed to drink *beer.* Well more for Georgie and me then!

There was a large ash tree in the corner of the lea directly opposite the pub. Georgie loved to climb that tree, and he knew exactly where he was going, up all those branches, and then safely back down again. This got me interested in climbing trees – but I wasn't going to attempt that one!

~

Scrumping with Georgie

A much easier way for me to experience the joy of climbing trees was to go up to the orchard, which was half way along Baker Street, behind Rand's Farm (owned by Mr. Rand of course). My mother used to joke about Mr. Rand, calling him Mr. Randy. All I knew about her going up there though was to go strawberry picking.

So, our next place of adventure was now the orchard. Being late summer, the buttercups and daisies were gone in the meadows, but now the pale pink apple blossom had turned to fruit, the apples were ripe, and ready for – well, little children to go and investigate!

There was a mad horse who lived in the orchard. It was probably living on his own that drove him mad. Horses need company just like humans, and it is so sad to see horses and ponies in fields on their own. Well this horse used to give Georgie and me the evil eye whenever he saw us. He was particularly evil when we were up in an apple tree – because he knew we had to come down...

At first I wasn't that good at climbing trees. This was a new adventure for me – Georgie would clamber up ahead of me, and I would follow precariously, scraping my knees on the bark. But I managed it though, and soon learned that climbing trees was actually good fun...

So we would sit up in the apple tree looking out for the horse, and eating the odd apple now and again. We had our own little joke: "What's worse than finding a maggot in your apple...?" "Finding half a maggot..." True – very true!

There was a hole in the hedge at the side of the orchard, just about big enough for a young child to scamper through. We would bide our time, waiting until that horse got bored and started to move away – and then we would make a mad dash for it! Sometimes he would see us and come after us, but we always got through the hedge on time to the field the other side. Oh how the adrenaline would be racing then. Well he never did get us. He was probably having a game with us, something to ease his boredom. But we didn't know that at the time.

~

The Brickfield

Down in the dip, on our way to school, was the brickfield. There were no bricks in there, nor was it a field, but that is what it was called. So this was our next adventure...

The brickfield was just a sort of rough area, and to get into it we would have to climb over the wide wooden gate on the side of High Road, and walk along a rough path that always seemed to be muddy. There was a camp in there that, although I knew it was there, I didn't know anything about. Georgie later told me that it was where a few of the local boys went to smoke – it was their secret place – so no girls were allowed!

Georgie has also told me that this camp was a masterpiece – it was dug out of a small hollow in the clay, and had a roof with a chimney, so there was a real fire in there. Georgie had gone along with a few of the older boys in the village – but they were happy for him to tag along with them. What adventures children – mainly boys – would have in those days! Even if I had been allowed to go in there though, I think I might have found it a bit scary...

~

The brickfield was always a good place to explore... There was nothing much in there apart from long grass, weeds and stinging nettles, but there were lots of wild rose bushes, known as dog roses, and they were what I liked about it – well I *was* a girl, wasn't I?

One day I decided to go down to the brickfield on my own to pick some of the wild roses to take home to give to my mother. Why I do not know, but that is how I was. I was happily walking around, totally on my own, picking the pretty white and pale pink roses when, just as I had a little posy to take home – a man stepped out from behind one of the bushes. He was dressed very roughly, wearing a crumpled brimmed hat, and he was just staring at me with a very strange look on his face. It wasn't quite the evil eye of the horse, but it was a look that alarmed me – and made me run as fast as I could – dropping all the roses in my wake...

I knew then that I must never go down into the brickfield on my own again.

~

Another time I was walking down the road that went past the brickfield – I was just about next to the gate – when a boy appeared, stopping me in my tracks. A new family had moved into the village, and I hadn't yet got to know them. He told me his name and said they had just moved in. He said that he had seen me before walking down the road towards Orsett. Having exchanged little snippets of information about who we both were, and what was around, he told me he was twelve years old, and then asked me about the brickfield.

"So shall we go down there and explore?" he asked me.

Yes, why not? Well, I wasn't going to be on my own this time...

We both climbed over the gate, and jumped down onto that track – as muddy as always. It was probably the trees that overhung it creating an arch, and thus holding back any drying rays of sunshine, that always made it so muddy.

We walked along the track and into the brickfield. I was feeling a little bit unhappy about it, because of how I had been alarmed by that man behind the rose bush before. But I was now with this twelve year old who was much taller than me, and no man would jump out on me with *him* beside me...

Suddenly he stopped walking...

"I've got a knife" he said.

"Oh?"

"Yes – a knife. Would you like to see it?"

No, I didn't want to see his knife, and already the fear was creeping in. I didn't know this boy, but he was older and much bigger than me.

So here I was, a little girl, welcoming a new-comer to the village, and trusting him. I really did want to show him around, especially as he was showing interest in the brickfield.

He delved into the waistband of his trousers – and pulled out – a sheath knife! He whisked off the leather cover – then waggled the curved knife at me.

"See – I said I had a knife" he told me menacingly...

I just flew – I absolutely flew – the flight reflex had come into force. Once again I was scrambling over that wooden gate as fast as I could, just like when the man had alarmed me...

I never went down into the brickfield again without Georgie.

~

The Sewage Plant

Georgie and I had so many adventures. There was hardly a corner of Orsett and the surrounding fields that we hadn't explored. There was one place though where we had never been – the sewage plant! What an adventure that would be...

The sewage plant was down in a field behind the brickfield. Well at least I had Georgie with me this time.

So off we went, through the brickfield, and then on to that place we had never been before. The way to the sewage plant was to walk along the sewer pipe that led to it through what seemed like a field of stinging nettles. Really, those nettles were higher than us – even though we were on the sewer pipe.

Georgie led the way, carefully putting one foot in front of the other on that pipe. Meanwhile the nettles were standing as high as us on each side, menacing and nodding, warning us that one false move – one slip – and we would be in their stinging clutches...

I have never feared stinging nettles like I did then! The film "The Day of the Triffids" was yet to be made, but looking back, those nettles really seemed like Triffids!

When we reached the sewage plant we were safe from those huge nettles. But now there was another danger – the murky sewage...

But here we were on our greatest adventure so far!

We walked around the edge of the whole plant, looking at all the strange things that we didn't recognise floating around in there. Never mind the smell – the danger was even greater... What if one of us had slipped in? What would have happened to us? Would we have drowned in the sewage? Probably! It would have been a long way back to get help walking along that sewer pipe through all those menacing, giant stinging nettles...

~

A leap of faith

Always on the look out for more adventures, one day Georgie told me that he had found a new place – a *secret place* – and only a few boys knew about it. This was going to be exciting, because it was near to a haunted house! So we walked down to the village and turned left into Pound Lane, so named because of the old stocks and pound, also known as "the cage", which still remained on the corner where Pound Lane met High Road.

I always found going past there rather spooky, especially as it had been used up until the nineteenth century for punishment, and sometimes for the most trivial of crimes. People who were put in the stocks were mainly there for humiliation, and subjected to whatever anyone wanted to throw at them – rotting vegetables and goodness knows what. They would have their shoes taken off so that people could tickle their feet, as a form of torture. Really, people could do whatever they liked to them to humiliate them. Also, as they were left out in all weathers, many inevitably died.

So going down Pound Lane was just the beginning of our latest adventure. We followed the lane round to Old Hall Farm, a sixteenth century farm house which, being rather dilapidated, did indeed look very spooky. It seemed uninhabited – apart from the ghost! We agreed that we weren't going to go anywhere near it...

I could hear boys' laughter as I followed Georgie round to the left, past a large copse of trees, and walked through long grass, through which a path had recently been trodden. We came across a large dank pond where the boys were, overhung by one of the larger trees, and surrounded by stinging nettles and brambles, which again had been partly trampled down forming a way through to this secret place.

An old rope hung from one of the branches of the large tree directly over the pond, with a knot tied in the end of it, making something to hold on to. The rope looked as though it may have been there for some time – but hopefully securely...

The boys there didn't mind me being with Georgie – they never did. They would let me play cricket, and even football, with them down on the "rec", the local name for the recreation ground. I think they liked the fact that I would have a go at most things – even though I was a girl. Besides, I was Georgie's friend – so that made it ok with them!

The boys were getting more and more daring as they took turns swinging over the pond, and the rope was getting more and more momentum. This looked like so much fun – but not the sort of thing I wanted to try though...

Then Georgie had a go. He loved being a dare devil too. Really, as with the sewage plant, if anyone had fallen into that murky pond, well, it would have been very dangerous getting *that* sort of water into your eyes and mouth. But no-one really thought about that. I don't think children did worry about the consequences of such daring then, they just enjoyed the challenge and the fun.

Meanwhile, I kept looking back towards the old house, hoping that nobody – or no *transparent* body – would suddenly appear.

"Come on Yvonne" Georgie beckoned, holding the rope for me. Oh dear, so what would I do? If I didn't have a go, then the other boys might call me a cissy, and not let me play cricket with them anymore. Worse still, they might not let me go to any other secret place they might find.

"Come on Yvonne" Georgie said again, "it's fun!"

So I very cautiously held on to the rope, and Georgie gave me a little push. My feet left the ground, and that was it – there I was hanging over the murky, dark green water beneath me. I didn't quite get the momentum going like the boys were able to, and I was just sort of hanging there, actually really afraid of falling. It was then that I heard the branch creaking overhead as I hung onto the rope, trying to get it moving like the boys did – but I was just swinging slowly. By now I could actually *feel* the branch creaking...

Panic set in – I had to be brave, and trust that that branch wouldn't *really* break – *would it?* I wouldn't *really* fall into the pond – *would I?*

I wanted to scream in terror, but I managed to keep a semblance of a smile on my face. I had been trained in that way at the pub.

I held onto the rope, and was swinging as much as I could – *creak* – *creak* – *creak* – then I took a leap of faith as they say. I don't remember landing back on the side, and I am guessing that it might have been a somewhat undignified landing – but at least I was still in the cricket team...

~

Conkers...

The long, warm summer days would turn shorter and cooler once we returned to school in September. The fields in which Georgie and I would roam and play would be hung with a heavy morning mist when summer turned into autumn. With days now spent at school again, golden October would soon arrive. The red and gold leaves of the deciduous trees were falling, and the woods that had been carpeted blue with the bluebells in the spring, were now carpeted in shades of russet.

The smell of wood smoke would pervade the village streets, as people would burn their garden debris, and woodland smelled of rotting fungi.

But no matter – there was still lots of fun to be found. There were the horse chestnut trees that lined the "rec". They rarely grew in woodland areas, but normally in parks, village greens, and formal places like that. Having been brought over to Britain from the Balkans some four hundred years ago, they tended to be planted formally, and have stayed in those places. By now their long white blossoms had turned into fruit – I am guessing that because their seeds, the chestnuts, are heavy and fall straight down to the ground, they don't drift to other places. Indeed, their spiny green cases have a way of keeping them where they are.

These horse chestnuts, so called because they were once used as medicine for horses, were a great source of fun. The thrill of finding these "conkers" was immense. Some would be lying bare on the ground under the trees, and some would still be in their prickly cases. Usually these would split and show the conker inside. It could sometimes be a bit precarious opening them without getting scratched, but that was all part of the challenge.

So we would either meet up with other children (mainly local boys) after school to play "conkers", or take them to school to have fun playing the game in the playground. We would thread them onto short lengths of string, and the game was to hit other children's conkers, with the intention of breaking them, until one person had one left – and that was the winner.

Sadly, it seems that children aren't allowed to be free to just *play* games like this any more these days... Now they are growing up being almost sedentary with their tablets and computer games. The only tablets I knew when I was a child were Beechams Pills!

As far as I am aware from my childhood, nobody ever got injured from playing conkers, climbing trees and haystacks, crawling through hedges, swinging over ponds – and Georgie and I never did fall in the sewer did we? We just had fun...

So That's Where Babies Come From!

July 1955

At the end of July 1955 I found out where babies really do come from. It wasn't a stork putting them under a gooseberry bush after all – that was all nonsense. They came out of the midwife's black bag!

I had asked my mother all about it, and she went all sort of red and just said "you'd better ask Nell". So I asked Nell, and with a twinkle in her eye and a little grin said "you'd better ask your dad..." So I asked my father and he told me all about it – how the stork flew across the sky, holding the baby in its beak, then placed it under a gooseberry bush. But hey – where did the stork come from anyway – and why put them under prickly gooseberry bushes? It all sounded very silly to me.

~

Nurse Ellis walked up the stairs, carrying a sturdy black bag, her round face rosy pink, and her navy blue uniform and cap all pristine.

"Where is she then?" she asked with an eager smile.

My grandmother led her along to her bedroom where my mother was going to give birth. I had seen Nell going along there earlier with white sheets and a horrible looking, brown rubber mattress cover. She also took a white enamel washing up bowl and a long, sinister looking tube.

"The baby's in the *bag*" Nell had insisted – "you will see it later..."

I wanted to go and see the baby being taken out of the bag, but I wasn't allowed to go along there.

~

I was sent over the road to stay with Valerie's mother, Mrs. White, where I was to spend the night. I loved staying at her house, even if it might have been that I was just being "got out of the way" sometimes, and Mrs.

White treated me as if I was one of her own. Valerie has told me that her mum loved me as though I was another daughter. If only I had been. I used to see her every day, because after school I would go to get the bread that she had kindly taken in for us. The baker used to come round in his van delivering the daily bread, but my grandfather had fallen out with him and told him where to go, so he wouldn't deliver to the pub anymore!

It was always Mother's Pride sliced white that was delivered. Well that was very handy for the pub, and we normally also had sandwiches at tea time. If we wanted anything more fancy though, we would have to go to the little bakers in Grays High Street, which would usually only be on a Saturday. But oh – that bread... There were cottage loaves, with lopsided tops that were always nicely burnt, farmhouse loaves, with dark crusts as well, delicious fruit loaf, and also seed bread, made with caraway seeds, which my mother and grandfather loved, but which I really couldn't eat. One day, knowing how much I liked dark crusts, my grandmother sliced some off the top of a farmhouse loaf for me. I really enjoyed it, but I was then so afraid that she might get into trouble for doing that...

~

Mrs. White had seven children, although not all were still living at home, and Georgie also lived with her. So she had a lot to do! Valerie and her sister Beverley would make bread and butter pudding a lot, and I loved helping them with that. I would help them butter the bread and cut it into triangles, then sprinkle dried mixed fruit and sugar over the top. I would help with anything in the kitchen when I was there.

We would have the wireless on while we were doing these things, and would sing along to the music. The songs that immediately spring to mind are "Cherry Pink and Apple Blossom White", "A White Sports Coat and a Pink Carnation" and, on this particular day, it was Slim Whitman's "Rose Marie", which had just come into No.1 in the charts. I was so happy whenever I was at Mrs. White's house.

I loved the whole house. It was a real family home, and always so welcoming. There was a front room, decorated with a trailing ivy pattern wallpaper on a white background, which I think Valerie and Beverley chose. This room was usually only used on special occasions like Christmas, and I remember a Christmas Day I spent there sitting in front of the fire, feeling so hot, and eating oranges with all the family. It was so simple, but so memorable...

The small living room at the back was always warm too, with its open fireplace. Mrs. White's daughters would hang their stockings up to dry from the mantelpiece – and I remember a time when they all got burnt and got stuck to the tiled surround!

It was in that little room that Valerie taught me to knit (along with my grandmother and Nell at home). At that stage I was just knitting scarves for my dolls, but I remember those cosy times, knitting and watching programmes like "In Town Tonight" on their tiny black and white television.

I would also love to brush Valerie's long blonde hair, and I would even plait it for her. I wanted to be like her, happy and carefree, and I wished my mother would let me keep my hair long.

"Why can't you be like Valerie?" my mother would say to me, being more of a statement than a question. Yes, I did want to be like Valerie – but she was six years older than me for a start, and also, if I could only be allowed to let my hair grow long again, then yes, maybe I could be quite like her.

"I don't know – what is a big girl like her doing going around with *you*?" my mother would also say, again more as a statement.

She had these things that she said quite often. I can't help but think that they were devised to make me feel that I wasn't good enough.

~

Whenever I stayed over at Mrs. White's, I always shared a bed with Valerie and Beverley – I would be in the middle, and they would moan at me for turning over so many times!

"I don't mind you turning over" Valerie once said, "but why can't you just turn over – and not go all the way round?"

I'm still trying to work that one out...

Their bedroom was all pale blue, with pretty floral wallpaper, and a pale blue candlewick bedspread. To have one of those was quite the thing then. The corner of the bedroom had a blue curtain draped across, forming a triangle where they kept their clothes. Clothes in those days were quality not quantity, well quality if you were lucky – but quantity – certainly not. Clothes rationing hadn't ended until the month I was born, and people had got used to having few clothes. So that little triangular wardrobe sufficed.

~

So this particular day, I was very happy staying over there – but I was missing all the excitement!

"I'm not allowed to see the baby come out" I told Mrs. White and her daughters with a sigh.

There were a few exchanged glances, and nervous smiles...

"The baby's in the nurse's bag – and I'm not allowed to see it." I sighed again. Phew!

~

"What would you like?" Mrs. White asked gently. "A little brother – or sister?"

"Well I don't want a brother" I replied, knowing how my mother kept saying that boys were so much better than girls. I needed a sister to be on my side. I just hoped that my mother had ordered a baby girl!

~

The next morning I was allowed to go back to the pub, and went upstairs to see the new baby. Even though it was July, there was an open fire flickering in the fireplace.

"You have a little brother..." Nell told me, as I peeped around the door.

Oh no... Not a *boy*...

My grandmother was in the room as well, and my mother was sitting up in bed smiling and looking happy.

"You can have a look at him", she said, and I went over to the white wicker rocking cradle. He was very sweet, and had blonde hair just like me.

"His name is Ralf" my mother said. It is a nice name, but I had never heard of it before. All the boys at school had typical English names, like George and Geoffrey, John and Robert. I never knew until recent years either just why she had named him Ralf – and I am sure as with the choice of my name, my father didn't have any say in it!

I sat on the pale green wicker commode (seat down of course), and my grandmother put baby Ralf in my arms. He was wrapped in a fine, intricate, lacy shawl that she had knitted.

"Mind his head" she said, "don't let it drop back." I instinctively knew how to hold him though. It was almost like holding a baby doll, but he was warm and alive, and breathing softly. I peeped inside the shawl and looked at his little fingers, so tiny and delicate. All was peaceful, all was quiet, and there was a new addition to the family.

"Can I have a sister now?" I asked my mother...

A couple of moments of silence... Then everybody laughed.

The Trouble With Seven Year Olds

It was the 26th March 1956 and my seventh birthday. I received my usual five birthday cards, which I collected from the post box in the door of the cook house. I never did know why that was the post box for the pub, but who I was to ask? I never knew either, why my birthday cards from my parents and maternal grandparents were stamped and sent by post as well – from the pub to the pub!

"Hmm, so you are seven years old now" my mother said later that day, handing me my present in a brown paper store bag with string handles. "Seven is a horrible age – especially with girls" she said, sniffing and looking upwards with a flick of her head. "You're going to grow all gangly now, your legs are going to get all long and thin – and you will start to get cheeky – oh *I* don't know what I'm going to do with you..."

But I wasn't going to get all cheeky. That would risk severe punishment. *"Never answer back – never ask questions – do as you are told – and don't ask why..."* It was always the same.

I opened the bag and took out my birthday present. It was a maroon corduroy pinafore skirt, the kind that had a bib going up from the waist in front, and crossed over with straps at the back. It wasn't what I had hoped for, like something to play with, but who was I to say what I would like for my birthday anyway?

"Thank you" I said quietly, reaching up on tiptoe to give her a kiss on her cheek. She turned her head away. She didn't do kisses, well not as far as I knew. "And mind – that's only for best", she instructed.

I didn't like that corduroy skirt. It was springtime, and the days were getting warmer, and I really would have preferred to be wearing a pretty dress for best. I remember wearing it over a jumper and going out of the pub through the lobby and into the sunshine. I didn't like it. I so much wanted to wear something pretty.

And why was I going to suddenly change? What was going to happen to me? Would it matter if my legs were going to grow all long and thin? Would it matter if they didn't?

Well the pinafore skirt was long enough to cover all eventualities. And as usual, was meant to last me for some years, whether I liked it or not.

"I don't know what I'm going to do with you..." always rang in my mind.

Sports Day At Orsett School

Summer term 1956

Sports Day was something to be feared. Although later on I was to enjoy playing rounders – I loved tennis, and I even enjoyed playing cricket with the local boys down on the "rec" – at this young age, my weak, spindly little legs couldn't keep up with my body – nor anyone else's it seems...

I was usually last in the flat races, and in the baton races I worried about letting everyone down because I wasn't as quick as the others. I couldn't quite manage the hurdles either, or "hurtles" as I called them then – possibly as I always banged my ankles on the bar!

The three-legged race was another one... There I would be bound to whoever – usually a boy as I remember – and he would go charging off on his right leg – whilst I would be limping sideways... Anyway, why did I always have to be the *left* leg...?

So – this particular sports day beckoned. The flat race went exactly as I thought – I was last of course. No matter how much my name was called out urging me on, it made no difference. The "hurtles" hurt as badly as ever, as I collapsed on the wrong side, somehow with both ankles knocking off the bar...

But then – the worst thing ever – and thankfully this was the last "sport" of the day. I don't remember having practised much for the *tarpaulin* race... Well actually, it was the last leg of the obstacle race on Sports Day – not that *legs* were actually needed in that part – more knees and elbows – and overall a sense of *direction*...

The whistle blew – and we were off! How exciting – or maybe not... Somehow I got through or over the obstacles, which were obstacles indeed – but not as quickly as everyone else. How could it be that at such a small school as Orsett School, I found it so hard to keep up with everyone else?

I console myself that maybe my mind may have been quicker than my body – I just didn't *do* sports days!

And then – the large, dark grey tarpaulin sheet that seemed to stretch forever lay ahead of me. Everybody else's bottoms were disappearing underneath, like little moles digging their way to their burrows. I reached the tarpaulin, still with the wriggling rear ends going through, but by the time I found the courage to actually go under it – everyone else had finished.

Nevertheless, I had to do it – didn't I? How could I give up now – how could I not follow through something I had started? How could I lose face?

I crouched down and crawled under that dark, smelly tarpaulin. Was this my first experience of claustrophobia? I didn't know what that meant then, nor the gagging feeling of finding it difficult to breathe...

Onwards I went though – but where to? The bottoms had all gone. I could hear people – Valerie, Nell, and whoever else may have come along – "come on Yvonne" and "come on Eee-vonne". Despite what my mother had told me, I now knew that "Eee-vonne" was actually being called out to *me*...

There was a little light peeping underneath the far end of the tarpaulin, but it was also peeping under at the sides... I wonder how moles find their way? They dig with their noses, but do they really know which way they are going when they go into the deep darkness? Yes, of course they do – but I am not a mole...

It was then that I realised that these people, whether they were friends or not, were all calling my name. Calling me onwards... I thought that everyone had forgotten me – that I really didn't matter.

But no – they were still calling me. Their voices were coming from my right – so I then knew which way I had to head to get to the finish. I emerged, somewhat like a turtle peeping out of its shell – and I was cheered tremendously. It didn't matter that I had so badly come last – I had *finished* – and not given up... That was what all the cheering was about....

Nanny Mandeville's House

August 1956

Florence Elizabeth Barker, my father's mother and therefore my paternal grandmother, was born to a wealthy family in Kensington. She grew up in a beautiful three-storey house in a very smart road in West Kensington. I can imagine her walking around those streets in a long skirt, little buttoned boots and a big feathered hat. That is just me being romantic, but I expect she wore something similar as a young woman.

She was a fairly plump woman, who loved hats like Nanny Felstead, had lovely clothes, and had lots of expensive jewellery. She was very elegant, and tended to wear smart, lower calf-length skirts, and pristine white blouses. In one of my aunts' words, she was "a little cut above everyone else in Grays". Despite her upbringing though, she was always very friendly, and would stop and talk to people as she walked down to the town.

Florence, or Nanny Mandeville as I knew her, moved to Quarry Hill in Grays as a young bride, having married my grandfather. Despite her family's wealth, as is the norm in my family (of which sadly I am also a victim), she was cut out of the family fortune. From what has been suggested to me by her youngest son, my late Uncle Ivor, it seems that her family didn't agree with her choice of husband.

~

Nanny Mandeville's house stood proudly at the top of Quarry Hill. The actual quarry was a mile or so away, but in this small town in a grey, industrial area of Essex, there weren't many quaint road names in 1895 when the house had been built. Grays was then a very small town, and the roads seemed to be usually named after places that they led to. For instance, Orsett Road led in the direction of Orsett, Palmers Avenue led to Palmers School, which happened to be in Chadwell Road, which led, of course, to Chadwell – who needed satellite navigation in those days!

The houses along Quarry Hill were lovely Victorian semi-detached, with all the ornate features of that era. The high ceilings, with beautiful ceiling roses, picture rails, above which was a deep patterned coving, and a highly polished mahogany banister to the stairs, which swirled into a curve at the bottom. Nanny Mandeville's house was the first one you could see as you walked up Quarry Hill. It had an old flint wall, six feet high, and covered with ivy, and a lovely garden that stretched out at the side of the house. It was the biggest garden in the area, with a large apple tree in the centre of the daisy strewn lawn. In springtime this was bestowed with white apple blossom, with its promise of an abundant yield in early autumn. It was wonderful sitting in the shade of that large sprawling apple tree in the summer, with the sun twinkling through its leaves, and the smell of lavender all around.

Nanny Mandeville loved the scent of lavender, and there were well established highly-scented lavender bushes, and peonies in a glorious shade of magenta, in the borders. There were other smaller fruit trees, shrubs and flowers, but these are the ones that stay in my memory.

~

My paternal grandfather, Henry David Mandeville, was from a small hamlet called Llanytidman, just outside Llanymynech, in the Welsh Borders. He was the son of David Mandeville, who was the son of William and Elizabeth Mandeville. William Mandeville is said to have once been the Lord Mayor of Oswestry, although I have no proof to substantiate that.

My Uncle Ivor also told me that my grandfather over-saw the building of the railway through the Welsh Borders and then through England. I have no idea how my grandmother met him, but they obviously fell in love and she left her family in West Kensington. I find this all terribly intriguing, and also very romantic.

My father never spoke to me about his family history. I only found out about it from Uncle Ivor, his brother, after he had died. The only thing my father told me was that he used to go to a farm in Wattisfield, Suffolk for the summer holidays – staying with his aunt and uncle Barker, and "lots of cousins". He loved those weeks he spent there; he learned how to ride a horse bareback, and would go lamping for rabbits in the evenings, still riding bareback, and carrying a rifle! He spoke as though they had been the happiest days of his life.

~

Nanny Mandeville gave birth to three sons in the early 1920's. Her first born was my late father, Douglas Henry David, and the second, my late Uncle Ivor, was the survivor of twin boys, the other twin sadly dying at birth. It is Uncle Ivor who has told me so much about the family history of which I have written here – and this was all after my father's sudden death in 1994. It is strange how it takes a death in the family sometimes to bring other family members together. Due to a falling out between my father and Uncle Ivor, I didn't see my uncle for many years, but there he was, telling me all the things I wish my father could have done.

~

On Saturdays or Sundays, my father used to take me to Nanny Mandeville's house. He would leave me there for the day while he either went to work doing overtime, or more often going to the Working Men's Club at the bottom of the hill. I don't know where my Grandad Mandeville used to be; maybe he was doing the same thing...

The house always seemed to smell of Yorkshire pudding, although I am guessing that was just on Sundays. These huge puddings, I was sure, must have hit the roof of Nanny's old grey oven. My father told me that her secret was to add an egg for everyone who was sitting down to dinner. So I imagine that sometimes they must have contained maybe six or even seven or eight eggs! Whenever I encounter that delicious smell, I am straight back there, walking into the hallway of that lovely welcoming house. Nanny Mandeville would always be standing at the door waiting – with her arms open wide for me. I loved her so much, and I know she loved me. She would give me the affection that I didn't have at the pub, and would make me feel special, rather than invisible.

There was a Grandmother clock in the corner of the hall, so named because it was slightly smaller than a Grandfather clock. It may have been slightly smaller but, at the height I was then, it looked very tall to me. I loved that clock, and would stand looking up at it, fascinated by its ornately patterned face, with inlays of mother-of-pearl, its pendulums, and the way that it chimed for each number of hours on every hour, and once on every half hour.

To the left of the hall was the "front room", where all the best things were kept. Behind that another reception room, which I only remember as having dark blue curtains that made it a little gloomy, and at the end of the hall was the dining room, which was also used as a sitting room. This is where I used to spend my time with my grandmother. It had a bay window that overlooked the lovely garden at the side of the house, and an open fire on cold days. This room then led on to the kitchen, with its hard stone floor – and the warm smell of roast beef and Yorkshire pudding!

Nanny used to make the most delicious rhubarb wine, and that was always a little treat for me. I would sip that from a tiny glass as we sat by the fire. We would sit chatting, and I remember my fascination with her collection of brass ornaments that adorned the mantelpiece – brass plates with raised images of sailing ships, two brass bells, one in the shape of a Dutch girl, candlesticks, and a set of brass chimes that rang harmoniously as you touched them. Every one of them was highly polished, and gleamed in the light that came in through the bay window.

Later we would sit at the dining table in that bay window, with its fringed, copper-coloured chenille tablecloth, and play Ludo and Snakes & Ladders. Such simple games, which were so good for learning counting, but always so much fun. If only children (and their parents) realised these days that so much pleasure can be had from such innocent little games.

~

The smell of lavender is also always very evocative of the house as well – there was always a fragrance of lavender water in the bathroom, as well as of the Imperial Leather soap she favoured. These lovely scents always remind me of Nanny's bathroom.

I remember staying there once with my parents. I must have been about two or three years old at the time, because that's when I had my very first toothbrush. It was white with a red, white and black "Mickey Mouse" at the top. Nanny had lovely white towels, edged with fringes, that enveloped me with their softness, and were so different to the well-used, frowsty towels at the pub.

I loved those days that I spent at my grandmother's house. When my father dropped me off with her, we would walk down the hill to the little sweet shop at the bottom on the corner. She always bought me a small pack of my favourite sweets there, some that we didn't have at our shop in Baker Street, nor anywhere else as far as I knew. Those little sweets are unforgettable – no matter whether it was Easter or not, they always stocked them. They were miniature chocolate eggs, filled with the softest toffee. There were only about eight of them in the pack, side by side in an oblong box, which made you know that these really were special!

~

Christmas was celebrated in the front room, where the family would gather. I remember one such time in particular – a tall, decorated Christmas tree dominated the corner of the room next to the bay window at the front. We didn't have fairy lights in those days, but it was resplendent with coloured baubles, lots of sparkling tinsel and a white clothed angel sitting at the top of the tree.

I was sitting on the settee, opposite the glowing fire, which warmed the room with its Christmas logs, and Nanny was serenely playing the piano. It was a beautiful piano, again with petal shaped mother-of-pearl inserts. Like Nanny Felstead, Nanny Mandeville had been brought up to play the piano too. But Nanny Mandeville's playing was much more classical. She was lost in her music, and we listened to her intently, watching her clever fingers deftly moving back and forth along those ivory keys.

Having sat momentarily with her head bowed slightly at the end of her piano playing, Nanny then went over to the Christmas tree to where the presents were. It was all very simple then – just one gift for each person, and all carefully chosen with her love.

My gift was a lovely book about the fairies that lived in the blackberry bushes. There were little elves too, who lived under the red and white spotted toadstools. The text was big, and the illustrations were pretty. I read it many times, always fascinated by the stories. They were all mystical little tales about goodness, and things being right in the end. Little tales to believe, and to give me hope.

But how could things be right in the end, when that lovely book was taken away from me? How could that happen when I was always being good? Where were the fairies to help me when my most treasured possessions disappeared?

I have never forgotten that book though. If only I could have kept it.

If only I could still read those large printed words all over again, taking me back to the magical land where fairies lived in the blackberry bushes, and elves lived under the toadstools.

~

One day in August 1956, I was seven years old, and sitting in the car park at the round marble table with the wrought iron legs, that was beneath the kitchen above. This was one of the areas in which families would sit when they came to the pub, and their children could sit outside with their fizzy drinks, paper straws and packets of crisps. But before the pub opened, this was my little place. It was where the living room door had once been, with its forsythia arching over, and the clover at its base.

Being August, it was hot, and the kitchen window above where I was sitting was open. Usually, at that time of the day, I would instinctively walk up Baker Street at the right time to meet my father cycling back home from work. I loved seeing his figure getting nearer and nearer as he cycled along. Then he would put me on the special little seat on his cross bar, and I would ride back to the pub with him, with my legs stretched out, and happy that my father was home.

But this day was different though. My father was home unexpectedly early. I remember it so clearly, even what I was wearing – it was a little black and white, dogtooth check pinafore dress. It had a pleated skirt, and with it I was wearing a pale blue, short sleeved jumper and a matching blue ribbon bow in my blonde hair.

I realised he was already home when I head his broken voice in the kitchen above, telling the family the dreadfully sad news... My father had called in to see Nanny Mandeville at some time during the day – but had found her – lying on that hard stone kitchen floor... She was dead.

"Let's not tell Yvonne yet..." I heard my mother say.

The thought of Nanny Mandeville dying like that, with no-one there to help her, was too hard to comprehend. How could such a wonderful woman suddenly die? What was death anyway? Was I never to see her again? Would the fairies look after her? Had the angels taken her?

I slowly got up from my table in the car park, and walked out to the street. There was an old brick wall, which was the street side of the garages. There was a spider spinning a web in a crevice in the wall. I stood watching it, and then I touched the web – and the spider ran, breaking my thoughts... I wasn't afraid of the spider, but I ran too – as fast as my legs would take me, up Baker Street – to where I usually met my father. But that day, I had to go back to the pub on my own...

It felt like forever, walking back down Baker Street, like being in a dream where my feet were stuck in mud, holding them down, and burdening me with the weight of that heavy mud. Even though I was only seven years old, I bore the pain of my sorrow on my own. I had to somehow hide my tears, for I was afraid of being caught "listening" to the grown-ups' conversation, which would incur punishment.

When I was eventually told some days later, my eyes were all cried out. No-one knew that I already knew... No-one was aware of the lonely emotional suffering and pain I had gone through – and all on my own...

Whitehall Road

September 1956

The next month, on the 3rd September, my parents bought their own house. It was a nice, typical Victorian, middle terrace in Whitehall Road, which was at the time a quiet little road in Grays. It had an old flint front wall, a garden gate, that squeaked as you opened it, and a small front garden, with the old path edged with large clam shells. London pride, with its large glossy leaves and slender pink flowers, was planted along the borders, and bright orange Chinese lanterns grew next to the front door. I was fascinated by the Chinese lanterns, I had never seen them before, and they looked as though they were made of paper. They then turned into a translucent white in the autumn, showing the black seed pods. As did the honesty that was also there, with its flat seed heads that glinted in the late summer sunlight.

It was a very warm September, and the smell of paint always transports me back there. My father made a good job of painting the house, and I had great fun stripping the old wallpaper off the walls, particularly when it came off in large strips – very satisfying! The front room, with its typical Victorian bay window, was brightened up with a yellow patterned wallpaper on a white background, which picked up the sunlight streaming through the window. Sadly though, that lovely room remained unfurnished, so was never used.

Behind that was another sitting room that looked out onto the long, narrow back garden, and next to that the kitchen, where we had the dining table. I had the larger of the two back bedrooms, and it was so much nicer than the little box room, with all the woodworm, where I had been sleeping at the pub. All I remember about it, was a small Victorian fireplace, with a black grate and a white surround, and my bedroom curtains, which were green brocade, with a little hint of pink in the woven design – as I say – just a hint! I did like having that bedroom though, despite how sparse it was.

I have no recollection of why I was suddenly being allowed to live with my parents, but I wonder if, just possibly, they had decided to try and live a "normal" life...

Whilst there, my mother went on to some kind of health kick. Virol was the order of the day – a new fad for my mother to give me, but it was quite common then. It was made of malt extract, a by-product of the brewing industry, and was a gooey brown mixture of the malt and other additives and came in a round brown jar. I didn't mind Virol though.

What I did mind was that I had to have a cod liver oil capsule every day. Not believing that her daughter could possibly swallow such a large capsule, my mother would put it in a jam sandwich for me to have when I came home from school.

The trick with having the cod liver oil capsule in a jam sandwich, was to bite the sandwich in a certain place – so that you didn't bite into the capsule... Oh that dreadful taste of biting into that capsule is something I won't forget! I should have done what I wanted to do, and just swallowed it whole with a drink. But no, I had to take it as my mother had instructed. Yuk!

When I had one of my numerous colds, I was always given a sachet of Beechams Powders on a spoonful of jam, which would always leave a white residue around my lips, that I then had to lick off. Had nobody thought of dissolving it in a drink?

This leads me on to cold sores... I was always getting them! Why was it only *me?* There must have been something very lacking in my immune system to be getting these along with mouth ulcers. As I have surmised before, the ulcers could have been caused by all the alcohol I had been plied with, even as a baby, when I was given gin in my milk to make me sleep. Now, as a child, I was getting cold sores.

These were getting worse and worse, and each time I had them they spread further around my lips. What was causing them? The only remedy for this, or so it was deemed at the pub, was to put neat real perfume on them... Nell used to do this. She didn't seem terribly bothered about putting neat perfume onto my lips with her bare finger. This hurt so badly!

One time every millimetre of my lips was covered in cold sores – they had somehow joined up and caused these long horrible blisters all the way round, and even extended out into the corners of my mouth. This time I really couldn't cope with the pain. This was the worst they had ever been. I couldn't eat nor drink without a straw. Anything against my lips was total agony.

I was sitting in the kitchen at the table. I had tried to eat some food, but couldn't. I started crying, and then I was sobbing.

"What are you crying for?" my mother scowled, but with some semblance of ridicule. Why didn't *she* get ulcers and cold sores? Why was it only *me?*

"It's my *cold sores...*" I uttered as best as I could, amidst pain and tears. "They hurt *so much...*" I mumbled, bringing my hand up to my mouth, but not touching it.

"Well that's nothing to cry about" – she said dismissively.

Oh, but it *was.*

~

Unfortunately, living in Whitehall Road meant that I had to leave Orsett School, which I loved, and move to Little Thurrock School in Grays...

I didn't even have a chance to say good-bye to Orsett School, and my friends there for, being a cash purchase, everything happened so quickly. My lovely grandmother had died so suddenly just two weeks previously, and had probably only just been buried – strangely, in the same grave as her father-in-law David Mandeville at North Stifford Church, so she didn't even have her own grave... As I was so young, I wasn't allowed to go to the funeral. I don't even remember it happening. No-one used to tell me these things until after they happened. And now I had the prospect of starting another school – and very soon.

There was a woman who used to come to the pub called Reeny Howard. She was a most unpleasant woman, and my mother and Nanny Felstead couldn't stand her. However, she had a daughter, Margaret, who was the same age as me, and she went to Little Thurrock School. So my mother asked Reeny if she would ask Margaret to look out for me when I first started. Well Margaret, a big girl with dark hair, did so for the first couple of days or so, but she soon told me that she was now just going to be with her own friends. So I was left pretty much on my own. I would stand at the edge of the playground watching the other girls play together in their little groups, and just wish I could be back at Orsett School.

Before long though, a lovely little girl called Emma made friends with me. It happened that she lived at Stifford Clays in a flat above a shop, and her grandparents lived in a delightful Victorian house in Orsett next to the policeman's house. We became good friends, and have kept in touch all these years. I even still have a letter from her that she wrote to me when we were seven years old. I have very few things from my childhood, but luckily, I had kept that in a box in Nanny Felstead's wardrobe...

This is what she wrote...

Dear Yvonne,

Thank you for your letter, I am sorry I couldn't write sooner but I have had a lot of things to do lately and I didn't get round to it. I have got a little present for you which I hope I can soon get to you. Must go now.

Your loving friend, Emma x

That is something I have always treasured, just one small sheet of pale pink paper with Emma's young handwriting in green ink. How many children these days would have something like that I wonder? Text messages are not something to keep forever...

~

The Headmaster at the school was Mr. Jenkins, a nice man who spoke with a Welsh accent. It seemed that so many teachers were Welsh then. I took to the lessons well, even the woodwork class, where we made things out of balsa wood. This was more for the boys of course, but they had to learn how to sew as well – just simple sewing though, nothing like the girls had to do.

It was there that I learned how to do smocking. I wonder how many children these days would even know what smocking was – let alone know how to do it! Little girls' dresses then would be smocked across the chest, giving the dress a natural gathering, and with the little puffed sleeves that these dresses always had, they were so pretty for babies and little girls to wear.

There was something so different there to Orsett School though, which was run by the Church of England. We had to do a lot of bible studies there, and I particularly loved The Gospel of St. Matthew, and the miracles of Jesus. At Little Thurrock School though, there wasn't the emphasis on the bible, and I missed that. To sum it up really, there was just something *missing*.

Although not as nice as Orsett school dinners, they were quite nice at this new school. What really churned my stomach there though, was that a rather plump girl called Susan sat opposite me at the refectory table. She had this "party piece" that she did with so much glee... She would fill her mouth with mashed potato – then squeeze it out the sides of her mouth. It was absolutely disgusting! At least that was one trick my grandfather didn't do... I don't know what was more stomach churning really, Susan doing that or my grandfather sitting opposite me at the kitchen table pulling yellow sinews out of pigs' trotters with his teeth!

~

My mother was never happy at Whitehall Road and, despite all the decorating that my father had done, she was never totally happy with the décor, even though she had chosen it all herself. One day she told my father that she wanted it stone-dashed! He seemed aghast at that suggestion, and said that you couldn't stone-dash a house like that, being built of lovely Victorian bricks.

"I'm having it stone-dashed" she told him firmly.

"But it will look different to all the other houses" he explained.

"That's why I want it stone-dashed!" she demanded.

And so – that is what was done. If my mother wanted anything – she had to have it. No matter what the expense or how strange her demand was – it had to be done...

It is still stone-dashed to this day – I expect it has proved too difficult to remove. And yes, my father was right. But he had to do as he was told...

Well the stone-dashing has remained, but the lovely little front garden, with its pretty flowers and clam shells, has now long gone, and has been turned into a concrete slab, with a wheelie bin taking pride of place – instead of the London pride...

~

Whitehall Road was a turning off of Southend Road, and there were some small shops along that part of Southend Road. I would be sent along with a note for groceries sometimes, carrying them back in a brown paper carrier bag with string handles. There was also a hairdresser's along there.

Hairdressing salons were so different in those days, where privacy and peace were prevalent. This one in particular had polished wooden screens between each styling chair. So they were relatively private, which was good, as ladies in those days didn't want others seeing their hair being permed and tinted...

~

One day my mother looked at me, frowning (not unusual), and told me to go and get my hair cut – like a parent might say to a son. Only I was still only seven.

I didn't want to have it cut. I wanted to let it grow again like it was when I was younger, and I really didn't want to look like a boy again.

"How do you want me to have it cut?" I asked her as she put a florin (a two shilling piece) in my hand.

"Just tell her to do it as she thinks", she said, dismissively.

Following my mother's instructions, I walked along to the end of Whitehall Road, turned left into the busy Southend Road, and went along there until I found the hairdresser's.

"My mummy said can you cut my hair please?" I asked the hairdresser, handing her the coin.

"Now, how would you like it cut?" she asked kindly, helping me up onto one of the chairs and putting a black rubber cape around my shoulders. I would love to have known her thoughts.

"Mummy said cut it how you think", I said resignedly. I looked at myself in the mirror. My hair was already short – how much shorter did it have to be?

I kept my head down as the hairdresser snipped away. And then I felt her brushing the back of my neck – with a wooden handled brush just like I had seen them use in the barber's...

Oh well – was I ever going to have long hair again?

~

Before long my mother said she didn't want to be at that house any more – she hated being in Grays – and being what she called a "Grays-ite"... She was going back to the pub.

So that is what we had to do. It was difficult for me, and it must have been hard for my father leaving the house that he had decorated so well. He was from Grays himself, and I imagine he felt that when they moved there, he was "going home".

Now though, we were all living back at the pub – and under the rule of my grandfather. What's more, it meant that I was back in that little box room – with the woodworm!

Unfortunately – I was still going to Little Thurrock School. Nell would get me up early and ready for school, and then put me on the bus in the mornings, giving the driver the tuppence ha'penny for the fare, and asking him to drop me off at the Oak, a pub at the top of Rectory Road, which is where the school was. So I would get off the bus there, then walk down Rectory Road to the school.

Coming home I knew that I had to walk back up to the Oak and go to the zebra crossing where there was a lollipop lady. Having crossed the road, I would go to the bus stop and had to wait for the No.53 bus that went through Orsett.

"Can you drop me off at the Kings Arms please?" I would ask the driver, handing him my other tuppence ha'penny that I had kept safe all day for the journey home.

I travelled like this for two years while I was at Little Thurrock School. I was ok, but how I wished I was back at Orsett School! I am guessing that because my address was still officially a Grays address, then I had to go to a Grays school. At least living back in Orsett again, I was able to see Georgie and my other little friends at weekends and holidays.

~

My first Christmas term at Little Thurrock School, I had been off sick and I went back to school towards the end of that term. What I didn't know was that it was the day of the Christmas party, and that was why girls in my class were wearing party dresses. I also didn't know that everyone had been asked to take something in to contribute to the party...

"Where is your contribution?" my rather snotty teacher asked. What contribution? What was it all about?

"What have you brought in for the *party?*" she emphasised, leaning over to me, knowing that I hadn't brought anything.

"Well now – as you haven't brought anything to contribute to the party – then you won't be going..." she said with a self-satisfied smirk.

Later that afternoon, we were all told to form a queue, in pairs, and to lead out of the classroom. I got up to go and join the others.

"Sit down Yvonne!" my teacher commanded shrilly. "You didn't bring anything for the party – so you can't go..."

So I sat back down at my desk, and watched all the other children leave the classroom, two by two, to go to the party. Some of the children were looking round at me as they left. I don't know whether it was with pity or condescending, but it was a truly horrible feeling.

It was quite dark in there too, because the teacher had even switched the lights off. Then the classroom door was closed, with the only light coming through from the hallway. It seemed as though everyone had gone home – but they hadn't – they were at the party.

I sat there at my desk for what seemed like ages. It wasn't *my* fault that I hadn't taken anything for the party – but I was being made to feel that it was.

I wasn't aware of the time, but by now I should have been on my way home.

After a while, my teacher returned.

"Come on" she said, as she opened the door – and led me off to the canteen. By then everyone was on the jelly and blancmange course, but that was ok. I sat down in my place at the refectory table, and had a little of whatever was left. There wasn't much – but at least I was *there*.

~

Parents were waiting at the school to pick up their children, and I started my walk up Rectory Road to the bus stop. It was really dark by now, I didn't have a watch, and I felt very confused. Then – I saw a familiar figure coming down the road. I looked – and I looked again – it was my mother! It wasn't as though she was relieved to see me though – she wanted to know what I had been getting up to, to make me so late going home. At least on that particular occasion she had actually come to find me. She hadn't even sent Nell. That was probably the only time in her life that she had shown any concern for me.

I blurted out what had happened, and how unhappy I was. All I wanted to do was go back to Orsett School. Surely, that wasn't too much to ask. I was living back in Orsett anyway. But no, all the time my address was down as Grays, I had to stay at that school.

At least the next Christmas my mother gave me a Lyons chocolate Swiss roll to take to the Christmas party – and so this little Cinderella *did* go to the ball...

Two Worlds

September 1956 to July 1958

To a young child the place where they live is their world. Even to children who live in cities and may never have seen a cow, their local streets, shops and alleyways are all their *world*. My world was Orsett and the surrounding countryside. The lanes I used to walk down, and the fields I used to explore. Well now I was back from a short time living in Grays town, but to the world that I knew.

I continued travelling to Little Thurrock School for two years, to-ing and fro-ing from the age of seven to nine. I still saw my friends in Orsett whenever I could, and occasionally I would be invited to go to Emma's home, the flat above a shop in Stifford Clays. I was never allowed to invite her home though. I don't remember much about Emma's father, but I remember her mother very well. She was lovely, and sometimes I would see her cycling past the Kings Arms wearing a grey coat and a headscarf, going down to the village to see her parents in Rectory Road.

I was invited down there once for Sunday tea. It was winter, and there was a very welcoming fire in the front room. The dining table was set out in there, all very nicely done with proper table mats and napkins – nothing like the newspaper we had on the kitchen table that served as place mats at the pub...

There was a large mahogany Victorian mantel over the fireplace, with little shelves and mirrors, all very in keeping with the lovely Victorian house. We were having cold meat salad for tea, which was unusual for me. But oh dear – I didn't recognise the meat... I quietly asked Emma what it was – and she said it was tongue! I really don't remember eating it, but I suppose I had to because it was very impolite to leave anything.

I still went to Sunday School early on Sunday afternoons. It was held in the Chapel, which was along Rectory Road from Emma's grandparents' house, at the end of the houses. No matter what the time of year, I remember it as always being so cold in there. I did love going though, especially as the bibles from which we read there were the type that had the occasional water coloured pictures in them. Whenever I see an episode of "Dad's Army", when they are gathered in the village hall, it reminds me of that hall, the bareness and coldness. It's a nice memory though.

Sometimes, when I wasn't at school, even though I was so young, I would walk down to see Reverend Godwin who lived in the Rectory opposite the Chapel. He had told me that I could go to the Rectory at any time if I needed to talk about anything, which was very kind, although I didn't know of anyone else who went to see him. It is only now, looking back, that I am wondering whether he suspected anything about the goings-on at the pub. Maybe he even *knew* some things, being the village vicar...

I would walk up the front path, through the large wooded garden. I would reach up to the round, black ironwork door knocker, and I can still remember the echo when I knocked, as if I was about to enter a hallowed place. His wife always answered the high oak door with a smile, and would take me into the front parlour. It was lovely in there with velvet Georgian style armchairs, and the high walls were painted in matt Wedgwood blue, with a border at the top of white Wedgwood-style figures.

I would sit there quietly, looking around me and up at those white figures, so typical of Wedgwood. Then Reverend Godwin would come and sit with me. Mrs. Godwin would bring us tea in pretty patterned china cups, and little biscuits on matching tea plates. He would always have time for me, asking me about school, and what I had been doing. I don't know what I found to chat about really, because I had to keep quiet about so many things, as I always had that threat of being taken away to a home, but it was always comforting talking to him, no matter what it was about. What's more – he was *interested*...

I have a little book called "Squirrel Goes Skating", by Alison Uttley, which is all about woodland animals and their adventures. There is a name plate in the front that says – "Awarded to Yvonne Mandeville – Orsett Congregational Sunday School – 1955". Something that Reverend Godwin had awarded me. Luckily that was one of the few things that I kept in my box in Nanny Felstead's wardrobe... At least that has survived.

Sadly, the lovely Chapel where I spent my childhood Sunday afternoons, reading about Jesus and the bible stories, did not survive, and has now gone. In its place are four large detached houses... The Rectory has also gone, and where it stood in that large wooded garden is a block of twelve, two-bedroomed apartments...

How can one world be turned so drastically into another world? Doesn't anyone have any feeling for these beautiful old buildings any more – for their history, their heart, and the memories that were steeped within their walls?

At least they live on in *my memory...*

~

One day, it was a Saturday, and my mother was in a particularly bad mood with me. I really don't remember what she was accusing me of, but whatever it was, I hadn't done it. She marched me off to the bedroom where my parents slept at the pub, and had a right go at me. I still couldn't admit to something that I really hadn't done.

"But I *didn't*" I was pleading.

Suddenly she hit me so hard around my head that I fell to the floor. We didn't have fitted carpets in those days, just lino and the odd rug here and there. My face went smack down onto the cold lino, and I felt pretty stunned.

At that moment my father came into the bedroom. He didn't say a word. He just picked me up and took me to the car. He got a few things together, and then drove off, taking me back to Whitehall Road.

I don't know exactly how long we stayed there, just the two of us, but it was probably a few weeks – and it was like living in another world...

Unfortunately, I had to have a door key and let myself in after school until my father came home from work. But then he would cook the most delicious meals, which we ate at the table in the kitchen. I would sit at the table and we would chat, while he fried the best steaks or lamb chops, always with fried onions, potatoes and a green vegetable – most of the time being Batchelors tinned processed peas! I did love them though...

He had worked in the butchery trade when he left the Royal Navy, and knew all the best cuts of meat. When cooking a roast beef dinner once, he had bought a very dark piece of beef – it really didn't look at all appetising. He told me though that the darker the meat – the more tasty it would be... And it really was!

Whatever he was cooking, and it always involved lots of meat, he would make what I called, and still do call when I make it – black gravy – a combination of Oxos and Bisto. Also, he didn't pour any of the cabbage water into it, like Nanny Felstead used to do! I loved it so much that I would have more after I had eaten, poured over a slice of bread. Better than any dessert I thought – now that was quite a compliment coming from a child.

Daddy told me all about how the animals were killed at the slaughterhouse in Grays where he worked. There was a pen outside the slaughterhouse on the pavement, strewn with straw – something to make the animals feel more comfortable maybe? A poor cow would be tethered, awaiting its fate as people walked by. It's not that I wanted to know, but he never saw a problem telling me these things. At least they had been killed humanely, unlike the poor victims of war that he had encountered whilst serving in the navy, fighting the Japanese in the Pacific...

I say humanely – well yes, physically. They were stunned first. But my father was never comfortable with slaughtering sheep. He said he would hold their head in his left arm, while he got the stun gun poised in his right. The sheep would always look at him intently with soulful eyes, knowing what was about to happen...

Well this was not the best of topics whilst eating beef or lamb!

Another thing he told me about his time spent working at the slaughterhouse, was all about *blood* – he seemed to be fascinated with it. He told me how if you get a bowl of blood and keep stirring it, it will go all stringy – did I really need to know that? And how did he find that out anyway? Why was he stirring blood?

Even more disgusting though, was that he told me – he used to drink it! I found that so hard to believe, but he went on to tell me that he took some home once and was sitting at the dining table – drinking it... Then his father came home – and saw him...

"You dirty bugger!" he apparently exclaimed, as my father relished the taste with bright, blood-red lips. But he carried on drinking it...

That was a very strange, and extremely disgusting side to my father, that I really didn't like. I never asked him *why??* Nor did I ask him why he stirred bowls of blood… I really didn't want to hear any more.

~

Despite our chats though, he never spoke about my mother, nor did he ever ask me about my feelings. But what if he had though? Would I have disclosed what I really felt about what went on at the pub, and how unhappy and lonely I was? Would I have told him how my grandfather hurt me by twisting my knee and elbow, and putting boiling hot spoons on the back of my hands and the insides of my wrists? I think if he had pressed me, I might have said something. But he never asked. As always, my feelings didn't matter. But at least he had picked me up and taken me with him to Whitehall Road.

Whatever the problem was between my parents at that time, I didn't know anything about it. I would like to think that the final straw was my mother hitting me to the floor, when I was still so young. I think there was more than that though, but it was between the two of them.

Or was it? Was someone else involved? I really hate to speculate, and my father was a very tolerant man, but had something happened now that was far beyond his tolerance…

What he did tell me though was that he just wanted to live a normal life, in a normal house, like most families… I remember his face when he was telling me that – he looked so sad and hurt.

Most of all, he wanted to get my mother away from the pub. I knew he hated my grandfather. In fact, I don't think I ever saw them speak to each other, apart from when my grandfather was being abusive to him. I think it was a sort of mutual jealousy, a conflict that I could sense over my mother.

~

I had been sitting at the kitchen table in the pub one evening when my father had come home from work. He was never "work shy" and would work all week at the cement factory, as well as do all the jobs that my mother and grandfather demanded of him. He was tucking into his meal, and relishing every mouthful, even though it had been kept in the airing cupboard since lunchtime.

The kitchen door opened – and my grandfather came in...

"Look at that lanky idle..."

Whatever the last word was, I cannot remember, so probably didn't understand, but it was something really derogatory.

"His plate is all piled up like a dog's dinner..." he snarled.

My father reached for the cruet, and sprinkled more salt and pepper onto his meal. Maybe this was his way of consoling himself against my grandfather's cruel remarks – and my mother's lack of defending him. He cut off a piece of roast potato, and handed it to me on his fork – even though it was just a small morsel, it was delicious, heavily salted and peppered, but a little sign to me that he welcomed my presence at the table.

~

Another time, my grandfather just suddenly turned on Daddy – he really laid into him and beat him up badly – while my mother stood by and did nothing about it. Badly injured, my father managed to get away from him, and hid down in the cellar. Of course, he never reported the assault, and just kept quiet about it. A bit like me really.

~

My mother and her father were always very close, and I could detect that she always put his feelings above my father's. I don't know why she did this – maybe my grandfather had total control over her. And somehow – she had total control over my father...

"For Christ's sake Joan..." I heard my father say many times, "put a lid on it..." and other things in that vein. "Lord – give me strength..." he often pleaded, gritting his teeth...

Then she would come out with something very hurtful and blasphemous. She loved her father, and if there was someone's side to take it would be his. Or maybe, that was the control he had over her. I don't know.

~

And so, it wasn't long before we went back to the pub. I didn't want to go. I was lonely anyway, but being lonely with my father was a better option than being lonely amidst all the people at the pub. Besides, being away from the pub, I didn't have to do physical work, and could concentrate on my school lessons. In fact, I felt like a normal child living in Whitehall Road, even though it was as though I was from a one parent family – and what they called "a latch key kid".

And so, there I was, back at the pub – in that other world – full of abuse, confusion and heartache. At least I was going to go back to Orsett School next term though.

The Local Characters

There were my friends. Georgie of course, and his aunt Valerie with whom he lived at her mother's house along with her siblings, well – whichever ones weren't married and hadn't left home. I had adventures with Valerie too, but as she was six years older than me, they weren't the sort of adventures I had with Georgie...

Valerie and I would go for long walks around the lanes, and over the fields, chatting all the time, a lot of it being about local characters. Sometimes she would take me to Gravesend to visit her sister Barbara and her lovely husband Vic, who lived on the outskirts of Gravesend. I had a great adventure there once (or not) – but I will talk about that particular one later.

~

There were also the customers in the pub, and the local people in Baker Street, High Road and Stifford Clays Road, who all knew me, and who all seemed to like me. When I would be walking up Baker Street or down High Road, or scooting along on my little Tri-ang scooter, there were always friendly waves and hellos as I went by. Some of the older people would spend much of their time leaning over their front gates, especially the men who really didn't seem to have much else to do – they would always call out to me, touching their flat caps, and sometimes I would stop and chat.

There was someone who I used to avoid though, well so did everyone else! Her name was Lil Oddie, and she was a very "odd" character indeed – she had long unkempt hair and always wore an old coat, no matter what the weather. She would walk around Baker Street and High Road, muttering to herself all the time – and always carried a suitcase!

The nearest anyone got to hearing anything she was muttering was something about going to find her mother, although they weren't sure, because they weren't that close! Looking back, she was a very sad character, and really someone should have tried to help her. But we children, and Valerie and her sisters too, along with everyone else who knew her, were always afraid to get anywhere near her. So whenever we saw her we would cross over onto the other side of the road.

I really don't know what happened to her. I can only hope that a Good Samaritan came along one day – and didn't cross to the other side of the road...

~

At the back of the Kings Arms was a large meadow, which was part of Mr. Bridger's land. Our garden ran alongside this and sometimes, when the meadow was covered with a profusion of buttercups and daisies, I would climb over the fence and into the meadow, and would sit there making daisy chains. At the far end of this meadow was a derelict windmill, which was also owned by Mr. Bridger. The windmill may have been disused, but it was a landmark, and in the summer evenings its outline would be seen in all its glory against the setting sun.

Between the pub and Mr. Bridger's house was a little narrow alley that led in the direction of the windmill. On one side of this alley was a row of very old thatched cottages. They were so tiny and yet, in their day I expect they probably housed large families. On the face of it, they were rather unkempt, but there was one in particular which certainly wasn't!

Valerie was friends with a young couple who lived in that distinctive cottage – Moira and Tom. They were an unconventional couple, the kind that Valerie liked. I liked them too, and sometimes Valerie would take me round there when they were both at home.

They also made the ice cubes for the pub in the little compartment at the top of their refrigerator, which I would collect on a Sunday for the Sunday lunchtime saloon bar customers. I feel sure that in return they would have been rewarded by my grandfather with whatever drinks they fancied! He did that sort of thing.

Having them making the ice cubes for all the gin and tonics that were being consumed was a necessity, because we didn't have a fridge, let alone a freezer – they were new-fangled things at the time, well in Orsett anyway. The nearest thing we had to a refrigerator was the pineapple-shaped ice cube holder that sat on the saloon bar counter...

~

Their tiny cottage was lovely, in a very arty sort of way. As you went through the very low front door, there was a little living room on the right, but ahead were two fishing nets complete with glass buoys. They were draped from one side to the other – the first, being a natural fishing net brown, hung from the right to the left, held back by a rope and a buoy, and the second one behind it, hanging from the left to the right was dyed purple, and again, held back by a rope and a buoy. So very different to the tie backs we have these days!

This was August 1957 and I was only eight years old, but already I loved their style. I had never seen anything like this before in someone's home. They told us that the fishing nets were authentic, as were the buoys, and even the little bits of rope. They came from somewhere I had never been before – another wonderful land – called Cornwall... Little did I know then how much that atmospheric county, that place where artists flocked, would mean so much to me one day...

So having gone through both the fishing nets, this led into the kitchen. There – right in the middle of the floor – was a rockery... There were rocks and plants there – oh how I was loving this couple!

The way to the only bedroom was via a wooden ladder that led upwards to a square cut in the bedroom floor, which you then had to somehow get through. Valerie went before me, and I followed on. However, I stayed at the top of the ladder, just looking into the bedroom.

"Come in Yvonne", they were beckoning, but I was afraid to go into their bedroom. Something instilled into me...

So I stood at the top of the ladder, as Moira and Tom showed Valerie their bedroom. Something that really struck me was that they had pink and white candy-striped sheets on their bed, something I had never seen before.

They were a lovely couple, and we would always sit and chat. They were very unconventional though, with Moira going to work (something which married women didn't do in those days) and Tom being a house husband (which married men *definitely* didn't do in those days!).

One Sunday morning when Valerie and I went round there to collect the ice cubes, Tom was sitting in the living room knitting a dress for Moira. It was a tube type dress, quite popular then and, as was the fashion, was going to end just below the knees. The knitting yarn was black with yellow flecks.

Although a little unusual, this was looking very nice as Tom knitted away in the armchair, while his roast was slowly cooking in the kitchen. It was all so strange, and so completely different to what I knew. But who was to say whose life was "normal"? Mine certainly wasn't at the pub...

A grey Siamese cat with a very sharp face and bright blue slanted eyes, so unlike the cats I was used to, sat on the long low black settee in front of the small square front window. I had seen her before – but always on a lead. Tom used to go to Grays shopping on the bus – and would take this cat with him! The two of them used to be quite a sight waiting at the bus stop, and I always wondered what happened if the cat got caught short...

But this was a special cat, wasn't she? Did she *ever* get caught short on the bus – or in the shops? I can only hope not!

"Hello Marnie" I said, as I sat on the floor next to that very stylish settee, and looked into the cat's eyes – but I didn't like what I saw. Her eyes were mean – *very, very mean* – and, as I lifted my hand to stroke her, she immediately lashed out at me, leaving a long scratch down the side of my hand to my forearm.

Well I never touched her again!

~

What I remember more than ever though, was that Valerie was already becoming very stylish. I loved the dress she was wearing that day, and I remember it so well. It was a sleeveless "shirt waister" dress, made of an ice blue sateen cotton (the very colour of Marnie's eyes) and had a script pattern all over it. We used to have fun trying to read all the words. I loved that dress, all clinched in at the waist with a self-fabric belt and with a little collar that stood up against her blonde hair.

As we walked back to the pub with me carrying the bag of ice-cubes, a song was in our steps...

"Wake up little Susie" by the Everly Brothers was in the charts, and had also been playing on Moira and Tom's wireless.

"Wake up little Susie – wake up little Susie" Valerie and I were singing, as we skipped along the street back to the pub. It didn't really matter that once I got back to the pub I would stop singing...

~

Sometime later Moira and Tom left Orsett to go and join the "Chelsea Set" – a group of people that were of great fascination to me, especially as that wonderful flamboyant character Oscar Wilde had lived there all those many years ago. I loved arty people like this, but I can't help but feel that Moira and Tom had influenced me in a way, when I was only eight years old...

When they left Chelsea they then moved to Beverley Hills – well, of course they did – and as far as I know, that is where they are residing happily to this day...

The Pub Characters

There was always Doob of course, Nanny Felstead's friend, who used to sit in the taproom with her by the fire, making her chuckle with his low whispers. He could make me chuckle too – just by looking at him – his old brown felt hat, with its brim pulled down over his face, his shiny shaggy jacket, and his huge purple nose, dotted all over with pock marks. But – he helped to make my grandmother happy...

There was Stan the scrap metal man, amongst other things. Well whatever it was, that was the sort of thing he dealt in. I really liked Stan, he was a nice man, and we used to play pontoon in the taproom using bottle caps as currency – the more bottles people bought – the more currency we had! He had two side-kicks – Wozzle, who was sort of non-descript in a way and very quiet, and Flash, who was also quiet, so I really don't know why he was called Flash! Maybe it was because he was good looking...

Then there was "Cripple George". Oh dear, but he knew that everyone knew him as Cripple George, and he really didn't mind – at all. That is how it was in those days. There wasn't any "political correctness", things like that. My grandfather even gave money to the "Spastics" every Christmas, so we had "Spastic" stamps on the backs of all our Christmas cards.

Cripple George used to come to the Kings Arms in his invalid carriage. This was a three-wheeler carriage with a black hood like a baby's pram hood. He would leave the invalid carriage in the car park, and then edge his way into the taproom very slowly, one normal foot in front of the other foot that wore a huge high shoe – so he must have had one leg shorter than the other, amongst other things.

People would send pints along the bar to Cripple George, which he accepted in all good faith, and he never once complained about what he was called. In fact, he seemed to like the way that everyone acknowledged his disability. How different it is now, with everyone minding what they say, for fear of offending someone.

The character that stays in my mind most of all though is a lovely old man who lived in a small house at the top of Baker Street – Arthur Kempster.

He was a real character, but very quiet and unassuming. He kept himself to himself, and didn't want any help from *anyone*. He had come from quite a well-to-do family, but I don't know what went wrong. At least he had his house, well it seems, a pair of houses – appropriately named "Kempster's Cottages".

I had never been in his house, but I can only guess that it was in a very bad way. Arthur would come into the pub at lunchtimes, and would always sit at the same place. He would order a pint or two, and would then unwrap his lunch – which consisted of a pound of raw sausages, a whole onion and a Swiss roll – always the same.

He would sit there eating the sausages raw, pulling at the uncooked meat through the sheep-innards casings, and sucking with gusto. He would slice the onion and eat all of it with the sausages, all with his pints of beer. He would then finish this off with the Swiss roll, which he would bite at whole, savouring it until it had all gone.

If you got too close to him, which I would try to avoid, you could see fleas jumping on his clothes. It wasn't just one flea, but several, and I only hope that they loved their host so much that they stayed on him – and went back home with him again...

I did like Arthur Kempster though, even though I kept my distance. He was friendly, and would love to talk – if anyone let him. He just seemed to be a poor old boy who had originally come from a good family, but had hit bad times in earlier years, and had ended up living like this.

One day I heard that he had been taken ill, and thus into hospital. We knew a nurse there who told us what happened...

Upon examination they found that he had never cut his toenails, well not for many, many years. They had grown round the end of his toes, and along under the whole length of them. So that explained the strange way in which he walked. He wasn't openly crippled like Cripple George, but his crippling condition was hidden, deep in his holey shoes.

Poor Arthur was also in such a state that he had to be fumigated and all his clothes burned.

Well after that, he never did come back to the pub. He no longer sat in the taproom drinking his beer and eating his raw sausages... He died quite soon after all that.

Poor Arthur. Is it always the best thing to take someone out of their comfort zone? Possibly it is. But in Arthur's case – it seemed not to be...

The Pond And The Crow

April 1958

The Pond and the Crow sounds like a good name for a horror film! Well this was an adventure that I had that did actually go wrong...

Valerie's older sister Barbara, and her husband Vic, had invited us to stay with them. As with all of Valerie's family, they welcomed me into their home as though I was indeed – *family*.

They lived just outside Gravesend and Valerie had taken me to visit them sometimes. We would take the bus to the Tilbury ferry, cross the murky river to Gravesend, go up those awful open steps over the water that I have described before, and then up the High Street to take the bus to Barbara and Vic's welcoming house.

This would be an even more exciting trip though – as this time, Georgie was coming with us – *and* we were to be staying for the weekend... One of those glorious times that was to get me away from the pub for a couple of nights.

The plan was that on the Saturday afternoon Vic was taking Valerie, Georgie and me to some woods near Meopham. This meant a very exciting ride in his sidecar – so Barbara packed us a picnic – and we were set to go. Vic had all the motorcycle gear – he really did look the part – a long black leather coat, leather cap and goggles, and thick black leather gloves – even though he had a sidecar attached to the bike!

So Valerie got on the pillion seat behind Vic, and Georgie and I sat in the sidecar – him in front and me behind. I had never been in one before, so a new adventure was about to unfold... Vic's gloved hands played with the accelerator on the handlebars, and we were suddenly off – with the sidecar rocking from side to side!

It was the last weekend in April, but not a particularly sunny day; in fact the sky was a light grey colour. The yellow plastic windows of the sidecar made everywhere look sunny though! As Georgie was in the front, he was pretending he was driving – I just hung on behind and we were having so much fun. As was Valerie, her arms clasped tightly around Vic, with her long blonde pony tail flying in the wind behind her...

So there we were, enjoying this new adventure as we travelled through the country roads of Kent, and I could see Valerie laughing with joy – as free as a bird.

~

The grassy area alongside the woods, where we were going to have our picnic, was covered with long established clusters of primroses, so many that we had to find a space amongst them to lay out the picnic. Beneath the surrounding trees were shy little violets, so delicate and fragrant. Bluebells, although prolific in numbers, were still tightly in bud, holding their promise for a glorious swathe of blue under the beech trees in May. So the primroses now held centre stage, glowing in their pale yellow hue, bringing a little bit of sunshine to us on that rather grey day.

Beyond this grassy area was a large pond which, being overshadowed with trees most of the way round, looked dark and rather murky. Not somewhere we wanted to go too near!

Even though the sun wasn't exactly shining, we still had a lovely time, enjoying our picnic, marvelling at the large amount of primroses all around us, and chatting. However, always looking for a new adventure, Georgie and I decided to go over to the pond – *to have a closer look...*

The pond was quite low down and there was a steep bank down to it. We weren't planning to go down there, but I think we must have wanted to see how close we could get... The April showers had made the edge of the bank very slippery and muddy – so guess who fell in?

I remember the horror of slipping down the bank – and straight into the pond! I fell back against the bank, and the water was up to my face. There was a large dead black crow in the pond with its wings spread out making it look huge. I was actually afraid of crows in those days, thinking they were the harbingers of, well, doom... And this crow was getting closer – and closer – to me...

It was very precarious for Vic to get me out, but he managed to do so before I went under – and what's more – before the crow got me...

What a to-do!

Having travelled back to Gravesend soaking wet in the sidecar, Barbara ran a bath for me, washed my hair, and brought me my night clothes. She then sat me by the fire, wrapped up snuggly in a blanket.

Valerie and George – as I know him now – still remember this little "adventure", but it's not one that I wish to think about too often...

~

On the Sunday morning Barbara and Vic were having a lie in, and when I got up I noticed their bedroom door open and Valerie was in there talking to them.

"Come *in* Yvonne" Barbara beckoned when she saw me standing on the landing. But I couldn't. I knew that I must never go into any adults' bedroom, well especially not when they were in bed. So I stood there in the doorway.

"Come *in* Yvonne" Barbara said again, tapping the bed, indicating that I was welcome to join in the conversation. But I still stood in the doorway. I felt so awkward, and feeling that I was doing something I really shouldn't do. How different were other people's lives to what I was experiencing living at the pub.

Later when we went downstairs, we went into their front room and Barbara played their new record on their equally new radiogram – it was "Tom Hark", a very unusual sound in those days, being made by a tin whistle band, but it was great. Valerie and I loved it immediately, and we were soon dancing around the room... ♪♪ *Dah dah dah dah – dah dah dah dah – dah dah dah dah – dah dah dah dahhhh...* ♪♪

How I loved being at their house!

~

I never saw Barbara and Vic again though, because sometime later they went to live in Los Angeles. Barbara wrote lots of letters back to her family telling them about her new life there. Apart from missing her family terribly though, something else that she missed so much were the English seasons. It was a little tedious having all year round summers...

Well, I don't suppose primroses, violets and bluebells grow in such splendour in Los Angeles!

Northcroft

In 1958 the house in Whitehall Road was sold, and my parents bought a bungalow in Orsett a little way down from the pub, called "Northcroft". I say my parents bought it, but I have been told that actually my grandfather bought the bungalow because he wanted my mother back in Orsett nearer the pub, something that my mother wanted too.

This was the Dr. Jekyll side of Grandpop. Or was it? Did he have some other motive? The kindness of Dr. Jekyll would feed the lust of Mr. Hyde, and when Mr. Hyde was dominant, he would go to the ends of the earth to satisfy his craving.

What my father didn't know, was that my grandfather also regularly gave money to my mother – and lots of it by the sound of it... This she kept hidden from my father.

~

Somehow "Northcroft" sums up something cold, dark and bleak, and that is how it looked at first. All it needed was a light but warm touch, injecting a little bit of life into it. Actually, my parents never used the house name, only the number. Maybe they thought it a little too depressing. "Northcroft" – doesn't it sound like a little croft, way up in Aberdeenshire? So romantic if that is where it was, with views of the rugged sea and the north winds blowing and whistling through the walls...

But this was in England – in Essex. It was one of a row of bungalows built in the 1930's, with a long narrow garden out the back, that led onto the fields, and the sloe bushes, where my father would gather the fruit for his sloe wine.

In the garden at the back of the bungalow was an old air raid shelter. It was an Anderson shelter, one of those dug into the ground, with steps leading down through the earth into its darkness and a rounded corrugated iron roof, covered with soil and grass for protection. The thought of a family taking sanctuary down there while the German bombers were flying overhead, I found rather disconcerting.

My mother never wanted to go down there, so my father had a plan – this was now his sanctuary – this was where he kept his secret whisky store, and fermenting home made wines. Oh those delicious wines – they were as wonderful as Nanny Mandeville's – rhubarb, damson, elderberry, and now sloe... She had taught him well!

There was no way Daddy could have left his home made wines at the pub, not with Grandpop prowling around. So on the pretext that he was tending to his wines, he would shut himself down there in the air raid shelter amongst his whisky bottles...

He took me down there one day. He could trust me not to tell anyone about this, because that was how I was being brought up – that I was never to say a word to anyone – about *anything...* There was just a narrow shaft of light coming through from the small doorway above, which highlighted the glint of the bottles. He poured a little drop of whisky into a small glass and handed it to me...

"Get that down you" he said, handing me the glass – "and not a word to your mother..." he added with a naughty grin.

Yuk! I just did not like the taste of the whisky, it was far too rough for my young palate. So Daddy downed it in one go.

"Ahh" he went, with a satisfied smile. "You don't waste a drop of this amber nectar". Then he poured himself another glass.

~

Despite having the bungalow though, my mother would still spend all day at the pub. My father would come home from work, not to his bungalow where he could have spent a "normal" life, but to the kitchen table in the pub, where he would have his dinner, which had been kept warm all day in the airing cupboard. At least the gravy was heated separately in a saucepan, so it was not congealed like the food.

Cabbage and sprouts would turn brown and yellow though – and the smell – it permeated the contents of the airing cupboard! So not many vitamins saved there then – at least some were in the cabbage water that had been poured into the gravy...

He would have a mountain of food, so much that any more, and it would have fallen over the sides of the rather substantial dinner plates. My grandfather would ridicule him – calling him a glutton.

Well, my father may have been a big eater, but he was also a neat eater. He didn't sit at the table eating like a pig like my grandfather would be, pulling at the yellow trotter sinews with his teeth.

At least my father taught me proper table manners, and how to use cutlery properly, working from the outside in, and then at the end of the meal leaving your knife and fork lying side by side, and not out at right-angles. He also said that if you would like more food, you would leave the fork with the prongs facing upwards – but if you had had sufficient, then you would leave your fork with the prongs turned downwards. I didn't know at the time that he had come from such a good family, who grew up with such niceties.

My mother's table manners though were more in the vein of no elbows on tables, and no talking at the table – at all. "Little children should be seen and not heard" she would say if I uttered the odd word. She would usually follow this with "I wasn't even allowed to *cough*". She would also remind me that when she was a child, if she uttered a word – she would be sent out of the room.

Although she was a stickler for table manners, they didn't extend to not taking food off of someone else's plate though. That someone else's plate – was always mine. I liked to save my best bit till last – but I soon learned not to! Usually that tastiest of morsels was my best roast potato – all crispy on the outside, fluffy on the inside, and tasting deliciously of whatever joint of meat it was roasted with. Suddenly – a fork would come down right onto that last potato – and it would quickly be whisked up into my mother's mouth... "Heh heh" she would grin, relishing every last bite in front of me.

~

Although my parents now had the bungalow, I was still living at the pub, and so was Ralf, who was now three years old. He was privileged though, being allowed to sleep in the large "spare" bedroom – but I was still in the woodworm room...

What Did You Do In The War Daddy?

The first time my father told me about his World War II days was when I was too small to reach the taproom counter and had to stand on a Smith's crisps tin. My father would be on the other side drinking his pints, and would tell me about his days in the Royal Navy. His pale blue eyes would water, and then tears would appear on his cheeks. He would tell me the same things over and over again. It was as though he needed to talk about it, but I was seemingly the only person to ask.

Later on, when I was older, he would sometimes take me to a special place. It was called Stanford Pit, and was a very old quarry that had filled up over the years with water. We would always go on our own, early on a summer's evening, and would walk precariously around the edge and find the place where we would sit and watch the sunset over the water. This was when he told me more about his navy days.

He had left his parents when he was just seventeen telling his weeping mother and angry father that he was going off the join the navy to "kill all the Japs..." He lied about his age, saying he was eighteen, and that was it – he was in the Royal Navy.

He served on various ships out in the Pacific Ocean: destroyers, aircraft carriers, and at one time a submarine. His stories were very explicit about what went on, but the one that stays in my mind most of all was when he was in Singapore. He was part of the group of servicemen who, when the war ended, went to rescue the women in one of the prisoner of war camps.

What he found was far, far worse than anything that I have ever seen on "Tenko". The things he told me may have been far too graphic for a child of my age – like the woman they found half dissolved in a bath of acid, her eyes still open in terror, and her mouth set in a scream.

Another story he told me, was about an officer's wife, who had had her nipples bitten off and spat in her face. But I was there for him – and he needed to talk about it.

I treasure my memories of those times with my father at Stanford Pit. To my mind, this was *our* place, without fear of being taken off to do some job.

But then, it was always back to the pub, and once again my father would be back to his pints – and under the rule of my mother and grandfather.

~

I think my father must have been quite an unhappy man. His memories of his times in the navy were of the trauma and atrocities that were carried out, but sometimes he spoke as though maybe his time in the navy had been the best days of his life. He was certainly very proud of being an old sailor.

He told me once how he wished my mother would live a normal life – away from the pub. But the Kings Arms *was* her life – even though they had the bungalow in High Road, she would spend each day and most evenings at the pub.

My father seemed to dull his mind with beer – and at weekends, if he wasn't at work, he would pride himself on having "eight pints before lunchtime". This was an awful lot of beer to consume...

One Christmas Eve in the afternoon, my grandfather came home from having driven along Stifford Clays Road. He told us that on his way he saw some old boy lying up on the bank, with his feet still in his bicycle pedals. Unlike the Good Samaritan, he had just carried on his way back to the pub – without stopping to see if the man was alright.

We were upstairs in the kitchen and my grandfather was looking out of the window. A tip-up lorry was reversing into the car park next to the pub.

"Look – there's that old boy I saw up on the bank!" Grandpop exclaimed – as the lorry lifted the truck at the back, and a man fell out onto the ground – followed by his bicycle. It was *my father*... Goodness knows where he had been drinking, because that wasn't his normal route home from work. What's more to the point is just *how much* had he been drinking, because he was well used to copious amounts of alcohol...

My mother decided to take charge, and somehow my grandfather and Nell managed to get him – into the garage... There they sat him on the running board of the old Morris, and handed him a large turkey.

Usually we wouldn't get a turkey until late on Christmas Eve when my grandfather would go to Romford market last thing to get one knocked down in price. This time though, he had probably "acquired" it, possibly doing a bit of beer bartering!

"Now you are staying there until you have plucked that turkey" my mother ordered, as my father fell forward onto the ground. Again he was pulled up and sat on the running board, where he sat with his head slumped down onto the turkey on his lap.

I was very worried about him, and went to see how he was several times. Each time I saw him he was very, very slowly, plucking one feather at a time. He sat there like that for hours. For all anyone knew he could have been injured – but my mother and grandfather had no mercy.

~

It wasn't always this sad for him – he did enjoy life sometimes. He was good at ballroom dancing, although my mother didn't dance. If only she could have at least *tried*. Sometimes at pub parties Daddy would dance, the waltz or something similar – with me standing on his feet. I loved those times, when he got me up to dance like that. Standing on his feet, with his right arm around me, and my right arm held high, I felt protected. I think he enjoyed that too, as he had no-one else to dance with. But usually he seemed to drown his sorrows with alcohol.

~

I think my father could be a bit of a romantic though. One spring morning my mother got up to find lots of daffodils in a crystal vase on the kitchen table. They didn't have any daffodils in their garden though...

Later, Daddy chuckled as he told me he had gone out in the middle of the night and jumped over a near neighbour's front wall... *That was where all those daffodils had come from!*

Just as well then that my mother never had the neighbours round...

My Ninth Birthday

March 1958

The only birthday party I ever had as a child was when I was nine. It was just a little tea party with a few childhood games afterwards, like pin the tail on the donkey, blind man's buff, that sort of thing. Now this was all very exciting, not only because it was *my* party – but also because my friends were actually allowed *upstairs* in the pub.

Ralf was only three, but he was there of course. There were also two of my girl friends who lived near the pub and who were the same age as me, Georgie, and Flora's stepsons, who were aged ten and eleven. The table was set out in the lounge, and there were chicken paste sandwiches, strawberry jelly and blancmange, and a lovely chocolate birthday cake with tiny pink and blue candles. That was the only birthday cake I had ever had.

Nell was in charge of the food, and my mother was around as well. So we all tucked into Shippam's chicken paste sandwiches. Children liked paste in those days, and didn't expect anything fancy. If I had some mustard & cress in with it, then it was even better – but just chicken paste, and also bloater paste, were particularly good. Then we got onto the jelly and blancmange. Unfortunately, as always, I had to have bread and butter with mine, which I never thought went together, but if I didn't have the bread and butter, then I couldn't have the jelly and blancmange.

And so I sat there, nibbling at the bread and butter, along with the jelly and blancmange. But it was difficult, especially as we had just had sandwiches. By now all the other children had eaten theirs and were eager to have the birthday cake. So the candles were lit, "Happy Birthday to You" was sung, Flora's stepsons gave me the bumps, and the cake was sliced.

Meanwhile, I was still struggling with the bread and butter...

Everyone was having "seconds" of my birthday cake, and I hadn't even tasted it. And then – when I was finally allowed to have mine – it was all gone... No-one had thought to save any for me – and it was *my birthday cake*...

~

But what fun afterwards though, especially when we played postman's knock. Well it could have been if it had been played fairly – we girls were obviously hoping to get a boy, but we only got each other. It's no fun kissing another girl on the cheek! And the boys were hoping to get girls – but they just got each other too. Then one more go... I was standing out on the landing being the "postman" and, to my delight, and to the giggles of the girls, Georgie came through the door – a swift little peck on my cheek – and then he was back in the room. So sweet. And all so very innocent.

Thinking about it, these three childhood games are all about not seeing what you are doing. These days, putting the pin on the donkey's tail would probably go awry, with grinning boys chasing the girls' bottoms with the pin, and with blind man's buff they would be touching each other up maybe. Goodness knows how postman's knock would be played now...

~

My birthday present from my parents was a record player. It was blue and cream with a lid and a carry handle, and it played 45 rpms, 78 rpms and 33 rpms. Someone also gave me a £1 record voucher, which with singles being 6 shillings and 8 pence, you could get three for that.

My favourite record at the time was "Diana" by Paul Anka, which had been released ten months previously. I was only nine years old, but I knew what music I liked!

So I knew I could get three singles with my £1 record voucher. I also liked Buddy Holly's "Peggy Sue", Danny & The Juniors' "At the Hop", Guy Mitchell's "Singing the Blues", Ricky Nelson's "Poor Little Fool" – and anything by Elvis Presley! At the time he was in the Top 10 of the charts with "Don't"... All grown-up songs for a nine year-old, but I loved them, and I could dance to them. But if I could have had only one record at that time – it would have been "Diana"...

The following Saturday my parents took me down to Grays to the record shop to spend my voucher. This was new to me, and all very exciting.

"So what are you going to get with your voucher?" my father asked.

"Well first of all, I want to get "Diana" by Paul Anka", I replied, almost shaking with excitement.

"Paul who?" my mother asked, with a sort of frown.

"Anka", I said.

"Never heard of him" she said shortly.

"But... I love "Diana" " I pleaded, "it's my favourite song..."

"No, you don't want *that*" my mother replied, "I don't know that one..."

My mother was always telling me "You don't want that". It must have been one of her most-used statements. She was always saying it. What she really meant was *"I* don't want that".

So we left the record shop, where I was surrounded by all this wonderful music on 45rpm singles, and went up the road to Woolworths, which had a small record selection – but all 78 rpms. My mother went through the 78s and found "At the Hop" for me – but it wasn't by Danny and the Juniors – it was by Paul Rich... I didn't want Paul Rich – I liked Danny and the Juniors! She then came back with Marion Ryan's "Love me Forever"... What?? And the last, but certainly not the least of her choices was... "Charmaine" – by Mantovani and His Orchestra...

So they were my birthday records. At least my grandfather had already got some Elvis 78s – those that he played in the bar occasionally – but which now he allowed me to play on my new record player upstairs – sometimes.

~

Nanny Felstead came from Southgate in London, a family of eight children, some of whom died during childhood, but four children remained. There was my grandmother, and her three brothers – Tom and Dick, but I don't recall the other brother's name, so I'll just call him Harry...

Nanny hadn't seen them for years, but one afternoon, Tom and Harry had both come to the pub to see her. They were both as short as her, and dressed in sharp, double-breasted suits and ties etc. They were real cockneys, just like her, and it had been a joy seeing them all so happy being together again. They were laughing and joking, and coming out with their own cockney rhyming slang, which to me didn't make any sense, but it did to Nanny! She was well away having such a happy reunion with her brothers, and I don't know why she never went to see them in London.

Well her other brother, Uncle Dick, lived in Bedfordshire, in a cottage at the side of a road. The frontage may have been a bit narrow, but he had a lovely garden that stretched out at the sides and at the back, and his main gardening pleasure was growing shallots!

It was soon after my ninth birthday that we went to visit him once – later that day wending our way home with a box of those shallots that he had kindly given us. Uncle Dick had a son called Bobby, who was fifteen years old at the time. I had met Bobby for the first and only time before then, probably just a couple of months previously. He had cycled all the way from Bedfordshire to the Kings Arms. I was upstairs in the pub kitchen and my mother was sorting socks, rolling pairs into balls, when Bobby appeared in the kitchen door. The doors were always open, but even so, I was very surprised to see someone I had never met coming through the door. My mother and grandmother were naturally delighted to see him – but I didn't have a clue who he was, no-one introduced me to him, and I didn't know what to say. So I just stood quietly while the conversation went on. He seemed to know me though, and I remember telling him that it was going to be my birthday soon, and that I was going to have a party.

When Bobby left, to embark on that long cycle ride home, my mother didn't go down to see him off. Instead she went back to where she had been standing at the kitchen table sorting the socks.

Suddenly, a rolled up pair of socks, which were rolled so tightly they resembled a cricket ball, came hurting across the room – hitting me right in the face...

"When someone comes to the pub" she shouted, "you go and greet them properly – you ask them how they are. You don't just stand there..."

Quite right I know. But at the time I was only eight years old, and when someone who I had never met suddenly came in through the kitchen door, I had been rather taken aback, and no-one had actually told me who he was. The shock and sting of that tightly rolled pair of socks, certainly made me know that never again was I to query who someone was, no matter who it might be. I would always have to greet any stranger who came to the pub – properly...

~

So there I was at Uncle Dick's cottage in the Bedfordshire countryside. I was pleased to see Bobby again; he was really nice, and he led me into the little sitting room at the back of the cottage, while my parents and grandmother went to inspect Uncle Dick's shallots...

"So what did you have for your birthday?" Bobby asked.

I told him about my record player and my record voucher, and he asked me what records I had got with it. I told him, and he sort of grimaced. "But what is your favourite record?" he asked, "what did you *really* want?"

"Diana!" I said, without any hesitation at all.

He smiled, and then went to his small record collection. He then came back with a record with, for some unknown reason, a cover that he had made himself out of newspaper. It was a Paul Anka EP, having four tracks on it – including "Diana"...

He gave me a lovely smile as he handed it to me... "It's yours" he said kindly...

I never saw Bobby again, but I still have that EP – it is one that I particularly treasure.

The Girl Who Came Back

September 1958

I returned to Orsett School in September 1958. It was only a small school, and most of the children knew me. I remember being told that I was known as "The girl who came back", which was quite warming really. It would have been awful if they had forgotten me.

The teachers had changed though, and there was also a new Head Master – Mr. Simpson. He had taken over from Mr. Patterson while I was away, but apparently I'd had good reports from when I was there before, and Mr. Simpson welcomed me warmly.

As there were so few pupils at the school, there were two years in one class – there were only thirteen in my year – Gordon Greig, Robert Thompson, Andrew Jackson, Roger Hall, John Newby, Geoffrey Head, Heather Warner, Pauline Brown, Robert Reynolds, Georgie Bilham, Elizabeth Harry, Stafford Wilson – and me – as they appear on my treasured Leavers' photo. So there we were, two years in one classroom.

That didn't matter though – we all got treated the same... Or maybe not! The brightest students sat in the front row, at desks two by two. There was Georgie Bilham, Elizabeth Harry, Robert Thompson – and me. I sat next to Elizabeth Harry, who was the local policeman's daughter. We were the front row children!

There was also something that would never be allowed these days. To say the very least – Mr. Simpson would not have lasted long at his job! It was a Dunces Corner at the back of the room, where anyone could be put as a punishment for not paying attention, or whatever. But in those days it was acceptable as a punishment. I remember Robert Reynolds spent quite a time in there, not because he was a "dunce", but because of the length of his hair. It wasn't that long really, just too long for what was acceptable for school. Well, at Mr. Simpson's school anyway!

"Into the corner Rosie" he would say to Robert, "and if you don't get it cut – I will tie a pink ribbon on it!"

For the boys who just weren't very interested in school lessons (and they were all boys) I feel sure the humiliation didn't make them any better, just even more reluctant to actually learn anything. But that is how things were. Again, at Mr. Simpson's school!

We also had our shoes inspected each day to see how shiny they were – and had to confirm that we had actually polished them ourselves. God help anyone who hadn't...

Then we were asked if we had cleaned our teeth! Occasionally there was the odd poor child who hadn't, so they then had a lecture on how to clean their teeth. The usual excuse was that there was no toothpaste in their house... "So use salt" Mr. Simpson would say, and then go on about how they had to use salt in the army to keep their teeth clean. Only cleaning your teeth at night was no excuse either...

"Don't you come into this class without cleaning your teeth first", would be the irate instruction.

So there was all this emphasis on teeth cleaning – but I don't remember Mr. Simpson actually asking if anyone had had a wash?? Crikey – with some of them – that would have started something!

~

I *quite* liked Elizabeth Harry, who I was sitting next to, and I knew her parents well. Her father, Mr. Harry the policeman, would cycle around the village and up to Baker Street, doing his rounds. He was a nice man, and would always give a wave and a cheery "hello", even though he was supposedly out looking for any potential trouble. But Elizabeth had this annoying – and very painful – habit of pinching my upper arm. It really did hurt – and she knew it did. I could tell by the look on her face when she did it. She would hold on to that pinch and make me squeal, and the more I squealed – the more she held on. So after the first term I was pleased to discover that Georgie was seated beside me in Elizabeth's place. Ah, peace at last!

~

Being back at Orsett School was blissful. Well apart from a certain person who sat behind me. His name was Geoffrey, a big boy, with the sort of grin that if he was looking in your direction – you knew you had better make a quick getaway.

With that grin firmly planted on his face, he would chase me around the school playground with worms – trying to put them down the back of my jumper... He never caught me though, I think he was a bit *too* big and lumbering to do that – thankfully!

So he devised another tactic to get me...

I was ten years old and sitting at my desk in class quite happily. Suddenly – I felt this horrible creepy sort of feeling on top of my head... I gingerly put my hand up to my head to feel what it was – and it was a dead *bat! He had put a dead bat on my head!!*

I was absolutely horror struck! Until then, I hadn't really been afraid of bats. Georgie and I would climb up the hay bales in the barn over the farm, and sit up there at dusk, chatting away, with bats flying all around us. I believed that they wouldn't actually touch us, so I felt fairly safe with them.

However, one day Valerie and I were walking down Fen Lane on one of our evening walks. Bats were flying around having a nose at us – they came pretty close – but didn't actually touch us. Besides, if they had, then they would have got Valerie first – as she was taller than me!

"Keep your head down" Valerie said, quite alarmingly. "If they get into your hair – they will never get out – and you will have to have it all *cut off...*"

And now – I had one... *On my head...*

Ok – it was dead – thank goodness. But I really hated the feel of having it in my hand – and then seeing what it actually *was!*

I don't blame the class for laughing – and Geoffrey was enjoying every horrible moment of it! I don't remember him getting told off for doing such a horrible thing either – but then another day he went a few steps further...

I had a nice, new, white "sailor collar" blouse to wear to school. One day when I was wearing it, my hair was not curled up quite as much as

Nell would normally do it. Or maybe it might have fallen down a bit. But there I was with my white blouse and my blonde hair hanging a little loose at the back.

We used thin wooden pens with detachable nibs in those days, which we dipped into inkwells in our desks. Suddenly – my head was yanked back – it was Geoffrey – and then he pushed my hair down his inkwell!

Of course, he was now in trouble – big trouble – with Mr. Simpson – but *that* didn't help *me!* When I pulled my head away – my hair – and my new white blouse – was covered in dark blue ink... Not only was it terribly humiliating – but I also had to go home with my hair covered in ink – as well as my new blouse...

Naturally, this caused a bit of a rumpus when I told my mother how it happened, and although I really don't recall what was said or done about it – Geoffrey didn't ever touch me again...

~

Winters at Orsett School were cold and bleak – well physically anyway. I still enjoyed my time there though, no matter what.

It didn't matter that in the winter months the bottles of milk all school children were given at the time solidified into ice, and then were put on the (rather unproductive) radiators to thaw, ready for the milk break – which was vile! I didn't like milk anyway, and this was the perfect reason to let me off having that little bottle of milk.

My hands and feet were always cold, just as they were in that stark Sunday School hall. It was hard to concentrate when you felt so cold, but I did. It wasn't really that much worse than waking up in the pub with ice on the *inside* of the window – and the cold dark bathroom that followed on from there. Ugh! The feeling of those harsh towels on my skin – and the one slimy face flannel, that was shared by whole household, and smelled of everyone else's ablutions... Just Yuk!

Then the one mile trek down to school, so many times in the snow – slipping on ice, and with snow coming over the tops of my shoes and soaking my socks – no wonder I got chilblains...

~

When winter turned into spring, our nature walks would start. Mr. Simpson would take us on these long walks over the fields and through the woods, pointing out to us the various plants etc. – just like my grandfather did with me.

"So what are these?" he would ask, pointing to a cluster of little bright yellow flowers. "Buttercups?" – "No..." "Primroses?" – "No..." "Celandines", I said confidently. Mr. Simpson beamed a smile at me... Oh dear... I felt very shy about being praised for my knowledge of wild flowers. It was all because of my country walks with my grandfather though.

Mr. Simpson asked us to write a poem about flowers. It is all so simple, but I have never forgotten my little poem, even though it is so long ago. This is what I wrote...

"In Spring – the flowers come up
The daisy
And the buttercup
The lovely Scarlet Pimpernel
And the beautiful
Bluebell."

Mr. Simpson read it out in class – he liked it. *But...* There was an addendum...

"It is all very lovely" he said, "but the rhythm at the end doesn't quite match – you need an extra word before 'bluebell'..."

Oh well, he was a hard taskmaster! I have never added that other word in.

No extra words can describe the beauty of bluebells – unless of course – their fragrance...

So here we go...

"And the beautiful *sweet* bluebell"

It still doesn't have the same, er, *ring* to it though...

~

An Easter Break...

Easter was always somewhat different for us Church of England school children. On Good Fridays we would have to go to Orsett Church for a morning service. Some of us would have to read from the bible at the pulpit about the Easter Story. I was always very nervous about doing that, but I *did* do it. Then when we came back down to our seat, we would be given a toffee – a little sweetener to look forward to for having done it!

Good Friday was always a bleak day – literally, as well as me always feeling sorry for Jesus. The day would always seem to be chilly and overcast, but it was very atmospheric for such a day.

The sun always shone on Easter Sunday though! Easter eggs then were somewhat different to what they are now. For a start – you had *one*. Well *I* did anyway. But it was something to be enjoyed – slowly... It would always be the same – a hollow chocolate egg, decorated with little mauve crystallised violets, flavoured with violet essence, very much like the lovely chocolates that were sold in the tiny sweet shop in Orsett village. They were little confections filled with pink and mauve fondant, and tasted of roses and violets.

I can't help but wonder how many of today's children will one day as adults speak in raptures about their Ninja Turtle Easter eggs...

~

It would be so lovely if passion flowers bloomed at Easter, as they were named after the symbol of Christ's Passion and Cross. But never mind, we can enjoy their beauty in the summer months, and be reminded of what Easter is all about.

There was a lovely elderly gentleman called Mr. Cleeves, who lived in Stifford Clays Road, a pretty little walk along the road from the Kings Arms. He was a quiet man, always well dressed for the countryman that he was, in a tweed jacket and hat. Occasionally, he would walk along to the pub with his walking stick to have a morning drink.

"Good morning Landlord" he would say, lifting his hat. He would quietly have his drink on his own, and then "I bid you good day" he would say, lifting his hat again, as he left to go back to his cottage.

I had never been in his cottage, not even his garden, in fact I don't know anyone who had been. The cottage and the garden were both very pretty, from what could be seen from the road, quite large and surrounded by a wall. The weather-boarded front was covered with Virginia Creeper, and the wall was covered with honeysuckle and roses that rambled over in abandon.

One summer morning, Mr. Cleeves came to the pub and asked to see me – he had brought me something special... I had never seen a passion flower before, and Mr. Cleeves had this perfect flower head which he picked to give to me. He explained how Jesus on the Cross was the large stamen in the middle, and the smaller stamens around were the disciples bowing in deference to Him. I was fascinated by his story, and always think of passion flowers – and Mr. Cleeves – at Easter. I grow my own passion flowers now, so each summer I am reminded again of this kind man's lovely gesture.

~

Back to School...

I loved being back at Orsett School so much. To have been taken away for two years had left a void in me, a void I didn't really understand at the time, but it was this dark void that was too wide for me to cope with at times.

Being back there though was joyful, and I was so grateful for those hours away from the pub. I was back with Georgie too, and he has even told me that he doesn't remember me ever having been away! Probably because we still used to go on our adventures out of school time, but being back in class and sitting next to him again was good.

Mr. Simpson decided that he was going to have class teams – and that Georgie and I were to be joint captains of the yellow team. Ah, I liked that. The colour of sunshine and spring flowers...

I was also given the privilege of being the mint monitor. This meant that on the days that we had roast lamb, which was normally in the early summer months, I would go to the Headmaster's garden – and pick the mint for the mint sauce. Now this involved some sort of strategy, because I had to gather it in time for the cooks to make the mint sauce – but to also have enough time to sit with Mrs. Simpson, the Headmaster's wife.

I would always go to the house first and knock on the door, letting Mrs. Simpson know that I was about to go in their garden to pick the mint, and she would always ask me into the house for a chat, and we would sit for a while in the kitchen, next to the old black cooking range where she had two chairs. I loved those times.

There was a long cord hanging next to the range, on which she had threaded many reels of various colour cottons, and sometimes she would sit there and sew while we chatted. It was such a simple way of storing cotton reels of thread, and she would pull off a yard of whatever colour she needed next.

Having chatted for a while, usually about school and lessons, I would then take the mint over to the Nissen hut over the road, which served as a dining room for the school, and then make it back in class to sing Grace...

It was only then that we could have the clatter of forming a file at the serving hatch – for the food for which we really were *truly grateful...*

~

School holidays always had at least one outing organised by Orsett Church. Affectionately known as a "charabanc" outing, we would usually go to Margate or Ramsgate at Easter and during the summer holidays, and the circus or ice-skating shows in London in the colder months. Nell would usually accompany me, I don't think my mother liked mixing with the other women – or *any* women come to that.

They were always really jolly affairs, with everyone singing on the way home... Songs like *"My old man said follow the van – and don't dilly dally on the way..."* and other old music hall songs. It was always great fun.

I have a rather amusing photo taken of me on one such outing. It was in Dreamland in Margate – I have a monkey sitting on my shoulder – and it is searching through my hair... I may be laughing in the photo – but I remember feeling very wary of this funny little animal. I don't think Jimmy or Freddie were with us – but if they had been, that little monkey would have had a really fun time going through *their* hair.

There was quite an incident at one time on the coach as we were going through London. We had all been given a boiled sweet, and suddenly everything erupted... Poor Georgie had accidentally swallowed his – whole!

Really, he was going blue, and the only thing to do was for two adults to hold him up by his legs and someone else banging on his back to dislodge the sweet from his throat. That was so scary, because he could have choked to death but for the quick thinking of people on the coach – at least the sweet came out.

~

So, by not wanting to join in with the other women on these trips, whether it was good or bad what happened, my mother missed out.

These charabanc outings were not for her, so she didn't experience the camaraderie on these trips, the jovial singing on the way home, not even the way that poor Georgie's dilemma was handled swiftly, and with the best possible outcome. But she also missed out on actually seeing her little girl laughing, smiling – and *having fun...*

If only I could have had some semblance of fun back at the pub.

At least I have the memory of kind Mr. Cleeves giving and explaining to me the story of the passion flower...

Mummies And Daddies

1957 to 1958

Although my mother would refer to my grandfather as "That Man" when she spoke *about* him – just as my grandmother did – when she spoke *to* him I would sometimes hear her call him Daddy. Sometimes she wouldn't call him anything. When she spoke to me about him she would call him Grandpop, or sometimes Grandpopsy-boysy, which was a more affectionate term. I always called him Grandpop, my grandmother Nanny, and my parents Mummy and Daddy – that is once I realised that my father *was* my father and didn't call him "the man who lives up the cottage" anymore!

On the Saturdays when my father wasn't at work, he would always have to have his "eight pints before lunch", and that is what he did. Then after lunch, he would go to bed in the spare bedroom and sleep it all off.

It seems that he may not have been the only person "sleeping" in that room either, as I have been told that my grandfather also used to let it out to anyone else who wanted a bed for an hour or two – supposedly with someone they should perhaps not have been in a bedroom with...

~

"Now be a good girl – and go and have a lie down with Daddy", my mother would tell me. "Then you can stay up tonight". Well I was usually staying up anyway, with lots of jobs to do in the bars.

I didn't want to go and lie down with my father for the afternoon. I wanted to be out playing with my friends. But no, I *had* to go and lie down with him.

I used to feel so uneasy about this. Despite my young age, it didn't feel right getting into bed with my father. I don't know why I felt that, because I didn't know that it really wasn't right. Maybe instinct was kicking in. I would lay there as stiff as a board, without moving all the time so that I didn't wake him up. Then later my mother would appear, and I would be allowed to leave the room. I would leave Daddy still sleeping off the copious amounts of beer, oblivious to the fact that I had ever been there.

I don't know why my mother made me do this. It wasn't natural for me to be in bed when I would rather be out with my friends. Maybe in turn my mother had had to do that too? I don't know. Maybe she thought it was *normal...*

~

One day I came indoors and couldn't find my mother...

"She's down in Grandpop's bedroom", Nanny told me, "they're doing the books – and don't want to be disturbed."

Usually they did the books at the kitchen table where everything could be spread out. Sometimes I would be roped in to help too. So they must have been pretty secret accounts that they were doing...

"Now you stay here with me duck" Nanny said, "and don't you go down there..."

~

My mother didn't speak much about her childhood, apart from her short time at school, and how when they moved to the Kings Arms just before the war, my grandfather kept her off school. She left school when she was just twelve years old – at my grandfather's behest. If anyone queried him, like the school board man who used to do the rounds sometimes, he would just say that she had been evacuated. So I think she must have had a lonely childhood, being shut in the pub.

One day she did actually talk to me about her school days though. She had gone to St. Chadd's school in Tilbury, and what got her talking about this was that one of my teachers at Torells had actually been *her* teacher at St. Chadd's. Her name was Miss Lee, a lovely lady, and apart from general teaching she also taught us ballroom dancing, and other dances like the Polka. She used to join in showing us what to do, and it was so funny, she would have to hold her large bosoms in place as she jumped up and down, to the great amusement of some of the girls!

Well Miss Lee was a woman that my mother had actually liked in the past. I know she liked my aunts, but they were family. In general, she just couldn't associate with other women. She would talk in a very derogatory way about women as though they were different creatures – and now here was I – one day going to grow into a woman myself...

Anyway, now my mother was actually *talking to me* – relating little snippets of her childhood. She told me about the huge black Alsatian dog called "Boy" that my grandfather had when she was a little girl, and that he shot him in the shed one day. She said how the blood was running out of the shed for days – thus confirming my grandfather's story that he had told me many times before. But why was the poor dog shot?

She also told me how she wasn't allowed to play with other children. This was in reference to when they lived in Tilbury. She would stand at the front gate watching them all as they played in the street. I don't know whether it was a regular thing or not, but she went on to tell me how she would be standing at the gate watching the children, and how my grandfather would creep up behind her – and pull her knickers down. The children would all find this highly amusing of course, and she would be left having to pull them back up again – in front of them all.

I can't help but feel sorry for the childhood that she had, especially for the humiliation that went with it. Goodness knows what else went on that she didn't tell me about. At least she had a very loving mother though.

However bad my mother's childhood might have been – I know that she was determined to make sure that I suffered too...

No matter how much I suffered though, I vowed that I would never treat *my* children the way I had been treated – and I never did.

My Boy ~ My Boy

October 1958

One day in early October 1958 it was like Groundhog Day... Nell was taking that horrible brown rubber sheet along to my grandmother's bedroom, along with the sinister-looking tube and the white enamel washing up bowl; the midwife was walking up the stairs – and I was sent over to Mrs. White's to stay for the night. It wasn't Nurse Ellis this time though, it was Nora, a midwife who was also a customer in the pub.

So why wasn't my mother giving birth in her own bedroom in the bungalow? Why was it going to happen at the pub again? Why couldn't she accept that she lived with Daddy at the bungalow – not at the pub with her parents?

At least I now knew where babies came from – I knew because a girl at school told me. They didn't come out of the midwife's black bag after all, that was as silly as a stork putting them under the gooseberry bush! No – they came out through a mummy's tummy button...

I had to make my own conclusions about how it got out. Ah, so that is why it's called a tummy *button*... You press the button – and out comes the baby... So how does the midwife get the baby out of the tummy button? And what's more – how did it get in there in the first place? Ah – that is what that horrible long tube was for...

~

"It's got to be a girl... It's got to be a girl... It's got to be a girl..." I kept thinking. Ralf was only three years old, but already he was thoroughly spoilt, and it was only going to get worse...

Something my mother did, not just once, but a few times, was to walk past me muttering...

"My boy, my boy – to me you're such a joy… Heh heh…"

I think it was the "heh heh" that got to me most of all. That sly little chuckle at the end that told me what that song was all about.

I enjoyed helping with Ralf though, and taking him for walks in the pushchair.

I wanted to have babies one day when I was grown up and married, especially little girls. Living at the pub, I was in a very male dominated environment. A boy would be wonderful later on, but at first I had some kind of strange feeling that one day I would have two daughters…

As well as a baby doll Nell had bought me, who I had named Rosebud, I had two smaller dolls, one with dark hair and brown eyes, and the other with blonde hair and blue eyes. I was sitting on the bed at the back of Nell's shop, dressing these dolls – the brown haired one in pink – and the blonde haired one in blue. Somehow it flashed into my mind that I was going to have two little girls just like that – and that there would be three years between the two. I have never forgotten that moment – that moment of realisation that makes you just *know* that one day this would happen. What this light bulb moment didn't tell me though was *how* this was going to happen – and I certainly didn't relish the thought of the awful tube being pushed through my navel!

~

"Oh no – not another *boy*…" I remember saying those words so clearly, as my mother told me I had another brother.

"His name is Colin" my mother said. I wonder whether my father had an opinion?

He was a very pretty little baby, but looked so different to Ralf when he was new born. Unlike Ralf and me, he had dark brown hair, so I suppose he had inherited my mother's and grandfather's colouring. I loved him, just like I loved Ralf, and he was like a little doll. I cradled him in my arms as I sat by the fire in the bedroom. But another boy though? My life could only get worse – especially as he grew up being known to others as my grandfather's *favourite*…

Every Picture Tells A Story

When Colin was about four months old, my grandfather arranged to have a professional photographer come to the pub to take family portraits. The family being my mother, my two brothers and me. Unlike most family portraits, my father wasn't included. I couldn't help but feel sorry for Daddy sometimes, especially as Grandpop treated him as though he wasn't there.

Now being just nine years old, I should have been wearing a pretty dress, creating an image that I would have been proud of throughout the years. Apart from the fact that I didn't have any pretty dresses, yet again, my mother seemed to be trying to make me look as awful as she could. Well, I looked absolutely dreadful. Not only did I look dreadful, but I also looked emaciated. I was so terribly thin, that I could have spent the last six months in hospital – or a cave! A pretty dress would have bucked me up, and would have made a world of difference to the photo.

Although Nell wasn't a hairdresser, she had a knack with doing hair, albeit in a World War II sort of way, and she had done my hair just as my mother asked. Of course, this was now fourteen years after the end of the war, and I *was* only nine years old. But nevertheless, my hair had to be done as per my mother's instructions.

With a tail comb and her finger, Nell wound sections of my hair round, making small sausage shapes (or maybe chipolatas?). Then she would pin each of them with a hair clip. This process was done with all of my hair, and I looked really silly... I did not like having my hair done like that – why couldn't it just be let loose? I was a young girl – so why couldn't I be allowed to look pretty?

Now we get down to my clothes... Oh dear, they were terrible, and I felt so awful wearing them. Even at nine years old a little girl wants to look nice, especially for a portrait photo.

I was wearing a dull beige boy's jumper that zipped up the front. It was made of a rough wool, and it was very itchy and uncomfortable. I hated it. With that I wore a dreary plain brown skirt, which ended just below the knee, and my socks were beige woollen knee-high, held up with garters. Nell made these garters with knicker elastic, so called because so many knickers had elastic going through the waist. You had to be careful that the elastic didn't get too loose or break, otherwise they would fall down – the knickers that is! Although they are not showing in the photo, I remember that my shoes were brown lace-up – just like a boy's.

So I was this merge of brown and beige, not good colours for a child of nine, and especially as I looked so ill. But why did my mother want me to look like that? Didn't she want to feel proud of me? Would she ever show that photo to anyone and proudly say that I was her daughter? Why *couldn't* I wear pretty clothes like other girls?

It is not a good photo anyway. My mother is expressionless and looking elsewhere, with baby Colin on her lap, looking as though he has slipped down somewhat and is about to slide off. Ralf was looking daggers at the cameraman, as though he was willing something awful to happen to him...

I was the only one smiling, and that's not because I was happy, especially as that awful jumper was itching so badly, but I knew I always had to smile when necessary. However, there were so many dark stories hidden behind my smile...

A Room Of My Own

My parents only used Northcroft for sleeping, and Ralf, Colin and I slept at the pub, Ralf and Colin being in the fourth bedroom, and me in the woodworm room. Nell was fully in charge of looking after us all, although my mother did spend all day at the pub. She just wanted to be with my grandmother – and my grandfather...

I have never – ever – had a bedtime story read to me in my life. Neither did my parents ever "tuck me in" at night. Nell has "tucked me in", but there were never any bedtime stories. She would get Ralf and Colin ready for bed, and then she would sing them lullabies...

> *"Little man you're crying – I know why you're blue*
> *Someone stole your kiddy car away*
> *Time to go to sleep now*
> *Little man you've had a busy day"*

But it wasn't *them* who ever had anything taken away – it was *me*... And it never stopped.

~

One day, I was over the moon – my parents told me I was going to live at the bungalow with them! Oh, glory be! They said I could choose the wallpaper and paint for my bedroom, and I excitedly went with them down to the decorating shop in Grays. Oh how I loved going through those wallpaper books! It was something new to me, and I had a full leash to choose whatever I wanted!

Even at that age I was good at art, and to choose the decoration for my very own bedroom was wonderful. I slowly turned the pages of those big wallpaper books, dismissing all the large, gawdy patterns. I knew that no matter how long it took, something would stand out to me, something that was *me*...

And then I saw it – it was a pale lemon background with tiny mauve flowers – it was so pretty, and very much *me*... The paint that I chose was a very pale lilac that blended in with the little mauve flowers. I now had a room that was totally mine – and all to my own design. I was *so* happy!

~

"I don't like it" my father said, as he painted the skirting boards. I felt awful that I had displeased him by not choosing a white or cream paint. But that very pale lilac blended so well with those little mauve flowers. I didn't want to upset him, but when it was finished, it all looked so pretty, and I was so happy that this was going to be *my* bedroom.

What it needed now was a mauve or lilac eiderdown for my bed. No-one suggested that I could have one, but that was what was in my mini-designer's mind...

One day the fair came along, as it did every summer, and Nell and I walked along Stifford Clays Road to where the fair was being held at Blackshots. Nell let me have a go on one of the stalls. It was a very simple one, where you drew straws to see if you had won anything. Although I am sceptical of these things, I know that they must give away *some* prizes – and I won one of them! They were all the normal trashy sort of things, but my prize was one of the *big* ones! I was only a *little* girl, but that was what I had won!

The stall holder showed me the biggest prizes on offer. One was a huge blue teddy bear, bigger than I was – and another was – a lilac eiderdown. That beautiful lilac eiderdown was mine! I remember walking away, so proudly holding that treasure, which against all odds had been the exact colour that I wanted for my bed.

"But what about the blue teddy bear?" Nell asked. No, I didn't want that – it was blue – and so therefore it was for a *boy*...

I carried the rolled up eiderdown all the way home, and was so proud that I had won it. And yes, it was put on my bed in my newly decorated bedroom, and I happily slept beneath its cosy warmth.

~

Some months later, I had come back from one of my "let's get Yvonne out of the way" trips for a few days, I don't remember where, probably over to Kent or to Mrs. White's, and I went home to the bungalow. As I went into my bedroom, I noticed that everything was completely different... Everything was *blue*...

The wallpaper was blue, the paintwork was blue, including the skirting boards, and there were two single beds in there now – both with blue covers.

I felt as though I had walked into the wrong house. It was disconcerting – disorientating... I just stared at the room in disbelief, unable to move.

"Ralf and Colin are sleeping in here now" my mother told me, unflinchingly. "You are going back to the pub..."

What??

It was no use even trying to protest. The dark deed had been done – my pretty bedroom was now totally blue...

~

I walked slowly and disconsolately back up to the pub. My head dropped downwards and my shoulders hunched. My arms hung unmoving down by my sides. All I could see was my feet as I took each heavy step.

I eventually reached the pub. It wasn't really that far, but it seemed to have taken a long time to walk up there. I went up those awful dinner-stained stairs, and reluctantly along to the woodworm room. I opened the door greeted by the smell of rotten wood and – *creatures*...

Were they still there? Yes, of course they were. Those little worms that hid in the holes that they made. Why didn't anyone do anything about them? Were they to be allowed to munch away until the whole of the dressing table collapsed into dust?

~

"No, you're not sleeping in there any more", Nanny Felstead told me without any emotion – "you are sleeping with *me*... "

And so, that is where I slept for the next eight years or so of my life. Sleeping with my grandmother in her drab bedroom, *in her bed,* where everything was coloured a dark shade of – green...

~

I asked my mother many times over the years if I could have my own bedroom – somewhere I could put up posters like other girls, and do my homework in peace. Somewhere that I could call my own – my very own little space... And somewhere where I could get dressed or undressed – in private...

But "No!" – that was what I was always answered with, despite my pleading and pleading, knowing that there was a spare bedroom...

"No – that is for when Ralf and Colin want to stay at the pub" my mother always said.

But didn't they also have what had been *my* bedroom at the bungalow? That pretty bedroom for which I had chosen my own wallpaper and paint, but which was very soon wall papered and painted *blue*?

And what happened to my lilac eiderdown? It was used as a – *cat bed*.

Nanny Felstead's Bedroom

1959 onwards

When I reflect upon Nanny Felstead's bedroom, I just see a dark sludgy green. It wasn't the same darkness as my grandfather's dark and foreboding bedroom where he kept his collection of weapons, some of which were on the wall, but a dismal, dark, cucumber skin green. I could describe it more as "avocado", but as no-one knew what an avocado pear was in those days, well not in my family anyway, I can only go by how I saw the colour at the time. Olive green would be another apt colour, then again, the only olive we knew about was the olive oil that we would buy in very small bottles from the chemist, to put in our ears when we had ear ache!

The wallpaper was dreary, some sort of green pattern on a dark beige background. The furniture was heavy dark wood, and Nanny's bedspread and eiderdown, although satin, were dark cucumber skin green, as were the curtains. I can't help but recall that the Victorians used arsenic in their colourants to make green, and actually caused great danger to people breathing it in. It was used in wallpaper, paint, and all manner of items. I assume there was no arsenic in Nanny's room though...

Next to the fireplace, there was an original Lloyd Loom chair, pale green in colour, a traditional design that went back to the 1930's. Nanny Felstead was very proud of that, and she really coveted it. There was a large heavy wardrobe with a drawer at the bottom, a chest of drawers, and Nanny's triple mirror dressing table. On this she kept her set of three crystal powder bowls – filled with her pale pink face powder – and hand crocheted silk doilies, which both she and her mother had made. On the mantelpiece above the fireplace stood an antique mantel clock, an arch design, with an inlay of mother-of-pearl. Above that was a small 1920's mirror, which hung from the picture rail by a chain. I couldn't help but find it all rather depressing though, and so different from my pale lemon and lilac floral bedroom.

Trying to sleep at night was terrible. The floor consisted of bare floorboards. There was a small rug, mainly for decoration rather than comfort, and of course, no carpeting. The floorboards would creak at night of their own accord, even though there was nothing walking on them – well I hoped there wasn't! But it could be pretty scary at times.

There were mousetraps in the fireplace, all lined up, ready for their night time killing. They were always going off in the night, clunking as they crunched the little mouse heads, and making their eyes stick out on stalks. Having had my grandfather make me look at a line of them on a cupboard once, when I was so little that they were at the height of my face, I could never bear to look at them again. What worried me so much though, was if any of them climbed up the wooden bedstead – and on to the bed. I found the thought terrifying.

Apparently mice sing like birds, although not audible to humans. Just as well really! I wouldn't want a night chorus going on all the time – telling me they were there... They are audible to cats though...

I really don't know where the mice were hiding, but they were *there*... Lots of them... No matter how many were caught – there were always more.

On day I opened my drawer in my grandmother's chest of drawers to get my pale green angora jumper – that she had painstakingly knitted for me on the tiniest gauge needles – and saw a mouse tail scurrying away. Alarmed, I didn't look to see where it went, but when I took out my jumper – there was a huge ragged hole in it – it had been turned into a mouse nest... Well I suppose angora does make a very nice soft nest!

I would lay there listening to the mouse traps going off in the night, knowing that their little necks were being broken and their eyes were sticking out, and there was always the fear of ghosts.

As well as the cellar, the bedroom end of the landing was also very spooky. I would go along to Nanny's bedroom to go to bed at night, and would feel all sort of *shivery*. I had to be grown up about it, and convince myself that there wasn't *really* a ghost lurking along the landing, but at times I could really feel its presence.

A few times as I was going towards the bedroom, The Old Woman (the cat!) was looking like a cartoon cat that had just been scared, literally stiff. Each time it happened she was in the same place on the landing – all her fur was sticking out on end, and her wild looking eyes were staring straight behind me... Shivery indeed.

So I had to go to bed, thinking these things – well *knowing* them – if I was to take any notice of The Old Woman.

The Old Woman was very wise though. She knew a thing or two. If she was alarmed on occasion at some entity appearing behind me, then who was I to question her?

It didn't help that there was a horrible framed picture in the taproom above the piano. It was of a butler bending down to a safe, looking round aghast at the translucent figure of "His Master" standing in the doorway. Goodness knows why my grandfather liked that picture and had it hanging on the wall. But as much as I tried to avoid seeing it, it was always there.

~

Over the road from Nanny's bedroom was a large ash tree, on the corner of the lea where I sometimes played with Georgie. The bedroom curtains were very thin, and when the moon was full, or in the right place, the ash tree would be shadowed on the bedroom wall opposite the bed. I would grip the top sheet, clutching it tightly in my hands up to my neck, looking at the strange, scary shapes that the tree cast on the wall. I knew I ought to keep my eyes tightly shut – but I couldn't. Sometimes there would be a hand, with long gnarled fingers, tantalisingly twitching at the wall. Then a face might appear. Normally the eyes would be closed – but then if they suddenly opened with the movement of the moon, then I would pull that bed sheet right up over my head..

~

It was one sunny summer's tea time, and all seemed to be unusually well in my world. The glorious summer's day had filled my mind and body with all the goodness that the sun delivers. I felt unusually happy. Well, as happy as I could be living the life I was. But sunshine always made a difference – well normally.

I was sitting at the kitchen table in the pub with my mother having tea. My tea was bread and butter with sticks of celery that I dipped into salt on the side of my plate. I was sitting at my normal place, at the end of the table opposite my grandfather's place, and my mother was sitting at the long end of the table. Every time I eat, or even smell celery, I am immediately transported back to that sunny teatime.

It may have been sunny outside, but as always, darkness loomed in my suffocating world in the pub.

I loved the celery, and I especially loved the salt as it tingled on my tongue. My mother was frowning as I savoured this simple delight, and then she came out with something so strange ...

"Enjoy your tea" she said, still frowning. "There are flying saucers coming over here tonight..."

"What are flying saucers?" I asked, stirring my tea and looking at the saucer that held my teacup.

"They are from another world" she said, narrowing her eyes.

'Another world???' I pondered, as I took another bite of the celery.

"And they are coming to get us tonight" she added, looking very serious.

Oh dear, I almost choked on my celery, and took another gulp of tea.

"They are coming to get us – *tonight*" – my mother emphasised.

So, was this to be my last meal on earth then, I wondered.

That night when I went to bed, I looked more intently at the shadows that the huge ash tree was spreading across my grandmother's bedroom. Why wasn't anyone trying to save me? Where was everyone anyway? I could hear the normal muffled sounds drifting up from the taproom below, so why didn't anyone else seem to be terrified of being abducted by beings in flying saucers?

I stayed awake all night, looking at the eerie shadows that the huge ash tree cast across the bedroom wall opposite me. Mouse traps were still clunking in the fireplace, just like they always did. And as well as being afraid of a mouse running up the wooden legs of that old bed – now I was afraid of flying saucers – and whatever they might hold.

The shadows on the wall wreaked havoc with my nerves that night. When my grandmother came to bed later, her mind was sodden with her normal quota of spirits, and she was soon out like a light. But still I watched those shadows as they moved mysteriously across the bedroom wall.

Of course, there were no space ships, no aliens, nothing like that at all. It was just my mother in her world of fantasy telling me things to frighten me – which she knew they would...

~

One night, I was in bed asleep and the bedroom door opened waking me up – there was a figure of a large man standing there... He was looking down at me, and I didn't know what to do. Then he turned the light on... Phew! – it was my grandfather. He told me I had to get up and go to the lounge. It didn't matter that I had school the next day. That never mattered to anyone. If I was required to do something – then I would have to obey – *and do it.*

In the lounge there was a new radiogram, very new to Britain at the time – well to our part of Britain anyway! It had wires going through the floor to two speakers on the wall of the saloon bar below.

I was required to put records on for the rest of the evening, until the pub closed. I remember feeling *so* tired, but I had to do as I was told. They were all singles, which in those days were quite short. So there was no time to sit back on the settee to relax between each one. There was a mixture of Winifred Attwell's honky-tonk piano music, which always went down well in the pub, and pop music of the time – including of course, the awful records I was forced to have for my birthday. At intervals I had to play advertisement records which we had been given by the brewery – subliminal messages to buy the beers!

"A Double Diamond works wonders
Works wonders, works wonders
A Double Diamond works wonders
So drink one today!"

And then another one...

"Skol lager – lively now...
And after...
De de de de...
Lar – ar – ger – Skol"

I did slip in the odd Elvis record too though!

It was only when the pub was closed that I was allowed to go back to bed.

~

It wasn't easy sleeping with my grandmother. She would usually get drunk on gin, and really I don't blame her, considering what she had to put up with. But after time she would drink gin from the optic, straight down her throat. One night she almost choked herself to death – really, she was in a terrible state. I would like to think that that may have deterred her, but I don't think it did.

Well, she would normally wake me up when she came to bed.

"Here duck" she would say sometimes, handing me a glass of Benedictine – "get this down you – it will make you sleep". Well it might have done – if she hadn't kept waking me up...

Sometimes she would stand at the bottom of the bed, wanting to sing to me – usually "I'll Be Your Sweetheart" – for she loved that song, just as my grandfather did. I would have to listen all the way through though – as she sang *all* the verses. Sometimes, even still wearing her hat!

Nanny used to be particularly merry on Friday nights when she went out for the evening. This was a total mystery to me, because I never knew where she went. No-one would tell me, and when I did ask she just said "The Ham and Beef Store!" with a little laugh. No-one would tell me where the Ham and Beef Store was either, and where on earth was there a food store open late on a Friday night?

So the Ham and Beef Store always remained a mystery. Everyone else seemed to know about it, and it was a source of amusement. Obviously, it had a totally different meaning to going shopping for ham and beef...

Everything that I didn't see with my own eyes was a mystery to me. No-one would tell me *anything*.

Now that I was sleeping with my grandmother, she could no longer have her boyfriend Fred sleeping with her at the weekend. Perhaps he was the bit of ham and beef she used to have on a Friday night?

When she did eventually get into bed – she wanted to chat. This would be late every night, unless she was totally out of it. It had been very many years since she had had to get up early for anything. But I had to be up early for school the next day, and sleep for me would be a long time coming.

She always had a large bottle of lemonade next to the bed – on top of the chest of drawers on *my* side. She wouldn't have it on the floor on her side.

"Pass me that bottle duck", she would say nightly, waking me up in the middle of the night. Then I would have to fiddle with the stopper with its metal leavers each side, as they were in those days.

Then I would have to wait while she guzzled that down, along with all those gases going down quickly into her stomach. When she had had enough she would hand it back to me, so that I could put it back on top of the chest of drawers. No wonder she didn't have any teeth...

~

She could have easily lost all her hair too. She would buy bottles of the darkest brown hair colourant and get Nell to put it on her hair with a toothbrush – then she would leave it on!

"You have to wash it off!" I told her one day when I saw this being done, and showed her the instructions on the packet.

"Wash it off?" she exclaimed "but then it will be grey again..."

There was nothing I could do to persuade her that it didn't work like that!

Then she was complaining because her hair was starting to fall out. I tried to persuade her to go to a hairdresser, saying that they could cut it and style it so that the thinning patches might be covered up. I also thought that she might take notice of what a hairdresser might say about what she was doing to her hair with the colourant.

"I'm not going to a hairdressers" she said most indignantly. "I'm not having anyone see my thinning hair!"

I didn't know much about hairdressers at the time, but it seemed the only solution for her. I told her that they are used to it, and probably saw lots of people with hair like that.

"Well – they're not seeing *mine!*" she said.

I couldn't help but wonder how long it would be before she started wearing hats behind the bar!

~

Another example of our home hairdressing would be my mother and grandmother's metal hair curlers, which were wound tightly around locks of hair and then clipped together. Worst of all though were the curling tongs – they weren't like today's tongs though – they were made of iron and had to be heated on the stove. Then the handles would be held with a tea towel to protect the hands. Nell used to do this as well for my mother and grandmother. To test that they were hot enough she would clamp them onto newspaper – and if it singed and turned brown – then they were hot enough...

So what with the neat hair dye, the metal curlers, and the iron hair tongs, no wonder my grandmother was rapidly losing her hair!

~

Talking of hair washing, this was another ritual at the pub, which I could only do when I had permission. We didn't have bottles of shampoo, instead we had "one wash" little pouches at the shop. There were a selection, but my favourite was one that I can only describe as smelling like lemon custard, and had *"French"* written across the pouch. Women would come into the shop to buy one little shampoo pouch, *just when they needed it...* There was no such thing as hair conditioner then, well not that we knew about anyway! Later on though I found a little miracle of a cream in a shop in Grays. It was the first time I had ever heard of "hair conditioner" and it was aptly called "Crème Silk". What a difference that made to hair washing, especially the combing through afterwards! Previously Nell would painfully comb out all the tangles in my hair, tugging and pulling with the wide toothed comb that everyone else used – but this Crème Silk changed everything.

So there I would be, with clean smelling hair, all combed through – without pain – and ready to dry... But – therein lay the problem. Nell would dry my hair for me – with the "Hoover", that very old vacuum cleaner with the brown bag used to collect all the dust and dirt – but now putting the nozzle on reverse. This was a well-known way of drying hair then – and I only hope the bag had been fully emptied before she did it!

This may seem like a far-fetched notion, but this method of hair drying began in the 1920's. I don't think anyone at the pub had realised that we had moved on a few decades since then!

~

Well going back to Nanny Felstead, Nanny also had the most *awful* wind! But they were not always loud rumbling hurricanes that rippled down the bed, sending a blast of over-warm air around my legs. Sometimes they were quiet – *very* quiet – and those ones were always the smelliest, contaminating the bed with putrid gasses from her bowels.

"The soft ones are always the worst!" she would chuckle, as I squirmed in disgust.

She would take a box of matches into the toilet with her, saying that the sulphur from a struck match would dispel the smell. But that was hardly something she could do in bed...

One lunchtime, Nanny was in the taproom, the pub had only just opened, and there was no-one else there, just a few round the other side in the saloon. Suddenly, she let out this really loud rip-roaring thundering blast, and then said –

"Where e'er you are
Where e'er you be
Always let your wind
Go free..."

The people in the saloon bar were roaring with laughter, and I expect that kept them in stories about the pub landlady for ages!

~

Another story, which probably did the rounds in Orsett about the pub landlady, was that one day she came indoors saying she had just peed over the drain near the cellar flap, which was just off of the car park.

"I had just squatted down and was piddling over the drain" she said quite indignantly, "when old so and so (a customer) came round to get his bike – and watched me!" Really, I can't see why she had to go *there,* when she was so close to the pub, and besides, we also had outside toilets as well. "I reckon I gave him quite a sight" she said, chuckling...

I wish I could remember who that customer was, but whoever it had been, she didn't seem at all bothered that he had seen what she was doing – and had watched her! Well, what else is a man to do when he sees the landlady of his local pub peeing over a drain – right in front of him!

~

Despite all these unladylike activities, when Nanny went out, she would dress up rather like a duchess – Coronation Street's pub landlady Annie Walker always reminded me of her. She *always* wore a hat, no matter what the weather. Felt hats in the autumn and winter, and straw hats in the spring and summer. She always bought her hats from milliners, who knew her and what she liked, and in fact, I think that her hats and her beautiful jewellery were her trademark. She loved going back to London shopping, which she and my mother did once a month. When I was able to go with them, like in school holidays or Saturdays, despite the long bus journey from Orsett to Grays, then Grays to Aldgate, then Aldgate to Oxford Street, she would always be dressed impeccably. No-one could ever think that she could be so unladylike at home sometimes.

She could go from cockney to duchess in an instant. At home she would call a hat a goss, and an umbrella a gamp. I would either be "duck" or "old girl". Well, "duck" when she spoke to me, and "old girl" when she was calling me. She really was quite a character, and it is so sad that my grandfather treated her the way he did. But he never kept her short of money though.

Her favourite shops for clothes were Ticehurst in Grays, Chiesmans in Gravesend, and a very individual dress shop in Leigh-on-Sea, close to her fur coat shop. It was at these shops that she would buy the dresses she liked to wear in the pub. Until clothing rationing ended in March

1949, my Auntie Hilda told me that Nanny would go to a place in Green Lanes, London, where she knew someone who would let her buy what she wanted without coupons – because she could afford it!

"Auntie Doll, have you any new dresses?" she would ask her whenever she went to the pub.

"Yes dear", she would answer, "come up to the bedroom and look through my wardrobe."

Auntie Hilda said that she loved doing that. Nanny would have the most exquisite dresses, and her excuse was always, "well I have to look right dear – being landlady of this pub..." She always wanted to look the part when going out as well.

Gloves were always a must – leather in the winter and cotton in the summer. When I was old enough I had to dress the same if ever I went out with my mother and grandmother. I was let off of the hat though – that was for women. But I still had to wear the gloves. And another thing – never wear black shoes in summer! That was a real no-no!

And then there were her handbags – always good quality leather ones, and for them she believed in quality not quantity. When she opened them, you could smell the rich leather – as well as Senior Service cigarettes – along with Lanvin's Arpége perfume. She loved her perfumes, and had told me how the American soldiers when they visited the Orsett Camp would bring her and my mother beautiful French perfumes and silk stockings. If only she would have sprayed a little Arpége around the bedroom when she was letting out all her gases!

Her beautiful jewellery though was another matter. My grandfather had bought her lots of lovely necklaces during the war, so they were all 1940's and earlier. The earlier ones were the most beautiful and so evocative of that era.

Something I am glad I don't have though is her sapphire and diamond engagement ring. Well, it wasn't *her* engagement ring as such, for it was originally for somebody else at some time. Nanny told me that my grandfather had got it when he was serving in the army in the First World War in Flanders – he had taken it off of a dead Jewish woman's hand – and later gave it to her. I really wouldn't want to be wearing that poor woman's ring on my finger...

~

Nanny Felstead, born Doris Elsie Caroline Tait, but always known as Doll, never spoke about her childhood, but it seems that despite her mother having given birth to eight children, five of which died in childhood, like my grandfather's siblings, the family were not badly off. They lived in London, and her father was a coachman for a horse-drawn carriage, and wore a top hat. So I expect he worked for a fairly well off family. Apart from that, she never told me about her young life in London.

I remember her mother, Elsie Tait. She was a small, very frail-looking woman, with hollow eyes, surrounded by darkened skin that looked even blacker against her deathly white face. She lived at the pub when I was a little girl. I remember her showing me these beautifully embroidered little shoes that she had had many years before when she was younger. They were tiny, and made of cream silk, with embroidery in pretty shades of pink and green. They had a lovely little "Louis" heel and, looking back at them, they could have come straight out of the Versailles Palace in Paris. She was very old and frail when she died, and as all her belongings were being disposed of, I asked if I could have those precious little shoes.

"They've already gone", I was told bluntly.

I have never forgotten them, and throughout my life I have favoured shoes with little "Louis" heels. I managed to find some with those pretty little heels some years ago. They are just plain suede, and with no embroidery, but I still have them – they will never have that same magic as my great-grandmother's shoes though.

Curiouser And Curiouser

I had been told all the usual stories about the stork and the gooseberry bush, and that I "would know some day" where babies came from, and this was normally accompanied by lots of grins and chuckles, which made it "curiouser and curiouser" – as Alice had said.

One day, I was walking along the landing, that long stretch of dreariness that extended from the front to the back of the pub, and I overheard my mother and my grandmother talking in the kitchen. I could sense that it was probably something that I shouldn't really hear. Oh dear – what to do – what to do? There was nothing for it – I was to stand there by the banisters and listen – despite any subsequent peril.

"I am expecting again", I heard my mother say. Then her voice lowered, and I didn't hear what she said next... Whatever it was, it was something very much just between her and her mother.

But then – I did hear something...

"Will you tell him to stop doing it Mummy?" she asked her mother, quite plaintively. It was almost as though she had gone back to childhood.

Although I knew that men and women slept together in bed, and babies were born, I didn't know about the mechanics of sex.

So what was my father doing that was so bad? And what's more – what was my mother doing asking *her mother* to tell her *husband* not to do something? This intrigued me, and if it wasn't my father doing whatever it was – then who was?

Well, whatever it was – or whoever it was – another little baby was on its way.

I didn't know about such things then – but did my mother have a miscarriage – or even an abortion? No-one ever told me anything.

I have never forgotten my mother's words though... *"Will you tell him to stop doing it Mummy?"*

~ 171 ~

Nanny And The Dress

O ne Saturday afternoon Nanny Felstead suddenly decided she wanted to go to the little dress shop that she liked at Leigh-on-Sea. I suppose these days it would be called a boutique. Individual dresses, and just one of each, all uniquely stylish.

So my father was summoned to take her and my mother, and I was also going along for the ride. I loved going to that little shop. Being in my young teens, the clothes were not for my age, but I loved looking at all the dresses and accessories.

As usual, to go to dress shops, I would put on whatever were my best clothes at the time. I liked to feel the part, even though I was so young. Going shopping always meant wearing my best coat, shoes and gloves, just like my mother and grandmother did.

The woman who ran the dress shop was always very welcoming. She knew my grandmother would find something special in there and spend some money.

Ah – but maybe not today...

~

My father was outside in the car waiting patiently for us. I expect he was thinking about how many pints he could have downed if he hadn't been taking us to Leigh-on-Sea!

"Nanny" I said, as she put her coat on and got her hat, "you've still got your curlers in..."

"Have I duck?" she said, putting her hat on...

Then she went straight to the car. My mother didn't say anything, even though my grandmother looked rather silly, with her head covered with metal clip curlers, and so different to how she normally looked when she went out. She got in the back seat of the car and as usual struck up a cigarette...

Goodness knows how much smoke I used to breathe in in those days. What with the smoke in the bars, especially the taproom, which hung in layers across the room, and staining the wallpaper and ceiling brown... Somehow though, despite all my family being heavy smokers, I have never been tempted, even though I have been pressured to put a lit cigarette to my lips, I never did.

~

Having travelled to Leigh-on-Sea at a steady 40mph, which was the speed limit that my mother had set upon my father, we eventually arrived at the little dress shop.

There were a few mannequins in the window, displaying nice dresses.

"Oh – look at this" my grandmother exclaimed, as she set her eyes upon a very smart-looking dress on one of the models. It was very nicely displayed, with what must have been lots of pins holding it in over the slender shape of the model. The dress did indeed look very nice. It was navy blue with short sleeves, and a large draped cream-coloured collar in what appeared to be organza.

I felt so embarrassed as we entered the shop. There was my grandmother with her head full of metal curlers under her hat, which was of a style that didn't cover them at all – and she didn't even seem to know... Surely my mother could have pointed it out as well. But no, I don't think my mother would have ever said anything to upset my grandmother.

Nanny asked about the dress in the window – was it her size? Yes – it was! This was a ladies dress shop that catered for, let's just say, more mature ladies...

By now the woman was looking down her nose disdainfully at my grandmother, even though she could very well be about to spend quite a lot of money on that dress. I don't know if she even recognised Nanny at first, and I certainly felt very uncomfortable being with her looking like that.

"But can I show you anything else?" the woman asked, waving her hand to the dresses hanging on padded hangers along the wall.

"No – I want *that one*" Nanny said, pointing to the window.

With quite a few deliberately long huffs and puffs, the woman summoned her assistant to help her take the dress off of the mannequin in the window. It seemed ages that they were doing that.

There – at last, was the dress, and she held it draped over her arms in presentation to my grandmother – although still looking down her nose.

Nanny looked at the collar, and then said – no, it wasn't of the material that she thought it was... She thought the collar was organza, and really, it did indeed look like organza when it was in the window.

The look on that woman's face! Having to put that dress back on the mannequin exactly as it had been would be a bit of a challenge. She must have known that Nanny was a good customer, but oh dear, I do think Nanny had let herself down that day, going into that shop with metal curlers in her hair

Well she may have known her fabrics and materials etc., but really, she didn't seem to know – or maybe care – that she had gone out looking like that.

Was this the first stage of her gradual mental decline? Maybe it could explain her unladylike behaviour at the pub – especially urinating in things and places that she really shouldn't have...

I will elaborate on this later...

Casting A Clout

It was a beautiful May morning. The mist over the fields had cleared and the early morning sunshine had broken through. I couldn't wait to get outside and feel that warmth on my skin, and breathe in the springtime air.

May blossoms were blooming profusely in the hawthorn hedgerows, and scented the air with their distinctive sweetness. I stood outside the Kings Arms on the pavement that curved round at the front, where I could see all four roads, which met at that very point.

To my right was Baker Street, starting with the Kings Arms car park, with its little arbours that the German prisoners of war had built for my grandfather, in return for beer and cigarettes. Behind that was our large garden, then our orchard, where the chickens and our bantam cockerel Joey roamed free. After that were my grandfather's two pretty cottages – Ivy Cottages – which had once been festooned with ivy of course, all those hundreds of years ago when they had been built.

When my grandfather took over the Kings Arms, just before the war in 1939, he bought the land adjacent to the Kings Arms car park, being the garden and orchard. That was also when he bought the two cottages. Next to them was our little shop that Nell used to run.

There was a beautiful laburnum just behind one of the cottages that brought the summer sunshine into the garden even on a dull day. A very old brick pathway led to the bottom of the garden, where there was a small shed on the left, and a chicken coop on the right, although it no longer held chickens. Next to the shed was an ancient elder tree, which was laden with elder blossom in early summer, and then elderberries in late summer. My father would gather these to make another addition to the selection of wines he used to make.

In the field behind the cottages was the dilapidated windmill, which had served to produce the grain for the bread all those centuries ago. This was always a remarkable sight when the sun set behind it. It was also a very eerie sight when silhouetted against a stormy sky...

The cottages were Listed buildings, and of great interest to local historians and students of local history. They went back at least to the 17th Century, maybe even earlier. My grandfather once showed me the deeds, or indenture, which were very old style script written with a special ink on parchment. The top was cut in a wavy line, and he told me that on the sale of the cottages the wavy line would have to match up with the other side, which I guess was held by the solicitors, and was a safeguard against fraud. This was a legal practice that went back to medieval times. They were fascinating to see, and to know how much they stood for. Today these kind of indentures are prized collector's items. I would love to know what happened to these ancient deeds to Ivy Cottages...

My grandfather loved those little cottages, he called them his dolls' houses, and in the front garden of No.1 he planted lots of sweet smelling wallflowers each side of the narrow front path. Their warm vibrant colours from yellow, through orange, copper, deepest red and purple, were quite a sight in the summer months. They would seed themselves, so each year there would be more, scenting the air, and adding to the prettiness of the cottages.

~

Beyond Ivy Cottages and Nell's little shop was a row of terraced cottages – they bowed slightly at the front, showing how very old they were, and all with the barest of little toilets down the garden. Mrs. Earl lived in one of them. She was eighty years old, and very ill. She had her bed in her front room by the window, so that she could see what was going on in the street, and who was coming to the door, which was always unlocked during the day. I used to go up and see her sometimes to talk to her. She was always delighted to see me going past the window, and she loved me going in and chatting to her. She was such a lovely lady, and I have found out since that she was very wealthy, and yet chose to live in a little cottage like that.

~

Straight ahead of me was High Road, which was my route to school, and where my parents and brothers lived. I so much wished that I could have a normal life like my friends. One where you lived with your parents, and were treated according to the age that you were, and not being told to do things beyond your age. My father told me that he also would love to live a normal life, like a normal family, with no pub being involved. But what my mother wanted – my mother had. My grandfather had bought that bungalow for her so that she could own her very own property in Orsett. This must have made my father feel awful, but at least he had bought the house in Grays, and I am told he later paid my grandfather back. It is sad really, that he had gone to all that trouble decorating the house in Grays just how my mother had wanted, but she didn't want to live there.

~

On the corner where Baker Street and High Road met was a triangle of grass, upon which was a wooden seat, where sometimes the local teenagers would sit to see whoever might be going by, and a very old black and white signpost, pointing in the four directions. As well as this though was something that absolutely revolted me – it was the pig swill bin, that was emptied at the most just once a week, but normally even less often. It was so totally disgusting, with all the local people putting their unwanted rotting food in there. Lifting the lid was utterly horrendous, with the putrid smell arising from the swarming maggots wriggling in their delight over their feast. So guess whose job it was to take any leftovers from the pub that even the dogs and cats wouldn't eat – like parts of cows' entrails, and the bones of pigs' trotters and skulls – and put it in the pig swill bin? It was *my* job – obviously...

To my left was Fen Lane, which led of course down to the fens. This was where my grandfather and I would walk the dogs, and Valerie and I would go for long walks. It was also where Georgie and I would start our adventures over the fields, and play with the frog spawn in the puddles after a spring rainfall. We would prod it with sticks and see what happened, and the frog spawn would join up in places. And we would joke about the tapioca pudding we had at Orsett School... Ugh! I wasn't afraid of frogs in those days, and we even had the resident toad on the rockery at the pub that, when I was a little girl, I would go to see in the mornings, with him always sitting on the same rock.

~

Behind me was Stifford Clays Road, with a row of tiny ancient cottages along a little alley, where Moira and Tom lived. I remember the rag rugs that some of the people along there had. They were made out of little strips of rags, and made with a latch hook latching the rags onto canvas. The effects could be very pretty, but not so much when they were used as door mats! One of the women who lived along there used to catch mice – and chop them up – and put them in the chicken feed! Well, I'm so glad she didn't offer us any of *her* eggs!

~

It was a lovely area in which to live. I just wished that I didn't have to live at the pub with all its rules, orders, restrictions, lack of privacy, pain, and unspeakable things going on behind closed doors.

But on this beautiful May morning, I was happy, standing outside on the corner and welcoming the sunny day to come. I was wearing a dress that I actually liked. It was sleeveless with a round neck and a slightly flared skirt. The fabric was pale lime green cotton with white spots, and it was as fresh as the new leaves on the beech trees. Because of that dress, I have always associated May with wearing that shade of green.

It is strange how these moments from long ago can linger in your mind for always. This is a memory that can bring me joy, and show me that whatever bad there is, Nature will come along sometimes and show you her beauty and warmth.

~

Looking back, I can't help but wonder why I stood so long at that juncture of cross roads that reached tantalisingly out from all four sides of the Kings Arms. Was there somewhere deep in my young subconscious that one day when I was older I would be faced with which way to turn – which road would be the best to take to bring me some form of happiness and to leave this juncture behind? Alas no... I never had that choice. I was to be led along a very bumpy road – with no return... No turning back – just forward into the unknown...

~

Nell was calling me – "Come on Yvonne – it's time to go to school".

I went from the early morning sunshine, back indoors into the dark brown gloom of the pub, and up to the kitchen where she was going to make sure my hair was just so. Oh why did I have to have it curled around and pinned into those little sausage-shaped curls? I just wanted my hair to be free.

"Can I take off my vest?" I asked her, sensing that it was going to be a hot day.

"No", she answered assertively. "Never cast a clout till May is out".

So what did that mean? Did it mean that nobody could hit anyone until June? I wasn't aware that no clouting had gone on that year...

"No!" Nell laughed. "It means you can't leave off an item of clothing until the first day of June – and that means – your vest!"

Oh, so I still had a while to go until I could leave off that itchy woollen vest! At least I was now past the liberty bodice stage as well – although only just!

What Nell didn't know was that what "Ne'er cast a clout till May be out" was a very old folk belief going back centuries. Possibly to the eighteenth century, or even before. *"May be out"* was really referring to – *not until the May blossom was in bloom* – which showed it was now warm enough to leave off an item of clothing ("clout" in Olde English) with no fear of it suddenly turning cold. Hawthorn trees were obviously very wise old trees, and knew a thing or two about the weather! A lot can be said for old folklore, and the spirit of plants.

Well here in Orsett the May blossom was certainly out – and the day *was* a hot one! We had all already danced around the maypole at school to welcome the onset of summer – one of those summers that were long and hot – as they always are in one's memory.

And so wearing my vest, I set off on the twenty minute walk down to Orsett School, past my parents' bungalow, and wondering whether my mother might just be looking out the front window to see me walk by.

Who's Calling?

As I have said at the beginning of my story, I was nine years old when I was first groomed to serve behind the bar. I learned how to pull the perfect pint, but I had to stand on a Smith's crisps tin to reach the till. I was shown how to lift the glass backwards, half fill it with beer, and then gradually bring the glass forward whilst filling it. This was to give it a good "head" which had to be the exact depth each time – not enough "head" and the beer was deemed as being flat – too much "head" and the customers thought they weren't getting a full pint!

My mother would put red lipstick on my lips and dark pink Bourjois rouge on my cheeks, and I was told to always *smile – no matter what any man said to me...*

At around the same time I was told how to answer the telephone.

First of all, there was the wall mounted telephone at the shop. It was black and heavy, and the type where you had to turn the handle. Goodness knows where Grandpop got it from, but it's the kind I have seen in war films, when everything is all very secret.

Thinking of that telephone in the shop brings back nostalgic memories of the coal fire burning in the corner of the little room out the back, and the smell of the oil stove that stood precariously in the way, and I was always afraid of brushing up against it when it was alight. This was for when there was a shortage of coal, and it would be lit instead of the fire. There was also Nell's treadle Singer sewing machine, and her ironing table where I learned to iron with the heavy black iron that had to be heated up on the fire.

There was also a bed, on which I would sit and play with my dolls, with a little window above it, where Nell would peep out and see whoever might be coming into the shop.

So this was the scene, and Grandpop was very proud of his telephone.

That was the first telephone I had ever talked on. Nell had told me to dial the number for the pub, and see what happened. It was fascinating hearing a voice that I recognised talking to me on the other end of the receiver.

~

Then there was the pub telephone, which was a large black "normal" telephone for the time, upstairs on a desk on the landing.

"Hello – Orsett 219 – who's calling please?" I would have to answer. Then I would go and fetch whoever was being asked for.

I can't remember exactly how old I was, although I think I was probably about ten, but I answered the phone and I could hear some heavy breathing... Then a very creepy sounding voice spoke...

"Will you take your knickers down for me?" he said, in a tone that made me shiver.

"*Pardon?*" I answered, unwittingly giving him the opportunity to repeat what he had just said.

I put the receiver down next to the phone and went along to the kitchen to get Nell.

"There's a man on the phone – asking me to take my knickers down for him?" I told her.

"Is he still there?" Nell asked, already on her way along the landing. As soon as she spoke though, he put the phone down.

A couple of days later he phoned again. Who was this slimy-sounding man? Was he a customer? Was he someone I was pulling pints for? Whoever he was, he knew my whereabouts. He knew that I answered the pub telephone, and he also knew when I was there...

"Will you take your knickers down for me?" he asked again. What was he expecting? Did he want me to answer and say where and when – or did he just want to know that I was doing that while he was on the phone? He couldn't see me... *Could he?*

This time I put the phone down on him immediately. So why did it all feel so creepy? He wasn't doing me any actual physical harm by saying these things. So why did I feel sick and unsteady hearing his words? Why did I suddenly become afraid of answering the phone?

Nell had a plan. She told me to carry on answering the phone as usual, and if he called again – which she reckoned he would – I was to say something like yes, or just a minute, something like that to keep him on the line, and then go and get her.

"Will you take your knickers down for me?" he was asking me yet again a few days later. There was no way I could answer in the way Nell had asked me to. I think I said something like "um..." then quickly put the phone down again and went and got Nell.

"Stay here" she said, as she metaphorically rolled up her sleeves, and marched along the landing to the phone. Of course I didn't hear what was being said to her, but she was listening... It seems that he thought it was still me, and that I really might be taking my knickers down for him...

What he was instructing to do next, I never did find out. Then I heard Nell's voice – she was speaking in a low tone, and I couldn't hear what she was saying.

"It's him – over the road" she said, having recognised his voice. He had been spying on me, and had been getting some sort of kick out of phoning me in that manner. Nell never did tell me what he was asking "me" to do. But "he won't be phoning again" she said triumphantly.

No, he didn't as far as I know.

To this day I am still very nervous about answering the phone...

Landlord And Master

Arthur Leonard Felstead was born in 1892 to a family of what was to eventually consist of ten children. His father was a railway policeman in North London, although like any normal policeman of the time, he had the handcuffs, the truncheon, and the power to use them if necessary.

His mother, Ada Felstead, was a most formidable-looking woman, who ruled the house with a "rod of iron" as they say – no-one would dare to upset her, be naughty or answer back, for the risk of her retribution was far too great to contemplate. Anyone who dared to speak, or even cough, at the table was immediately banished from the room, or rapped over the knuckles with her punishment stick that she kept next to the table.

As a boy my grandfather roamed the streets where he lived in North London, looking for mischief, sometimes even barefoot. These are the stories he told me when I was a little girl, and the photo I have of his mother confirms to me just how strictly she had brought up all those children – well the ones that survived babyhood and childhood that is.

~

He had been a Gunner in the First Middlesex Machine Gun Corps during the First World War, and had fought at the Somme. During the Second World War now being landlord of the Kings Arms, he was Chief Fire Warden, and the only person allowed out after curfew. He still had his warden's helmet and gas masks that he kept in a cupboard in his bedroom, and he would bring these out to show me from time to time. I found the gas masks terribly scary things to look at though. As necessary as they were at the time, they looked like monsters' faces to me. He put one on my head once. It felt terrible and, being a child, I was really terrified of it. I also couldn't stand the smell of it on my face, and I really didn't like looking like what I deemed to be a monster...

~

My grandfather was a stout man, with plump jowls and a full pouting lower lip, so much resembling Alfred Hitchcock, although he did have a full head of hair. He had brown eyes, and was proud of his thick, silver grey hair, which he kept immaculate with lavender scented Brilliantine. Every evening before he opened the pub doors he would sit in the kitchen and would summon his mistress Nell to comb his hair. She knew exactly how he liked it, and would sweep it upwards and backwards, with a generous dab from the green Brilliantine pot. Nell would button his white detachable collar on to his shirt, and then with an extra dab of Old Spice aftershave on to his cheeks, and a straightening of his waistcoat he was ready to greet his customers.

He could be quite a charmer, and women seemed to be drawn to him. If there were women sitting at a table on their own while their husbands were at the bar, which usually was the case, my grandfather would make a point of going over to them and pandering to their vanity.

"What fine young wenches we have in here today" he would tend to say. Or "what a bevy of beautiful maidens I see before me". And "what a vision of loveliness we have here..." The women always loved it. There were always so many giggles amongst female customers when Grandpop was around.

~

My grandfather was standing at the saloon bar counter, wearing his neatly pressed white shirt, gold cufflinks and sleeve garters, which held back his sleeves to the perfect length. His slick tie had been carefully tied by Nell to his exact requirement, and the buttons on his waistcoat were done up, but leaving the bottom one deliberately undone – he knew how to dress. As always, Nell had been on her knees polishing his brown brogue shoes – despite everything, she adored him.

It was a Sunday lunchtime, and saloon bar men were bringing their wives, women, whoever, to the pub for their gin and tonics. Grandpop was standing there surveying the scene, and puffing quite regally at his Havana cigar. He knew what he was doing – that was why he was in the saloon bar...

The cigar smoke filled the bar with its expensive Cuban aroma. They were the kind of cigars that needed a proper cigar cutter to nip off the top, which my grandfather would do with great aplomb, checking that the cut was perfect. This was his grand side. The side that only happened when he was surrounded by his "beautiful bevy of fine young maidens", or whatever else he chose to call them.

A couple of women had gone over to the counter, leaning over and whispering to him amidst naughty-sounding giggles. Both of them were stroking his slicked-back silver hair.

"Look at those fornicating old wocs" Nanny said to me. "All they want is his dough..."

That translated means "Look at those fawning cows – all they want is his money..."

I had asked her once what a "woc" was – "spell it backwards" she replied...

My grandmother certainly had her own unique vocabulary!

~

Something my grandfather loved to do, was to make a woman feel special by giving them a drink called a "Bleeding Heart". This was a small, fan-shaped glass of advocaat, to which Grandpop would cleverly add a heart shape with cherry brandy. With a very deft flick of his wrist he could drop cherry brandy into the advocaat in the shape of a heart. The heart would then slowly bleed into the advocaat as it was sipped.

Nanny Felstead never had a good word to say about him. In fact I think she *hated* him.

"Look at that man" she said one evening when he was standing in the taproom, his hands behind his back as he waited for the first customers to arrive. "He thinks he's lord and master over us all..."

"I am..." he said, even though he was supposedly hard of hearing. "Lord and master – *of all I survey...*" turning round and looking straight at her.

"Hmm" Nanny sneered dismissively. She was risking it, but Grandpop was usually in a good mood when he was waiting for his customers.

One day my mother asked her why she ever married him. "Because he was always so nice to me" she said. So he had charmed her too. Strangely, they were living together when they got married, which would have been quite a scandal way back in those days. Despite the way he treated her though, she stayed by his side. One day she told me that if she left him, she would no longer be landlady of the Kings Arms, a status that meant so much to her.

Nanny used to take advantage of the situation when he went out. She would sit upstairs in the lounge, in her armchair overlooking High Road, where she could watch people to-ing and fro-ing. "Look at that old woc", she would say, as she watched various women walk down the road.

"Look at her arse", she would comment sometimes, beckoning me to the window to see who she was referring to. She loved sitting there, in that chair, and could be so funny sometimes – especially when she was having a nap...

"Just having a quick doss duck", she would say sometimes, sensing that I had entered the room. Then she would go straight back to sleep – with her mouth wide open... I actually saw a fly go in it once. I can't help but wonder how many other flies had gone in there that she hadn't known about!

She would have the electric fire on – all three elements, and would sit and smoke to her heart's delight. My mother and I would be on full alert for when my grandfather pulled back into the car park.

"Quick – here's that man!" my mother would warn.

Then it would be all systems go... The electric fire would be turned off – all traces of cigarettes would be removed, and Nanny would strike a match saying the sulphur would mask the smell.

"Doesn't it get on your wick", Nanny would say despondently, as she sat there trying to look innocent.

Then we would hear Grandpop plodding up the stairs, and we would all hope and pray that he didn't detect anything, and that the glowing red elements of the electric fire would die down sufficiently before he came in...

I can't help but wonder whether Grandpop ever did detect any cigarette smells or see the last remaining glows of the fire, but my mother and I were always pretty good at covering things up. His sense of hearing was a different matter though...

"He never hears what I say *to* him – but he always hears what I say *about* him!" Nanny said one day. I think that maybe Grandpop feigned deafness a few times!

~

"A household of women" the pub was once described to me. Well I suppose it was once another mistress moved in... My grandfather ruled the roost though, the cock presiding over all the hens – cock of the roost – a very apt description of him!

There had been another bird in the pecking order once though – a friend of Nell who had set her sights on my grandfather, this cock of the roost. What was it about him that was so charismatic to women? Well, he must have had something, because Nell and her friend had a fight over who was going to have him! Never mind that he had a wife – my grandmother – but it seemed that the hatch was open to any hen that wanted to share his perch. Apparently Nell won.

My grandmother never referred to him by name. To her he was always "that man" or "Lord and Master". To me though he was Grandpop. Well when we were out of the pub that is. He was very much a Jekyll and Hyde personality. The loving grandfather when we went out walking the dogs, or going for rides in the countryside, and Mr. Hyde whenever he was back at the pub.

The countryside rides with me in his car were for him to meet up with various landladies of pubs in North Essex. He would leave me in the car with a bottle of Amber Orange, which I drank through a white paper straw, and a packet of crisps. He told me I couldn't go in someone else's pub at my age, and so I was happy sitting in the car for an hour or so waiting for him. Well happy enough. I didn't know what he was really getting up to at the time!

Actually, I do remember a time when I was allowed to go into one of these pubs, after he had been in there for an hour or so... That particular landlady must have known I had been sitting outside in the car, and wanted to meet me. I stood at the counter, and I will never forget the strong smell of pickled onions on her breath as she leaned over and spoke to me – the top of my head was just about at the top of the counter – that is how young I was.

~

If my grandfather could get away with anything untoward – anything at all – then he would. And really, I can't think of anything that he *didn't* get away with. He loved telling us the tale about the saloon bar customer who would compliment him on his sherry...

"A nice drop of Harveys Landlord", he would say, savouring the warm taste of what he thought was his favourite sherry – and had paid for – not knowing that it wasn't Harveys after all. My grandfather would chuckle knowing that what he was really drinking was the cheapest sherry he had – poured into a Harveys' bottle!

He got away with other things along those lines too, like putting the slops into the mild – for which customers also unknowingly complimented him on his good beer – although my father knew what he was doing. He didn't seem to care though – until the day that he found out that something else had been put in the slops... Oh dear, that is a story that is so difficult to tell...

~

As she got older, with my poor grandmother's arteries slowly but surely hardening and affecting the blood flow to her brain, she wasn't always in total control of what she was doing. What with her alcohol consumption as well, she sometimes did very strange things...

I can only assume that she knew what she was doing the day that she peed over the drain by the cellar flap – and then complained that one of the customers had seen her – and watched her! We all thought at the time that it was just laziness, or even some sort of daredevil thing that she wanted to do. But knowing what happened gradually later, that could be very much to do with her slowly-degenerating mental state. As far as I know though, no-one knew that at the time.

There was the time when Mrs. Eades' Christmas pudding bowl (she always made our Christmas puddings in return for a large bottle of stout) was behind the bar waiting for her to collect. No-one knows how often my grandmother might have done this, but one day she was found urinating into the pudding bowl – then tipping it into the slops! I had never seen my father's face look so disgusted as when he was told about this. His face contorted into a screwed up eyes, nose and mouth like I had never seen him look before. He always enjoyed a pint of mild and bitter – but whatever went into the slops – also went into the mild... Not so mild then...

Then there was the day that there was a saucepan of stewed apple waiting on the stove. My mother went to heat it up – and it felt exceptionally heavy...

"There wasn't this much in there earlier" she remarked quizzically.

She peered at it again, and then she smelled it... To her disgust as well, she told me that she had seen my grandmother using a saucepan for urinating – and now she had done exactly that – into the freshly stewed apples...

~

My grandfather always knew when inspectors were around. They were always different people of course – but Grandpop could always tell – he could "sniff them out", as he explained. Somehow he had the knack of making sure everything was present and correct the moment they entered the bar. How he did it though, I really don't know.

"Hello sir – what can I do for *you?*" Somehow, his charm would take over, and if the gin or vodka was somewhat watered down, it never got detected.

So he carried on doing such things, charming inspectors as well as women. Well apart from the time he was beaten up badly by a gang in the hallway because he was having an affair with someone's wife. It seems that he was just unlucky that time, because usually he would get away with it. Affairs for him were just a way of life, no matter how much hurt he caused to all concerned.

It has been suggested to me by someone who knew my grandfather at the time, that my mother wasn't his only child. And when so many of my possessions that were taken away from me were given to other local girls, it somehow makes sense.

"Money talks" my grandmother would say, seeing him take out a large bundle of notes from his pocket, and flick off a few to give to some woman who might "appreciate" it.

"Look at him" she has sneered – "he thinks he can buy friends..."

Well whether he "bought" friends or not, he *did* have people in his camp.

~

Sometimes he would have "lock-ins". He seemed to be quite popular for this, as without any strict drinking and driving laws in those days, people would enjoy having a few more drinks after time – and "one for the road" – which was pretty normal then.

One of his "friends" was a local high ranking Inspector in the police, and he liked a bit of an after hours lock-in too!

One night there was a raid – I say a raid, but it wasn't how raids are seen these days. It was after hours and there was a gathering of men in the saloon bar, including the Inspector. There was only the minimum amount of lights on, in fact, the light was mainly from the open fire, and a few lights behind the bar. All the curtains were drawn – as usual – and everyone was having a really rather good time. The later it got, and the more alcohol they consumed, the merrier they got.

Suddenly, there was a banging at the door. Someone – I think it was Nell – answered it, and a few policemen burst in, and went straight to the saloon bar.

"Oh – I'm very sorry Sir" one of them said as they saw their Inspector – and so they went...

I can't help but wonder though – what did they think of that little girl standing there in the bar – watching all this going on? Didn't it occur to them that at such a late hour I might have been there – under sufferance? Wasn't that more important than a few men having after hours drinks?

~

So that would often be my evenings and night times, being forced to stay up, doing the tables and the washing up and drying of the glasses.

Daytime though would sometimes bring out the Dr. Jekyll in my grandfather – and this was the grandfather that I liked and felt comfortable with.

Grandpop and I would take the dogs for long walks around the lanes, and he knew every bird and wild flower that fluttered or nodded in the hedgerows. I learned so much about nature during these walks down the lane with him – he would point out things to me all the time. "Look at that little bird" he would say, suddenly stopping in his tracks to show me a mother bird tending the fledglings in her nest. Or "look at the little chaffinch – pretty little thing isn't it."

In the spring he would point out the primroses and violets growing wild in the grass verge, the yellow celandines growing in the ditches, the white aconites, and later the bright pink and luminous white campion. Wild, sweetly-scented honeysuckle was also abundant in the summer, winding its way through the hedgerows, with the white and pale pink wild roses – I have always associated honeysuckle and wild roses together.

The dark deadly nightshade, with its deep purple flowers and poisonous black berries, was also of interest. I knew I must never ever touch that. Just by eating two of those black berries has been known to kill a child. Two to five berries can kill an adult. Surprising then that its called "Belladonna"... Goodness knows what Italian women used to do to their eyes when they used it as eye drops to dilate their pupils to make them look more seductive! Belladonnas they may have thought they were, but could they actually see themselves in the mirror?

In late summer we would go blackberrying. I would carry a creamy white-coloured pudding bowl, veined with thin grey lines from where it had been boiled so much, and Grandpop would pull down the top branches of the brambles with the hook of his walking stick for me to pick, telling me that the best blackberries were the ones at the top, furthest from the ground. I would then take them home for my grandmother to make her delicious apple and blackberry pies. These walks were the only time he used a walking stick, other than when he used his heavily gnarled and twisted one to keep Butch in order!

He also taught me how to garden, not just recognising every garden flower and shrub, and how they grew, but basics like how deep to plant bulbs, how to properly prune a rose bush, and how to tell a weed from a seedling. I used to love helping him to garden, and going for those long walks with the dogs.

~

Indoors though things were very different. Very different indeed. My grandfather ruled with an iron fist (sometimes literally). The main victim of his gross violence was my grandmother, but I have also known him to be violent towards his mistress Nell. War seemed to have seeped into his blood, and in some ways I don't think he had ever really left the battlefields. Not that I am making excuses for him though, because although he could be so charming, he was a very violent man at times, with an uncontrollable temper that verged on sadism.

His cruelty to my grandmother was unbelievable, and there were many things that I witnessed that he did, not only to her, but also to Nell. But, as I said earlier, Nanny only stayed with him because she didn't want to lose her status as landlady of the pub and really, it was the only life she had known since their marriage. I used to wonder how Nell stayed with him too, but she was besotted with him. Moreover, there was also something very dark and strange that kept her by his side...

From early days in my childhood, and until I was about seven years old, Grandpop liked me to go into his bedroom each morning, and get into bed with him while Nell was up cleaning the pub and making cups of tea, which she would bring into us. Grandpop loved to reminisce. He would tell me stories about his childhood in London, playing in the streets of Cricklewood, sometimes barefoot, because he didn't always have any shoes. His parents George and Ada were very strict, especially his mother who sounded very cruel, and she kept a stick next to the dining table ready to hit any of the children's arms if they had their elbows on the table, or if they even dared to speak while eating. My mother had told me how as a child she wasn't even allowed to cough at the table, let alone talk. The rule about no elbows on the table though still applied to me.

Grandpop would also tell me stories about his time spent fighting in the trenches in Flanders and at The Somme. He got trench foot from having permanently wet feet by being constantly in mud. Drinking water was hard to get too. He told me how he took his billy can, which they used for eating out of as well as drinking, to a river to get some water to drink. He stood there drinking – then saw a dead cow floating down from upstream!

Other stories he told me are very hard for me to repeat. I absolutely love France and the French people, in fact I would live there if I could.

But he said that when the army was in the villages, the women would sometimes lift up their skirts and pee at the English soldiers. He said that always made them chuckle. Well I suppose that was innocent enough then, and the women were maybe only having fun. There was something else though that was particularly awful...

One night when he was in the trenches, it was dark and he had peeped up above the trench and was looking across no-man's land to the German trenches. He had his machine gun at the ready, and stood there – watching and waiting. Fairly soon a German soldier came up out of his trench, and with his back facing no-man's land, he squatted – doing his business...

"I aimed my gun right at his big fat arse", he told me with a wicked grin, "and then I shot him".

He loved telling me that story, but it always bothered me. The thought of that poor man relieving himself in the dark, not knowing there was an English soldier aiming straight at him, is so terrible. To me that is not war, it is not conflict, it is not a fair battle. But to my grandfather at the time, it really was war – getting rid of the enemy in any way that you could – even at their most vulnerable. And what was he doing telling me all this anyway? Did he enjoy telling me these things? He would tell me these same stories, over and over again, along with accounts of the atrocious conditions – and the blood and literally guts of war, with tears streaming down his cheeks. I can only think that, whether they were wicked grins, or tears, through me he was living it all again...

Grandpop also used to sing to me and teach me songs so that I could sing along too. Songs like one of his and Nanny's favourites – "I'll Be Your Sweetheart" – including the verse which begins...

"One day I saw two lovers in the garden
A little boy and girl with golden hair"

He liked singing "Little Man You've Had a Busy Day" and "The Little Boy that Santa Claus Forgot", which I always found so sad because I thought it was true. Then there was "Run Rabbit Run Rabbit Run, Run, Run" which was a jolly song to sing, but that worried me a bit about rabbit pies!

He also liked Paul Robeson's "Old Man River", and he would go into a deep baritone voice to sing that to me. Well I didn't try that one! One day he taught me a new song...

I was going for a walk with Valerie along Baker Street...

"I've learned a new song" I said enthusiastically. Then in my innocence I started singing it to her...

"Roll me over in the clover – roll me over, lay me down, and do it again."

Oh dear, to this day I have never forgotten her scorn!

"That is *so rude!*" she said frowning at me like my mother. Well how was I to know that rolling over in the clover then doing it again had anything other to do with, well, just rolling over in the clover!

~

Well this must all sound like a lovely start to the day. In a way it was, but looking back with what I know now, and from what I remember from when I was very very young, it may not have been the healthiest thing for a little girl to have to get into bed with her grandfather every morning. My family and Nell all knew what he was like, but never worried about putting me into any potential danger.

Despite the stories and the songs, Grandpop's bedroom was a very scary place. He had a huge dark wooden desk in front of the window, which looked over to the lea, the farm and the lane where we used to walk down to the fen. Well that was fine, but it was so dark in there. There was a large dresser next to the fireplace, and an ornate and very heavy looking wardrobe. The walls were dark, and festooned with weapons – guns, knives, a walking stick that had a concealed spike at the end, his sheathed Japanese sword, and his father's truncheon and handcuffs from his days as a policeman in North London. He had a little Derringer gun that he kept next to the bed, fully loaded, and he would chuckle as he told me that dare anyone break into his pub! He also had a rifle that was fully loaded, and said that he would shoot at their ankles! As I say, it was a scary place for a little girl.

I found *him* very scary too at times. I was only too aware of what his temper was like, and how he could "turn" in seconds. Dr. Jekyll would suddenly turn into Mr. Hyde – and *hiding* was the best thing to do when that happened... He never used his fists on *me* though. With me it was more subtle, in the form of "torture", which was excruciating. This took the form of putting boiling hot spoons on the back of my hands, or worse, the tender insides of my wrists.

Sometimes at breakfast he would be sitting at his end of the table, stirring his black Camp coffee, stirring and stirring until the spoon was really hot. "Come here girl" he would beckon, and I knew I had to leave my place and go over to him for the torture. There was to be no resisting, for I always had to do exactly as I was told, standing there, holding out my hand for him, and yet – no-one ever stopped him.

Another form of torture would take place on the landing. Sometimes as I walked along the long landing to the bedrooms, I could sense him creeping up behind me, he was so intimidating – and he knew that *I* knew that something very bad was about to happen. He would then twist what he called my "funny bone", being my elbow on my right arm. Funny bone? Yes – very *funny* for him. This was the most unbearable pain of all, and yet no-one ever stopped him from doing it. I would be crying out loud while this was going on, and being pushed back against the wall or the banisters. My elbow would be sore for ages – but why didn't *anyone* come to intervene when they heard my cries of pain?

He also twisted my kneecap on more than one occasion, again utterly excruciating. One of these times was when I was sitting in the kitchen in the armchair. I saw his menacing eyes as he came over to me, then he just grabbed hold of my right knee and twisted it. Again, I was crying out in pain, but even though others were in the kitchen at the time, still no-one stopped him. Now, my right knee is bigger than my left, and causes me a lot of pain sometimes. I *know* that this must go back to those days, so I am never going to be free of the memories – none of them. I never knew why he wanted to hurt me so much, and nor why my mother used to let him.

Chinese burns were another thing he liked to do with my wrists, again so intolerably painful. He knew all the pressure points on the body too, probably something he had found out during the War. Sometimes he would appear behind me and forcefully push his middle finger into my back between my shoulder blades. I know it was his middle finger, because he demonstrated it to me once. He would also flick his thumb on my head sometimes as he walked past me – again, the right spot to cause pain. *"Tum-ti-tum-ti-tum..."* he would go, as he just carried on walking down to his bedroom. No matter what he did – he really knew how to hurt.

~

Bath times at the pub were awful. No water could be wasted, although goodness knows why. My grandfather didn't have to pay a separate water rate, but he had this thing about wasting water. Maybe it went back to the war.

As well as baths, when I was younger, my mother would give me a top to toe wash every evening in the kitchen – with everyone else there. I had no choice though.

"Lift your leg up" she would say, as she washed each leg in turn with the slimy flannel that everyone else used. Even at such a young age, I didn't like lifting my legs up in turn in front of everyone. I had already got a sense that what was between my legs was deemed to be private. Then she would powder me between my legs – "Don't want to get chapped" she would say, making me feel that even more attention was being brought to my little naked body.

~

There was no such thing as bubble bath in our household, and the only water softener was soda crystals, which we also used for washing up. I usually had to have my grandfather's bath water, which always smelled horrible, and had a layer of scum on the top. This was probably due to his use of a pumice stone to get rid of the hard skin on his feet. I actually felt dirtier getting out of it than before I got in. I was sure he peed in it too.

A daily top-to-toe wash at the sink was far more effective than getting into my grandfather's bath water! However, there was also no lock on the bathroom door. The unwritten rule was, if the door was closed, then someone was in there.

My body had started changing, albeit slowly. I was pre-puberty, so nothing was changing dramatically, but instinct told me that there were parts of my body that I didn't feel comfortable about anyone seeing.

The closed door was not an unwritten rule to my grandfather though, and what used to happen to me, had also happened to Flora when she had stayed there between the ages of nine and twelve.

My heart would sink as the door opened...

"Tum-ti-tum-ti-tum" he would go, and I knew it was my grandfather.

Just as Flora had done before me, I would sit uncomfortably in the bath with my arms criss-crossed over my young body. Flora has told me that she must have been developing at a younger age than me, and therefore had small breasts forming. Even so, I instinctively did the same as what she has told me she had done. It was so embarrassing.

It was always the same thing he would do. He would go over to the toilet, undo his trousers, and there would be an almighty torrent into the bowl... He must have been saving that up for ages, because each time he did it, it seemed never ending.

And the smell – it was awful. Too many barley wines consumed every day maybe...

The froth would still be there later... He never flushed the toilet, the chain hanging from the overhead cistern remained untouched. Can't waste water...

Then he would turn to me – tuck himself back into his flies and slowly do up his buttons. Then he would pat himself... And stand there looking at me, with my arms crossed over my young chest, and always terrified of what might happen next.

"Tum-ti-tum-ti-tum" he would go again when he eventually left the bathroom.

I can remember that hum to this day, and it still makes me shiver... *"Tum-ti-tum-ti-tum..."*

~

I could never say anything to my mother who, being second in command, ruled with a permanent frown of disapproval, and the ever present threat to me was that if I ever spoke a word of what went on, then I would be taken away to the children's home run by the nuns. As I have said before, all the children I knew lived in fear of the nuns, and when sometimes we would see them walking two or three abreast along the street in our local town, we were so afraid of them that we would immediately cross the road. This fear was probably very unfounded, but the threat of what might happen to me was always there.

~

One day my grandfather taught me a life lesson. Well actually I think I taught myself. In 1956 when I was seven years old, something new came into the shops. Grandpop came home one day proudly showing us his latest gadget – a Jif lemon. He seemed thrilled to bits with it! Well I was intrigued too about how much like a real lemon it was. Very soon though I lost the top... That little yellow thing had rolled somewhere in the kitchen, but try as I might I just couldn't find it. I put it back in the pantry hoping that Grandpop wouldn't notice.

Well of course, he very soon did! He went on the rampage wanting to know where the top of his Jif lemon had gone. No-one knew – except me. I crept down the stairs, out of the pub, and then slowly started walking up Baker Street. I felt physically sick and afraid. I knew that someone was going to be punished for this, and it was either going to be my grandmother or Nell – or both.

After a while of looking down at the pavement and pondering I went back indoors. I knew what I had to do. Things had calmed down and Grandpop was in his bedroom. I went along to his bedroom and knocked on the door. I was never allowed to enter any bedroom without knocking first, and waiting until I was asked in.

"Yes?" he said, with a degree of agitation in his tone.

I slowly opened the door and went into the room. He was standing at his desk writing.

"Well?" he said, still sounding agitated, but still writing.

"Grandpop" I said slowly, feeling as though my stomach was going to fall to the floor. My hands were tightly clutching the sides of my skirt as I tried to get the next words out. He carried on writing. "I am really sorry", I confessed, "but it was *me – I* lost the top of the lemon."

He put down his fountain pen and stood for a few moments staring out of the window. Then he turned to me. "Well my girl", he said, looking down at me over the top of his round horn-rimmed spectacles, "because you have been so honest and have owned up – then I am not going to punish you." He then just turned around and carried on writing.

~

Grandpop used to write a lot of letters, mainly in the form of love letters to his lady friends. I knew this because my mother told me. She would sometimes sneak into his bedroom when he was out and read what he had been writing. One day I was sitting at the kitchen table drawing. Grandpop was out, and my mother came in looking flushed.

"Copy this" she urged, handing me a letter in my grandfather's writing and a notepad. "It doesn't matter what it says – just copy it."

I dutifully copied this long letter, so carefully written in my grandfather's beautiful handwriting. I didn't know much of what it was about, but I didn't like reading his words of love and passion to a woman I didn't know, and I felt very uncomfortable doing it.

How could my mother have exposed me to such things? I know she knew that at the time I didn't know about such things, but to make me copy all this word for word, was very wrong for a mother to make her young daughter do. I actually found that quite traumatic, having to obey my mother, but also being disloyal to my grandfather. I also found it traumatic having to read and write about things that as a young girl, I knew nothing about...

~

Another lesson I learned through Grandpop's actions was never to throw away any letters or other paperwork without first tearing it up. One day when we went on one of our walks we went in the opposite direction and went up Baker Street to the rubbish tip. The place was swarming with squawking seagulls and smelled terribly. Grandpop walked around with the dogs sniffing everywhere, until he found something of interest. He would prod at things with his walking stick, somehow knowing there was a letter or two in that particular pile of rubbish. Then he would read it... I think he got to know a lot about local people doing that! So I have always torn any paperwork that I was discarding into little pieces before throwing it away. There might be other people doing the same thing as my grandfather!

~

As I have said before, my grandfather took over the Kings Arms in 1939 just before the War. It had a small car park, a large garden, and a large plot of land next to that which he bought. This then became an extension of the garden.

He had also purchased the property next to the orchard, which was a very old building called "Ivy Cottage". He had apparently bought this as an investment, but also as somewhere to which he could retire in the distant future. It had been a cottage with a baker's incorporated next door – there was a large brick bread oven behind it, which had a small black iron door, through which a flat, shovel-like article called a "peel" would be pushed holding the dough to be baked.

Ivy Cottage was then made into two cottages, with outside toilets and no bathrooms, and I clearly remember the huge brick bread oven at the back, which was later made into a kitchen. The ancient well, which had originally held all the water for both cottages, was still there, just outside in the garden.

The cottage on the left became No.1 Ivy Cottage, and what was the baker's became No.2. During the time that the cottages had been built, people had been a lot shorter, and therefore the ceilings were very low.

When my parents married in 1946, my grandfather said they could live in No.1. So to make it more habitable, my father dug the floors down deeper, while he and my mother lived with Nanny Mandeville in Grays.

The cottages had a lot of character, and their long history had made them even more appealing. At the time they had been built in the 1600's, Baker Street didn't exist – it was a stream. All in all however, they were two very pretty cottages, and that is where my parents went to live until 1956.

I say lived there, but my mother spent most of her time at the pub with my grandparents. She had grown up with the pub way of life, and didn't really like what she saw as "normal life".

The woman in No.2 Ivy Cottage was a widow, Hilda Jobson, who lived there with her daughter Celia. She had a lovely large, sand-coloured dog called Flossie. I think was probably a Labrador. Mrs. Jobson would sit me astride Flossie, and she would carry me round her garden. She must have been a very strong dog, although I *was* just a very little girl.

Grandpop liked her too, and he was always going up to see her. He liked seeing his tenant, and making sure she had everything she wanted...

~

I can't remember how old I was, possibly nine or ten, but my father said he was going to make me a dolls' house. I was thrilled to bits about this, because it was something I dearly wanted. He was making it for me in the cook house, and each day when he came home from work, I would go in there with him, watching him gradually build this house for me. He would take me down to the Doll's Hospital in Grays, which also sold parts for making dolls' houses and other toys. I loved that little shop. I remember Nell taking me down there to have a doll mended. It was little Rosebud. I think one of the dogs had chewed her leg, and she had to go to hospital. She had also lost most of her hair and needed a wig. Nell took me down to collect her, and there she was – sitting on a shelf waiting to be taken home – right as rain, and with a full head of hair!

The dolls' house of course, was not for dolls of that size, it was for the tiny family of dolls that were going to inhabit it, and give me hours of joy going about their business in their new home. I was going to be mother doll, and I would have children, and they would have a daddy, mini dogs and cats, and we would all live our little mini lives happily for ever after.

Each week I would go with my father to that little shop and help him choose what I wanted – the windows, which were green with diamond-shaped leaded lights, the door, which was also green, the wallpaper and floor coverings. Last of all came the choice for the roof tiles. Daddy had taken weeks making this dolls' house for me, and with the roof finally on – it was complete.

I came home from school and eagerly rushed to see my dolls' house. It wasn't in the cook house any more – so it must be in the pub. Daddy must have put it there in a special place, waiting for me. I went upstairs, looking around to see where he had placed it. I felt frantic – I couldn't find it... "Mummy – where is my dolls' house?" I asked my mother, who was sitting in her usual place in the kitchen with my grandmother.

"Grandpop took it up to the Jobson's" she said, "he gave it to Celia..."

Honky-Tonk & Skiffle

The Kings Arms was very well liked by the locals – the taproom and the saloon bar customers, although entirely different people in each bar, all seemed to enjoy coming to the pub. On summer evenings we could see people walking over the fields from Stifford Clays and Blackshots to come to the pub. Some would bring their children, and they would sit outside. I used to like being outside talking to the children while their parents enjoyed their evening's freedom in the pub. It was up to me to talk to them and make sure they were ok, even though I was only a child myself.

My grandfather once had the idea to get a donkey so that *I* could give the children donkey rides. I was dreading that, but thankfully it never happened!

There was always a lot of litter. No-one seemed to think twice about throwing their litter on the ground, and children took their behavioural patterns from their parents. My part in keeping everything tidy was to gather up the empty bottles and glasses, and pick up the litter that the families who sat outside threw to wherever they may land. The Smith's crisps bags, with their little blue salt wrappers, the white paper straws in the bottles of fizzy drinks that would be used as darts, and just thrown into the air. Every packet of crisps, nuts or sweets that they had had, the cigarette packets, the yellow dog-ends – all would be thrown so indiscriminately onto the ground.

There was lots of it – but I had a stick with a spike on the end of it, which my grandfather had devised – how thoughtful of him! It could be a little humiliating at times, picking up all this litter, with more being thrown down. But that was how things were then. Well in my world anyway.

Once I was punished for something, goodness knows what I had done – or rather *not* done – but I was confined to staying upstairs on a Saturday evening, watching the families walking across the fields and so much wanting to be down in the car park with the children. But I had to stay up there all evening, even though it was one of those lovely evenings that followed a hot summer's day. That particular evening, I actually would have rather been picking up litter...

~

Grandpop loved the gramophone player. He was the only person I knew who had one at the time, but as I said in a previous chapter, it meant work for me sometimes.

The customers loved honky-tonk music, such as Winifred Attwell and Russ Conway. Sometimes someone would play the piano in the taproom, usually honky-tonk style – and once they started they couldn't stop – because there would be pints of beer lined up all along the top of the piano to ensure that they carried on!

So it could be very jolly in the pub, but I hated the times I had to serve behind the bar.

Around the late fifties and early sixties a new kind of music was on the scene – skiffle music. Lonnie Donegan had hits with "My Old Man's a Dustman" and "Does Your Chewing Gum Lose its Flavour on the Bedpost Overnight", which everyone seemed to love.

So my grandfather decided to have a skiffle group come and play in the taproom every Friday evening. They would play a lot of Lonnie Donegan music, as well as other skiffle. I found it amusing that they used a wash board to make music, as this is what I used to have to use when I was helping with the washing!

This all went down very well, it was fresh and new, and what was more, it was a little different to what was normally on offer in pubs at the time. I suppose these days they might be called a "Lonnie Donegan Tribute Band"!

~

Fewer people were learning to play the piano, which had once been the main source of home family entertainment, and there wasn't much to see on television either, with just two channels at first, and then BBC2 coming along later – still at the time in black and white, as Britain didn't get colour television until 1967.

Watching the television upstairs in the lounge in the evening was quite a ritual. We could only turn it on if there was something in particular that we wanted to watch, which a lot of the time, depending on my grandfather's mood – it was what *he* wanted to watch. He loved the "Black & White Minstrel Show", which began in 1958, especially when they were singing Al Jolson songs, and "Sunday Night at the London Palladium" – especially if Tommy Trinder was on. We would be summoned to watch these programmes with him, totally in the dark, and no-one dare move while it was on, not even to get up to go to the toilet. We certainly weren't allowed to eat anything of course!

"Don't you *dare* come in here with those" my mother scolded as I went to go into the lounge with a packet of crisps. Even if I had just opened them I would have had been sent straight out again – let alone sprinkle the salt from the little twisted blue bag over them and giving them a shake!

And so the ritual would begin. Grandpop would have the best seat, on the settee directly opposite the television screen, my mother would sit next to him one side, and I would sit the other. My grandmother would sit in her armchair – whether she could see the screen properly or not.

Grandpop's favourite programmes though were, unsurprisingly, boxing and wrestling. These would be on after the pub had closed, and everyone would all sit in the little snug bar at the end of the taproom watching them on the television in there, while eating a cheese on toast supper, which Nell and I had prepared – accompanied by the delicious pickled onions that Nell used to make. So depending on whether I was upstairs trying to sleep, or helping with the supper, and then watching the television, I got to know the boxers and wrestlers of the era – my favourite being a wrestler called Ricky Starr, who was also a ballerina! He was good looking and much more appealing to me than the rougher ones!

Grandpop loved anything to do with violence and weapons. One day he bought Ralf and Colin a pair of red boxing gloves each – "Now go and knock the hell out of each other" he told them. So that's what they did. I never liked seeing those boxing gloves around.

For my seventh birthday he gave me a – pop gun! A pop gun is like a rifle with a cork in the end attached to string. It is operated by air pressure, so when the trigger was pulled the cork would fly out with some degree of force. Now, what was I supposed to do with *that!* I remember walking round the car park, just firing it at nothing to please my grandfather. At least Ralf was only a baby then, and Colin wasn't even born, so it couldn't be used against me!

Why give me a pop gun for my birthday present though? I was only seven years old, so why couldn't I have had a pretty little doll or something like that?

Boys Will Be Boys!

1960s

Ralf has never liked his name, maybe it might have had something to do with him finding out that our mother named him after one of the German prisoners of war who were held at the army camp down on the fen. Apparently, according to Ralf, our mother had a close friendship and quite a passion for this young German. Well she must have done, if she had named her son after him! As always, my father wouldn't have had any say in it. He was from a family where sons were named after their fathers and grandfathers, with their father's name being their second name, and either of their grandfather's names being their third. So having been fighting in World War II, it must have been quite an anathema to him for his son to have a German name (just as well really that there weren't any Japanese soldiers held down on the fen!).

I remember the army being at the camp, and the war was still very much in everyone's minds. People would still talk about it as though it had only been yesterday, and some still had their air-raid shelters in their gardens. So children were growing up wanting to know all about what went on. The more gruesome the details – the more they seemed to enjoy it.

Ralf used to get ribbed at school about having a German name, and also wearing little National Health glasses. He was also very fair, and a little Germanic looking.

"What with my name – and my German style glasses – who was always playing the Nazi?" He told me a few years ago with a little laugh!

Colin, on the other hand was the complete opposite to Ralf in looks. He was the image of our grandfather in photos of him when he was young. He had brown eyes, and dark curly hair that almost hung in ringlets when he was very little. His thick brown hair stayed with him as he grew up, and the older he got, the more he looked like Grandpop.

He was Ralf's sidekick, and always into mischief, and both of them always got away with *everything...*

One day when he was at Orsett School, it was the day that Nurse Day was doing *"examinations"*. Oh dear, what an awful day that used to be. I remember us having to get undressed down to our pants, and stand in a line to be examined. I hated it when Nurse Day pulled the top of our pants out and looked in them. It was only very briefly, and I suppose she was checking that we were the sex that we were known to be. Nevertheless, it was still highly embarrassing, as young as we all were.

I had long left the school by then of course, and now it was Colin who was going to be *examined...*

He wasn't going to have any of this! So when Nurse Day was due to arrive – he went missing. He was gone for hours, and people were getting worried, searching everywhere for him. He was finally found hiding – in the coal bunker!

I don't know whether he ever did get examined, but it would have been quite difficult examining him when he was covered from head to toe with black coal dust!

Another time, I don't know what was in Colin's mind, but somehow he set fire to the leather settee that was in the fourth bedroom. Luckily it was discovered in time, because it could have burned the pub down if it had really taken hold – but no-one told him off for doing that.

~

It wasn't only the way my brothers would get away with all sorts of mischief – and sometimes blame *me* – but the way they were brought up to disrespect me made me feel worthless. I felt worthless anyway, but this just compounded it. The way they treated me seemed to be seen as a sort of amusement... *"Boys will be boys..."*

But what about *girls being girls?* Why couldn't I have the respect that their older sister *should* have had?

They were allowed to choose where they wanted to sleep – either at the bungalow in their blue bedroom (hmm), or at the pub in the large fourth bedroom. I had gone from having to sleep in the tiny woodworm room, to having to sleep with my grandmother – *in her bed.*

I had no privacy whatsoever. They knew, as I did, that if a bedroom door was closed – then you must not go in there. However, sometimes I would be in Nanny's bedroom either getting dressed or undressed, and they would suddenly burst in the door – and they wouldn't go away. No-one would do anything about it, and it was just as bad if I was in the bathroom. They told me once with great glee, that they used to watch me through the keyhole sometimes... I hated the very thought, it was *so* embarrassing – and upsetting. I had suspected as much at the time, as I had heard them, so all I could do was stuff something in the keyhole when I was in the bathroom, and just hope that no-one managed to push it through.

My mother should have understood how I felt. It certainly wasn't easy for me growing up like this. It was always "boys will be boys" that she would say dismissively, whenever I tried to complain about them. And "you're old enough – and *ugly* enough to know better" she would scold, if I tried to reprimand them myself. That second remark stayed with me for years, and even though I was certainly *not* ugly, I had very little self-esteem.

No matter how much I tried to please my mother, by always doing as I was told and being made to help with the cooking, cleaning, washing and ironing, not only at the pub, but also polishing at my parents' bungalow down the road – "and don't forget the chair legs" – she often called me a "useless article". But what is a useless article? Well useless is being of no worth whatsoever, and an article is merely an object. I grew up with that notion.

Doing the polishing wasn't just a fairly quick task either, because the polish was in a wax form in a tin, so it took quite some time getting just the right amount of polish on to the duster, neither too little nor too much. The good thing about it though was that it smelled lovely, especially Johnson's Lavender wax polish. Mansion Polish in a red tin smelled nice too, although I did prefer the lavender. After all the work of rubbing it well into the wood, it was a good feeling to leave the bungalow smelling nice and gleaming.

~

When I look at the photos of me as a child, I can see a pretty little girl with blue eyes and wavy blonde hair. I want to hug that little girl, and protect her from pain. I want to give her a bedroom of her own, and let her keep her dolls, teddies, books and anything else she held dear. I want to tuck her in bed safely, kiss her goodnight, and read her bedtime stories that I never had. I want to dress her in the pretty pink dresses like other little girls wore, and tell her that one day, many years ahead, there would be a very special man who would tell her every day that she was beautiful.

~

At dinner time, which was always at lunchtime, I always went to the toilet and washed my hands beforehand, as I had been instructed to do from a very early age. The three of us children used to eat first at weekends, followed by the adults later. One day we were having a lovely roast dinner, and when it was put on the table I was in the bathroom at the time, washing my hands. When I came in and went to sit down to eat, I found that Ralf had poured some of my bottle of fizzy Amber Orange drink over my dinner.

"Now why would he do that?" my mother asked when I went and told her. Meanwhile my dinner was getting really cold, and slopping in fizzy orange drink. "Oh well, *boys will be boys*" she added, and left it up to me to sort out what I could do with my meal.

It may sound as though I hated my brothers – but I didn't. I was always very nurturing, even from a young age. Besides, they were my *brothers...* It was the way that they were being brought up, and encouraged to disrespect me, that upset me so much.

~

When I was at senior school, the brown leather satchel that I had had when I first started (a left-over from Orsett School) had to be replaced with a larger bag to hold all the books I had to carry around with me. It was dark blue with a zipped top, and held everything that I needed.

One day, I arrived at school and opened my bag – my God – the smell of faeces was unbelievable... I looked in my bag – and there seeping through my books and everything – were these runny turds... I don't normally speak like this – but I am showing my utter disgust and revulsion...

I sped off to the toilet as quickly as I could to get rid of them – moving them though only made the stench even worse. Then I had to wash my books the best I could – bearing in mind I wrote with a fountain pen in my exercise books, and the ink ran with the slightest contact with water – whilst also hoping that no other girl would come into the toilet. Well I did the best I could.

This meant though that there was no way I could use those books, lying in this squodgy mess in my bag. So I zipped up my bag again, and just hoped for the best.

My teachers were not at all pleased with me when I told them I had forgotten my books, and I got into trouble for that.

Obviously going home on the bus that day was pretty awful – and highly embarrassing, with my bag smelling of faeces. It had sort of ripened throughout the day, and by now was even more disgusting than when I first discovered it that morning.

I told my mother about it – and showed her the mess. The bulk of it was somewhere in the sewers at Torells, but the utterly disgusting state it left behind – was in my bag...

"I wonder how that happened" my mother said, with a look that made me feel that she might be guessing. "You know you shouldn't move, er toilet, as it makes it smell even more..."

Yes – I *knew that!* I just wished I had left it as it was – and taken my bag home to open it to clean it. But of course, I had tried my best to rescue my books and pens etc., and just made the whole thing even worse.

"It must have been a cat" my mother then ventured. Oh really. So how then did a cat decide to unzip my bag, climb into it, squat, do its business, and do the zip up again?

Well no. Cats may be so very clever, but they couldn't actually perform anything quite as clever as that!

"*Someone – put it in my bag...*" I tried to explain...

"Now who would do that? my mother said, as dismissive as always. "It must be a cat". She didn't even want to see the stinking mess that had flooded my school bag, and my wet school books. She could have at least offered me some sympathy, and even said she would buy me new books. But no.

So that was the end of that. Surely she could have said that she would ask those two boys if they *"knew anything about it?"*

My books needed to be dried out, and the awful smell had to somehow be removed from my bag. I had the most terrible night trying to sort all this out.

The teachers were equally as displeased with me the next day when I told them that I had accidentally left my books out in the rain – and that was why they were damp and curly at the edges. Big trouble again. I still have the dictionary I had in my bag at the time – with its telling brown edges seeping into curly, once soaked pages... At least it doesn't smell. I had done a good job with all the cleaning...

I never spoke about this to my brothers at the time. They would have denied it even if they had done it. I would have also got into trouble for accusing them of something that my mother wouldn't have believed they would do.

~

My grandfather liked to keep the kitchen knives really sharp, and would use the iron knife sharpener regularly to keep the blades as lethal as they could be. My father would always sharpen the carving knife before carving the Sunday roast at the pub as well. Consequently with all the sharpening going on, the blades would gradually take on a different shape, curving menacingly over the years. Also, there was a knife sharpening man who used to come round sometimes. He would take the whole array of knives and sit there sharpening to his heart's content. Thus there was never a blunt blade in the pub!

One of these knives, which my grandfather was particularly proud of, was a little parer. It was lethal! I had to use it for preparing vegetables and peeling potatoes, but I was really afraid of even holding it.

One day all the family who were at home were in the kitchen. It could be nice sometimes when it was like that, the family together and talking. Everyone was sitting at the kitchen table, with someone in the easy chair, and I was standing with my back against the pantry door. Suddenly – I had the most tremendous shock... Ralf was standing at the other end of the table and looking at me with menacing eyes...

The next thing I knew – that little lethal parer hit the pantry door – very close to my face. He had had a good aim, or more likely I was extremely lucky, because it couldn't have been more than three or four inches away from my face. If it had hit me, I could have been killed, or at least blinded if it had gone into my eye.

The shock was so great that I don't remember much about what happened next. All I can remember is – the sound of laughter... Yet again, no-one chastised Ralf or reprimanded him in any way, and he must have been very proud of himself.

~

I am actually finding it very difficult writing about these things. Ralf and Colin are my brothers after all. It is difficult to comprehend though just how they were allowed – or encouraged – to treat me in this way. I don't think that children are naturally wicked. Wickedness is something they learn from adults, although not all children succumb to such wickedness. It is just that Ralf and Colin were *encouraged* to treat me this way. To disrespect and upset me – and to do these terribly awful, distressing, and highly dangerous things.

Which leads me on to something that happened when I was seventeen...

As soon as I had my seventeenth birthday, I applied for a provisional driving licence. My father was teaching me to drive, and I enjoyed those driving lessons, especially being able to spend some time with him away from everyone else. I was well versed in road sense from all the cycling that I had done over the past few years, and took to driving straight away. I was overjoyed that my father said I was a "natural" on the road, with my positioning being good, and my whole approach being as relaxed and confident as a learner driver's could possibly be.

We would get back to the pub, and he would sing my praises on this new challenge in my life. I was happy, and as I was working, I was saving as much money as I could to one day be able to buy a little Mini – just like Twiggy's! Of course, this would have probably taken a few years, but I enjoyed driving so much – and it was something I knew I could *do*.

One day – one dreadful day – I had been out driving with my father, and pulled into the pub car park. I will never – ever – forget the sight of Ralf suddenly running right in front of the car...

I slammed on the brake having to do an emergency stop – not a practice one – but a very real emergency stop – to save hitting my brother. Ralf thought it was great fun, but I was so shaken up, I stopped driving immediately. Although I have tried again since, to this day, I don't drive. That memory has always stayed with me.

~

Some years ago, when my brothers and I were talking about the things they got up to at the pub, I asked them – *why did they did they do the things they did?*

"It's like the time I jumped out in front of you when you were learning to drive" Ralf said, with a little grin... "It's because you're our *sister*..."

Sums it all up really.

Aunts And Uncles – Or Not!

Going back to my grandfather's family and his youth, he was born to a family of ten children, although four died in childhood, which was quite normal in those days – the other six however, James, Cecil, George, Arthur, Doris and Nance all survived into adulthood.

Jim left the house one day at the beginning of World War One, on the premise of going to get some fish and chips. What he was really doing though was going off to join the army in their fight against the Germans... Sadly – none of the family ever saw him again...

~

I knew Uncle Cecil, Uncle George, Auntie Doris, and Auntie Nance though. Uncle Cecil was married to Auntie Cissy – a rather amusing combination of names, which could be a little tongue twister for some people! They would come to the pub sometimes, and like both my grandmothers, Auntie Cissy could play the piano and sing. No matter what other tunes she might be asked to play, she would always play "You are my sunshine", the old song written in 1939, and sing at the top of her voice, along with the customers. They were good times when Uncle Cecil and Auntie Cissy came over.

Uncle George lived in a Victorian house in Romford, and occasionally Grandpop took me to visit him. We often used to go to Romford, primarily for Grandpop to call into the Ind Coope Brewery for business reasons, while my mother and I would go to Romford market.

I loved Romford market. It was a hive of activity, with hustle and bustle everywhere, and people calling out offering their wares. It was a good source of second-hand records, and all manner of interesting things. Grandpop had his favourite stalls where everyone knew him, and he would love to get a bargain – like large tins of broken biscuits! When it got dark in the late afternoon in the winter, the stalls had hurricane lights, which in the weeks leading up to Christmas would make the Christmas decorations and bunches of holly glisten and sparkle. My memories are full with the smell of Cox's apples, oranges, and paraffin lamps for the stall holders to keep warm. I remember them so well with their red cheeks and fingerless woollen gloves. Late in the afternoon on Christmas Eve Grandpop would go there to get the Christmas turkey, which by five o'clock would be reduced right down to clear – and he would always get one! It wasn't that he couldn't afford a full priced turkey, but he loved a bargain and thought it worthwhile to go all that way to save some money!

One day when Grandpop took me to see Uncle George he was lying in a bed in his living room. It was a dingy room, badly lit, and with a heavy feeling of illness pervading. Uncle George was dying of consumption, more widely known as TB. It was a highly infection disease, but there I was, still a child, in that death room, saying good-bye to Uncle George. He told me that there were a few books that he wanted me to have, and he had them on a table next to his bed.

One was "The World Film Encyclopaedia", published in 1933. This is filled with interesting facts about the films and stars from 1922 to 1932, and fully illustrated with black and white photos of the very glamorous stars, studios, scenes, theatres and maps. A wonderful book to have.

Another was a copy of Jane Austen's "Pride and Prejudice" which, although originally published in 1813, was a 1946 publication with rather amusing line drawings and watercolour illustrations. This somewhat lightened the rather heavy reading for a child of my age, but introduced me to Jane Austen's world.

The final one was Kathleen Winsor's "Forever Amber", originally published in 1944, but this was a third impression dated 1949. This was also heavy reading, but I found it fascinating learning about Newgate Prison and what conditions were like there. The part of the book that has stayed in my mind most of all though, and which I sometimes think about, is the part where the couple stroll slowly into a field, and where Amber experiences physical love for the first time. It didn't describe exactly what they were doing, but somehow I could sense the passion between them. That was so romantic, and wistfully hinted at how making love for the first time should be... I don't know how many times I read those paragraphs...

Interestingly, the green hard-back cover of "Forever Amber" is covered with very aged teacup stains. So I can only think that Uncle George had kept that book on the top of the pile next to his bed!

Strangely, whenever I have touched those books throughout the years, with each one of them I am transported back to Uncle George's deathbed. Because of his illness and how worried I was at the time about getting the illness myself, I have always washed my hands without fail each time I touched them. So it took me rather a long time to get through "Pride and Prejudice"!

~

Auntie Doris was a very kind and lovely lady, and I used to love going to see her. She lived in a Victorian semi-detached house in Enfield, with a long garden at the back. Although the surrounding area has now changed somewhat, her house is still there, and still has the same front door with its stained-glass window.

Once in a while, Grandpop would suddenly get the urge to go and see his sister, so he would get together whatever family were around at that particular time, and then we would all go to Enfield... Sometimes Grandpop drove, sometimes my father did, depending on whether or not he was at home.

"I must go and see poor old Doris" he would say, even though she was only a little older than him, and off we would go. In the early days of my childhood my grandfather's car was a black Morris, the type with the running boards, brown leather seats with vertical stitching, and small amber coloured indicators that flicked out at the sides. Those indicators always amused me. Later on in 1959 Grandpop became the proud owner of a Ford Anglia Deluxe, newly manufactured and very modern! It was a pale aqua colour with a cream roof. Looking back, I much prefer the old black Morris that used to chug up Bread and Cheese Hill. But times were moving on, and so were cars.

Whether we went in the Morris or the Anglia, getting to Enfield in those days wasn't a quick journey; it meant going across the Essex countryside, then through Epping Forest to Waltham Abbey, and stopping off at what seemed to be every country pub on the way! We had an AA badge on the car, the domed type of the era, with two "A"s entwined in chrome on a yellow background. This meant than whenever an AA man came along on the other side of the road on their motorcycle they would salute! My grandfather or father would always acknowledge this, and the AA man would smile as he drove past. How different things were then.

Well, eventually we would arrive, and would be greeted by Auntie Doris' smiling face. Then after an hour – and it was always an hour – Grandpop would suddenly get up and say that we were going. So, always disappointingly for me, off we would go on the long drive back to Orsett.

Dear Auntie Doris, she was a very lovely lady. Somehow though in her later years her mind wasn't quite as it used to be. One day she arrived at the pub – she had hitch-hiked all the way from Enfield – and she was still wearing her apron and fur-trimmed pink slippers! "I just wanted to see Arthur" she said, and went on to say how some kind lorry drivers had given her a lift in their cabs. These days their first thought would probably be to alert the police, but as I say, things were so different then. So having eventually arrived at the Kings Arms, it was then my father's job to drive her all the way back again...

Grandpop also used to write long letters to his sister Doris, which he would sometimes read out to me. These would be all about their childhood and his feelings for her. I don't really know whether he ever posted them to her though, because one day he read this long and very lovely letter that he had carefully written to her, then turned to me and said "she won't want to read this silly stuff" – and then tore it into little bits. I felt so sad.

~

Auntie Nance lived in Tilbury, not the most salubrious of areas at the time, but she too was a lovely lady. She had the sort of house where her bike was kept in the hallway, and the ladders were hooked onto the wall going up the stairs – well I suppose it was a practical thing to do!

On New Year's Eve 1955, when I was six years old, we were invited to Auntie Nance's house. She was wearing a maroon coloured dress that had large wet stains under the armpits, which gradually grew bigger as she rocked a baby in time to the music. I don't know who the baby was though, but I can only guess it was one of my younger cousins.

Jimmy Young's "Unchained Melody" was being played over and over again on the radiogram, and whenever I hear any version of that at all, it takes me back to that night – the bright overhead light in the front room, the bike in the hall, the ladders up the stairs, the laughter, and the warm sense of family, something which I missed out on so much at the pub.

My cousins, Lyn and Ann, Auntie Nance's granddaughters, were there, along with other aunts and uncles. Lyn and Ann had been bridesmaids earlier that year, and they were wearing their bridesmaids' dresses. They were both full length, with puffed sleeves, and were so pretty. Lyn's was lilac and Ann's was peach, and I watched them with envy, as they held out the skirts and did the odd little twirl.

I had never been allowed to have anything lilac, and I remember sitting on the settee with Lyn and telling her how much I loved her dress. Goodness knows what I was wearing at the time, but it certainly wasn't a party dress. When I asked her if I would be having it one day when she had grown out of it, like I had her other clothes handed down to me, she said no, Ann was going to have it. Of course it was logical that her younger sister Ann, who was also younger than me, would have her clothes – maybe the hand-me-downs that I used to have from Lyn were just the ones that Ann hadn't wanted.

So I was sitting there, looking down at my hands in my lap, feeling downhearted and rather foolish for having asked, when suddenly the music stopped –and a very different sort of music came on... It was some sort of foreign music, loud and very exciting. It was then that my Uncle Jim (not Grandpop's brother) appeared in front of us wearing just a real grass skirt and a Fez, and doing the sand dance! Then he was in the centre of the room doing the hula-hula. Everyone was in fits of laughter – and he really could do the hula-hula!

Well I said that he was my Uncle Jim, and that's what I always called him. But I have recently found out that he was not an uncle at all – he was one of Auntie Nance's boyfriends!

I don't know what attraction men had to Auntie Nance, but it certainly couldn't have been her strong-arm muscles – nor her ability to crack walnuts with her teeth! One of her daughters, my Auntie Hilda, has recently told me a tale about what went on at the pub one day...

My grandfather may have been very popular with the ladies, but when it came to the men, it could sometimes be a very different matter. He had apparently been having an affair with a married woman, but her husband found out about it, and organised a gang to go to the pub and beat him up. They had suddenly burst in and waylaid him in the hallway that led to the bars. Auntie Nance was at the pub at the time and realised what was going on. Grandpop was being beaten up very badly, but she rolled up her sleeves – and dived in herself – laying in to all the men!

My grandmother was fully aware of what was going on, but she just gently took Auntie Hilda's hand. "Come along dear", she said, very calmly, and leading her away... "Let's go round to the bar... Now, what would you like to drink...?"

~

My grandfather's mother Ada – my great-grandmother – lived at the Kings Arms for some time after her husband died.

However, one day, my grandfather bundled her into his car and took her to his sister Nance's in Tilbury.

"I'm dumping her here with you" he told Auntie Nance, "I'm not having her gossiping about what goes on at the pub..." and then he just drove off.

I wonder what stories she was telling...

Respect Her Possessions

One of the worst ways to be cruel to someone – is to take everything they love away from them...

The physical torture at the hands of my grandfather, although extremely painful and humiliating at the time, and something I have never ever forgotten, didn't hurt me as much as having everything I loved, and had made, taken away from me.

Something that I never had was respect, and neither were my possessions respected as being mine. My feelings never mattered to anyone. The nights I sobbed myself to sleep didn't matter. I have already mentioned my doll's house, which I still remember to the smallest detail, but there were so many other things that were given to me – then all too quickly given away. It was so heart-breaking seeing other children enjoying my possessions – things that were thoughtfully chosen for me, and given to me with love.

My doll's house, was not the first thing to be given away. My teddy bears and dolls gradually disappeared, along with many other things.

My dear Auntie Hilda married her husband Uncle Paddy the day after her eighteenth birthday in May 1952. He was in the RAF, and was stationed in Malaya at the time. After their wedding Uncle Paddy was sent back to Malaya, as the independence hostilities were still ongoing, and there were still rebel units carrying on fighting.

After a couple of years, along with other RAF wives, Auntie Hilda had the option to go out to Malaya to be with Uncle Paddy, and so she travelled all that way by ship. This took weeks at sea, but eventually she arrived in Malaya. She has recalled that where Uncle Paddy was stationed, which was where they lived, she could still hear gun fire in the jungle. She was there for two years, and when she returned home, she came home with her baby son. I absolutely loved Auntie Hilda, and I could tell that she loved me. In fact, she has told me recently that she *always* loved me. She also said that I seemed so nervous all the time, and very lonely.

I was only young, but I still remember her coming to the pub upon her return, and bestowing me with gifts that she had so thoughtfully bought for me in Malaya.

My eyes were all aglow at these wondrous things that she had brought back from this mysterious far away country. There was a pretty toy Koala bear, with grey fur (I hope it was fake!) and with paws and a little round nose made of black leather. It had delightful big eyes, and cute little ears, and I loved it. There was a set of three hand woven square baskets, which all fitted inside each other. So it was a real surprise opening the big one and finding another inside it – and then another... I found them so intriguing. There was a straw coolie hat, with ribbons that tied under the neck. The most beautiful of all these gifts though was a paper parasol, beautifully hand painted with pretty watercolour flowers in shades of pink and green, and with a handle and spokes painted with a jade green wash. To this day, shades of pink and green are Auntie Hilda's favourite colours, so I know she would have chosen that carefully, something that she loved herself, but gave to me... I had never before seen anything such as these gifts that she had brought all the way back from this far away place...

I loved that little Koala bear, and I would walk around cuddling him. He was so soft, and his large eyes were so expressive. I felt that he loved me too. The last time I saw that little Koala bear was when I sat him on a cabinet in the kitchen. He looked so sweet sitting there, with his lovely eyes, shiny nose and little paws.

But then he was gone. Where was my little bear? No-one seemed to know what had happened to him – and I never did find out.

Gradually Auntie Hilda's other gifts to me also disappeared. The square baskets, the coolie hat, the beautiful parasol – she had chosen them for me so carefully, and had brought them back by ship all the way from Malaya – they all went. I have never told her they were all taken away from me. But then there are very many things I have never told her – nor anyone else – until now...

~

Once I knew that my father was actually my father and not just "the man who lived up the cottage" I used to go up to Ivy Cottage on weekend mornings to see my parents. My father used to wear this long full length, rather grand looking dressing gown. It was dark green, with a shawl collar, a fitted waist with a tie belt, and against the dark green was a small pattern of yellow flowers – he must have brought it back from the Far East in his navy days! He was a very heavy smoker at the time, and collected these pretty little inserts in Players cigarettes. They were the size of the cigarette packets, with exquisitely embroidered flowers on white silk. He was very proud of this collection, and used to let me play with them. I would lay them all out on the floor, putting them in various orders, and learning about the flowers that were depicted. The day that he gave them to me, I absolutely treasured them, and I kept them in a box at the pub...

Something else I used to play with at the cottage was a picnic basket full of my baby clothes. They were so beautiful, most of them having been knitted by Nanny Felstead on the smallest gauge knitting needles – little pure white dresses and matinee jackets in intricate lacy patterns, with the tiniest pearl buttons.

I loved to dress my baby doll Rosebud in my baby clothes, and I became very adept at putting her tiny arms into the sleeves, and doing up the buttons. This was all up until the age of about five, and then my mother let me have the basket of baby clothes at the pub.

I kept my baby clothes safe in their basket, and always kept them neatly folded. I really treasured them, even though at the time I didn't know much about babies. But they were always so special to me, and I knew that I had worn them.

There was a girl who lived up Baker Street called Elaine. She was older than me, but we were friends in a way. I was eight years old at the time, and we played "Libraries", swapping our books. We even made little library tickets. This was towards the end of 1957, and the few times I spent with Elaine were somewhat different to times spent with my other little friends.

I still loved my baby doll though, little Rosebud, and dressing her in my baby clothes. Even at eight years old, you still love your dolls!

One day, I went to get my basket of baby clothes – but it was gone...
Again, I was frantic. Not only were they my baby doll's clothes – but they
had also been mine, and my grandmother had knitted them so patiently.

I asked my mother where they were... "I gave them to Elaine" she
said, with no feeling in her voice whatsoever. "She is having a baby – and
I felt sorry for her."

So that was that. Elaine had my basket of baby clothes, and I was
never allowed to query anything. She was about thirteen years old, maybe
even younger. Then she disappeared. I heard that she had gone to a
home somewhere. This might also have been the same home that I had
been threatened with if I "told" anything to anybody. I don't really know
if it was the same one though. Sadly, I never saw her again.

I heard that she had returned one day, but she didn't have a baby with
her. I never saw her on the street, nor did I go to call for her. Maybe I
wasn't allowed to see her. Then, sometime after that – I heard that she
had died...

I never did see my baby clothes again, and have never known what
happened to her or how she died.

What I do have though, is one of her little books that we played
libraries with. It is a little green book called the "Observers Book of Trees
and Shrubs" In the back is written in pencil in Elaine's handwriting...
"Y. Mandeville 28/11/57 – Return in a week's time."

I don't know how I still have that little book, but that was the last
time I saw her. Maybe I wasn't allowed to go to her house again. It is
something to remember her by though, and it is nice knowing that when
she died she still had one of my books too.

I only wish I knew what had happened to my basket of baby clothes...

~

When I was six years old and in the second and last year of the infants at
Orsett School, we were taught how to embroider. The stitches were quite
big, probably five to an inch, and the needles were fairly blunt, with an
eye big enough to take embroidery wool. We were learning cross-stitch,
which I have always loved to do, on embroidery canvas. I was making a
bag, covered in various rows of patterns in shades of pink and blue, two

of each. When I finished it, the teacher lined it, and showed me how to plait a handle using all the shades of wool.

I very proudly gave this to my mother. I can't remember what her reaction was, but I hope it was positive...

My mistake! Years later I found that she hadn't treasured it as I had hoped – she had given it away to some other child to keep their rather grubby pens, pencils and crayons in...

~

Going forward a few years, fashion in Essex was always a little behind the times! On one of our trips to Gravesend my mother bought me a felt "circle" skirt in Chiesmans, a well-loved department store in Gravesend High Street. She liked it! "Circle" skirts were popular then, and so called because they were cut out from a square piece of fabric as a complete circle, and therefore had no seams. A circle cut out in the middle of the fabric formed the waist. Mine was made of turquoise felt, with an appliqué going around the hem saying... "See You Later Alligator..." so was obviously very much a homage to the Bill Haley hit. I can't help but think that maybe it might have been old stock though – but then again the phrase had stuck, and people were still saying "See ya later alligator" when saying their goodbyes anyway. In fact that phrase stuck for years!

What this needed though was a full net underskirt to give it the volume of the skirts other girls were wearing at the time. I had seen them walking along the street, wearing these skirts with little bolero tops, sparkling white socks, flat little pointed toe shoes, and the skirts brushing against each other as they passed. To have one of these underskirts would have been perfect under my felt skirt. I could then dance and twirl with my skirt atop this bubble of frothy net, and I would be like all these other girls. Think Peggy Sue in "Peggy Sue Got Married"!

I had also just started at senior school. There was a semblance of a uniform, but nobody wore it. Maybe being maroon and blue had something to do with it! But really, the girls at that school weren't at all interested in a uniform – neither were their parents. What they were wearing though when I first started at that school, were these huge skirts billowing out over the net petticoats. One of my first memories there was seeing girls walking through the corridors with their skirts actually touching as they passed too.

I thought that as my mother actually *liked* this skirt, she would allow me to have one of these net underskirts. But no, she didn't. I never wore the felt skirt to school, and even I didn't think it was appropriate. But I so much wanted one of these voluminous net underskirts!

~

One day another woman came into our lives – and into my grandfather's bed. She was Mrs. Binns, the landlady of a hotel in Grays, and who I had first met when I was nine years old, when my grandfather took me to the hotel to meet her – and we ended up coming home with Butch! Like the Kings Arms, everything in her hotel was sort of "brown", and with dingy stairs leading to the ballroom upstairs. I remember the smell of stale beer, and stale cooking. Everything smelled – well stale... A bit like Mrs. Binns really...

~

One day my grandfather brought Mrs. Binns to the pub. It wasn't unusual for him to bring a woman home, but this time he had something else in mind... This was the day she became entrenched in the pub...

They just walked up the stairs – and then brazenly along to his bedroom.

My grandmother was in the lounge, sitting in her armchair where she could look out of the window. Her eyes were just staring into the distance down towards the village, but they were not focusing. She had tears in her eyes, and even when I spoke to her, she didn't respond.

I went into the kitchen and Nell was sitting at the table. She was sobbing, crying her eyes out, as my grandfather and Mrs. Binns were in the bedroom that she shared with him. I felt so sorry for her, even though she too had done this to my grandmother. Now the same humiliating thing was being done to her...

Suffice to say for now, Mrs. Binns moved into the pub as well, and slept with my grandfather, who kicked out Nell to sleep in the woodworm room between his bedroom and my grandmother's. It was a very strange time for all of us but, as usual, I just had to accept the situation. I have been told that my grandfather liked "three in a bed", so maybe Mrs. Binns and/or Nell might have taken part...

Three in a bed or not – I didn't really know what that meant at the time. I was used to three in a bed anyway, with Valerie and Beverley. What did *I* know what went on amongst adults? Well, as I have since found out, it wasn't always adults...

"Never go into a bedroom when the door is shut" is what my mother had instructed me, no matter who was in there. So I never did. I didn't know all the, er hmm, ins and outs of such things, even though I had had contact with my grandfather's genitalia when I was about two or three years old, and sight of my grandmother's boyfriend's too, when I was a little older.

~

Strangely, I really liked Mrs. Binns. I think it was more because she liked me though. Well, she was very kind to me, and showed me a lot of affection, which I didn't get normally. She took a lot of interest in me, would talk to me about what I was doing, and smiled at me a lot, which meant so much to me.

She really liked my new skirt, and said that what I needed was – a net underskirt. Yes! I did!

Very soon she gave me a large shopping bag. In it was not just one – but two net underskirts. One had layer upon layer of powder blue net, just like I could see peeping under the skirts of other girls as they swished along the pavements. The other was pale pink, not quite as many layers, but was so pretty, embroidered with a pale silvery-grey flocked pattern and a scalloped hem.

I absolutely loved them, and was oh, so very grateful. I put them on hangers and hung them from the top of my grandmother's wardrobe – the only place in "our" bedroom that I could put them – so I could look at them, looking forward to the day that I would be wearing them. Nanny was happy with them hanging there. She liked them too, and although Mrs. Binns was yet another rival, she didn't mind at all that she had bought them for me.

One day I came home from school, and went straight up to my grandmother's bedroom. I loved those two underskirts, and loved thinking about the times I would be wearing them. I would put them on and walk around the bedroom, imagining that my skirts would be swishing just like the other girls. I just loved looking at them anyway – and knowing that they were *mine*...

This time though – they weren't there... I looked inside the wardrobe – but no, they weren't there either. So I frantically asked Nanny where they were...

"Your mother gave them to Jean over the road" she said, quite matter of factly, and not even looking at me. Why could she not even look at me – or even given me a sympathetic hug? Why couldn't she intervene when my mother and grandfather gave my things away? Maybe she was afraid of my mother as well as my grandfather? Well, my mother and grandfather certainly were very close.

Jean lived over the road from the pub in one of the same row of council houses as Elaine.

How could my mother take my pretty net underskirts from my grandmother's wardrobe – and give them to someone else? How could my grandmother let her do it? These thoughts went over and over in my mind. How could *anyone* allow that to happen? It was my dolls' house, my gifts from Auntie Hilda and my baby clothes – all over again. Why – just why – didn't anyone stop her? And what was Jean's mother doing taking them anyway?

So there was Jean – walking around – with a full skirt billowing – with *my* net underskirts...

~

Last night I dreamed I was dancing around the house as my pale blue net underskirt swirled around me. It rustled and swished, and I was so happy. All too soon though – the dream ended...

~

Shopping in Gravesend as well as Oxford Street was very popular with my mother and grandmother. They loved shopping – well, for clothes, hats, gloves etc. Although Gravesend High Street wasn't like Oxford Street, with its wonderful stores and expensive clothes, Gravesend had a few little shops as well as the Chiesmans store, which they liked. It was also so much easier to get to than going on that long bus journey to London.

There was no Lyons Corner House where we used to go for afternoon tea, nor Pathé Pictorial that we would call into afterwards. But going on the ferry across to Gravesend was always a delight as well, and it made the day rather special. Much more special than shopping in Grays, where the only department stores were Ticehurst and Joyes, the latter being a very old-fashioned store that still had the little cylinders to put your money in that would whizz up just under the ceiling across to the cashier's box. Well it was ok for things like corsets and stockings, but didn't have the sort of dresses that my mother and grandmother liked.

Oh dear – those corsets! They were a pale pink skin-toned concoction with "stays" that kept them in place. The stays were a little like men's collar stiffeners, only much longer and far stiffer. They would always be removed when washing so they didn't bend, and then they had to be eased back into the seams that potentially held all the wobbly bits in place.

The corsets had suspenders for stockings (not at all glamorous though), and fastened at the back – with great difficulty! Mummy and Nanny would always get dressed in the kitchen for the evening stint in the bar, with Nell easing flesh and pulling fasteners at the back, to give what they deemed to be a more desirable silhouette. How they were able to breathe in these contraptions, I do not know. No wonder Nanny nearly choked herself when she was swigging gin from the optic...

They had no sense of modesty either. It didn't matter who was in the kitchen at the time seeing all this going on. Even my brothers remember the ritual. What I found so amusing was that my mother always wore her bra – *over* her vest!

~

And so, here was another shopping trip to Gravesend..

I am not sure exactly how old I was, but I was around twelve or thirteen. With Grace Kelly around, my mind was already turning to elegance. My

"See You Later Alligator" skirt had long disappeared, and I don't think I grew out of it. Being made the way it was, it was quite flexible around the waist, and really I was a thin, skinny little thing – a matchstick with the wood shaved off, as my father used to call me...

Well. We went into Chiesmans, as usual, and I saw from afar a dress – calling to me. It was navy blue with white spots, had a slightly scooped boat shape neckline, short sleeves, and a scooped corded waistline that matched the neckline. The skirt was gently gathered from the waistline, and it was the most desirable dress to me. I loved it instantly, they only had that one – and it was in my size. It was meant to be!

My grandmother, obviously realising how taken I was with it, kindly bought it for me...

The first time I wore it, I had to ask Nell to help me. It had a long back zip, which I had never had before, and I needed her to do it up for me.

"Your very first grown-up dress", she said proudly, slowly zipping up that long zip for me.

I absolutely loved that dress! I think I wore it maybe a couple of times – but then it also disappeared – goodness knows where. And I didn't even have a photo taken wearing it...

~

One day Nanny Felstead went to Leigh-on-Sea to buy a fur coat. She loved shopping in that Essex town near Southend-on-Sea. There were some nice little shops there where she would buy her very individual dresses to wear behind the bar. Well one of them was a fur shop, which only sold fur coats and stoles – before then it had been the place to get the awful whole fox furs that women found so fashionable in the 1940s. Both my grandmothers had worn them to my parents' wedding in 1946 – and no-one had ever thought anything of it. I am guessing that to own one, and to wear it hanging over your shoulder, with its dead face, staring eyes and little paws for all to see, may have been a symbol of wealth or style. I don't think the protocol of wearing dead animals came into it then.

Well Nanny spent a lot of time choosing her fur coat. She chose a very dark brown one, lined with golden coloured silk. Nanny loved that coat, and she was very proud of it.

This fur coat came in a large cardboard box, which sat on her bedroom floor next to her dressing table. Nanny gave the box to me, and told me that I could put all my things in it, which I did, well apart from a few books that I kept in her wardrobe. My things consisted of so many *things*... Books, pencils, crayons, watercolour paints, oil paints, paint-by-numbers pictures of the bridges in Venice that I had done in the past, Barbie teenage dolls, their clothes, some of which I had made myself. There were "Mirabelle" magazines, which were a more grown-up version of "Jackie", with photos I had cut out of Elvis, and covered with cellophane so that they looked like real photos.

I also kept in there the beautiful embroidered flower silks that over time my father had collected from the cigarette packets, which I loved and which had helped to teach me the names of the world of flowers. There was my stamp album too, in which I had stuck lots of stamps that a customer's air hostess daughter had sent to him on her many long haul flights.

One day I came home from school (*things happened* when I was at school...) and went into Nanny's bedroom to go to my box – but it wasn't there... Really, my whole life at that time was in there. My baby doll Rosebud, teddies I had been given by aunts, and even a golliwog, had long gone to who knows where? But this box was now filled with all my more grown-up things, things that I loved and treasured.

Panic set in. *Where was my box...?* It was a horrible sickening feeling that raced down to the pit of my stomach.

I asked my grandmother where it was...

"Your mother had a bonfire today..." she told me – again not looking at me...

~

My grandfather used to like my paintings, drawings and sketches, and would tell me I was "clever". Later, he also liked to watch me type, and would marvel at touch-typing. But he was the only person at home who was ever interested in what I was doing.

One day he pinned a large sheet of white card on the hall wall. It was about five feet long by two feet wide, and he asked me if I would paint him a picture in watercolours. I was delighted – I saw it as a commission!

He said he would like a picture of a Geisha girl, so I set about doing that. I drew the picture first, the Geisha girl holding a fan, and wearing a long flowing kimono. This was going to give me plenty of scope to use colours that I loved.

Each day when I came home from school I would do a little bit more, and it was gradually coming to life. Of course, standing on the landing doing this, I had to make sure that Grandpop wasn't anywhere around – there was no way I could cope with a twist of my funny bone whilst doing that!

But at least I knew that I was doing something that was being appreciated.

"This is going to be a famous painting one day" he said, as he stood admiring my work – (or perhaps not...!) But he was saying that quite earnestly, even though I knew that it was just a fantasy.

And so my painting carried on. It was taking me ages though trying to find time to do it, with all the other things like homework, and the jobs around the pub I had to do after school.

"It looks to me as though you had better hurry up and finish it" Grandpop said to me one day when I walked up the stairs and saw him looking at it. "Otherwise it's going to be famous for being called 'The Unfinished Painting'!"

So each day I carried on adding a little bit more, and making my Geisha girl look actually quite beautiful. I still had more to do though.

One day I came home from school, and as I walked up those dark and dingy stairs to the landing – my painting had gone...

So where had it gone? Nobody knew – absolutely no-one. If someone had taken it down, they would have kept it safe somewhere. But no, it had totally disappeared.

Maybe my brothers had done something with it, or to it – or maybe my mother had destroyed it, or just thrown it away as she had with so many others of my treasured possessions. If any of these had been the case, then no-one would have told me what had happened. My mother and brothers could do no wrong. Surely Grandpop hadn't done anything to it after all the compliments he had bestowed on me – but maybe Mr. Hyde had...

Gina

Two dresses and a pair of stilettos!

Mrs. Binns had a son called Martin. He was the tall, dark handsome type, and was a rally driver, driving all over Europe. His wife Gina was very petite, and always wore very high stilettos to make her look taller. Unfortunately, all those stilettos did was to make her calves bow outwards, so she had a very strange way of walking. Although thinking about it, I recall that a lot of women had calves like that through wearing such very high-heeled shoes.

With Martin travelling all over Europe, Gina was left at home with their little girl Heidi, who was two or three years old, so Gina asked me to go and stay with her a few times, which I really enjoyed. They lived in a long wide bungalow on an estate in Kent. It was quite distinctive because it was painted pink! It had quite a large frontage though, and lay well back off the road.

Upon reflection it was a very "sixties" style, which was a rather refreshing change from living in the dark, dank atmosphere of the Victorian Kings Arms. What is more, I could sleep in a bedroom on my own when I was there!

Gina was an Avon Lady, although I really don't think she went from door to door – I think she just sold to people she knew. I used to have such fun going through her Avon box, and trying on various things that she suggested. I particularly liked the cream perfumes in those pretty little pots. My favourites at the time were "Somewhere" and "Topaze", both of which smelled all fresh and creamy. So I had lots of fun with Gina, and we got on as well as I would have done with an aunt that I loved.

I had great fun with Martin too sometimes when he took me for a spin in his bright red MG. We would go whizzing along all the roads around Wigmore. There were no speed restrictions in those days! Oh how I loved it!

~

One afternoon Martin brought a rather special lady to the Kings Arms. They came into the saloon bar just after the pub had closed at lunchtime, so there were no customers in the bar. It was Pat Moss, someone with whom he went rallying sometimes. She was really lovely, with short brown curly hair, and she spoke really well. I really don't know the circumstances that made him bring her to the pub to see us, but it was good meeting her and also knowing that she was Stirling Moss' sister, or Sir Stirling as he is now!

~

The first time I went to stay with Gina my parents took me over there. They were interested in seeing the bungalow anyway. Strangely, I felt very homesick when they left, although goodness knows why. Gina was lovely, and so was Heidi. I would take her for walks in her pushchair and I loved looking after her.

One day I walked along to the local chemist, and looking in the window I saw a tin of L'Aimant talcum powder. The tin was as pretty as the scent. So I bought that with my pocket money to give to my mother. I hope she liked it as much as I did.

One of the times when my parents came to pick me up, Martin was home and that evening he was sitting on the floor playing with Heidi. The next day he had totally disappeared. It seemed that he had left the country.

I was at home obviously, so didn't know what Gina was going through. If only I could have gone and stayed with her again, but of course, I had to go back to school.

"How can he sit on the floor playing with that little girl – knowing he's never going to see her again", my mother said scornfully upon finding this out. Well there was obviously something – or maybe *someone*, who he considered far more exciting than Gina. Maybe his sense of adventure was calling him, and living in a bungalow in suburban Wigmore was not to his liking at all.

I don't know how soon Gina found out what had happened to him, but the next she heard from him was later in the year when he sent Heidi a coat – from New Zealand. No-one had any inkling about what Martin had planned, not even his mother. So now Gina was living on her own with Heidi.

~

The time came that I was able to go and stay with Gina again, and Mrs. Binns wanted to stay too, so my grandfather took us both over there. Very soon after we arrived, he and Mrs. Binns went into the bedroom where she was going to sleep. I sat on the settee and Gina sat in an armchair. It was all very embarrassing really, well for Gina anyway, and I felt embarrassed for her, even though I didn't exactly know what was going on behind the closed door.

Sometime later they both emerged from the bedroom – as bold as brass, and my grandfather left... *"Tum-ti-tum-ti-tum..."* touching his flies like he often did, probably ensuring they were done up.

Unfortunately, Mrs. Binns came and sat next to me on the settee... The stench exuding from her was overpowering. I had never smelled anything quite like it before, nor have I since, and it was making me feel sick. The nearest I can get to it is the smell of the lights being cooked in the cook house.

Gina and I just sat looking at each other. I didn't feel I could move until Gina did, and she didn't seem to know what to do or say either. I don't think we could have spoken with that smell under our noses.

The next day Mrs. Binns said she was going to cook. As she had been the landlady of a hotel for years until she left to live at the Kings Arms with my grandfather, I assumed she must have known all about catering. So – this was going to be good... Wasn't it?

Gina and I took Heidi out for a walk in the pushchair, and left her to it. When we came back, the meal was waiting for us... It was *sausage stew*.

Considering the strange things my grandmother cooked sometimes, like pigs' trotter stew, I should have been used to this. But... Mrs. Binns hadn't browned the sausages before putting them in the pot to boil, and they looked as raw as they did when they went in. This also meant that fat and grease was floating on the top – along with the sausages... It was *awful*... I think I went hungry that day!

~

Mrs. Binns wasn't the best person to have around when I was trying to eat – as was proved to me one day back at the pub.

The old grey coal-burning stove in the far corner of the kitchen served to heat all the water for the pub, so it had to be kept going all the time. This also provided a good means for making toast. A long iron toasting fork, that had somehow turned black and crooked over the years, was always kept beside it leaning against the wall, and I enjoyed making toast in that way. So I would hold the bread on the toasting fork down low over the red glow. To my mind this was the best kind of toast ever.

So there I was sitting at the kitchen table, enjoying my hot buttered toast. The golden butter melted obligingly into the thick slice of bread, and I savoured it as one of the more simple joys of life.

Suddenly the door opened behind me – and Mrs. Binns walked past me across to the stove – carrying a *used sanitary towel!* She had made no attempt to cover it – she was that kind of woman. She lifted the lid of the stove – and put the sanitary towel in there, closed the lid, then went out.

Somehow, my toast didn't seem so appetising any longer...

~

One day my grandmother was washing her face in the kitchen, and using the communal face flannel.

"Ugh!" she exclaimed, looking at the flannel in disgust. "*That woman* – has been using this to wash her old fannackerpan.." she said, putting it down, twitching her nose with her mouth turned down in disgust.

"What's a fannackerpan?" I asked innocently.

She didn't answer – but my mother giggled...

~

The Chinese dress

One day, when I was thirteen years old, Gina came to the Kings Arms
with two of her dresses for me and a pair of her shoes. They were cocktail
dresses, and as she was so petite they were only a little bit big for me. One
of them I really liked. It was a Chinese dress, in an aqua colour sateen
with a bird, flower and Chinese writing design on the fabric. It had a
little stand-up collar, fastened in the front with "frog" fastenings, and had
a very high slit going all the way up the leg. It was a very beautiful dress,
but I didn't really think I was going to be wearing it!

The other dress was turquoise lamé, sleeveless and with a cowl neckline,
which of course, hung low on my little chest! So I really didn't think I
would be wearing that either.

The shoes were black stilettos, and the heels must have been at least
four inches high, maybe even five. They too were a little bit big for me,
as I only took a size 3 shoe then, and when I tried to stand in them, I just
went lurching forward.

However, before long my mother had me wearing the Chinese dress
behind the bar – and also the shoes, which caused me to wobble, and I
had to hold my hands out to steady myself. I must have looked *so* stupid!
It was only when I lurched forward a few too many times, nearly tipping
into the slops tray, that I didn't have to wear them any more – well not
for a while that is...

So there I was, thirteen years old, behind the bar, having to wear this
dress which may *possibly* have suited me more a few years later. Gina
must have had all good intentions, but that *high slit up the side?*

~

Most of the girls in my class were now wearing bras. The straps could
be seen through tops, and a few even wore black bras which showed
deliberately through white blouses. To my mind this is one of the most
awful faux pas of dressing. But what they were doing was showing that
they were big enough to wear bras – even at thirteen.

I was concerned that my vest might be detected, and my friend Alison
– who I had first met at Little Thurrock School – felt the same. So we
decided to appease our mothers by wearing them to school, then take

them off when we were there, and keep them in our bags until we went home. Well ok, but I still wanted to wear a bra like the other girls. So I very bravely plucked up the courage to ask my mother if I could have one.

"What do *you* want a brassiere for?" she asked me mockingly. "You've got nothing to put in it!"

Somehow, my father got wind of this, and chipped in at some time when my request had been mentioned.

"All you've got are gnat bites" he said chuckling, referring to my tiny pink nipples that were just beginning to grow on my small developing breasts. How did he know that? He was obviously just guessing, but I didn't like hearing that at all.

By now, Alison had persuaded her mother to let her have a bra, albeit a tiny one. But it *was a bra* – and had straps that just might be seen by the other girls.

One day my mother gave in, and took me off to the British Home Stores to buy me a bra. It had to be one of the smallest ones of course, but at least it fitted me. She bought me two, and I chose pure white cotton broderie anglaise. They were really comfortable, and I felt so grown-up – and what's more – like the other girls in my class.

Still my mother wasn't happy though. Even though the bras fitted me, she instructed Nell to make some padding for them to make me look – a bit bigger! I didn't want to look bigger though – I just wanted to be *me*...

~

The turquoise lamé dress

One of my second cousins was getting married, and his wife-to-be Ellen had asked her best friend, my other second cousins Lyn, Ann, and Gillian, and me, to be bridesmaids. My bridesmaid dress was lovely, very "couture" in style, and made of peach taffeta. I had a little spray of peach silk flowers in my hair, and the groom had bought all the bridesmaids a pretty necklace, a lovely string of crystals. Dressed up in that I certainly looked older than thirteen!

Ellen's parents seemed quite well to do, their house was really nice, rather posh, and with expensive looking rugs hung on the staircase wall.

I had been there before without my parents, and my mother had asked me what their house was like.

"It's really posh" I said, recalling the nice things that they had, "and there are rugs on the wall going up the stairs."

"Rugs on the *wall?*" my mother asked disbelievingly.

"Yes", I said, "a bit like they have at Hampton Court".

I didn't really mean that the house was like a grand palace, nor that the rugs were as large as those there, I was just remarking on the rugs on the wall, because I had never seen rugs on the wall in any other person's house before. It struck me. I liked that.

When my parents eventually went there, my mother told me off afterwards saying I had exaggerated about how nice the house was, and said that "it's nothing special at all!" Well it was to *me* – and what's more it didn't have dinner stains on the wallpaper, like we had upstairs at the pub.

~

So there I was in Ellen's parents' house, upstairs in her bedroom getting ready for the wedding with my cousins. I felt so awful when I took off my petticoat to get into my bridesmaid dress – a bit of the padding in my bra stuck out, and I could see that Lyn had seen it. She didn't say anything though. Why on earth had my mother told Nell to sew padding into my bra? Having two pretty white broderie anglaise bras was enough for me – I didn't feel right with padding. Especially at that age. But that's how my mother wanted me to look – a child with a woman's body...

However – worse was to come.

That evening the reception was being held at a very posh hotel, and although I thought I might still be wearing my bridesmaid dress, my mother told me to get changed – and put on Gina's turquoise lamé dress – along with her shoes. Lyn told me how lovely I looked, but I knew I didn't. I didn't want to look like *this*. I felt as though I was in fancy dress, and of course, those shoes...

~

With Martin living in New Zealand, Gina was now having to move house, and so she found a council house in Lowestoft.

Meanwhile, my grandfather had been trying to get her into bed. I expect that is why she moved so far away. I knew this, because my mother and grandmother were talking about it in the kitchen one day. It didn't matter to them that I happened to be there as well. Maybe I was invisible? Well invisible to them? Once they got talking about something like that, maybe everything turned invisible.

She had obviously turned him down, and it seemed that he took his revenge by telling people that she was a lesbian. He wasn't used to women turning him down!

"What's a lesbian" I asked innocently, suddenly making them realise that I was actually indeed in the kitchen with them.

My mother struggled for words. She didn't just ignore me though.

"Errmm... A woman who loves other women", she stuttered.

Oh... Black marks for Gina then. My mother *hated* women – except for my grandmother that is...

Well Gina loved *me* anyway – I knew that. She was so kind, and would do anything to make my life staying with her a little more pleasant than it was at the pub. I think she had picked up on a few things – although I would never have said anything. I am just glad though that I never innocently asked her if she was a *lesbian!*

I really loved Gina, and I didn't like hearing these things being said about her in spite, even though I didn't know what they meant.

~

I was good at painting and drawing, anything creative. At around this time I painted a portrait with my oil paints. It was of a woman wearing a big puffed sleeved, burgundy coloured dress, very much in the eighteenth century style. It was a head and shoulders portrait, and down to the waist, which was pinched in and laced. I painted the face, a pretty looking woman with brown eyes, but instead of giving her long flowing hair, I gave her short dark hair, which was actually a strange thing for me to do.

One day, I had been working on the painting and it was on the dresser in the kitchen drying, when Gina came in, having come to the pub to visit us. She stood looking at the painting quizzically, but with a smile on her face.

"Is that *me?*" she asked, a little diffidently.

"Yes!" I said. Well of course it was. I don't think I realised just what I was painting until I painted the face – and recognised it... That was why I gave my lady the short dark hair – like Gina's.

"Ooh – can I have it?" she asked.

Yes, of course she could! If I had kept it, it would have only disappeared before long anyway.

Some time after that I went to stay with Gina in Lowestoft. The house was very plain, and probably built just after the war – but Gina had made it look nice. Home fashions were a little strange then, and she had plastic curtains in the kitchen and towelling curtains in the bathroom. It wasn't the best of looks, but I suppose it made sense! And it did have a fireplace.

Unlike a lot of older houses in the sixties, the fireplace hadn't been ripped out and replaced with plywood, or whatever else people thought looked better than a fireplace – so it made the front room nice and cosy. As I walked into the room – there was my painting – framed and in pride of place over the mantelpiece. I was so happy that for once, something I had created had not been destroyed or thrown away...

"Thank You For The World So Sweet
Thank You For The Food We Eat"
– Or Don't

Bartering

On the whole, I suppose it is fair for me to say that we did have *some* nice food at the pub. We always had roast dinners on a Sunday, usually a large succulent joint, like rib of beef, leg of lamb, crispy strips of breast of lamb, or belly of pork – complete with teats, I dread to say – but which would crackle up nicely.

I would usually mix the Yorkshire pudding, which my grandmother would make in a large baking tray, black from years of use. I also learned how to make sage and onion stuffing and apple sauce for the pork, which involved me grating a lot of breadcrumbs, chopping up eye-pricking onions, and mixing them all together with dried sage – the only concession to today's ready-mix accompaniments being the dried sage; not forgetting having to collect, peel, pare, chop up and mix with just the right amount of sugar to make the perfect tart apple sauce, the Bramley apples straight from the tree. All these things I would do – well I wasn't at school on Sundays...

My favourite was the roast lamb and mint sauce, made with fresh mint that I would go up the road to Mrs. Crosby to collect – large fragrant bunches of mint straight from her garden. We were also given fresh peas, runner beans and other such summer delights by local people.

I soon learned how to deftly chop the mint with a large knife onto the breadboard, and with the addition of malt vinegar (the only vinegar available then) and a little sugar, it would turn into that delightful sauce to go with the lamb. All this produce was given to us usually in return for beer – normally draught, poured straight from the tap into those old lemonade bottles with the stoppers that clasped over the neck.

My grandmother didn't do any actual work around the house, and she even preferred to sit on the customer side of the counter in the bars, but she was happy to cook. I learned a lot from her, but I really did have to do my share! My eyes used to water cutting up the onions for the stuffing, and it was even worse when I had to grate the horseradish, which we grew in the vegetable garden.

Mondays, was always cold roast meat with bubble and squeak and home-made pickles, and I enjoyed that too. A particular favourite that my grandmother cooked was spicy bread pudding, with lots of currants that burnt at the edges, making those parts the best bits, well for me anyway. What put me off though, was that my grandfather didn't have the best of table manners, and he loved to cut off a slice of bread pudding after dinner – with his dinner knife – thus leaving a smear of potatoes and gravy along the part of the bread pudding where he had cut it. That was so disgusting.

I loved stewed fruit and custard, the fruit pies that my grandmother made with slightly burnt crusts from the old mottled grey gas stove that she cooked them in, and the crunchy sugar on the top. All the fruits were from the garden and I would normally be told to gather them – the windfall apples, the plums and the rhubarb...

As well as all the bartering that went on, with fresh vegetables etc. in return for beer, Mr. Haynes, who lived over the road also provided us with lots of the summer flowers that we had in little vases on the round tables in the saloon bar. It was my job to arrange these lovely scented flowers, which was no task at all, as that was something I loved doing.

Mr. Haynes' front garden was a work of art in the summer, with an immaculate front lawn with borders of red salvias, white alyssum, and royal blue lobelia. Harry Haynes was obviously a very patriotic man! He was so proud of his immaculate garden, and all the local people admired it. He grew flowers for cutting in his back garden, usually carnations, pinks, Sweet Williams, French marigolds, and dahlias, most of which were delightfully scented. As always, he was also suitably and quite justly rewarded with beer!

The gamekeepers would also barter in the same way with pheasants and grouse, those so called "delicacies" of which I wanted no part, and that would be left to mature and "ripen" on the landing for ages, just laying on the floor. I had to literally pick my way carefully through these dead, but beautiful birds. I hated it!

There were other meats too, which I just could *not* eat...

Run rabbit run rabbit run run run...

Behind the summer house and in the vegetable garden, we had a chicken coop. We were very self-sufficient in lots of ways, growing our own fruit and vegetables, even growing our own meat! This was normally in the form of the chickens who also provided us with free-range eggs, but we even had our own colony of rabbits as well for a while. They lived in the large oblong caravan that my father had built. He had built both of the caravans that we had in the garden, although the larger one was not done out for sleeping in like the smaller one. Maybe that had once been the intention, but it stood empty – until the rabbits came along.

It soon became full of rabbits, as they bred, well, like rabbits! These poor things though were bred purely for the meat that they would provide, although at first I didn't know this, and I saw them as pets. One day, when the rabbits had long gone, my father told me that when I was little, if I happened to find out that it was a rabbit in the cooking pot, I always refused to eat it.

"I'm not going to eat that poor little thing" he told me I would say. So therefore, I would have to go without.

Food hygiene!

In those days dinner was cooked at lunchtime, and anyone who was not present for dinner would have their meal kept on the hot water tank in the airing cupboard until they were able to eat it. The smell in there would be awful sometimes, especially if sprouts were on the menu – they were the worst thing for permeating the linen and towels with food smells.

Teatime though was always at five o'clock, well, for anyone who wasn't by then having their over-heated dinner. So if I had to go without dinner, there would usually be paste sandwiches or more often, bread and dripping, the latter being what I particularly liked, especially with Bovril spread on the top. Beef dripping was my favourite, with lamb being second, pork sort of following, although that was particularly runny, but I really couldn't eat any poultry dripping.

So then it would be just bread with sometimes a little bit of cheese, but usually with pretty rancid butter, as we didn't have a refrigerator. Butter that has melted in the heat and then reset, really doesn't complement anything – no matter how lovely the bread might be!

Any produce that had to be kept cool, and used on a daily basis, like the butter and cheese, especially when I was at school and so wasn't available to go down into the cellar, would be kept on a marble slab in the pantry, which had a fine grid in the back wall to let air in – supposedly! Marble is good at keeping cool – when everything else is getting overheated!

In the summer, along with the butter going rancid – the cheese would sweat. This was always very off-putting, with wet blister-like globules all over the cheese. Sometimes the cheese would be nibbled by mice. That bit would be cut off though, but I still didn't like the thought of the mice running over it. Sometimes the bread would have a great big hole going through it, again, nibbled by mice. So bread and cheese for tea wasn't always a good option!

I remember my mother telling me how she had gone into the pantry to get some pearl barley to put in a stew. As she went to pick up the packet she saw a mouse in there – looking out of the see-through plastic window on the front! Dare I hope that the packet was thrown away? I can't help but think that it wasn't.

Eggs, bacon and sausages would be kept in the pantry too, the sausages being made by Mr. Dodd, the butcher down in the village. Nothing was kept covered though, just laying there on open plates, so if any mice or flies got in, there would be a problem – well to me anyway! I often saw bluebottle eggs on the sausages – and these sausages would then be fried on darts nights, and given out sizzling on sticks to the darts team... Little did they know!

We didn't have any foil or cling film then, and if I covered any food up with a plate, it would just be taken off again.

"No point making more washing up" I would be told.

I suppose my family did do their best to keep the flies down, but I think it was mainly down to the lack of a refrigerator. We always had a sticky yellow fly paper hanging from the kitchen ceiling. That would always stay up until it was totally covered in flies so turned black. It was so disgusting!

Sometimes my grandfather would go on a fly raid with a canister of DDT pumping it from what resembled a bicycle pump attached to the canister. After some years this was changed to Flit, but that was as choking as DDT with the way that he sprayed it so copiously.

One day, Grandpop very proudly came down from the hen coup with a few hens' eggs that hadn't hardened. They couldn't be cracked obviously, so they had to be cut with scissors through what would have been the shell. Well I was having nothing to do with them! I don't think anyone else did either – apart from my grandfather!

Maybe he had DDT'd the chicken coop sometime...

~

Bottles of milk, delivered daily by the milkman, who really did wear a peaked cap and a white overall, and did indeed whistle while he worked – unless my grandfather had had a go at him that is – would be kept in buckets of water on the landing... Just as well we had such a long landing...

Any excess food supplies would be kept down in the cellar in what was called "the safe". This was a cupboard with a wire mesh over the front. This wasn't a "safe" as such, but I am guessing it was so-called because it supposedly kept food "safe" from going off.

I remember the day when I came home from school, and my grandmother and Nell were in the taproom with my mother. This was unusual for an afternoon, because my mother and grandmother would normally be resting, watching the television, or asleep, and Nell would be up in the shop. This time though, I think Nell had been alerted – and summoned – on that old black wall mounted telephone – to come down to the pub – and quickly...

My grandmother and Nell were administering copious amounts of brandy to my mother to revive and calm her down, and stop her from passing out. She was sitting with her head between her legs, trying to breathe, and was deathly white. Nell said that she had seen the ghost of the previous landlord, who had hanged himself down in the cellar – walking up those cold cellar steps...

So from then on – my mother deemed that it would be – *me* – who would have to go down to the cellar "safe" to get any cooled produce. Oh how I hated going down those steep narrow steps, with the whitewashed stone walls, and the dank smell. I was always terrified, *especially* knowing that the previous landlord had hanged himself down there – and that my mother had *seen* him.. That was a very scary place to have to go to indeed.

At my young age, I couldn't help but believe that ghosts really did exist, and that the pub was indeed haunted – and now my mother's experience confirmed that to me...

~

I don't know why, but the cutlery at the pub always smelled so awful. It was a smell of drains, or something like that. It was probably because the washing up was done mainly with soda crystals, or maybe it might have been whatever metal the cutlery was made of? It was actually nice looking cutlery, with cream-coloured bone handles, although I wouldn't want that sort of cutlery nowadays. Once I was able to go down to the town shopping on my own, which was probably when I was about eleven, I went into Woolworths one day and bought a knife, fork and spoon just for myself, with my pocket money. The handles were pale yellow plastic, and I kept that set separate from all the rest, washing it up myself.

Another thing that I didn't like was the breadboard. It was a large square wooden board with a decorative groove around the edges. Unfortunately, as it was never washed properly, things coagulated in the grooves. One day I was so disgusted by this that I got a sharp knife and went all around the grooves digging all this stuff out. My mother told me off for doing that – saying I was making a mess of the breadboard!

So back to what I was eating! As a treat, if I was lucky, I was able to have stewed or tinned fruit after tea with jelly. Sometimes it would be jelly and blancmange. I loved that, the wobbling red jelly and the pink blancmange – maybe that should have been called *rosemange...* But always, I had to have bread and butter with any dessert of that kind, which made it rather less pleasurable than it should have been. Goodness knows why I had to have bread and butter as well – but I *had to.*

In the evenings I could have a packet of Smith's crisps, those lovely crisps that at the pub were known as "chips", and which had those little blue bags of salt in the packets that were twisted at the top. It wasn't so enticing somehow once the little blue bag had been changed to be a small flat square packet.

Sometimes I was allowed to have a beef pie or a pork pie, which we had delivered each day to sell in the pub. The beef pies were kept hot in the airing cupboard, along with any other food that was kept hot (well warm!) in there – there were no food inspectors in those days! Sometimes, when I was at senior school, I would be given a leftover pork pie to take for my lunch, and very often, as I bit into it – it was mouldy. Therefore, yet again, I would have to go without.

I wasn't there at the time, but one lunchtime my grandmother happened to be behind the bar, and her double set of false teeth (which looked to me like a set you could buy from a joke shop) were playing her up, so she took them out and put them in one of the paper bags. One of our regulars came in for his normal pork pie, and away he went. A short while later he came back with the bag with the pork pie in it – and also my grandmother's false teeth!

"A good pub this is", he said handing over the bag, "not only do I get a pork pie – *but also the teeth to eat it with!*"

The Day of the Egg

We always had supper at eleven o'clock when the pub closed. Once I was able to help in the kitchen, which was at quite an early age, and after washing up the glasses, Nell and I would make melted cheese on toast, with home-made pickled onions. We would mix pieces of cheese with milk in a saucepan, bring it it to the boil – stirring all the time – and then pour it over the toast. So food was always on offer, albeit at the said times, but it was often used against me as a form of punishment. What for though, I really don't know.

On summer evenings, and after all the field women had gone home, Nell and I would go pea or potato gleaning. I really enjoyed that, and it was a great sense of achievement adding to the food stock. Even now the smell of fresh peas fills my senses with the pure delight of pea gleaning on a warm summer's evening, and sitting outside podding my gain into a white enamel bowl.

In the early autumn mornings, Nell and I would go mushrooming – always at around seven o'clock. I knew exactly which fungi were edible, and which weren't. We would go over the fields knowing that the edible mushrooms mainly grew in and around the cowpats. One might think that this would be a most unpleasant start to the day, but I did enjoy going over the fields in the early morning mists that hung low over the fens.

The mushrooms were solely for my grandfather who would breakfast at ten o'clock, as no-one else seemed to eat them. He would consume them with gusto, along with fried eggs from the chickens.

His eggs were always fried in lard, or sometimes dripping, along with green back bacon that was sliced to his liking by the Home and Colonial shop in Grays. Unfortunately, the eggs would be covered with ominous black bits from the mushrooms – which may or may not have had something to do with the cowpats!

Unlike the poor rabbits, the hens were free to rummage around in the dirt, picking up this and that, the grain I would scatter for them, and pulling up worms. There were white hens, and brown ones, the eggs being the same colour as the hens... I wasn't always happy about having an egg for breakfast, because I used to gather the eggs from the coop sometimes, and knew that they came out of the hens, but didn't really know why. Sometimes there would be a double-yoked egg, which was a treat to my grandfather, but to me it was – twins!

When he had boiled eggs, which he always preferred to do himself, he liked having his Camp coffee made with the water that his eggs had been boiled in – complete with bits of feather – and brown bits – saying it was good for you!

Well it wasn't good for the rest of us, so he had that disgusting concoction to himself!

Living with the hens there was a really horrible little bantam cock called Joey. Oh how I hated him! He was a crafty little thing, and had a real dislike for me, and would chase me and peck at my ankles when I was sent to the orchard to pick apples and plums etc. He would always catch me, or would lie in wait for me, and suddenly appear and run out at me. I really couldn't see the use of having a male chicken, but I was told that he was needed to help to make the little fluffy yellow chicks that hatched occasionally, and that would then grow up to be chickens. Well the female ones that were kept anyway. Grandpop only wanted one cock, of the fowl kind that is (er-hmm) – and that was Joey.

Well one morning, when my mother happened to be at the pub around breakfast time, I was given a boiled egg for breakfast. I remember it had a very unpleasant smell, and I wasn't at all happy about having to eat it. I sliced the top off with a knife, and put my teaspoon into the yolk. I was even more disgusted to see that there was something in there. It was only a small thing, but it looked rather ominous to me.

"Get it down yer girl..." my grandfather said from the other side of the table, when I said why I couldn't eat it. "It's only a bit of meat..."

A bit of *meat*? Well, that did it. There was no way I was going to eat that egg.

My mother agreed with my grandfather, and she told me that if I didn't eat it – and all of it – then it would be put in the airing cupboard and I would have to eat it for my dinner.

And so, the egg was put into the airing cupboard and kept warm. Then, at dinner time, when everyone else was having whatever was on offer that day – I was presented with the egg.

I sat there for absolutely ages, resolutely refusing to eat the offending egg, and the smell just got worse – and worse.

"Right!" my mother said, in that very commanding way – "you shall have it for your tea then."

So the egg went back into the airing cupboard, where it was slowly reheated for tea – and then presented to me again, while everyone else had sandwiches or whatever.

Well I didn't eat that egg, and so I had to remain hungry.

Obviously, I have never forgotten *the day of the egg...*

Scenes of Horror

In the chicken coop, their perch was a rounded length of wood, rather like a broom handle, which stretched from one side to the other, and the hens would look very contented in the early evenings when my grandfather shut them in for the night. They would sit all along the perch side by side, with their talons curled around it, their heads down, and their eyes closed. I often used to look up at them and wonder how they could hold on so well when they were asleep!

One morning though, Grandpop asked me to go up to the hen house with him because he wanted to show me something. I had no idea that it would be something so horrific... A fox had managed to get in during the night, and there was blood, feathers and gore all over the place. All the lovely hens that I used to feed were all now dead or dying...

Why Grandpop wanted me to see all this, I do not know. But then again, why had he wanted to show me close up the row of dead mice with their eyes popping out?

My mother was just as bad though.

One day my father, who had worked in a slaughterhouse when he first left the Royal Navy, brought home a pig's head. He wasn't working at the slaughterhouse then, but he knew all about butchery. I didn't see the head, but he told me what he had in the bag, and that he was going to make some brawn, which is something my family loved, although something else that I could not eat. I knew all that went into it, and the sight of the bright pink meat set in jelly would turn my stomach.

My father went into the kitchen with the pig's head and closed the door. I made myself scarce, as I could imagine what was going on behind that door with all the things inside that head.

Hours later I returned to the pub, knowing that by now all the disgusting things would have been done, and it would be safe to go back. My mother actually seemed pleased to see me.

"Yvonne" she said, smiling, "you like bulls eyes, don't you?"

Oh – "bulls eyes", those lovely minty black and white sweets that we sold in a large jar in the shop. You would suck them enjoying the outer coating, and then you would get through to the lovely chewy bit inside.

"There's a couple for you in the kitchen on the table" she said, and then walked away, grinning...

So I went to the kitchen.

The awful smell of the brawn was overpowering, but my little treat awaited me. I went to the kitchen table, and there – staring right at me – were the two pig's eyes...

From head to toes

My place at the table was always opposite my grandfather and, as he was a rather messy eater, we had newspaper at our places on top of the white linen tablecloth, instead of table mats. Grandpop couldn't be singled out alone, so we all had to eat like that when he was there.

Nothing was ever wasted and, as well as table mats, newspaper was also used as toilet paper. The pages would be torn into four, and hung from butchers' hooks on the overhead cistern. It was even used like this in the pub toilets. To make it softer, I would crumple the newspaper pieces and rub them with my hands – my hands would be covered with newsprint – the mind boggles, it really does. I remember "The People" and the "News of the World" being the worst for newsprint, and they were also the hardest. The "Morning Advertiser" was somewhat better!

Well back to the table, Grandpop was bad enough at mealtimes anyway, and if he didn't like his dinner he would stand up shouting "what is this muck?" – and throw it right across the kitchen, through the kitchen door, where it would hit the wall on the other side of the landing. Luckily for me, I wasn't usually there when he did that sort of thing, so it never hit me. I used to see the aftermath of it though...

The wallpaper on the landing took on a very strange pattern, with brown gravy stains etc. streaking down the wall. And what with the ripening pheasants given to us by the gamekeepers – in return for beer as usual – hanging around in the autumn, the pub landing was at times a very unpleasant place to walk along.

I have always been very "sensitive" as to what I am eating, even from an early age, and as with the rabbits, I couldn't eat the pheasants either, nor venison, and to this day I cannot eat any kind of game. I can't help but think of the *games* people play to catch and kill these poor creatures.

The landing wasn't the only place that Grandpop used to throw his dinner – sometimes he would throw it down the stairs.

I remember coming home from school one day, and saw all the mess down the stairs. We lived above the pub, and although the stairs went up from the lobby which customers would come into from the back of the pub where the car park was, there was a door at the bottom, so no customers ever saw beyond that door. I started to pick up the pieces of broken plate and dinner, which were all over the stairs, all the way down.

"Leave it old girl", my grandmother called from the landing, "let him pick it up himself". So I made my way through it as best as I could.

That dinner stayed there for days that time, although it did eventually go. I suppose the dogs and cats cleaned it up.

So mealtimes weren't always very pleasant, and even less so on the days that my grandfather had one of his favourite dishes – pig's trotter stew!

I suppose my grandmother did what she could to clean them, but there always appeared to still be dirt between the toes as they went into the pot. I have never actually eaten a pig's trotter, but I have been given the gravy and vegetables from the stew, which I would sprinkle with neat curry powder to make it more palatable, but I would keep thinking about the dirt between the toes...

My grandfather really made a meal of them though, and he would love pulling out the bright yellow sinews with his teeth, slopping and squelching as he did so. Then he would chomp on the trotters until not one morsel of meat was left. It was sickening, especially as I was sitting opposite him.

I would think up plans though, to make barriers that I could sit down low and hide behind. There was usually a loaf of bread on the table, and I would stand that up on its end in front of me, or a bottle of milk if Grandpop wanted a cup of tea with his meal. So it was a bit like making my own fortress in front of me. It never really worked though – the sound effects summed up all that was going on.

I knew that I couldn't leave the table until I had eaten my dinner, and I would push food round and round my plate trying to make it get smaller and smaller. That didn't work either. Neither was I allowed to speak at the table.

"You're lucky" my mother always told me, "I wasn't even allowed to cough. If I uttered one word – I would be sent out of the room." Well having been told that, I don't suppose I coughed at the table either, but I'm sure I must have heaved a few times...

Other jams and jellies

Being true born Londoners, my grandparents loved – er – *jellied eels*. My grandmother knew exactly how to make them, and would pot them into what resembled half size jam jars. The sight of the green jelly and the black jam of the eels was *so* disgusting. Needless to say, I have never even tasted them, let alone eaten them.

My parents would take me with them when they went shopping in Grays on a Saturday, or sometimes I would go on the bus with my mother. There was a fishmonger at the top of the High Street, and that is where the eels were sold. I think we only got them if my father was with us, as he knew what to look for in an eel, and then we would take a few of them home alive in some kind of plastic bag – to be jellied...

The eels would be kept in the large butler's sink in the kitchen, where they swam around, not knowing their fate. Then, my grandmother would take them out one by one, putting them on the chopping board, and holding them down with her left hand, she would chop off their heads with the other – but the eels would still be wriggling and slithering around...

Chop – chop – chop – she would go, all along the body, until the eel was ready for the cooking pot. I only witnessed this once – but once was enough. How anyone thought this would interest me, I do not know. But it is another one of those awful sights I have never forgotten.

Foul Fowl

Although I had so cruelly lost my bedroom at my parents' bungalow, I would often be walking down there to see them when they were there, especially when my father was home. I would help him with the garden, seeding vegetables, planting spring bulbs and bedding summer flowers. I just liked to be with him whatever his project happened to be. Watching him mixing cement for the new front path was interesting – the way that the right amount of cement, sand and water would all come together as he would turn it over and over with a small spade.

"A nice bit of *concrate*" he would say, "every garden needs a nice bit of *concrate*..."

His accent could be so amusing sometimes!

~

One day a large structure appeared in the back garden, it was slightly elevated on a concrete base, and built of wood and wire – lots of wire... It was the kind of structure that I wonder might have needed planning permission, but no matter – what my mother wanted – my mother got...

"Your mother wants chickens" my father explained, shaking his head, and huffing and puffing as he knocked the final nails in.

"Chickens?" I asked, looking at this huge frame. "But we've got chickens at the pub..."

"She wants her own" he sighed. "But she doesn't want them running around the garden..."

"Oh – but what about the neighbours?" I asked, thinking that there might be trouble ahead.

"What *about* the neighbours?" he said, more of a statement than a question.

Hmm – I thought that Leonard Leonard next door might object. Now, Leonard Leonard is not a mistake – it really was his name. Maybe his parents, when they named him, didn't want him to be called by his surname at school...

~

And so, the chickens duly arrived – and they were *enormous!* I don't know where they came from, but they were probably a job lot that had lived a horrible life so far, as they seemed severely traumatised. Unlike the docile chickens at the pub these ones, with their evil-looking red eyes, accentuated by their white feathers, seemed to be mentally disturbed!

They were huge, but their feet were far too big for their bodies. Having been in there once to feed them, my mother refused to ever go in there again, and so it was my father's job. Even he found that the way they flew at him, head height, and with their talons out in front, was rather daunting. Just by looking at them, I could see that these creatures were not normal.

So why had my mother wanted chickens?

"I'm not eating my own eggs" she said, meaning the chickens'. "They've got to go..."

My father came up with a brilliant idea...

"I'll wring their necks one at a time" he said enthusiastically, "and then we can eat them..."

"I'm not eating my own chickens!" my mother exclaimed.

I never did know what happened to them...

~

The building didn't go to waste though, because there was space underneath it. This space served as a hiding place for my mother's cat who was heavy with kittens. The father was one of the feral cats that used to frequent anywhere where there were pretty young intact females. Cats can be so clever sometimes, for these feral cats knew that when their kittens were born, if they found them, and ate them, then the mother would no longer be happily caring for her litter, but looking for more – which is where they came in again...

Sure enough, the feral Tom sneaked round – looking for his woman. Sadly he found her, with her kittens – and ate them.

So my father shot him.

My Grandfather's Garden

The main garden at the pub was mostly an expanse of lawn, bordered with flowering shrubs, and fragrant old-fashioned rose bushes, pale pink, white, and the deepest crimson, with petals so soft they felt like velvet.

From springtime right through to late summer days, there were always flowers in bloom – bright yellow forsythia, that still glowed in the sunshine when the flowers dropped and the lime green leaves appeared. Lilacs followed, the sweetest smelling lilacs I have ever known, from the purest double white, through to deep purple, with all the shades of, well lilac, in between. Then came the deliciously scented philadelphus, or orange blossom as I knew it then. No wonder the Queen Mother chose to wear its fragrant white flowers in her hair on her wedding day.

There was a hazel tree, with cob nuts that I would pick and eat fresh in the autumn, an elder with its fragrant fronds of white flowers in the summer followed by the darkest black berries, and a small raised group of stones that was filled with earth and built around another tree, underneath which a solitary white hyacinth delighted every spring.

There was the large rockery behind the conservatory, and the extensive lawn, of which my grandfather was so proud that my mother told me that when she was younger, he would make her pick up every single rose petal that fell upon it.

At the end of the lawn was a summer house, in which we kept calico coloured deck chairs and tennis racquets. This had a rustic trellis window, and was covered in white morning glory, which opened its petals to greet the morning sun.

At quite an early age I learned how to play tennis. My father taught me, and I really enjoyed it. The car park, with the washing line that was strung across it, made a good tennis court when the line was brought down! There was also a nine foot wide expanse of wall across the back of the pub, with no windows. This blank wall was as high at the roof, and it became another good place in which to practice. Somehow though – the wall always won!

Behind the summer house was the chicken coop, which was also at the beginning of the vegetable garden and orchard. There were apple, plum and damson trees, and a Bramley apple tree that had a parasitic mistletoe that grew on it every winter, which would be brought indoors at Christmas, and hung up in the doorways to the bars, giving customers the perfect excuse to have a Christmas kiss!

Sometimes my grandfather would have already collected it, but more likely, he sent me to get it. It grew on the Bramley apple tree, quite high up, which meant I had to climb up a little to be able to reach it. Strangely, it had always grown on the same meeting of two branches – did this symbolise what this mysterious plant was all about? It was very pretty with its evergreen leaves on a deciduous tree, which of course would no longer be evergreen once it had been plucked from its host. At least the leaves remained green for the duration of Christmas.

Its little white berries held their own legendary magic. My grandfather would chuckle as he hung the mistletoe up under the door frames to the bars. I knew that any woman or girl walking under it at the same time as a man, would have to succumb to a kiss. It was apparently the man's privilege to do that! Something to do with fertility – and a man's dominance over a woman. So I would avoid walking under the mistletoe if ever I saw a man coming towards me.

~

There was the vegetable garden, growing whatever my grandfather, and father, fancied growing, including potatoes, so new, and so fresh, that we would rub off their skins with our fingers, cabbages, and all manner of salad items. I particularly remember walking through the tomato plants when I was so small that they were taller than me, and smelling their delicious aroma. No tomatoes these days could ever taste better than those.

Rhubarb grew profusely, and although my grandmother didn't do any housework, she didn't mind cooking, and would make rhubarb and apple pies, to which she would always add cloves, giving it a strong spicy aroma that goes so well with the fruit.

As with every working garden, there was a refuse heap, and every year scarlet and orange nasturtiums scrambled over it in all directions, creating an oil painting of colour, belying what lay beneath. A little like the oil painting of happiness that my grandfather and mother painted to the customers, and the village people. Although I was sworn to secrecy, at least I had this garden to enjoy.

~

One day, when I had just started senior school, I was on the bus coming home down Baker Street, and I got up from my seat at the normal place to ring the bell to indicate that I wanted to get off. I walked through the bus to the front, and we were alongside the cottages, but somehow I wasn't "home".

This wasn't what I knew...

This was an alien place...

I just stood there looking out of the bus window in disbelief and utter despair.

What was once our garden, the wonderland that taught me so much about plants and wildlife – was now just *gone...*

Just a vast, bulldozed devastation of rocks and rubble, sad limp dying trees and once flowering shrubs.

No more would I have this little bit of paradise, my heaven away from the rigours of life at the pub.

No-one had warned me this was going to happen.

No-one had told me my grandfather was making this into another hard and grey – car park.

Big Fish In A Small Pond

1960 was a most horrible year for me. In fact I think it was the most awful year of my childhood.

It was the year that I left Orsett School and started at Torells, which, to my mind at the time, was the beginning of a four year reign of terror. It was also the year that I came dangerously close to my life being ruined forever. What happened then though was at the end of 1960, and this was still summer.

The education that I had received at that little primary school was a wonderful start. We were taught many things about the world that many children of primary school age at the time didn't even begin to learn until they went to secondary school, one of these subjects being physics which I found fascinating. We were also taught how to write in old-fashioned script, for which I actually won a handwriting prize. My handwriting is still in a similar style today.

One day, in that final year there, Mr. Simpson asked me what I wanted to be when I grew up.

"I'm going to be an air hostess" I told him proudly.

"Well that's a very good profession to have", he said with that lovely smile of praise that he so often gave me. "You will be a good one", he added, to my delight.

"The girl with the crowning glory" he had once referred to me in class, meaning my thick blonde hair. Maybe he could envisage, even at that early age, that there might be a little bit of glamour to me when I grew up, as well as my adventurous spirit.

With all this in mind, in July 1959, I had been awarded a "Progress Prize for Class Subjects". It was a book called "Shirley Flight Air Hostess" by Judith Dale.

From that book I learned all about the Recruitment Board, the trials, the mock-up flights, and much more. I also learned that to become an air hostess I had to be fluent in three languages, preferably English, French and German. French and German were both taught at the local grammar school, and to get there I knew that I had to pass the "11-Plus" examination.

I loved writing stories as a child, although they were more fact than fiction, and based on the countryside. One of the stories that Mr. Simpson praised me for was one that I had written about my observations of the countryside, and how pansies looked to me like cats! They had such personalities – smiling when the sun shone, and drooping a little sadly when it rained – just one of the quirky little things that I had added into my descriptive writing. To have one of my stories read out in class meant the world to me – even though I felt highly embarrassed – and slid further and further down into my seat!

So I was thrilled to bits when I had the examination paper placed in front of me – and one of the writing options was to write about a walk in the countryside!

I passed! Mr. Simpson told me that it was my writing that had impressed the examiners. So there I was, all set to go to Grammar School, and to pack in as much learning as I could to get my wings...

~

As usual at the end of that summer term at Orsett School, preparations were going on for the Open Day, and we were practising our country dancing. Part of it was Scottish country dancing, and I was actually quite good at doing the Scottish sword dance. So, despite my terrible shyness, that was going to be my *pièce de résistance* at the end of the Scottish section of the dancing.

We made our own tartan sashes in needlework at school, and the girls were also given pieces of white cotton material, cut out in a pattern for a Scottish country dancing style blouse with a drawstring neck and short drawstring sleeves. All very Eighteenth Century milk maid style really. I say "given", but I'm sure our parents had to pay for the material. Anyway, we were supposed to make this at home with our mothers, but Nell helped me to make it. She and I were normally given the mundane needlework jobs, although my mother had actually taught me how to darn socks. She quite liked doing that. Darning socks was a sort of weaving, using a domed wooden, er, sock darner, and as men's socks in those days were made of wool, and the leftover war ethic of "make do and mend" still being very much in use, that is what we used to do (oh those darn socks...)

Unfortunately, I used to get terrible chilblains then, even though it was summer. Those awful things, they would itch and swell, and become really very painful, especially with all the dance practice we had to do. As shy as I was though, somehow dancing like that, and enjoying it, took me into another world, my own little world, where I could be *me...*

Open Day came, and although I enjoyed the dancing, despite my shyness, my feet were hurting so badly. Nevertheless, I did it and with a lot of encouragement, actually managed to do the sword dance. Up and down, up and down, my hands on my waist, my hands in the air, up and down, up and down, between the swords, up and down; but oh dear, how my poor toes hurt being on tiptoe!

Soon though, it was time to leave that lovely little village school, and on Leaving Day our Headmaster Mr. Simpson gave us leavers (all thirteen of us) a little talk about going to the next school.

"Now, you have all been big fish in a small pond here" he said, glancing around seriously to each of us in turn, "but when you get to your next school you are going to be little fish in a *big ocean*". How true that was to be.

~

That last day we all took our brand new autograph books into school, well the thirteen leavers that is. These were small books with pages of various pastel colours, which were to be treasured forever. It was interesting to see which colour page each person chose – pale pink, pale lemon, pale green or pale blue. Each colour seemed to suit the person who had chosen it. As well as the other leavers' autographs, the teachers, Mr. Simpson included, all wrote some little thing, even if it was just "By hook or by crook – I'll be last in this book" etc., I also asked Mrs. Harry, Elizabeth's mother, if she would sign it for me.

This is what she wrote:-

"If you have friends
Then treat them as such
Don't let your friends
Know too much.
For if your friends
Should turn to foes
Then all the world
Your business knows..."

"Hmm – *see*... What did I tell you...", my mother said firmly... "Don't ever tell anyone *anything*..."

Well – after all these years, *I am now...*

~

Mr. Simpson's remarks on my leaving Orsett School report, says "*A pleasure to have in the class*", which maybe comes from the fact that it was *a pleasure for me* being in that class, and at that little school that I loved so much. He then goes on to say – "*Yvonne works hard and thoughtfully. Whatever the future holds for her – she should do very well – in every way.*"

If only I had had the chance...

~

That summer was idyllic, with long hot days spent with my friends. My friends were my saviours, as were the surrounding fields that Georgie and I would explore. But that summer also brought with it some devastating news... The local grammar schools in Grays were not accepting any more girls – boys yes, but there had been many more girls born in the "Baby Boom" just after the war. Therefore, they weren't taking any girls from the villages. Three of us had passed the "11-Plus", Robert Thompson, Elizabeth Harry, and me. Robert was obviously able to go to Palmers Grammar School for Boys, but the only option offered to Elizabeth and me though was to go to a technical college in Ockendon. This was two bus rides away, and meant us going from Orsett to Grays on the No.53 bus, then catching the Romford bus which went through Ockendon on its route. Elizabeth was going to make that journey, so I could have travelled with her.

"No, you don't want to do that" my mother told me, a phrase which had become quite a habit with her, and so my parents decided I was not going to go there. I can see their concern, but they never talked about it with *me* to see how *I* felt about doing that journey every day. I wasn't even asked – as always, I was just *told*. They protested to the authorities that if I couldn't go to Palmers Grammar School – then I wouldn't go to *any* school...

My mother had left school at the age of twelve, so she probably didn't know much about senior schooling and all that went on. It was 1939 and just before the war when my grandparents moved to Orsett and took over the Kings Arms as landlord and landlady. She said that the School Board man came round at times, but her parents just told her to hide, and told him that she had been evacuated and had gone to live somewhere else. Somehow they got away with it. This was now 1960 though, and the school boards were a little tougher on truancy then!

They gave my parents an alternative, which was that I was to go to Torells Secondary Modern School for Girls in Grays. To my mind, to go there was not much better than going to Borstal – or what I had heard about it that is. Again, my parents protested and threatened to keep me off school. I can't help but wonder whether my parents thought that going to school was an option... Maybe my mother had it in mind that my grandfather might step in and take matters in hand, saying that I had "gone away" and kept me contained at the pub in secret – just like he had done with her...

They were then threatened with prosecution, and by now the offer of going to the Technical College in Ockendon had been taken away. And so, two days later than everyone else – I went off to Torells, that dreaded establishment that I could only think of as "Borstal".

I think those Borstal boys, who we used to see working in the fields on that country bus route in Kent to Flora's, caught my attention every time. They were always out there working, and I had never seen prisoners before. I think that it was the fact that I was so often being threatened with being "taken away to a home" if I "told" that made me want to try to see if I could see them. In fact, I think they may have been happier than me. Unlike me though, they couldn't go "home" at night, but my instant aversion to Torells, and indeed my fear of going there, was very much like a punishment to me for something that, unlike the Borstal boys – I had not done.

Looking back, I think they had a far better life there than I might have done at the *nuns' home for naughty girls...*

Now I was going to *Torells...*

~

As well as leaving Orsett School, this was also to be the last summer I would spend with Georgie. We didn't actually plan to meet up again once we had gone to our new schools. He was going to Torells Boys' and I was going to Torells Girls' – *and ne'er the twain shall meet* – the stretch of no-man's land between the two schools – made sure of that!

I don't think you think about things like that at that age though. You just know that that person is *always there*. It hadn't even occurred to me that at the end of that summer, we wouldn't go around together again. But we spent that summer holiday still going on our innocent adventures, and over the barn. We didn't even speak about the possibility of not seeing each other again...

~

One Sunday morning I was sitting at the kitchen table making the batter for the Yorkshire pudding. Now I don't know whether it was the act of breaking the eggs into the bowl that prompted my mother, but she suddenly said – "Now that you're going to the big school – have you heard about *courses?*"

Yes I had heard about courses. I knew from reading my "Shirley Flight Air Hostess" book, that to become an air hostess I would have to be fluent in French and German. So although I would be taking the commercial *course*, at Torells, which also meant I would be learning French, I would also have to take a *course* in the German language, either at evening classes or at a college.

"No, *courses*" she said, irritably, "*monthly courses*. It's what happens to *big* girls – Valerie would have started them – hasn't she said anything to you?"

No, Valerie hadn't. It wouldn't have been the sort of thing she would have been talking to her little friend about anyway.

I think my mother would have preferred it if I had already known about these "courses", because she seemed highly embarrassed telling me that one day I would find a little drop of blood in my knickers, and that would be the start of them. She also said that they would stop when a woman "falls for a baby", as the blood was then used to *make the baby*. She didn't tell me anything about conception though. "You'll learn all about these things at big school" she said dismissively.

To give her her due, she did go on to say that I would find that hair was starting to grow under my arms, and "down there", as she put it, casting a quick glance down to my lap. Ah, so that explained the ginger shock when knickerless Nell had done cartwheels one day in the car park!

I can't help but wonder whether that is why the men in the taproom would lean forward, their eyes all agog when Nell did the can-can on the bar counter! She loved doing that, and she loved the attention. Sometimes she would jump up onto one of the tables and can-can on there and the men would whoop with glee – she was pretty shameless...

~

Around about this time I was getting lots of nosebleeds. Nell would normally deal with it, putting a key down my back, which was commonly thought to help nosebleeds, and telling me to lie down. Lying down was probably the worst thing to do when having a nosebleed. No-one seemed to know about stress and high blood pressure in those days.

One afternoon I was having a very copious nosebleed in the saloon bar after the pub had closed at lunchtime. For some reason we were all in there, everyone sitting around with a couple of after-time customers – and the bleeding suddenly started.

"Quick – get a key" Nell said, as all this blood was gushing out of my nose. Someone put a key down my back, and just before I was told to go upstairs and lie down – my father suddenly came out with a bit of genius...

"The problem with her is – *that it's coming out the wrong end...*"

I was *so embarrassed...*

Was this true? Was this what was really happening?

Was I *a freak?*

Strange Things Are Happening To Me

December 1960

This awful "worst year of my childhood" wasn't only about going to Torells though. Even when the Christmas holidays came along, it still wasn't over with.

I may have been dressed as a little girl when I went to school, but at home my mother was still putting make-up on me to go behind the bar.

"Now don't you take any notice of what any men might say to you", she had told me since the age of nine when I had first been made to serve behind the bar and pull pints. Just smile nicely and say "*yes?*" when they come to the bar and they will tell you what they want, she had said...

I hated it, and preferred to be around the taproom side if I had to be behind the bar at all. There was something different about saloon bar people, well, in general that is. There were a few nice people who I knew and they were kind, but sometimes we would get strangers in there, and I would be very wary of them.

A couple of men had started coming to the pub – they were strangers too. They said that they had moved in to a house on the Stifford Clays estate. I really didn't like the look of them, nor the expression on their faces when they leered over the counter at me.

They frightened me.

One evening they came in the bar and asked me how I was. I had to converse with people if that was what they wanted, otherwise my mother would be very angry with me. At that particular time I had more chilblains, which were really bad, and as I had to keep standing there, my feet were hurting all the time.

"I've got bad chilblains" I said, explaining why I wasn't looking happy.

One of them, called Trevor, told me that fresh urine was a good cure for chilblains. "I've got plenty for you" he said, leaning over towards me with an awful slimy-looking grin. "And I've some for you too" his friend Terry chipped in.

My mother and Mrs. Binns, who were both behind the bar as well, were in fits of giggles. Oh yes, it was *so* funny. Or not. *I* didn't find it funny.

I just felt awful.

~

Christmas came and went, in its normal uneventful way. My grandfather would have the option for an extension licence to open on Christmas Day. Goodness knows why he always took it up, because the pub was practically empty on Christmas Day. The day would usually pass being very boring, and Christmas dinner would be served just like any other dinner – the family taking it in turns to eat. Which is a shame really, because a lot of work had gone into plucking the turkey, which was my father's job, and the cooking of the turkey, served with all the trimmings. I would be commissioned to make the stuffing, which meant grating a loaf of bread into a large earthenware mixing bowl, chopping a couple of onions and boiling them, and then adding dried sage. To have all this preparation just eaten in separate sittings didn't seem right – especially on Christmas Day.

Mrs. Eades, a lovely plump woman who lived down the road, would make a large Christmas pudding for us every year. She would bring it up to the pub in a thick, cream-coloured pudding bowl, that had fine grey lines going through it from the many years of having been boiled for hours. Nell and I would make mince pies and sausage rolls on Christmas Eve, although sometimes Nell would leave me to it! Sadly though, Christmas was all a bit of a non-event really.

Christmas evening, a few locals would come into the off-licence to get bottles of stout, but then they would just go back to their families. I used to envy people having proper family Christmases, but this was how it had to be.

And then came New Year's Eve, the best night of the year at the pub. Grandpop would get an extended licence until one o'clock, and we always had a big party with lots of singing and dancing going on – all the normal sort of things, "Knees up Mother Brown", "The Hokey Cokey", "The Conga", leading all the way through both bars and out onto the street. Then at midnight we would all be out on the street with people who lived along the road banging dustbin lids. We would all stop to listen to the boats sounding their horns down on the river. It was magical knowing that those boatmen on the river were sharing something very special with us. I loved New Year's Eve.

But oh dear, sometime towards the end of the evening, well, ready for the midnight bells – Terry and Trevor arrived. I avoided them as much as I could, and I went outside to enjoy the celebrations. Then, once it turned midnight, I went back indoors, and they said they were going. Phew!

However...

My mother told me that they said that they had a party going on back at their house – and that they wanted Mrs. Binns – and me – to go back with them! Mrs. Binns was going, but I said I didn't want to. I was happy as I was, having just been outside enjoying all the celebrations. What's more though, I had an awful feeling about Terry and Trevor. And why were they at the pub – when they had a party going on at home?

"Of course you're going" my mother told me, "they've come all this way to pick you up". I asked her why wasn't *she* going.

"*I* don't want to go to a party" she said, "now come on, they want *you* to go... *So you're going...*"

I very reluctantly went into the lobby where a very excited-looking Mrs. Binns was waiting expectantly. Her face was all wet, being a mixture of her thick make-up and anticipation. We waited for Terry and Trevor to bring the car round. Then Nell joined us. Now I don't know whether she had been invited as well, or whether she decided to come along to keep an eye on me. I don't know, because I never asked. I was never allowed to ask the whys and wherefores of things. I couldn't help but be scared about going somewhere with these awful men – but at least now – Nell was coming too.

Mrs. Binns was wearing a gawdy, copper-coloured, lurex dress, the same colour as her hair. And Nell was wearing her normal behind-the-bar attire of a low-cut see-through lacy top, that left nothing to the imagination really. She had also had a spray of Goya's Black Rose perfume, which she had been given as a present at Christmas. I really didn't like that one. The scent was too deep and dark. Little did I know then though, how much that suited her...

"Mind they don't take you in the fuzzies! – *heh heh* " my grandmother called out, as we left. I had heard her make little jokes before about being "taken in the fuzzies". I didn't really understand exactly what she meant by that, and I assumed it was something to do with bushes...! Oh well, maybe it was! It did worry me though, hearing her call that out when I was leaving with those two scary men.

The road along to Stifford Clays was pitch black, there were no street lights, and I kept looking out for bushes... I felt sure something awful was going to happen. I couldn't actually see any bushes in the darkness, but I knew they were there. But hey – why was I so worried – we were going to a *party*...

We got to the house and just like the lane, it was in total darkness. Something shivery came over me, this feeling of total fear. My instincts were telling me to flee – but Nell and Mrs. Binns were going inside. Terry and Trevor went ahead and switched on a couple of dim lights.

If only I could have made my escape, but by now it must have been about 2am and, as always, I was doing as I was told.

Terry and Trevor were in the living room. Then they put on some music. So this was the *party* then – after all.

Nell sat down on an armchair next to the fireplace where there was a dreary two-bar electric fire, and I sat on a dining chair, all very prim and proper, with my hands clenched together in my lap. There was no way I was going to be able to relax. I am guessing they must have played other records, but the only one that stuck in my mind was one that I thought was rather "rude". I had never heard it before, well of course I hadn't, it was all about a man turning into a woman! It was really weird, and about things I had never heard of. I have never heard the song since, but I have never forgotten the chorus – it is firmly imprinted in my mind... *"Strange things are happening to me"*, and Terry and Trevor kept playing it over and over again – before they got onto the *slow music...*

~

Mrs. Binns was dancing with Terry, and Trevor tried to get me up to dance. I didn't want to, but he made me.

"Come on dance!" he kept demanding gruffly, pushing me a bit. *"Dance... Dance..."* This wasn't normal dancing as I knew it, this was smoochy sort of stuff, and he was pulling me tightly against his body. I really didn't want to do it. While all this was going on Nell was just sitting in the armchair – watching. I kept looking at her, she was just looking back at me expressionless. I remember feeling embarrassed that she was watching me being made to dance with this awful man. His hands were moving around a bit, trying to make me move with him, and he kept leaning down and pressing his face against mine. He kept trying to kiss me, and I was very aware of feeling the wetness of his mouth on my face. All the time though – Nell just watched. How *could she?* Wasn't she there to look after me? If only she could have stepped in and rescued me. But no, she just carried on *watching...*

I remember looking at Terry, who to my mind seemed the less obnoxious of the two, with a sort of look that was saying "help me". I thought that he might rescue me, because it might be better to dance with him, as I knew I *had* to dance, but he was enjoying himself with Mrs. Binns.

Trevor soon got tired of me, and grabbed Mrs. Binns from Terry. She was much more willing to do this smoochy stuff.

Terry seemed to be ok at first, well comparatively that is. He wasn't trying to hold my body as closely to his as Trevor had been. Then, Trevor and Mrs. Binns went upstairs. The stairs went straight up out of the living room, and I don't think there could have been a door on the bedroom, or else they didn't even bother to close it. We could hear noises coming from the bedroom, and soon Terry was also trying to kiss me. First he was kissing my cheeks, and I didn't like it. He seemed to be putting saliva on me, and then he was trying to kiss my mouth. By now, his hands were moving over me too, and he was gripping me very firmly to him.

I kept trying to look at Nell to get her to step in, but she still sat there in the armchair. Maybe she didn't know what to do, or maybe she just thought it best to let it all carry on. I really don't know. What I do know though, is how embarrassed I was feeling again that Nell was watching this happening to me.

Meanwhile, the grunts and the giggles were still going on upstairs in the bedroom. I felt really afraid.

"Stop it!" I said, when he tried to kiss my mouth again... *"I'm only eleven"*.

Thank God I had summoned up the strength to say that.

So Terry, with a little shove, let me go – and went upstairs and joined Trevor and Mrs. Binns in the bedroom.

Nell and I sat there in silence all the rest of the time they were up there. Sometimes she looked at me, then looked away. I really didn't know what was going on in her mind. There were more grunts and giggles going on now, and the bed was banging loudly against the wall all the time.

Eventually, the three of them came downstairs, Mrs. Binns brazenly dishevelled, and obviously having no shame in front of me.

When we got back to the pub Mrs. Binns went upstairs straight away and joined my grandfather in bed. I joined my grandmother in bed, and Nell went to the little bedroom in between the two. So far, it had been the worst night of my life. But did anyone realise that?

Probably not.

I could have been viciously raped by those two awful men. Would Nell have done anything about it though? I would hope that she would have done, but she didn't do anything at the time to stop what was going on.

And what about Mrs. Binns? She certainly wouldn't have, because she was apparently up for anything – the grunts, the giggles, the bed banging against the wall... Looking back, I don't think she would have even done anything to help me if they had forced me up to bed as well...

But Nell??

No wonder I was sworn to secrecy about things that went on...

~

The next day I met my mother in the pub lobby.

"So how was the party then?" she asked, with an enquiring expression, bordering on a grin... "Did you have a good time? *Heh heh...*"

"No!" I said, looking down..

"Well you must have done", she said. "Come on – tell me what went on".

"There wasn't a party at all" I said, not knowing whether she was aware of that or not. She didn't seem at all surprised though.

"So what did you do?" she asked inquisitively.

So had she asked Nell and Mrs. Binns about it? Probably not as she was asking me. Although maybe she was just curious as to what I felt about it. I knew that I just had to tell her myself. Being my mother, I hoped that she would realise what I had been through...

"They were trying to make me dance – both of them – and I didn't want to" I blurted out – "and then Mrs. Binns went upstairs with those two men..." Well this got her attention.

"So what happened then?" she asked, in a knowing sort of way. She looked interested, and I didn't like the look on her face. There was no look of horror or concern for me as a child.

"Well there were lots of noises", I said immediately being transported back to that living room – being so close to the foot of those stairs.

"What sort of noises?"

"Grunts – and giggling – and..."

"And what..."

"Well... A lot of banging against the wall..."

My mother started giggling. Oh that was *so* funny, wasn't it.

But *I* didn't think so. It really had been the worst night of my young life.

~

My mother didn't ask me if I was alright? She didn't seem to care about my feelings – the horror of arriving at the house and realising that there wasn't a party after all. Then those two men trying to kiss and fondle me; hearing some sort of sexual activity going on just up the stairs, with apparently an open bedroom door. I didn't even know really what they were doing, this threesome doing things that were apparently taking place on the bed. All I knew was that I was terrified that they were going to drag me up there with them...

Looking back, I know I came very close to being raped – not only by one man, but probably both of them... I was only eleven years old, and yet it was speaking up for myself at that particular time, that saved me. It could also have been the fact that there was a ready and willing woman involved...

But what was Mrs. Binns doing? Wouldn't she have cared if they had forced me upstairs to join them on the bed as well? Would she have just looked on if I had been raped? She was hardly in any fit state to intervene – or was she really that bad that she might have joined in gleefully?

And what about Nell? What was she doing – watching me struggling with these two horrible men, and not making any move whatsoever to stop them? Why did she just sit there – looking at me – not saying a word??

Apart from my grandmother, Mrs. Binns and Nell were the two women that I trusted most in the world. They both looked after me, cared for me, and made me feel safe. So how could all this have happened?

Why didn't they do *anything??*

A few years ago I was told just what Nell was all about... She is long gone now, and I still love her, with the love of an innocent child that I once was – but I can no longer respect her memory...

Yew Trees ~ And Revelations...

As I said at the beginning of this book, my name Yvonne, as well as having the meaning "Cinderella" – also means "yew tree". "Operation Yew Tree" is rather poignant to me...

The day, a few years ago, that Flora told me what her mother and my grandfather really were, I went into some kind of shock. I could not fully comprehend everything she had just been telling me.

I was absolutely distraught.

I cried and cried, so much that I was finding it hard to breathe, and I found it very difficult to focus on *anything – anything at all...*

All I could think about, was that I had been brought up by *paedophiles...*

"Oh *yes...*" Flora confirmed, when I managed to ask her if that was really true.

Had I really been brought up by *paedophiles?*

"I think you were being *groomed*" Flora said, "that's maybe why you were taken to that so-called *party...*"

I had been talking to Flora on the telephone when she told me. I had told her that I was writing a book about my childhood...

"It's not all sweetness and light" I said, a little diffidently, having been sworn to secrecy all those years ago. "I am writing about the *dark* things too..."

"Yes – you write about all those horrible things that went on!" Flora said.

I was very taken aback. I didn't know anything about what happened to her as a child during the times that she spent at the pub during school holidays...

To be told that my grandfather and his mistress Nell, who I loved and respected – were *paedophiles* – and that Nell took her daughter *to bed* with them when she was just a child, was too hard to take in...

As Flora told me more about what they used to do, my head was just spinning, trying to register what she was saying... Somehow, the room had become a misty grey blur, that not even the beauty of the summer flowers in my vase could penetrate.

This gross abuse ruined her outlook on life. It was only when she plucked up courage to tell her grandmother, with whom she was living, that she didn't have to go and stay there any more.

My mother was in her late teens then, and must have been aware of what was going on in my grandfather's bedroom – as did my grandmother. Flora feels pretty sure about this – but neither of them did anything to help her – just as neither of them did anything to help me...

The pain of the physical torture – and the mental torture – that my grandfather and mother would regularly inflict upon me stays with me always, along with other things that I really didn't understand, but thought were "normal".

Flora was now quietly crying as she was telling me these things that had been done to her. She also told me that she had only until now told her grandmother and daughter about what had happened to her all those years ago. And now – she was telling *me*...

~

With great difficulty, but with her blessing, I am relating what Flora told me went on. And yet – her story needs to be told.

How was Flora to know, at nine years old, that what happened in my grandfather's bed was wrong, when she had no knowledge beforehand of what "having sex" was all about?

How was *I* to know, at two years old, that what my grandfather was making me do was wrong?

Instinct had told me though that it was not right having to get undressed in front of men late at night sometimes, even though I was pre-puberty. However, I had to do as I was told. As with everything, I was always under the threat that if I "told" I would be taken away to a "home", which was always described to me in horrific detail.

As it was with me, Flora told me that every evening that she was at the pub, she would have to sit in the bar until the pub closed. Also, like me, she wasn't allowed upstairs in the evenings.

"I *hated* being naked in front of people" Flora told me, saying that she too had to get undressed in the bar. Then, she said, her mother would take her upstairs to bed – the bed in which she slept with my grandfather...

That was how she found out about "sex".

Flora described what would happen. They would be "doing it – having sex" she said, next to her in the bed – "sometimes him on top, sometimes her on top", and all the time my grandfather would be pleasuring himself even more by "fingering" Flora "down there..."

She said how she hated it – *absolutely hated it* – but there was nothing she could do. She was after all in bed with her mother as well...

Flora lived in fear of these times that Nell would pick her up and take her back to the pub with her, primarily it seems, to satisfy her and my grandfather's perverted urges. Then came the day that they went too far...

"I woke up in the middle of the night" Flora told me, "and found that as I was sleeping, he had pulled me down to the bottom of the bed – my legs were spread apart – and he was *licking me – down there...*"

When Flora returned home to her grandmother she was crying as usual, but this time she couldn't take it any more and told her grandmother what they had been doing to her.

Of course, her grandmother was appalled that her daughter – *her own daughter* – could do such a thing, and told Flora that she would not allow Nell to take her to the pub ever again.

However, Nell and my grandfather were not going to have their paedophilic, and indeed incestuous, urges quelled...

When Flora was twelve years old, Nell contacted her and asked her to go to the pub for a week, saying that she and my grandfather were going on holiday. Somehow, against Flora and her grandmother's better judgement, Nell was allowed to pick her up and take her back to the pub. Unfortunately, *it was a trick...* They weren't going on holiday – *after all...*

~

I think it is because I mentioned those *"dark"* things, that Flora suddenly felt able to confide in me, knowing that I had been through quite a lot at the pub as well.

"But it was worse for you" she said. "You had to *live* there..."

And yet – why the shock? Hadn't I seen the signs? Well maybe. But at the time, I didn't know what a *paedophile* was. As is normal with most children, I had to accept that my life at the pub, and indeed the way I was so badly treated, might have been normal. But really, I didn't know – because I was also told never to say a *word* about what went on there...

Flora has told me that I was always such a quiet and shy little girl, and seemed so nervous all the time...

Looking back, as hard as it is sometimes for me, everything is clicking into place. Things that went on that I didn't understand. Things that I instinctively thought were *wrong* – but didn't know *why*...

My family knew what they were doing, and that is why I was sworn to secrecy. If Flora had said anything about what was happening to her, then her mother and my grandfather could have very well spent many miserable years in prison. Which is what several elderly men are enduring right now – in some cases maybe, for much less a crime than what Flora and I had to endure.

Operation Yew Tree... Indeed...

The Lipstick

One day I was sitting at the kitchen table doing whatever I was doing – it may have been painting, drawing, writing, whatever I was engrossed in – when my mother came in and put a lipstick in front of me.

"Put that on..." she instructed.

The lipstick appeared to be new – she might have chosen it especially for me – or maybe it was a wrong choice for her. It wasn't her colour though, so I think the former option was probably the case.

I took the top off, and looked inside. There was a pointed luscious looking lipstick – that looked as though it needed to be enjoyed! I pushed the little knob at the bottom up to expose the lipstick. Some of them were like that in those days. Well the more reasonably priced ones that is. It was only the expensive ones like my mother wore – Helena Rubenstein in all their shades of red – that you twisted at the bottom to expose the lipstick.

It certainly wasn't *my* colour though. At the age of twelve I shouldn't have been wearing lipstick anyway, but being made to, a pale pearly pink would have been more in order.

I sat peering at this lipstick. It was bright tangerine – or more blood orange, in my opinion.

I didn't like it. I hadn't actually seen a lipstick in that shade before.

"Put it on!" my mother repeated – "and leave it on until your father comes home..."

But why?

I went off to the bathroom, and looked in the mirror above the sink. My face was pale, my eyes were tired, and I looked emaciated. There was no way that applying a simple lipstick was going to make me look or feel any better.

I pursed my lips – and applied it. My lips looked like a cupid's bow. The small curves being exaggerated by that awful vampish colour.

I went back to the kitchen to where my mother was waiting.

"Now, don't you look nice... Heh-heh..." she said.

No, I didn't. I looked like a tart. Or whatever I thought a tart might have equated to at the time.

I went back to what I was doing. I was still a child, doing what children do, drawing, painting, or whatever.

Later my father came home. The lipstick was still coating my little lips.

"Your lips look very kissable today..." he said when he saw me...

I ran back to the bathroom – and rubbed frantically at my mouth. When I looked in the mirror I saw the awful stain I had made across my mouth and chin – the colour of a blood orange...

My Little Nellie

Nell had a very kindly face – soft, round and smiling. Well, smiling visually when she wasn't being hurt by my grandfather, either physically or mentally. I have seen many things that have been done to her. I have seen her crying with pain and anguish. Yet, she still stayed at the pub, despite the way she was treated sometimes.

My grandmother took advantage of her, and so did my mother. But really, they had good cause. There are not many wives who would allow their husband's mistress to move in with them, and sleep with him in his bed.

So why did Nell put up with all this? What was it that kept her by his side? My grandmother stayed with him because she didn't want to lose her status as landlady of the Kings Arms. But what was in it for Nell? What was it about my grandfather that appealed to her so much? Why had she left her home and young children to move into a household where the wife still lived, and who treated her like a skivvy? This was something that once I was old enough, I began to ponder. And yet, throughout my childhood I had accepted the whole thing as being *normal*...

Everyone liked Nell. In the little shop that we had next to Ivy Cottages, and which she willingly ran despite all the work she had to do at the pub, she was seen as the kindly lady who weighed out the vegetables, the fruits and the sweets, and who had a chair in the corner of the shop for anyone who wanted to stay awhile and chat...

She would listen to other women's problems, some rather intimate – especially the woman with the growth hanging down between her legs that wobbled as she walked! Although as I have previously said, they didn't know she was passing these confidences on.

The things I have heard when sitting in the kitchen with Nell, my grandmother and my mother, sharing a pot of tea! Women's talk it may have been – but I was sometimes there – and I think they thought it was all going over my head. But not quite! Wobbly things between a woman's legs? What were they?

It was only because of my grandfather's and my grandmother's boyfriend Fred's naked bodies that I had encountered, and that I had two little brothers, that I knew that *boys and men* had wobbly things between their legs! But a woman? What on earth could they have been talking about?

~

Another thing that my mother and grandmother were talking about in the kitchen over my head – they seemed to think I was either totally deaf or invisible as usual – or maybe didn't really care – was something that Nell had related to them one day...

There were two women who were neighbours and they had fallen out, because one of them had accused the other of being after her husband. It seemed that sometime they had come to blows. In those days women rolling up sleeves, trying to show forearm muscles that meant business, went on.

Well the wife won.

At least they had a fence between their gardens, but this didn't hide – the washing line...

The wife told Nell that to get back at her neighbour for being after her husband and apparently giving him a bit of a come-on, every time she hung his pants out on the washing line, she would look over at her neighbour's window, who she reckoned spied on her all the time, and passionately kiss the crotch of his pants!

~

My grandfather always called Nell "My little Nellie". He obviously loved her very much, even though he was so cruel to her. Well, he was very cruel to all of us at times – except my mother and brothers.

"Why did you marry him?" my mother asked my grandmother one day, when he had been particularly violent towards her. This was the day of the wet tea-towel being pulled around her neck – and the greasy pot of water that she had been cooking the bacon joint in, being tipped over her head.

"Because he was always so nice to me..." she answered.

Well, he could be quite a charmer when he wanted to be, and in old photos he does look rather handsome. How could my grandmother have known then what a monster he turned out to be at times? Maybe she should have seen the signs? For the signs are always there – whether we take notice of them – or not – as I found out to my detriment some years later...

Nell, however, must have known what he was like. After all, her sister Lil had been taken in by his charms, and had gone to live at the pub with him before Nell joined them.

"This really isn't on, Arthur" Auntie Doris told my grandfather when she realised what was going on. He took no notice – he liked having three in a bed, especially as they were sisters...

Nell obviously shared his weird sexual activities, although I never knew the truth about this until recent years. There was always something very strange about her...

~

Although I didn't realise at the time, I was far too young to know about these things, looking back, I noticed there was something not quite right about Nell on a few occasions when we had other babies and little children come to the pub. Nell was always willing to take them on for a day – she had a knack of keeping children amused and happy. Whether she was paid to do this I do not know. She seemed to enjoy having the little ones in her care though occasionally. She was known for her love of children, and people trusted her.

I trusted her too. She was the archetypical kindly woman. Her round face, permed hair, and short plump stature, summed up the essence of old-fashioned motherhood. The comfortable old chair with the well-worn cushions that she had in the corner of her shop, was there for the local women to sit and chat, and talk about their husbands and their many intimate problems!

So, being trusted to her care, little children would sometimes be left with Nell for the day.

I can't really recall any little girls being left with her, but I do remember little boys...

Sometimes she would bathe them and get them ready to be picked up by their parents later in the evening. She was very kind like that. Sometimes they would be bathed in the bathroom, and sometimes in the old butler's sink in the kitchen.

Once I went into the kitchen. There was a little boy in the sink and I saw her pulling back what I later found out was his foreskin. I didn't like seeing it at all, but Nell told me that it had to be done. The little boy wasn't protesting, he was splashing his little arms and legs, seemingly totally oblivious to what was being done to him. I turned away and went back to whatever I had been doing. The image of that little red tip being exposed like that, stayed with me. It was horrible.

I now know that this shouldn't have been done anyway. It can cause many problems, including infection, and contrary to what Nell thought – problems in later life. But she did it. I only saw it being done the once – and that was enough.

Another time, I was walking along the landing and Nell was in the woodworm room with two little boys. A lot of giggling and playful shrieking was going on. The two little boys were lying on the bed naked, and Nell was nuzzling their genitals in turn.

"Broooo-mmmm... Broooo-mmmm..." she was going, really pushing her face into them, and shaking her head as she was doing it. They seemed to be loving it – they were too young to know any different. To them it was all a game. I don't know whether this was a normal occurrence or not, but to me, as young as I was, it just didn't seem right, and made me feel rather uncomfortable..

To this day, I can't help but wonder – what on earth did she think she was doing? Did those little boys ever refer to it? Probably not. They were far too young to remember – or were they?

~

When I was about five or six years old, I used to get very sore on my bottom and between my legs. This must have been caused by the printing ink on the newspaper that we had to use at the pub for toilet paper. Even when my family discovered Izal toilet paper, which we also had at school, it was so slippery on one side and scratchy on the other – it even smelled of the disinfectant that we used to clean the toilets! This toilet paper was appropriately known as "shinies"! Amusingly, across the top of every slippery square was written the words "Now wash your hands please". Did people *really* have to be reminded to wash their hands after going to the toilet?

So, a combination of black newsprint and later disinfectant impregnated toilet paper, must have caused all this intimate soreness (well I am guessing that was what it was).

Sometimes it would make me cry. Well Nell was always to hand with the pot of cream. She would lay me across the bed in the woodworm room, either on my front or my back, depending on where the soreness was, spread my legs, and liberally apply the cream. I thought it was normal to have cream put into my bottom, even though it felt odd. It also felt rather odd having it applied between my legs. I suppose though that at the time nothing else could be done to ease my soreness. The time that I saw Nell enthusiastically nuzzling those little boys though, made me feel that something really wasn't *quite right*.

Who knows what young children think about these things? They trust adults to help them and to do what is right, without even thinking about the possibility that the trusted adult might even be *enjoying it*.

There came the time when I didn't complain any more about my sore bottom or the soreness between my legs. Even at such a young age, something was telling me that something wasn't quite right.

~

I don't really know what to make of "My Little Nellie". Outwardly, she was always smiling and fun loving, especially when she was up on the bar counter of the taproom or the tables doing the "can-can", which was obviously to the delight of every man in the bar – and she loved that. Living at the Kings Arms obviously suited her, even though she had to be up at six every day to clean the pub before making breakfast.

There may have been a very deep sadness within her though. How could anyone leave their three young children to go and be someone's mistress in the house that he shared with his wife and daughter? If she wasn't deeply sad about doing this, then there must have been something very strange and sinister.

Nell had given birth to a baby when she was a teenager, and unmarried. It was a little girl. No-one seems to know the truth about what happened though. Did the baby die – or was she killed? That is a deeply sad notion to ponder, but no-one really knows. What people did know though, was that she buried the poor little soul in allotments somewhere in a dark corner of Kent near her home...

I can't help but wonder how often this sort of thing might have happened in those days. Were some girls and women so keen to hide their pregnancies – and then dispose of the baby? And who was this little mite's father? Was he the soldier in the photo that she had shown me so many times, along with a photo of her three children? That is of course before her handbag in which she kept them was wickedly stolen.

~

Sometime later, Nell became pregnant again – this time by a sailor. She gave birth to another little girl – and named her *Flora*...

Whenever the sailor's ship was coming in to Chatham Docks, Nell would go to the quayside, holding her baby, wrapped in a finely hand-knitted white shawl. Flora's father though was always alerted to this, and would somehow be let off the ship at some other place so he wouldn't have to be confronted by her. At these times she didn't know what had happened, and would wait there for ages holding her baby. My mother and grandmother spoke about this in my presence many years ago. I think that, as usual, they thought that what they were saying was just going over my head, but these things made me curious about what had gone on. In recent years Flora has confirmed this sad story to me.

Nell eventually married Flora's father when Flora was three years old. She still feels embarrassed that she was born illegitimately. How times change! Then along came her two younger brothers. Her father wasn't the best of fathers to her, which added to her childhood trauma. Flora and I have since realised that we had somewhat similar experiences as children. Not the same, but the emotional scarring was there for both of us. No wonder we have such a very special bond.

The marriage lasted until 1950 when her father divorced Nell citing my grandfather as co-respondent. This was heard in the Divorce Court in London, and being regarded as a "poor person", Flora's father didn't have to pay any costs.

~

Flora has told me that she would have loved to have had a sister – that little baby girl that is buried somewhere in Kent, without even a little wooden cross. Did Nell ever go and kneel at her grave at twilight when no-one else was around? Did she ever put flowers on that little bit of ground that was her grave? I don't suppose anyone would know that – other than Nell. Exactly where that little grave is – only "Little Nellie" knew...

The Court Case

At this point, I must add in a combination of what I have been told by Flora, and what we have found out from old press archives.

First of all my mother had mentioned this to me shortly before she died. She told me that there had been a "big" court case in London regarding the divorce between Nell and her husband, which also involved my grandfather. According to my mother it had made the News of the World and The People, which were eminent Sunday newspapers at the time. They would grab these big stories, and my mother said it was one of the biggest stories in those days. Unfortunately, she didn't tell me what it was all about at the time, I could tell it was something she didn't want to discuss with me herself but, deep down, she wanted me to know. She just said "Go to Somerset House – and look it up..."

She should have said "The British Library", but try as we may, we haven't found anything in either of those two newspapers. However, there *was* another newspaper that *did* print what had happened.

It is a very interesting story...

~

"Bedroom story 'quite incredible' says judge" was the headline.

Flora was fifteen then and had long since stopped going to the Kings Arms. Her grandmother had taken care of that when Flora, after three years of sexual abuse, eventually told her about what she was going through with her mother and my grandfather.

Flora was nonetheless called to Court though as a witness to give evidence against them, although I don't know what she was expected to say... Her grandmother, with whom she was living along with her two younger brothers, dutifully took her on what was then a long journey by bus and train to London, and before going to the Court, Flora clearly remembers being taken to Madame Tussaud's. Having left there they walked in the direction of the Court. It was then that Flora noticed her father walking in the direction of the Court too.

"You're not going..." her grandmother said suddenly, spotting Flora's father. He was on a mission, and was using his daughter in his favour to sue my grandfather.

"They'll pull you to bits!" her grandmother said – "we're going home – now!"

With Flora having been spared the trauma of giving evidence against her mother, and having to say things that she really didn't understand, let alone talk about, her father was then left without his most important witness.

So, the Court case proceeded without Flora – but *my* grandmother *was* called to the stand...

My mother told me that my grandmother committed the criminal act of perjury, and denied that anything untoward had gone on – she knew that if there was any scandal involving an underage child, my grandfather would lose his licence, and she didn't want to relinquish her status of landlady of the Kings Arms.

The divorce case went ahead and Flora's father gave his testimony...

The newspaper report went on to say that he told the judge that he had returned on leave from the Navy and found his wife in bed with the landlord of the establishment where she was working. Why he went there I do not know... Maybe he had arrived home in Kent and then been told where his wife was? Whatever the reason, he had gone to the Kings Arms.

He claimed that he had watched his wife and my grandfather in bed for about ten minutes... Whether or not they were aware of him standing there watching is not known – or shall I say – not reported. Strangely, he made no protest, and then apparently retired to another bedroom and spent the night smoking.

He then declared that the next morning he, his wife and my grandfather all had breakfast together...

It seems that he didn't tell Nell, nor anyone else, what he had watched them doing, and only told his solicitors four years later. It was then that he decided to divorce his wife and sue for damages from my grandfather – apparently £500 – which was an awful lot of money in those days.

The judge said at the time "this is just about an incredible story as one can imagine." Yes, indeed.

When I read about this recently my heart shot down to my stomach. I didn't know that this revelation would affect me so badly, especially with the way I had been brought up at the pub. I actually felt sickened – totally sickened – knowing that the family into which I had been born were this decadent. Even though I grew up with the foreboding darkness of the Kings Arms and all its secrets, including the awful things that I had to endure, I am still cringing with the revelations of these other bad activities that had gone on.

Dismissing my grandfather from the suit, the judge found that Nell had deserted her husband in July 1946, and granted Flora's father a divorce. The claim for the £500 in damages against my grandfather was also dismissed. The judge concluded by saying that according to Nell's evidence, the alleged bedroom incident between her and my grandfather was only in her husband's imagination...

Maybe saying that he had stood and watched the sex act between his wife and my grandfather – for ten minutes – hadn't given him the credibility that he had sought. Besides, what husband would do that?

The Day We Discovered Toilet Rolls!

One day my mother discovered Andrex toilet paper. There was a newly-opened supermarket in Grays (*old Grays that is!*) and my mother went off to investigate this new way of shopping. Until then we had relied on supplies to the pub, the produce that Nell sold in the shop, and meat from Dodd's the butcher down in the village. There was also the pie man who brought fresh pork pies and steak pies to the pub, which would be heated and then kept in the airing cupboard to keep warm! No health & safety in those days then! But then again, would a Health & Safety Inspector actually look in the airing cupboard?

Toilet rolls are now an accepted daily essential, and have been for decades – former footballer Francis Lee made a fortune out of them. If there was ever a daily essential in life – apart from our "daily bread", then it has to be toilet paper!

Well my mother went off to the supermarket and came home with something new – it was a pink Andrex toilet roll. Just one – wrapped individually – well there was no point buying more than one if it wasn't as good as newspaper or Izal!

My mother let me try it – and hey – I was in toilet paper heaven! It was as soft as its pale pink colour depicted. This wasn't going to be around for long just being the one toilet roll. So my mother hid it and only let selected people use it – of which, thankfully, I was one. So for the first time in my life, I was in on one of her little secrets – maybe it was the only time...

Well the toilet roll ran out of course, and the next Saturday my mother took me to the supermarket to do some shopping with her. She had found a pack of not one – but two pink Andrex toilet rolls! In those days there weren't any plastic bags for packing your shopping, well not that I can recall. Marks & Spencer put our purchases into brown paper bags with string handles, but as far as I remember regarding other shops, we would take our own proper shopping bags, or more usually, a shopping basket.

This was the first time I had ever been in a self-service shop. I am sure my eyes were wide with wonder, seeing the packed shelves with so much to choose from, and so many varieties of each product.

So there we were in this new supermarket, queuing in one of the narrow aisles that led to the checkout. Then it was all down to the checkout girl (and they *were* all female then) looking at the price on the ticket, and tapping it into the till – there weren't any bar codes in those days. So if any inaccuracies occurred, it was all down to the checkout girl.

When we eventually reached the checkout, my mother got quite agitated, and told me to get hold of the toilet rolls first.

"Put them in the bag first" she said, and I'm guessing her face was as pink as the rolls! "Now – push them right down to the bottom of the bag" she said, "we don't want anyone on the bus seeing us with, er, toilet rolls" she whispered.

~

Toilet rolls weren't the only unspeakable items of the time. The word "knickers" always caused a chuckle, no matter what had caused what some deemed a "rude" word to be mentioned!

On some of our little sorties into Grays town, we would walk up Grays High Street, wait at the level crossing if a train was on its way, and then go over onto the other side of the town. That is when we would go to "Joyes" the shop that sold all the strange looking corsets, and other such items that worried me about being the day when I would grow into being a woman. Did I really have to be pushed, pulled and laced into one of these awful contraptions?

Well, just the other side of the level crossing was a shop called "Pollards". I don't remember ever going in there, because it wasn't the sort of shop my mother would normally frequent.

Out the front, spilling well onto the pavement, there were boxes of all sorts of things, anything really that I think Pollards could get their hands on.

At weekends, there was also a boy, obviously doing a Saturday job, always standing at the front...

"Come and get your knickers ladies" he would call out, holding up all manner of strange looking underwear, like bloomers, things like that. He would also hold up tea-towels – I never could quite see what they had to do with knickers!

He was a geeky sort of lad, very thin and gawky looking, and with thick, black-rimmed glasses.

"Come and get your knickers ladies" he would call out every time he saw us walking by. Hey – that got to me every time! There was no way I would want to wear underwear sold by someone like that, and in that sort of fashion. It would be *so* embarrassing.

"That boy's looking at you again" my mother would say, each time we walked past the shop. Huh – what? Well, I wasn't looking at *him!* I used to avoid his gaze every time we walked past – on to Joyes, where my mother could buy her flesh coloured "big" knickers in privacy!

~

These were the Saturday afternoons that my mother and I would go down to Grays on the bus because my father would be working. Sometimes though, when he had a Saturday off, he would take us in the car, and would walk around with us. Having been in the butchery trade just after the war, well in a *slaughterhouse,* he knew all about meat.

"The darker the beef – the better" he would say when helping to choose the Sunday joint, adding that it would be much better if it had been *hanging* for longer since slaughter...

Then it would be the fish monger's – and the *eels,* being the complete opposite, having to be kept fresh – and chopped up alive... *Ugh!*

So these shopping trips when my father accompanied us were not the sweetest...

Going home by car, my father, whether it was then or earlier years, would always take a diversion around one of the back streets. He would park the car on the left hand side of the road, then walk across to the barber's. I knew it was a barber's because it had the distinctive red and white striped pole on the wall.

I never understood though *why* – when he came back to the car – he hadn't had a hair cut...

Maybe he had got something for the weekend – Sir?

The Worst Thing To Wish Upon Someone...

One night, it was after time, all the customers had gone home, and I was upstairs. Suddenly, I heard a lot of ranting and raving coming from the saloon bar – it seemed to be going on and on...

I rather diffidently crept downstairs to see what was going on, and stood at the bottom of the stairs hoping I would get the gist of it. Well I didn't have to try too hard – my grandfather was absolutely raging and shouting abuse at my mother.

I couldn't just stand there, and went out into the lobby and stood in the open doorway to the saloon bar.

"... And I hope you get cancer – and die a slow and very painful death..." my grandfather was shouting.

Goodness knows what my mother had done to deserve this abuse, especially as they were always so close. At the time, it was the worst thing I had ever heard said to another human being.

My father brushed past me and went upstairs.

Ralf and Colin had chosen to stay at the pub that particular night and were in the fourth bedroom. I didn't know what to do. I was looking from Mummy to Nanny to Nell, and they were all looking back at me while my grandfather was still carrying on... No-one tried to usher me out of the way. For all anyone knew, he could have suddenly turned on *me*... Everyone knew he wasn't averse to inflicting pain on me at times.

My father came downstairs with Ralf and Colin in their pyjamas, and beckoned my mother to the door. She too brushed past me, without a second glance. Then they took my brothers down to the bungalow with them for the night – and left me to it.

I just turned and ran back upstairs to the relative safety of my grandmother's bedroom – and hoped my grandfather hadn't seen me.

Overall though, knowing what a violent and sadistic mood my grandfather was in – why hadn't my parents taken me down to the bungalow with them? Didn't they care what might have happened to me?

I wonder whether my grandfather remembered saying this, when my mother died two years before he did – with bowel cancer – a very painful death indeed...

Be careful what you wish for...

PART 2

EARLY TEENAGE TRIALS

A Small Fish In A Big Ocean

The girl who came late...

Having once been "the girl who came back" when I returned to Orsett School after being at Little Thurrock for two years, at Torells, I was now "the girl who came late"!

The fact that I had started two days late got me known as this straight away. When I was asked why, I innocently told them that I had passed the 11-Plus examination and should have gone to Palmers Girls' Grammar School – and not Torells.

Oh dear... Oh dear... Big mistake. This got everyone going, and I was very soon crowded by girls, all apparently wanting to get a glance at this new girl. Girls were asking me questions, I was trying to answer, whilst all the time wondering why I was being seen as so *different.*

The initial interest soon turned into little sneers and other such things – nudges on my shoulders that made me jump, things like that. I felt as though I was on some kind of whirligig, turning around and around. It was as though I was like a little sparrow, suddenly finding itself in a crow's nest. Or maybe a little lame duck – as I was later called...

Finding out that I lived in the pub didn't help either. What was I to say when I was asked where I lived? I didn't know then that my parents had always put my address down as being the same as theirs – the bungalow...

Why had my parents never used the Kings Arms as my address? Was there some bad connotation attached to the pub? I really didn't know. All I knew was that it was where I lived...

My mother, in her usual dismissive way, told me to ignore them, saying that they were just "jealous" of me. I didn't want anyone to be jealous of me though. And besides, they had no reason to be. How could anyone be jealous of me living in a pub?

More to the point though, how could anyone be jealous of the way I was dressed!

I knew, and could feel deep in my soul, that I shouldn't be there. I should have been at Palmers Grammar School. I should have been wearing that smart navy blue uniform, and feeling very proud.

There was a school uniform at Torells, maroon and blue, but to wear it was optional. It was far too late to buy me a uniform anyway, and besides, hardly anyone at Torells wore it. I wore a white blouse, a cardigan that my grandmother had knitted for me, and as it still fitted me, I had to wear the blue and white striped skirt that I had worn in my last year at Orsett School.

My mother bought me a navy blue gabardine raincoat with a hood, but oh dear, it had to last me the four years that I was going to be there, and was so big it went almost down to the ground. Nell sewed the cuffs back for me because they hung well over my hands, but that coat absolutely swamped me.

Moreover though – horror of horrors – the new shoes my mother bought me to wear to this school were what I called "pancakes". This was because they were so flat! They were navy blue childrens' sandals, the type with the wide T-strap – like Start Rite sandals! They were awful, and I felt dreadful starting at the "big" school wearing those, especially when I found that all the other girls were wearing normal shoes.

There was even worse to come. I grew out of them fairly quickly – well, I think I exaggerated how much they were starting to pinch my toes – because I just wanted to get rid of them. I even tried to scuff the soles, dragging my feet on the ground when I was cycling sometimes.

"There's plenty of wear left in them yet", my mother said, turning them over and looking at the rubber soles. Then my father got a Stanley knife – and cut the toes out!

No matter what the weather, that was how I had to go to school, until they fitted no more. No water ever penetrated those sandals though – when it rained or snowed I was given a pair of see-through plastic overshoes that did up with press-studs to keep my feet dry... I hated those things! But what could I do when I had the toes cut out of my sandals...

~

My mother then had a thing about my hair – and made me wear a hairnet to school. The hairnet wasn't as thick as Ena Sharples' in Coronation Street at the time, it was finer than that, but it still came down onto my forehead. I looked so stupid. The first day I wore it I kept it on – because my mother told me I had to. But oh dear, the jeers I got from the other girls. What on earth had got into her head though? She did have some very strange ideas.

"Always dress correctly" my mother would insist whenever we went anywhere together. It always had to be my best coat, best shoes – and gloves. Somehow though things were rather different if I was going somewhere without her...

~

I think that there is a lot in favour of school uniforms, and I feel sure I would have felt so much better if we had all been dressed the same. That would have given me a feeling of *belonging* – which I never had. My mother might have still made me go to school with a hairnet on my head, and my father might have still cut the toes out of my shoes when they got too small, but I feel my parents would have been promptly told not to send me to school like that.

School uniforms even up all classes throughout the spectrum of rich to poor, so no child has to feel poorer than any others. They may be expensive to buy at first, but with having to wear the same as everyone else, it saves all the business of fretting about what to wear to school, and whether your clothes are as good as what the others are wearing. So with there being no competition in the "fashion" stakes, it saves a lot of money in the long run.

I would have loved to have worn a school uniform. It would have made me feel more "part" of the school, rather than just the "girl who came late", having to say why, and therefore not really fitting in.

I remember my mother telling me one afternoon about how proud she was of my cousin Lyn, who was one year older than me, going to Grammar School. She went on about how lovely she looked in her uniform, which was a grey blazer, grey pleated skirt, red and white striped blouse, and a red tie. I felt envious of her, and my mother's pride in her. But Lyn's uniform was very much the same as that of the technical school that had been offered to me... So would my mother have been as proud of *me* if I had been wearing a school uniform? I will never know...

~

Not all the girls there were bad though. In fact there were a few really nice ones. But with friendships being formed during those crucial first days that I had missed, and with girls being girls, I was pretty much on my own to start with.

Once I had settled down in my class with the other girls at the top of the stream, I soon knew to keep with them, and not go near any of the other ones. I also realised that it was not a good thing to tell anyone else that I had passed the 11-Plus – and I never did. That was another secret I had to keep, even though I was very proud of that achievement...

~

And so – it still carried on. Throughout my years there I was made to feel as though I was "odd". From an odd family maybe, but I really didn't think there was anything odd about *me...*

I longed to be like the other girls. Not the way some of them behaved, but I just wanted to *belong...*

~

So all these things brought me an awful lot of attention – and in a way that was most unwelcoming. One of the first things that happened was when I was in a toilet cubicle, sitting on the seat, and I heard some giggling. It was then that I realised there were girls in the next cubicle standing on the toilet looking down at me. As soon as I looked up and saw them – they pulled the chain of my toilet – cisterns were high level in those days. It was so humiliating.

Other times they would look under the toilet door at me, and to this day I am still nervous when going in a public toilet if there are children around. The fear has never left me.

~

Forming lifelong friendships...

How had fate deemed it that I would not go to a Grammar School? Life was so unfair. *Everything* was unfair to me during those years.

"Not fair..." my father would mimic me whenever I complained about my situation, whether at school or at home, "like the hairs on a black man's chest" he would add with a chuckle. Then that would be the end of it. There was no point at all complaining. If ever I said *"well..."* in trying to explain myself, my father would always answer "A well's a deep hole". So that would be the end of that. My mother and father always had their same stock answers.

"You're old enough and *ugly* enough to know better", my mother would scold stony-faced. It was always the same if I dare to chastise my brothers for their torment. Calling me that did nothing for my self-confidence, and for years I really did think I was *ugly*. I must have been – because my mother told me so...

Looking back at old photos of when I was a child though, I can see that I was a pretty little girl. Well, up until I went to Torells. It was then that I was looking very gaunt, and often ill. I was even sent to school when I had German measles because no-one believed I was that ill.

My grandfather always wrote my excuse letters for not attending school. This was because he had beautiful handwriting, and my mother said it would have more credence if he wrote them. If he deemed me well enough to go to school, even if I was ill, he would say that if I stayed home – then he wouldn't write me an excuse letter. So I spent many miserable days at school, when I should have been tucked up in bed at home. I don't know how the teachers didn't notice, but somehow I managed to keep my feelings to myself.

~

My dear friend Emma, who I had met at Little Thurrock Primary School during the two years I was there, was now at Palmers Grammar School – where I should have been too – and although we still stayed friends by means of birthday and Christmas cards, we didn't see each other any more during those following years.

However, that other pretty little girl called Alison, who I had also met at Little Thurrock, was now at Torells and in my class. Like me she was very shy, and maybe a little too timid for the other girls. One day we were both alone in the playground at lunchtime, just wandering around, looking at the ground and, with me at least, feeling like I was in the Borstal exercise yard. Well we started talking about how we had recognised each other from Little Thurrock, and that as they say, was the beginning of a beautiful friendship...

I say beautiful, but in the way that we mentally clung to each other. We went through puberty together, bought our first eye make-up together, sneaked into a shop to secretly buy a rose scented Mum Rollette together, even though neither of us needed it. We talked about boys for the first time together, and *loved Elvis* together.

When we had to be apart for any time, we would write letters to each other. When we got to around fourteen years old, we would write about our excitement about a forthcoming dance, where we would dance together – around our handbags. We also wrote about boys who might have been looking at us, nothing else – just having a boy looking at you was enough. It was all so sweet and innocent. This friendship has lasted throughout all these years – albeit from afar – except... I had to keep my many home secrets from her, not daring to tell her what went on at the pub...

~

And so – there we were at Torells, Alison my only school friend now. Unfortunately, she wasn't always there. Whenever she was off sick for any reason, she would be at home for at least two weeks, sometimes three. She had persuaded me to take sandwiches to school, rather than have the school lunch, and we used to eat those together in the playground. As we were the only girls having sandwiches, I spent lots of times in our "sandwich corner" (which we affectionately called "samwij corner") on my own.

Sometimes on a hot day in the summer term, I would lay on the grass during lunchtime, and look up at the sky. Fluffy white clouds would make their way gracefully across the azure sky and I would ponder about the universe. What was beyond? Where did the galaxy end? Were we, the earth, the moon, and all the other planets and stars – all in a big bubble? If so, what if the bubble burst... And then – what was beyond the bubble? Were there more bubbles?

~

Valerie had left Torells a couple of years before I started, and Georgie was at the Boys' School. Oh dear the rules in those days. The tennis courts separated the Girls' School from the Boys', and each side of them were green swards that were there purely to keep us all apart. When we left school in the afternoon the girls were let out ten minutes before the boys – so that they could make a quick getaway before they came out. Didn't work! I am sure this doesn't happen these days...

I always wanted to get away quickly anyway to get home. I was always in front of the other girls, trying to avoid having my headscarf pulled off and being laughed at. Or anything else being pulled off for that matter.

~

One day I had the humiliation of being punished for something, which yet again wasn't really my fault. I had been picked to ring the bell at 3.45pm to mark the end of the school day. When I first started Torells, I knew that I needed a wristwatch. Whether going by bus or cycling, it was best to know the time. As it happened I had a late pass because I lived in Orsett and the buses were not reliable, so if ever I was unable to be at school by the designated time, I would show this to the prefects on guard at the main gate.

True to form, my mother wouldn't let me have a watch. She would say that I *could – maybe – some other time –* and this was her stock answer to whenever I asked her. She even promised me that she would buy me a marquisette watch, which wasn't really what I needed, because it was a dress watch. I just needed a plain wristwatch that kept good time and was reliable.

My father understood my need for a watch, but he couldn't go against my mother and buy me one. So he gave me one of his old watches which didn't have a strap. As was normal in those days, this was one that needed to be wound up every day. I kept it in my purse, which I kept in my school bag, and every time I wanted to see the time I had to get it from there. It wasn't a simple thing.

So this particular day when I had to ring the school bell – I had to go to wherever the bell was kept, strictly on time, and ring it at 3.45pm. Oh dear – what happened? I had excused myself from class to go and ring the bell, and for some unknown reason my teacher didn't query me – even though it was before 3.30pm... (Didn't she know that it wasn't really time for the bell?) No wonder my father no longer used that watch, because it was totally unreliable.

So there I was ringing the school bell, letting out all the girls fifteen minutes early... Surely someone could have stopped me?

I was in deep trouble for this, and the next day I was punished by having to stand under the clock in the hall at 3.45pm until every girl in the school had filed past me to go home...

I couldn't help but hear the sniggers as they passed me...

I still have that watch. It may be a reminder of that terrible day at the school that embarrassed me so much – and as unreliable as my family – but it was my father's...

~

Cycling became one of my big passions then, along with tennis – and Elvis...

To my utter delight I was bought a bike. I think it was second-hand, but that really didn't matter. It was a metallic red Raleigh bicycle, and I took to it straight away. All I had to do was get on the saddle and put my feet on the pedals – and away I went... It came so naturally to me.

I couldn't wait to get home from school – and onto my bike! First of all I would cycle all around Orsett, roads that I knew all too well, and road sense and the Highway Code came to me all so naturally. Then I would cycle along to Stifford Clays and back. There were lots of corners along that road, but no matter, I knew what I was doing – and was happy.

One evening I decided to be a little brave and cycle to Horndon-on-the-Hill, which wasn't as far away as I had first thought. I cycled down to Orsett and then through the Whitmore roads, then onwards to Horndon. I saw such pretty houses that I had never noticed in such detail when being a passenger in a car.

Little by little, I ventured further and further. Next it was Laindon Hill, and Langdon Hills, where bluebells grew in the woods in profusion. It was hard work getting up Laindon Hill. The only way to cycle was in first gear, so I would usually walk up with my bike. But oh the joy of freewheeling back down again...

The sense of freedom would course through me... I was at one with nature – and myself...

From there I ventured further, and one evening I found myself at the outskirts of a new town – it was called Basildon. How had I cycled that far? Yes – I had! The sign told me where I was. I had heard of Basildon, but had never been there before. From where I sat on my bike, my legs astride on the ground holding my balance, there lay before me a totally different landscape to what I was used to. I could see that it was indeed a rather different town to what I knew.

The houses all looked sort of *square* and in hues of grey – actually a bit like Grays in colour. Unlike Grays though, in those days, these houses were all rather more like boxes. I couldn't help but think of Pete Seeger's song "Little Boxes", which was a hit at the time. He was right! But there wasn't a green one – and a pink one – and a blue one – and a yellow one – they were all *grey*...

~

Unfortunately, Alison couldn't ride a bike, neither could she play tennis. It wasn't her fault. She was so delicate, and hadn't been brought up in a predominately male environment like I had. Her mother had warned her (and me when I was at their house) never to go near any boys – the complete opposite of *my* mother who *preferred me* to have boys as friends. Her bright blue eyes would smile at me whenever we met up, showing me that we were best friends... So always being paired with Alison at school meant I didn't have anyone to play tennis with.

Maybe I should have spoken up and told the games teacher that I really *really* wanted to play tennis, but I was always too shy to speak up for myself. So it was back to the pub car park and the washing line to play! I used to practise and practise in the car park, hitting the ball against the back of the pub. Having the wall hitting the ball back to me though wasn't quite the same as a human being!

As well as my father, who taught me how to play, there was also a chap who used to come to the pub from Orsett Heath for a drink on Friday evenings. I think his name was Brian. During the summer months we would have a game of tennis in the car park. He always called me "Butter Fingers", because once when I was about to serve – I dropped the ball. And so the name stuck! It is funny how things like that stay in your mind.

My family had at some time taken tennis quite seriously it seems, because they kept many racquets of differing weights in the summerhouse. I was assigned the lightest one. I felt very sad that I couldn't play tennis at school though, and sometimes I would resent having to just sit on the grass next to the tennis courts with Alison, watching the other girls play.

~

That first year there our Form Teacher was the PE/games teacher. I didn't like her at all, and I was pretty sure she didn't like me. Maybe she thought that I was no good at her subject. If only I could have been able to show her! But as I said just now, I was always too shy to speak up for myself.

Being our Form Teacher, she would take the register, and the odd other lesson now and again. Her way of calling the register was somewhat different to the others in that she would say the surname and then the first initial – which didn't always sound quite right. I was obviously Mandeville Y (which was fine as long as it wasn't pronounced as a question) but poor Pamela Pizzey – there was always a little giggle in certain areas of the class when *her* name was called out!

There were other reasons why I didn't like this teacher, not only because she didn't even give me a chance to play tennis, but she had a rather nasty little side to her...

There was a girl in our class who had a slight speech impediment – that is she couldn't pronounce "CH" only "SH", so words like cherry would be sherry, cheese would be sheese, and so on. One day this particular teacher called this poor girl out to the front of the class and asked her to go to the Deputy Headmistress' room – and ask for a CHIT... That poor girl, she didn't come back to class for ages...

~

Let the games begin...

Going out on to the hockey pitch was like walking into the Roman amphitheatre. Of course, there was no Emperor saluting me as I was about to get slaughtered, but I knew that I was no match for the other gladiators.

Alison had the best idea – she refused to take part in the games...

Always trying to please, I tried, I really did. But the other gladiators would go for my ankles, and despite my padded hockey boots, they always seemed to hit the right spot. I had enough of this, and so I went to the games teacher and asked her if I too could opt out of games. She didn't seem to be as compliant with me as she was with Alison. Maybe she enjoyed *the games...*

So we came up with a good idea! We said that we would really prefer to walk around the perimeter of the games field instead of playing these games while they were going on. Somehow the teacher agreed. So that is what we did. We *were* exercising after all...

There was also indoor PE though! I actually liked climbing the ropes, and could climb quite high – until the day I slid down rather too quickly and burnt the insides of my hands. I was absolutely no good at vaulting the horse, and would just end up splayed up against its behind, just like Alison!

And then there were the showers... I had never had a shower before, only baths, and the feeling of all that water showering down on me over my head was something I had never experienced before – nor had Alison. The main problem though was that we all had to be *naked...* You can't have a shower with your knickers on!

Although Alison and I didn't look at each other, we knew that we were both pretty flat-chested at the time, compared to some of the girls. A girl even laughed at me in front of the others – and said I looked like a boy! No-no-no! I *wasn't a boy!* Despite what my mother would have liked, I didn't have dangly bits between my legs, like my brothers, my grandfather and Fred Sawger... But neither was I sprouting breasts during that first year at Torells.

There was one girl who definitely had breasts though. She was very proud of them – and also whatever else she had. She would sit on the floor of the dry area of the showers, with her legs wide apart and knees bent, showing off a black bush of hair between her legs. Other girls would sit with her, chatting away, (of course they did!) but I found it all so embarrassing – and Alison did too. What's more, during the showers the PE teacher would stand there watching us – all the time. It didn't seem right to me.

And so – we got out of PE. Instead we had to go to the library and read books. Right up my street!

At least during that first year at Torells I came first in class in three subjects – English Language and two other related subjects. It made up for the comments that I got (I feel rather unfairly) for Games and PE!

~

There were certain girls at Torells who just saw the whole business of going to school as a joke. They would get up to all manner of things to get out of lessons. Feigning stomach aches was popular, and looking back I can see that they knew that this wouldn't be questioned too much. But one day the Headmistress said in assembly that there was something very serious going on at the school.

She explained that it had been brought to her attention that there were some girls making themselves pass out by dubious means to get out of lessons, and that it was gradually spreading around the school

The practice meant pressing just below the ear lobes and above the jawbone on both sides of the head – and if done in a certain manner, this would result in the girl passing out. This might not have been just girls doing it to themselves – but to others. However, if the wrong nerve was pressed for more than five seconds – it could result in death. So this was a warning to all the school.

Fortunately, none of them were in our class, so maybe we all had a little more intelligence than to do that. Alison and I had never heard anything about this going on before then.

At least with my grandfather's knowledge of nerves and pressure points – he hadn't done *that* one to me...

~

In all my time at Torells, whenever there was a parents evening, I would put out my books in order on the top of my desk, just like all the other girls. But my parents never came... I knew they weren't going to come, but still had to do it. I have never forgotten the sadness I used to feel doing this, and imagining all the chatter in the classroom as parents looked through their daughters' exercise books and spoke to the teacher about their progress. Were my parents so disinterested in me and what I was doing to show themselves up like this? I will never know. All I do know is that on those evenings life went on as usual at the pub, and no-one ever thought about how I must be feeling.

~

I had Alison though. On Saturday afternoons, I would meet her at her parents' house in Little Thurrock, and we would walk down into Grays shopping. Alison would be armed with a pepper pot that her mother would insist on – in case we got attacked!

It was only pocket money shopping so more window shopping really, but it was fun looking at make-up and things, and buying some little thing now and again. It was what the other girls did as well anyway, and was a ritual on a Saturday afternoon. So we would walk up and down the High Street, looking in shop windows and seeing other girls walking by, usually in pairs also. There would be a lot of chatter and giggling going on with the other girls, as boys eyed everyone up, but Alison and I had strict instructions from her mother – not to go near any boys...

That was unavoidable though, because to get to the main shops along the High Street, you had to walk past the "Queen's Hotel" on one of the corners. That was where the boys hung out! Well there was no point us crossing the road to miss the boys was there? Of course not!

"Standing on the corner", was a hit song by The Four Lads in 1960 – and was very appropriate for this strange sort of pretend mating ritual that was going on, especially as they *were* watching us go by and giving us the eye...

What they used to do was choose a couple of girls to follow – and that's what they did. No-one ever said anything, they just followed behind until they got fed up and looked for other girls to follow. It was all good fun really, and it was a pretty poor show if no-one followed you!

"They're following us…" one of us would whisper to the other with a little smile. We didn't even have to turn round to know this – we just *knew* – we could feel their presence…

Somehow our gait in our little white, pointed-toe shoes would take on a bit more confidence, and we would be more aware of how we were walking…

I think that, like cats, the boys had their territory… We would usually get as far as the railway crossing – then realise that they were no longer there. Maybe, because Alison and I didn't actually turn round and look at them by the time we reached the crossing gates, that was their cut-off time! Oh but it was fun – while it lasted…

These days it would probably be deemed to be sexual harassment, which is sad really.

~

Harassment from grown men though was another matter. One day I happened to be walking across the field on the footpath that I used to take to Orsett School. A girl I knew, Linda, happened to be taking the same route, and we were happily walking along chatting away. It was unusual for me to be walking through the field with someone else, because apart from the times I was with Georgie, I was usually on my own.

Suddenly we noticed a man standing at the other end of the path… He was just standing there.

"Quick" Linda said, "he's got his willy out…" and we turned on our heels and ran as fast as we could back the other way. I didn't look at the man long enough to see who he was, but if we had got nearer to him, would I have recognised him – and moreover, what would he have done?

~

Torells continued to be a right pain. Not only were the girls as a whole a problem, but I found some of the teachers to be a little odd.

Alison and I referred to one of our Maths teachers as Digit – because he was always going on about digits – but then came the time when he got really into mensuration. Oh dear – that mathematical term caused a bit of a stir! Yet still he carried on, and would chalk it in large letters across the blackboard. Mensuration this... Mensuration that... He loved that word!

He also knew that it caused some element of discomfort amongst the girls in class – and also a lot of giggling – nudge-nudging – and knowing looks...

I think he liked that though. I have since heard the odd story about him and from what I have heard, some of the girls fancied him – and made it very clear that they did. I just hope that no-one ever led him on too far...

~

There were a few teachers that I liked though, and really this proves to me that if you like a particular teacher, then you could do very well at that subject.

Our French Mistress, Miss Marshall, was an elderly lady with short grey hair. She didn't stand for any nonsense, but she was lovely. Under her guidance, I did very well at French. She made it so interesting though. It wasn't all about getting the vowels right and learning the verbs, but it was also learning about the French culture.

Sometimes during French lessons, she would go into a world of her own – back to her time spent in France – and the French man who was her only ever boyfriend. She would go into raptures about him, lovingly mimicking his voice, always in French. Some of the girls would be giggling behind their hands, but I was always enthralled. Unfortunately I really don't know what had happened to this wonderful Frenchman who had stolen her heart – because she told us the story – in French!

All I could gather was that she had been very much in love, and that there had never been – and would never be – another man for her. It is all so very sweet – but also so *sad*.

~

Music lessons were a new thing for me, and they started in that first year. The music teacher was quite nice, and she loved playing the piano in the music room where the lessons were held. She particularly loved it when we would sing "Jerusalem" in assembly, because at the end she would go off into the dramatic finale, totally in a world of her own...

I enjoyed music lessons and was fascinated by music notes, how to read them, and eventually how to write them. But I never quite gelled with it, in fact none of the girls did! I wish I had done though, because both my grandmothers played the piano beautifully, and could read sheet music. All I could gather were the highs and lows of the notes, and how long a note had to be held for. My grandmother kept telling my mother that I should have piano lessons, but I never did. I think that well brought up girls in her day had to learn the piano, it was part of their social education. Sadly for me though, it didn't happen.

At the beginning of that term the new school choir had to be chosen, which meant we all had to stand up individually and sing on our own. This was quite a terrifying ordeal! I absolutely didn't want anyone laughing at me and making fun of me, especially as there were 44 of us in class. Not all the girls could do it, and some collapsed back onto their seat in sheer terror. I *knew* that was going to be me too. At least I wouldn't be alone in that though.

My turn came and I stood up quivering in my shoes. The song we all had to sing was –

"Green green green's the colour of my garments
Green green green my only wear shall be
If you have me tell you why I love it dearly
My true love a gamekeeper is he"

"Come on Yvonne" the music teacher was beckoning, as I stood there trembling in some sort of haze. I knew I had to start on the right note, otherwise nothing else would follow. If I started too low, I would sound more as though I was talking. If I started too high, I would sound as nervous as I was and would get no further. So I took a deep breath, and just let my voice do what it was going to do – I started on the right notes, and the rest just followed on...

"Well done Yvonne" the music teacher said as I sat back down on my seat. Nobody said a word, but I was so pleased that I had actually done it!

~

Later, I found out that I had been chosen for the choir, and it was such a good feeling to know that someone thought that I could actually *sing* –

being part of something was what I really needed. Singing in harmony with other girls, and producing sounds together was really fulfilling. I was also put into the descant section, which made me feel a little bit special, as well as being *chosen*. It was rather like being chosen back in the infants at Orsett School in 1954 to be Mary in the nativity play.

Also I enjoyed the challenge of learning a new way of singing the hymns I knew so well. I especially liked singing the descant for *"All things bright and beautiful"*, and to this day, if ever I find myself singing that hymn – it is always the descant version! So I have to think carefully if ever I happen to be in a church congregation singing!

However, this new found pleasure meant choir practice, and this took place after school for an hour one day a week, as well as in music lessons. I did this for a while, but very soon my mother took a stand.

"You don't want to do that" she said scornfully. But I did! Why was she always telling me that things I enjoyed – I didn't want to do! It was crazy. It was also very cruel, because I had to leave the choir straight away.

~

Another teacher I particularly liked was Mrs. James, the needlework teacher. I enjoyed her classes too, and loved needlework and embroidery.

Then one day in the fourth year, which was my last year there, she said we were all going to make a dress to wear on Leavers Day. This meant learning how to use a paper pattern, and do the correct fitting etc. Well, Leavers Day couldn't come soon enough for me, but at least I had these two teachers that I particularly liked.

The paper pattern was standard for schools for the time, but I liked it, and was looking forward to making my dress – and being in line with the other girls. It had a round neckline, little cap sleeves, and darts that went down to the waistline. Then a gathered skirt was to be attached.

Mrs. James brought in a selection of approved cotton material in different colours. These were all of a small floral pattern in symmetrical lines or squares, which were chosen to make cutting out the dress simpler for first-time dressmakers.

I excitedly told my mother about how I was going to be making my dress, what it was for, and the subtle colours and patterns of the fabric. I knew she wouldn't allow me to choose pink or lilac, but there was a pale lemon pattern that I liked.

"You don't want any of those!" she said, without even seeing them. "You don't want – you don't want" were words she said to me many times. But I *did* want... I wanted to have something similar to the other girls. And besides, those fabrics had been chosen for ease of cutting.

But no!! My mother took me to a store that sold dress materials – and chose the fabric for me. It was a large pattern of bright turquoise exotic flowers on a white background. It didn't matter what my needlework teacher had advised – it was what my mother wanted.

The fabric proved to be very difficult to cut and match, although I did manage it. But it need not have been that difficult. Besides, when it came to Leavers Day my dress was so different to everyone else's. At least my parents didn't buy the class photo, but as always, they never did...

So yet again, my mother had her way.

Years later she asked me to make *her* a dress... So I took her to a department store that sold dressmaking fabric, and she chose the pattern – it was a very similar style to the one I had made at school, but without the gathered skirt! I asked her to choose the fabric that she wanted – and she chose a small leaf patterned fabric... If only she had let me choose one of those for my own dress I had made at school...

~

Being forced to go to Torells, meant that my only option really was to go into the commercial stream. So in my fourth and last year there I was in form 4C1... 4C1?? I had been in the A1 stream throughout! But the C in this case meant commercial – phew!

Despite my unfulfilled desire to become an air hostess, I quite liked learning to type. In fact, I was actually good at it, and picked it up quickly.

Again, this was helped by the fact that our typing teacher, Mrs. Power, was very nice. So there were three teachers that I liked, and I got on well with each subject that they taught.

So French, Needlework and Typewriting. They were some of my best subjects. I got on well with English Language as well, and also my favourite – Art – but our art teacher was a little strange, and the best art I did whilst at Torells was illustrating my exercise books!

Class 4C1 were learning to type on quite antiquated Imperial manual typewriters. They were the only ones around at the time anyway. They had a delightful way of going... Patter – patter – patter... PING! as you shot back onto the next line. And dare you make a mistake! This was a real no-no – and involved a lot of discreet rubbing out with a typewriter rubber. If copies were needed, this meant having a carbon paper between the top sheet and the copy paper, and if you made a mistake – then it would show up on the copy paper anyway. So the whole concept of typing was accuracy – accuracy – accuracy first – and with speed coming along soon after...

Mrs. Power was a lovely lady and, like Miss Marshall, was quite elderly. Although in those days "elderly" could have meant something somewhat different to these days. They were both still teaching, so obviously well before retirement age.

Copy typing meant *not* looking at the QWERTY keyboard – just at what you were copying. We weren't allowed to even glance at it. Mrs. Power's method of teaching typewriting was to do it *mentally*.

"Just think of daffodils" I remember her saying... "and the words will flow straight through to your hands..."

That didn't sound logical at first – but somehow it worked!

~

My grandfather was very interested in me learning to type, and he wanted to watch me do it. He was fascinated about how copy typing without looking at the keyboard worked. One day he came home with an antique Underwood typewriter for me. The 'a' jumped a bit, but that didn't really matter. So after school I would sit at the kitchen table practising typing.

One day my grandfather was out, and for some reason I sat at his end of the table. I don't know why, maybe it was something to do with the light – but *nobody* sat on my grandfather's chair. My mother was in the kitchen at the time and all was unusually calm. Suddenly, my grandfather burst in the kitchen door, and looked daggers at me – sitting in his place. I immediately got up and went to my end of the table, where I sat on my chair, leaving my typewriter where it was...

I'll never forget the look in my grandfather's eyes as he stood – they were wild... He picked up my typewriter and held it above his head – aiming it at mine... I just sat there, completely still – and looking back at him. I don't know what he saw in my eyes that made him put it down. But if that typewriter had hit me, it would have certainly killed me.

"I thought he was going to throw that at you" my mother said, quite calmly, as he left the room.

Yes – so did I... So why didn't she try to stop him?

~

During the fourth and last year at Torells, not only did Alison and I go to the "pictures" whenever an Elvis film was being shown, but we started going to the Thurrock Technical College dances. Our very first time there was a very new experience. First of all, at the bottom of the steps to the hall, stood a student of the college.

"Come on girls – show me your heels", he would say, before letting us going into the hall. Every girl then wore stilettos of varying heights, and they all had steel tips in those days. So we had to have rubber caps to put on our heels, even though ours were very low, so we didn't mark the wooden floor. Every time we went there he checked our heels, and he was rather nice. He always smiled at me, and Alison and I, not knowing his name, would refer to him as "Heels"!

So that very first time we bought our heel caps from the "heel cap" desk, and up we went into the hall. Music was playing, but everything was dark...

"When are they going to put the lights on?" we pondered. But they never did – it was meant to be dark – but Alison and I had never experienced a proper "teenage dance" before!

Well I am glad they didn't have ultra-violet lights, because our shoes were white – and we would have had every foot movement glowing in the dark. Yes, we really did wear white shoes – and we also danced around our handbags. True Essex girls we were then!

So all the girls would be dancing together, while the boys hung out being wallflowers, slumped against the walls – and watching. Alison and I got our own dance together and, as shy as I was, I really enjoyed dancing. Besides, we were dancing in the dark, and couldn't really see the boys who were there – in the shadows!

~

Writing those words "dancing in the dark" reminds me of something I did when I was about seven years old.

I have always loved music and dancing, and still do. Being so shy as a child though, I found it very difficult to dance in public. The feeling was there within me, but it was oh so difficult to cut that cord that held me back. Even now, it takes a lot for me to get up and dance, even though the rhythm of the music is titillating my soul. I have to feel very comfortable with the people who I am with, and have to feel pretty sure that they aren't going to tut or make fun of me. Once the right kind of music gets hold of me, the spirit of the rhythm takes over and I am dancing forever, literally dancing the night away.

Dancing is the way I can express myself, swaying to the rhythm of my favourite music, going where the music leads me, and if I am at home, singing along too.

I first learned how to dance by dancing on my father's feet as he led me around the room at parties at the pub, but waltz music was only a small part of music played at the pub. It was normally Winifred Attwell, Russ Conway, people like that, belting out jolly piano music to get people up dancing. So, my first steps doing the waltz were on my father's feet.

It is not only ballroom music that gets into my soul though, it is any music that I love, and which makes me move my whole body in a rhythmic way. I can be an angel spreading her wings, or I can be a sexy señorita doing the bossa nova. Whatever I am being, I am being taken out of myself, into another world where all that matters is the magic I am feeling. And yet, maybe what I am really being – is my true self.

When I was about seven years old, not only did I want a pretty dress that would make me feel like a princess, but I also wanted to dance. This wasn't dancing around on my father's feet, or doing the hokey-cokey. This was me – wanting to express myself through dance.

It was early one winter's evening. It was cold and misty outside, and darkness was falling rapidly. I had a lovely cherry red coat, with a round collar, and a waistline that flared out in gored panels. This was going to be my dancing dress... I put it on back to front. It was a little uncomfortable, and I couldn't do the buttons up properly, but to me it felt like a dress. And then I went outside...

I danced around in the car park, cold, dark and misty, but I felt wonderful. I was a dancer – and I swayed to the music in my mind, and then I took more steps, turning and swaying, reaching up with my arms, and down to my legs, then twirling round and round, covering the whole car park – all the time – just dancing...

Nobody knew I had done that. In fact no-one had missed me. Moreover, no-one had seen my happiness at being allowed to be myself, and expressing myself and my soul in my mind's music.

~

I was overjoyed the day I finally left Torells. Other girls were crying – but not me. And by the way, my mother was right – that navy blue raincoat I had when I first started did still fit me!

I went and said goodbye to Mrs. Power, and she got a piece of paper, which she wrote on for me...

> *"It's all very well to be pleasant*
> *When life goes along like a song*
> *But the man worthwhile*
> *Is the man who can smile*
> *When everything goes all wrong"*

Well, I have always managed to smile – no matter what was going wrong. So maybe I am worthwhile – after all.

Foxes, Hounds, & Pheasant Beaters

I have never been comfortable with The Hunt – the cry of the hounds alerting that they had found the poor unfortunate fox...

My grandfather acquired a fox once, well twice actually. The first time had been years before I was born. Somehow he had this fox, and the story I have been told by one of the victims involved, was that he sneaked into a bedroom one night when two girls – young female relatives – were sleeping in a bed together, and put the fox in the bed... Well at least I wasn't one of them! This was my grandfather's rather warped sense of humour. If he could terrify a woman or girl – then he would...

I do remember the second one well though – he was kept as a pet indoors in the pub, but I don't recall his name. Although I was always on the foxes' side when it came to The Hunt, this fox took an instant dislike to me. He was young and I suppose he just wanted to play, but he used to lay in wait for me when I came home from school – and suddenly – I would be the prey! He would chase me, and no-one ever stopped him. Maybe he was getting his own back for one of his pack being horrifically killed, but whatever it was – he wanted to get me! He knew I was afraid of him – and that the tables were turned and he was the hunter... "Let the games begin..."

How I hated that fox! Well, it wasn't really him, the poor creature; I hated the fear that I would feel whenever I came home from school – knowing that he was there – somewhere...

No-one took any notice of my fear. "Pain is all in the mind" my grandfather would say, if ever I complained if I got nipped on the ankle by the fox or Joey the demon bantam. So why did he used to torture me the way he did if he thought that pain was all in the mind. Well I suppose he enjoyed inflicting the pain, and now he was using another medium.

It is just as well that you don't automatically get rabies from a fox bite, especially one that was kept indoors. It is also just as well that he wasn't with us long enough to grow bigger.

One day as I let myself in the door, foxy was waiting for me – he chased me and frightened me so much that I ran into a case of Babycham glasses that had been delivered that day. Champagne in those days would be served in wide shallow stemmed glasses, and Babycham glasses replicated that style. They had a little Babycham logo on the glass, and at the time it was a very popular drink – especially served with a maraschino cherry on a little paper parasol! It was really a perry, but female saloon bar customers loved it, and I suppose drinking out of glasses shaped like champagne glasses made them feel sophisticated – along with their long cigarette holders!

I think there was more concern for the broken glasses than the cuts and scratches on my ankles, but at least I had shoes and ankle socks on. Luckily I had only broken a few glasses, but it really wasn't my fault!

Well foxy had to go, and quite right too. He couldn't spend his life in captivity, shut up in the pub all the time. He couldn't be let loose in the wild either, he would have no chance of survival.

So soon he was on his way. But where was he off to? Another landlord and landlady from another Essex pub appeared one day – along with a reporter from the Thurrock Gazette! They wanted to make sure everyone knew what they were doing... And therefore the next week there was an article and a photo of my grandfather handing foxy over to them. So his life was still destined to be spent in captivity. Poor little thing. I only hope they didn't get fed up with him – and put him out into the wild.

~

I hated the fox-hunting days. These were not town foxes that can now be such a nuisance, but rural natural living creatures, raising their cubs in their lairs.

The Meet would be held down in the village, but with the stables being in Baker Street, their first port of call would be in the saloon bar of the Kings Arms, where they would raucously get tanked up with whiskies. Meanwhile, the hounds outside – sometimes up to seventy of them –

would be howling and getting very excited in anticipation of what they were about to do. Maybe not quite so excited as the hunters though!

I have to admit that the sight of the huntsmen and women was impressive, with their scarlet coats, white stocks (cravats), and black velvet caps. Some would wear black coats with top hats or bowlers. Someone might think they looked more as though they were off to some royal pageant, rather than about to go charging over the fields for a kill.

What is it with the landed gentry and their hangers-on that they feel they have to hunt and kill? Is it in their blood that they love to see and smell the blood of an innocent creature that has just been ripped to bits?

~

It was the same with the shoot. This used to take place down on Orsett Fen. Large four-wheel drive cars would arrive – Jeeps, Land Rovers and the like – this being the status sign of the people inside, with their tweed jackets and caps, and loaded rifles.

The pheasants are raised to be shot, with the beaters striding through the bracken, sending them out of their nests only to be shot dead as they emerge from their cover. Unfortunately, pheasants are such slow flyers, they find it hard rising into the air, and don't manage to get up very high. So therefore they really are an easy target for anyone on a shoot.

I remember an episode of "The Animals of Farthingwood", which was first broadcast in the 1990s, and was a fascinating childrens' programme about the animals that lived in the wood. The series was really interesting, with the animated animals going about their lives – mostly good – but sometimes perilous. Seeing the hedgehog that we had got to know being squashed on the road by a lorry, wasn't one of the best episodes!

Well we also got to know and love a brace of pheasants, which mate for life, and the series showed them always together. One day though the female got shot – the shooters being the baddies of course. Her mate was looking everywhere for her – and then he found her – dead. It showed him seeing her roasted, on a tray on a window sill – and then distracted, he was shot himself... This was the saddest episode of that series that I ever saw. I doubt very much that any pheasant shooters would have ever watched "The Animals of Farthingwood"...

Unlike the foxes though, at least they get eaten. So their short lives have not been totally to no avail. I only hope that a few shooters' teeth might have been broken on the shot as they ate...

~

The foxes were not hunted to be eaten, but purely for the pleasure that it gave the hunters – and probably the status that went with being part of the Hunt.

So being fully inebriated with downing their whiskies at the Kings Arms, off they would ride down to the village, where they would "meet" again for more jollity.

And then it would begin. The Master Huntsman would blow his horn, and the horses would be galloping off across the fields, with dozens of hounds in tow. I hated hearing another blow on the horn when a fox or vixen was spotted. That sound, along with the call of the hounds alerting that they had found a fox, would resound up the lane if they were in the vicinity.

That poor terrified fox – when that pack of hounds set upon him – he had no chance. His poor little body being ripped to shreds, while for the most part he was still alive. Then the hounds would be praised, and his beautiful brush would be cut off – a trophy for the Hunt.

Sometimes, I couldn't help but wonder if it may have been a vixen that was caught, and then I used to worry if she had some poor little cubs somewhere, being left alone in their den to die.

As Oscar Wilde once said when describing his thoughts on fox hunting – "The unspeakable in pursuit of the uneatable"

Tally-ho.

Someone Called Elvis!

1960 onwards...

I really can't see how that at such as young an age as eight, I was being mesmerised by some young man on the big screen – someone called Elvis! The only film I had seen as a small child was "Pinocchio", and I think that was when I was five years old. I have never forgotten walking into a cinema for the very first time. Everything was dark, except for the screen and as the film had already started, the first image I remember is Pinocchio's nose stretching!

After that I was being taken to the cinema (or pictures as we called it then) on a fairly regular basis. There were three cinemas in Grays – the Regal, the Ritz, and the State – and there was another in Stanford-le-Hope – the Regent – which because we advertised their posters on the street side of our garage wall, gave us two free tickets each week. So there was quite a choice of cinemas to go to!

Usually Nell would take me to the pictures. When we went to the Regent we would always call in to a little teashop on a corner somewhere beforehand. We would have a cup of tea and a cup cake – I remember they made the most delicious "butterfly" cakes, which were always my favourite. When we went to one of the cinemas in Grays, we would stop and get a large bag of hot roasted peanuts from the man who cooked them on the pavement on a brazier. Everybody bought these, and so there was always the sound of cracking peanut shells and peanut munching going on all the time.

Before the film actually started though, the sound of organ music could be heard, and then the organist would gradually be raised up from out of the orchestra pit, playing the organ. It was all very sedate – apart from the peanut crunching that is.

Sometimes the ice cream lady would come around, and stand down by the screen, shining her torch down onto her tray. We always had the little tubs of really nice ice cream, which we ate with the little wooden spoons. I must say, I wasn't that keen on licking those little wooden spoons – I always thought I might get a splinter...

I remember being told that my Auntie Nance always took a tin of pineapple and a can opener with her to the cinema. I can't imagine anyone doing that now!

~

The first Elvis film I saw, originally released in November 1956 in America, was "Love me Tender". That was when I first saw Elvis! At the time he still had fair hair, and the film was in black and white anyway. But he was already very handsome. His voice was rather good too! Then the next year it was "Loving You". This time in colour. Nell and I would sit there staring at the screen – with smiles on our faces for the whole of the film.

Valerie loved Elvis too, and sometimes she would come with us – so three females, all of different ages, would be sitting there mesmerised by this gorgeous man...

Once I started at Torells, Valerie had already left school and was now at work, so now Nell and I were going on our own again. Then, once we were around fourteen Alison and I would go together. So from 1957 onwards, I saw every Elvis film that ever reached Britain, which I am guessing is pretty much all of them.

Alison and I even sent Elvis a postcard once. We wrote something nice on it for him, and decorated it with lots of little flowers – roses I think – which we both drew, all around the edges. We did all this in Alison's bedroom, then crept out of the house so that her mother didn't know what we were doing – our hearts all a-pounding in case she caught us! Then we sneaked to the post office along the road, and bought a stamp. It didn't matter that we would never receive a reply – we just wanted Elvis to know that there were two girls over here in England thinking of him – along with millions of others of course...

~

It seemed that everyone in those days went to the cinema. At first there was only the BBC on television, and that was only black and white. Then in September 1955 when ITV came along, there still wasn't really much to choose from for evening entertainment. So the cinemas had a lot of custom, even though there were four in the area.

It was also the choice of most people's first dates. It was fail safe really, with different films to choose from – and there was always the back row... The only thing I liked about sitting in the back row though, was that there was no-one behind me! I can't help but think that not many boys asked a girl out to see an Elvis film though – she wouldn't have been able to take her eyes off the screen!

~

At the end of every cinema showing, when the final credit had disappeared at the top of the screen, no matter which cinema we were at, we would all stand up and observe the National Anthem. As far as I remember no-one tried to skip the credits and escape – everyone was pleased to stand there in respect for our Queen.

From 1960 onwards, Shadows music like "Apache" and "FBI" etc. were played in the interval. I always found the Shadows music to be so exciting – it sort of summed up being out for the evening. This went on right through until Alison and I were going to the cinema. The lights would come on, and we would look around to see if there was anyone we knew. We never did see anyone though, probably because we always went upstairs in the circle.

When we were about to leave Torells we said that whenever we went to the pictures in the future, we would always look around the cinema to see if we were both there. There was a Scottish girl in our class at the time, who we couldn't understand, but her accent fascinated us. She was always saying "Och-aye..." things like that. So Alison and I agreed that if one of us saw the other one in the cinema – we would call out "Och-aye the noo!" Daft, weren't we?

~

My love for Elvis has never waned. I now have every record he ever made, as well as every film, and my lifetime ambition has been to go to

Graceland. If he was still alive today (which I sometimes wonder if he may be), he would still be as handsome. Even if his eyes were tired and his hair had gone – he would still be "the most 'handsomest' man in all the whole wide world", as I used to call him as a child, all those many years ago.

So what happened to all those photos of Elvis I carefully cut out of Mirabelle magazine, and covered with cellophane to make them look like real photos? They were all in my grandmother's fur coat box – the day my mother had the bonfire...

Grow Up – And *Don't* Act Your Age!

Summer 1961

It was still usual for us all to go to the pictures almost every week. Nell or Valerie would take me to see "U" certificate films, usually on a Friday, and my parents would always see the "X" certificate films whenever they were being shown, usually on a Tuesday.

It was a summer's day, and I had a new white cardigan that I had worn to school. Unfortunately, I somehow managed to get a splash of blue ink on the placket – right where it would stand out the most! I tried to get it off with water whilst still at school, but that was turning it into a paler blue smudge, which was spreading by the second.

So I smuggled it back home in my bag, and went straight to the bathroom where I had a brilliant idea! I covered the mark with toothpaste – voila! Although it smelled of peppermint, it would save me from being scolded until it was washed – maybe Nell would work her magic... It was just as well it wasn't Signal with its red stripes...

It may seem strange that I should talk about this little insignificant incident of my life, but it was that very day that something odd was to happen, something that I had never experienced before.

It was a Tuesday, my parents' day of the week to go to the cinema. Early that evening, my mother told me to put my new cardigan on. Phew – that was a close one! The ink stain was still covered with the toothpaste, and as long as I was careful it might just stay like that.

~

"You're coming to the pictures with us", my mother informed me as we got into the car.

"Oh – what are we going to see?"

"It doesn't matter", she said.

We parked the car and walked along to the State cinema, and as we got nearer I saw that the film was "World by Night", which was an Italian film, one of those that was supposedly a documentary, but was really an excuse to show scenes that would be cut from a normal film.

"But it's an "X" film!" I exclaimed, "I'm not allowed in".

"It doesn't matter", my mother said. "Just stand up straight and act as though you're eighteen".

Well I was used to having to look and act older than I really was, serving behind the bar etc. – but this was a little different.

"Pull your cardigan round you" my mother said, looking down at my flat chest. Hmm, that was close...

My cardigan did absolutely nothing to cover up the fact that I didn't have the body of an eighteen year old. I felt awful. On one hand I was intrigued about what an "X" film was all about, and what I was about to see, but on the other hand I was highly embarrassed.

The manager of the cinema was standing by the door as usual, greeting people in, but more likely sticking to the censorship code.

"She's not allowed in" he said, putting out his arm in front of me. I knew that he recognised me from going to the "U" films, and he must have also recognised my parents for their penchant for "X" films.

"It's a little near the mark" he said, with a grave nod to my parents.

My parents took no notice whatsoever, as we walked past him.

"Well that's up to you" he said. I felt terrible. I hadn't chosen to sneak into a cinema to see an "X" film.

My parents headed to the back row of the stalls. This was very unusual, as on the rare occasion that they had taken me to see a western or a war film (usually one set under the sea) they had always gone in the circle upstairs, as all of us had, but this time it was different. As intrigued as I was, I was really wishing I wasn't there.

"Leave your seat up and sit on it like that" my mother told me as she and my father were putting theirs down. "You need to look bigger so no-one notices you".

So there I sat, sitting as high as my parents. It wasn't very comfortable but I could put up with that.

~

The film was all about what went on around the world by night. The seedy night clubs, the strip joints, things like that. I found it intriguing, especially women showing their bare breasts etc., but obviously it wasn't as explicit as films shown these days. As embarrassing as it was to me, being only twelve years old, my parents weren't shifting in their seats showing any awkwardness whatsoever.

What it was that my parents were trying to show me, I really don't know. Why should I be seeing women taking off their clothes and baring their breasts for men? Was this what women did?

"Can I have one of your peppermints?" my mother asked me...

Oh dear... *What peppermints??*

~

September 1962

One day at the beginning of the autumn term in 1962, I came home from school (as was always the scenario when something untoward had been going on!) and my mother was nowhere to be seen, which was very unusual.

"Where's Mummy?" I asked my grandmother, as she sat watching "Liberace" on her own. They both loved Liberace, or "Liberarsy" as Nanny used to call him! I don't think she ever realised the significance of her mistake in her pronunciation of his name...

"It doesn't matter", she said, being the usual answer whenever I wasn't to know the truth. As I wasn't to know where my mother was, this made it all the more intriguing. I sat with my grandmother looking at the television screen, but not really seeing Liberace's nimble fingers, miraculously flying along the keyboard, churning out the music that mesmerised Nanny. She loved his music, his grin, his smile, his face.

"He is so lovely, that Liberarsy" she said, in a world of her own, but with him.

The programme ended, and I opened the curtains, letting in the sunshine that would have obscured the face that Nanny loved to see.

I stood looking out of the window, wondering where my mother was. There was no point asking my grandmother again, because "it didn't matter". But yes, it did to me. That very short answer made me realise that yes, it did matter – but I wasn't to know.

A large car drove into the car park. The couple in there stayed sitting in the car for a while, and then they got out... It was my mother, with one of the customers called Len.

~

My mother was always in a good mood when Len came to the pub. If she saw his car drawing in to the car park, she would rip out her curlers, smack on her lipstick, and go rushing down to the bar. She would be so happy talking to him and, dare I say it, flirting as I now know it.

Things were different though when he came to the pub on a Sunday lunchtime and brought his wife with him. They would sit all cool and sedately at a table in the saloon bar drinking gin and tonics, before they went back home to have their Sunday lunch, which they had set on a timer, something that no-one else seemed to have in 1960's England.

They would talk about their annual trips to Jersey, and how much they loved it there. Such was my inexplicable affinity with France, and doing well at school with the French language, the French/English amalgamation appealed to me, and the German occupation during the war was intriguing. Jersey to me sounded like a wonderful place to go, and I would ask them questions about it whenever I could.

They were wealthy, with a new "ultra-modern, sprawling bungalow", complete with all its ultra-modern appliances, such a far cry from my grandmother's little 1940s grey stove. And of course, Len's distinctive car...

~

I stood at the window watching... They hugged, and then they kissed. It wasn't just a quick social kiss, but a long, more passionate kiss, which made me feel that there was something between them.

My mother came upstairs. She was smiling and happy, and also very flushed. This was no red Bourjois rouge that blushed her cheeks. This was a blush of something else, something I didn't really know about. But I knew that whatever had caused this blushing and smiles was something untoward, and against my father.

"Why are you looking at me like that?" she asked when she eventually settled down. My grandmother was happy and in a good mood also, sensing that her daughter was showing all the signs of a joyful indiscretion.

"I *saw* you" I said, not really believing that those words were actually coming out of my mouth.

My mother was aghast.

"What did you see?" she asked, all a-fluster, but also showing anger.

"I saw you kissing" I said. I really don't know how I said that, especially risking incurring my mother's wrath. But the words just came out.

Didn't she realise though, that by exposing me to all these things that went on with adults, that at some time I just might notice something – and actually say something about it.

"Don't you ever tell your Dad", she said, with a threatening look that sent her pink cheeks to white.

I knew enough about life, even at that early age, that I would never want my father to find out that my mother had had a somewhat romantic liaison with someone else. He would have been so terribly hurt, and really, it was not up to me to take any part in my parents' relationship.

It didn't stop *my* hurt though. I had never seen my mother kissing someone passionately before.

When my father came home from work, as usual I went to meet him. He rode down Baker Street on his bike, and then we walked into the car park together, chatting as usual.

My mother was looking out of the kitchen window. Her eyebrows were narrowed and her mouth was turned down. The flush of romance had long left her face. But would I be saying anything to my father? No, of course I wouldn't.

I kept her secret, and always have done – until now...

~

Very soon, I had a wonderful surprise. It was now September, and the days were gradually getting a bit chillier. Maybe it was because of this, I don't know, but my mother had suddenly decided she wanted to go to Jersey – and NOW!

She probably wanted to experience a bit of the life that Len's wife had every year. There was no holding back. My father had to book the flight from Southend and that was it.

"We are going to Jersey" my mother told me. "And you are coming with us..."

Oh! Wow!

But why – why was *I* being given this privilege of going to Jersey? Could it have been anything to do with what I had seen?

Ralf was now seven years old and Colin was four. It was usually them who had preferential treatment but now, all of a sudden, I was asked if *I* would like to go on holiday with my parents.

Oh yes! This was so exciting, and what's more I would be going on a plane for the first time. I could see what the air hostesses were doing first hand, and not just go by what I was reading in a book.

"Where are we staying?" I asked my mother, my eyes and heart all aglow.

"Wait and see" she said, "but it will be a nice hotel – and it will be lovely".

~

Southend airport was pretty stark then, and nothing like what I had imagined airports to be like. But it was great, I enjoyed being there, and taking in all the atmosphere of what was going on.

It was a very short flight. I sat with my mother, and my father sat behind us. All the time, being my mother's first flight as well as mine, she was so nervous that she picked the strap of her rather nice cream leather handbag to bits. Really, by the time we arrived at Jersey airport, the strap was so ragged it was hardly of any use.

So had she enjoyed the flight? I don't think so! But she *was* doing what Len's wife did regularly – and she *was* having just a teeny bit of that way of life too...

~

We arrived at Jersey airport. Everything looked sort of grey, with square buildings and concrete.

"Now, you stay here" my mother instructed, as we got to a building that sorted out accommodation. But... Weren't we booked in – to a lovely hotel??

"Your mother said we'll sort out where we are staying when we get here" my father told me, not looking terribly pleased with her plan.

"Just stay there" my mother repeated, and they then went into the office to try to sort something out. I don't know, but perhaps she was hoping to find the hotel that Len stayed in.

I sat on our one and only suitcase that held our belongings for the week, just waiting – and waiting – my head in my hands, as I stared out across the concrete...

Len and his wife always stayed in a fabulous hotel. We knew that, because they had told us so. Somehow though, the prospect of this wonderful hotel welcoming us was getting bleaker and bleaker the longer I sat there.

After about an hour, they emerged from the "accommodation" building.

"Come on", my father beckoned as we headed for the car hire office.

But where were we staying? How had my mother just assumed that we really didn't need to book a hotel before arriving?

It was a small crummy guest house that was available – with just one bedroom, which had a double bed and a single. So where was my lovely hotel room that I could enjoy all on my own and with the privacy that I wasn't getting back at the pub?

Sharing a bedroom with your parents really isn't right, especially when you are thirteen years old.

I wasn't used to getting to sleep early, with my grandmother coming in and disturbing me at the pub, so I just had to lay there and try my hardest to get to sleep, knowing that my parents were in bed – next to me...

~

I have memories of going around Jersey by car – it only takes an hour or so to drive around the whole coastline. I loved Jersey and its history. But I have no recollection at all of where we would eat, nor anywhere we might have gone in the evenings.

I can only think that as Jersey's licensing laws mean that no-one under the age of eighteen can even enter a pub – let alone drink alcohol in one, I must have stayed in the guest house while my parents went out in the evening. There is nothing else they would have done. My father loved his drink, and my mother loved being in pubs.

Surprisingly, my mother bought me a little set of mini lipsticks at a perfume shop in St. Helier. I was thrilled to bits with them, and I also loved the perfume she had bought herself – "Quelques Fleurs" by Houbigant. It was beautiful, as the name suggests, in a very flowery way, and so unlike the usual spicy perfumes that she favoured.

I have this very evocative memory of my mother smelling of flowers, and me clutching the little pack of mini lipsticks that she had bought me, as we strolled through St. Helier.

"Now, put one of those lipsticks on" she suddenly instructed – and put your hair up! Then she gave me one of her necklaces of large beads, far too large for a child of thirteen.

I was wearing what was called a shift dress in those days, and that was the day that we stopped at a pub.

So there I was all done up, supposedly looking far older than my thirteen years. I have a photo of me all done up like that – I did *not* look happy! Other photos taken of me on that holiday show me looking natural and happy. I was away from the pub...

"Now, stand up straight" my mother instructed again, "and try to look as though you are eighteen". And so, we ventured in.

"Go over there and sit in the corner" my father said, apparently gasping for a beer!

The barman was looking over to me, and then back to my father. A little interchange of words went on, and then my father came back with the beers.

"He said you were underage and not allowed in" he told us, "but I said you have been very ill – that is why you are so small – and that we have brought you out here to recuperate" he added, taking a swig of his beer with a grin.

All I wanted to do was enjoy being a young teenager, finding myself in this new world that stood before me – not to be pushed into being an adult long before my time...

Four Little Paws And A Bushy Tail

It was the UK "big freeze" of 1963, with the coldest temperatures on record in central and southern England for over 200 years. I could no longer cycle to school because it was too dangerous, but buses were still running, albeit rather later and more infrequent than usual. At least I could stand at the window in the lounge upstairs in the pub and watch for the bus to come round the corner at Hill Farm. This gave me enough time to get down the stairs, out of the pub, and step precariously across frozen Baker Street to the bus stop over the road. It was just as well that I could see the progress of the bus from the lounge window, otherwise I feel sure I would have been frozen to the path waiting at the bus stop.

~

Torells was even bleaker in all this bad weather. The uninviting, stark greyness of the building with its steel-framed windows did nothing to welcome shivering pupils into its walls. At least there was one room though where a little more warmth could be felt – the DS room...

Domestic Science was a little daunting to me at first, but I was used to helping with cooking at the pub, so I did know what I was doing. What bothered me most of all was the concern that I might have to handle raw meat. I had always been able to steer clear of actually touching raw meat at the pub, even though my mother would have probably found that most amusing. But even she wouldn't have been able to chop up live wriggling eels like my grandmother did... Nanny was used to all that though, coming from London, the city of jellied eels. How anyone could eat them, especially with the green jelly that formed with them in the pots is beyond me. Just as well then that Grays didn't savour them as one of its traditional dishes!

~

Early DS lessons had been mainly theory; kitchen cleanliness and hygiene, things like that. How to use an oven, and how to light it and the gas rings with matches were very basic things as well, but of course necessary if you are going to cook!

We wore the bibbed aprons that we had made in needlework in the first year. They were chambray blue and we had decorated the bib with cross stitching colours of our own choice. The colours I chose for the embroidery were lilac – and black.

"Black?" Mrs. James our needlework teacher asked quizzically, rummaging around in her box for a skein of black embroidery silk. I was the only girl in the class to choose black, so the skein hadn't been used before. My lilac and black cross stitch design looked very pretty though.

Our DS teacher was also very pretty. She had been the Carnival Queen for Thurrock in the recent past, and had long dark lustrous hair – not the normal look of our teachers! Whilst I was in her class she got married; it was winter, and in the snow. She told us that she wore a long red velvet dress and a white fur cape – she would have looked wonderful. Why she carried on working at Torells teaching girls how to cook, and moreover hygiene and cleanliness in the kitchen etc., I do not know.

~

Having gone through all the theory of Domestic Science, a term which makes cooking sound really rather important and much more than just serving up meals, we were then going to cook our first dish. This was potato soup, something I had never had, but which turned out to be rather delicious. We had been asked to take in jars to take the soup home with us, and I shared some of it with my mother and grandmother.

"That's smashing duck" Nanny said, relishing the taste. And yes, it was rather lovely – even though it was vegetable!

~

In pairs, with Alison as always being my partner, we shared cooking benches which we naturally had to clean before leaving class along with washing and drying cooking utensils etc. Kitchen hygiene was paramount! We also had one cooker between two girls, and each pair had to look after it, completely cleaning it as well before we could leave the class. Of course, Alison and I would leave it spotless – we wouldn't have left it any other way.

On one occasion, we sat on the stools at our bench with arms folded, satisfied that we had cleaned everything and so could go home.

"You haven't cleaned your cooker" our teacher informed us as we sat there waiting to be dismissed.

"Yes – we have Miss" I said quietly, but confidently. I did like her, and she was lovely, but I didn't like being accused of something I hadn't done. At least Alison was being included in whatever this "crime" was to be.

"Come over here" our teacher beckoned, summoning us both over to the cooker with the rest of the class looking on. There was a horrible sticky brown mess spread on it – goodness knows what it was. How had it got there? Alison and I looked at each other totally perplexed...

"We didn't do that..." we sort of said in unison.

"Well, you are responsible for cleaning this cooker – and you will stay here until you have done", she commanded.

Hmm, such a pretty teacher who we admired and respected – but here she was accusing us of leaving our cooker in an extremely dirty state. So we just had to do as we were told, stay behind while all the other girls filed out to go home, and clean up whatever it was that had been put onto our cooker. We didn't even think about looking round to see if there were any sneering, guilty-looking girls walking past – so we never did know who did it...

~

Our second dish was steamed apple pudding, made with thickly sliced apples and *beef* suet. That was equally as good, and it didn't really occur to me that beef suet was actually – from a cow... But that's what suet was in those days – I don't think vegetarians existed. Sometimes though, being a natural carnivore can have unforeseen consequences...

~

During that lesson we had been told something absolutely disgusting and distressing about what we were going to learn to cook the following week.

We were going to prepare and cook rabbits... I had never been able to eat rabbit at home – let alone *prepare* one. I really fretted about this. Alison became unwell and was off school, which meant she would be away for at least two weeks, so I would be at the bench on my own without her sharing such a horrible task. I really could not have done it anyway, and I know I couldn't have even entered the DS room knowing those poor rabbits were in there, waiting to be *prepared* and then *cooked*...

To explain simply, as it implies in Deuteronomy, animals with paws may not be eaten – that includes hares, which of course includes rabbits...

~

The night before the next DS lesson, I didn't sleep at all worrying about this, and as well as having to do such an abhorrent thing, I felt sure that someone would play a practical joke on me... I knew about these practical jokes when preparing such things from what had happened with the pig's eyes that time, when my mother tricked me into seeing them on the kitchen table by telling me they were sweets...

I hoped and prayed throughout the night that something might happen to stop me going to school the next day, but Nell got me up as usual, and I headed to the freezing cold bathroom. I couldn't feign illness, because that wouldn't work, especially as I still had to go to school most times that I was unwell.

"You're well enough to go to school" my grandfather would say, "so there'll be no excuse note for you..."

I stood at the lounge window waiting to see the bus come round the bend at the top of the hill. I waited there for some time looking out of the window, but there was no sign of a bus. Then it occurred to me – there were no cars moving either. I went outside to see what was going on, and one of the women over the road told me that no buses were running that day... *Phew!*

We had had even more snow overnight, and it had been so heavy that a huge snowdrift, many feet high, had formed at the junction of Baker Street and the A13 – and Orsett was *cut off*...

Hmm – what, like the rabbits' paws?

The Deck Chair

It was a lovely summer's day, as days always seemed to be in the school holidays. Rain would be kept aside for the coming school autumn term, bringing with it the chill of autumn. But today, it was a lovely day. Everyone was out, or so it seemed. My father was at work, Nell was looking after the shop, my mother was somewhere with my brothers, and Grandpop was – well, wherever he might have been that day...

I was dancing around in the lounge upstairs to one of my favourite songs that I was playing on my tiny record player. I don't actually remember what it was, maybe a 78rpm or maybe a 45rpm, I really don't know. But it was something that got my thin legs moving, my little feet tapping, and my waist a-twisting. It was probably Elvis – or was it The Beatles...? Ah yes, those four lads from a place I had never heard of until now – somewhere *up North* – called Liverpool – or *Liverpoooool* – as they pronounced it, with a sort of "glug" in their voice, which I really can't accurately describe...

I couldn't help but think though, that their hair cuts, which were so different to Elvis' and the local lads, looked more like the "pudding basin" cut, that was prevalent in the early part of the century, where mothers would put a pudding basin on their child's head – male and female – and then cut around it... I have an early photo of my mother with a pudding basin cut when she was a young child, but these new "Beatle" cuts were, well, their very own Beatle Style...

The lounge door opened as I was swirling around in my own little world, surprising me so that I nearly tripped over the marble hearth of the fireplace, now redundant until the winter.

"Come on old girl" Nanny was saying, wearing a lovely floral summer dress, and of course, a matching summer hat.

"Now, we're going to get that next bus – and we're going down to Grays duck" she said, with her ageing eyes smiling kindly behind her butterfly rimmed glasses. She was wearing her raspberry-red lipstick which in a way helped to widen her now thin lips, and her three-row necklace of pearls. She was all dressed up to go to... Grays.

~

"I'm going to buy you whatever record you want" Nanny said, with a look that was showing me that she wanted to please me. Could she have been aware of how unhappy I really was – and that dancing brought me the joy in life that I was otherwise missing? I think that she was wise and very kind, behind the facade that she had to adhere to in front of my grandfather and mother. But now, they were both out, and she had the freedom to do whatever she wanted – within reason that is...

The number 53 bus stopped as usual at Congress House, aka the Co-op, and I thought we would be going to the record department in there, but no – another record shop had opened on the High Street, and that is where we were heading. How Nanny knew about this, I do not know, but she loved music as well – even though it might be *pop*.

"What I really, really, really would like" I said quietly and gratefully, "is the Twist and Shout EP by The Beatles..."

"You can have whatever you like duck" she said, already taking her purse out of her fine leather handbag to pay whilst I waited excitedly for the assistant to get it for me.

~

Clutching my record as we walked back down the High Street, Nanny slowed down when we got near to the toy shop. This didn't only sell toys, but art equipment etc. This was where my parents had bought my Paint by Numbers set a few years previously. It had been two pictures on canvas of The Bridge of Sighs and another bridge across the Grand Canal in Venice. It may have been Paint by Numbers, but I enjoyed doing it, and in a way it had taught me all about shades of buildings, water, etc. Sadly, I had put those two paintings in my box – the one that was sent into flames by my mother sometime...

"Now, what would you like?" Nanny asked, looking in the display window on the left-hand side of the little entrance way to the shop. I had no idea that she wanted to treat me to something else.

"Ohh!" I gasped. In front of me were all manner of art utensils – oil paints, water colours, art brushes, pens, pencils – they were all there. But then, something distracted my attention from this wonderful selection... Just inside the shop door I could see another array of colour – Hula-hoops in red, yellow, green and blue, were leaning against the counter. My mind was on my new and very precious EP – "Twist and Shout" – I could do a lot of twisting with a hoop to that!

I chose a blue one, and with me carrying it in what may have been a slightly clumsy way, we headed back to the bus stop to catch the No. 53 back home.

I couldn't help but be a little concerned getting on the single decker bus with this large hoop, but I carried it along to our seats, half way back where my grandmother liked to sit. I clutched onto it, hoping that it wouldn't stick out too far for anyone to trip over – and all the time in my other hand holding tightly onto my Beatles EP.

The bus driver was revving to go – but then suddenly a wooden apparatus with red and white stripes came into view at the front of the bus. Inch by inch it was being pushed slowly up the steps. There seemed to be a lot of huffing and puffing going on, as this thing very slowly manifested itself.

While all this was going on, the bus conductor with his cap of authority was tapping at his ticket machine... Hmm – what was this object being brought onto his bus? It was so funny, and Nanny and I sat there having a little giggle to ourselves.

A *deck chair* then emerged, followed by Mrs. Lovett, who lived just along the road from the pub... She looked at us and smiled, then slumped down into one of the front seats, her deck chair leaning across the aisle...

"And you were worried about bringing your hoop on the bus" Nanny said with a smile...

The Great Escape

Summer 1963

In 1963 there was a film called "The Great Escape" starring, amongst many others, the lovely, late Steve McQueen. To my young mind, he was the star of the film, and to me it was all about telling the story of his character's great escape from his German captors, doing all his own stunts with fantastic motorcycle feats. He was a good-looking chap, not in an Elvis way, but just darn down to earth good looking!

Meanwhile, as well as my earlier attempts at "escaping" from the pub as a little girl late at night, I had now, for a while, been having an "above board" one week escape from the pub each year – down to Brighton with Nanny Felstead.

This was her great escape too, and she would go to the same apartment every year, for two weeks. It was a nice apartment, but only had one bedroom... Uh-oh – I still had to sleep with her... So there was *no escape* there!

The first week I would go down to stay with Nanny, and the second week – her boyfriend Fred would join her – er hmm – in the same bed. I think it's just as well that I had the *first week*...

So, there was no escaping sleeping with my grandmother, but it was good to get away from the pub for that week each summer.

The apartment was in Preston Park, a lovely area of Brighton just outside the town, which meant a bus ride to get there. Just over the road from the apartment was the actual Preston Park, and we would go for walks around there in the morning sunshine.

My parents would take us down there. We would normally go over to Kent on the Woolwich car ferry, which was always exciting and a great start to the adventure, but sometimes we would go through the Blackwall Tunnel or over Tower Bridge if the car ferry wasn't running for some reason. Taking the London route could be exciting too, especially at times when Tower Bridge would be up to let the ships glide through underneath.

Having crossed the river, the normal route would then be through Tonbridge, then Tunbridge Wells, past the Pantiles. Here there were little art studios, with unusual paintings by local artists, and the local well-heeled women dressed up even for food shopping, and carrying the ubiquitous shopping basket, so reminiscent of the time, as they shopped at little local food shops.

It all seemed such a sedate and well-off sort of life, observing these things as we passed through. I wanted to be like that one day – when I was older – those women made wearing navy blue and emerald green together look stylish.

Then, when we reached Sussex, yet another world opened up. A world where huge rhododendrons bloomed in abundance, lining driveways that led to big houses. That was a world that I hoped to experience – one day...

The Sussex Downs were a joy to behold. It was the area where Virginia Woolf and her friends lived in their very artistic, but also very decadent style. The place where Oscar Wilde would come and visit, and all manner of things would go on in a lovely house, there in the heart of the Sussex Downs, called "Charleston".

"Charleston" – what a lovely name for a house that held such art, and memories of such a bohemian way of life.

Well these were all things that I was yet to find out about – one day – maybe...

~

But now, I was still in my early teens, a long, long way away from even knowing what the words decadent and bohemian meant. Although I loved art – and Elvis of course – I also already had a passion for shoes. This was all in my mind though, because I had to have what my mother chose for me – good sensible shoes that would last – even if I grew out of them! It must have been my love for my great-grandmother's little Louis heeled shoes that made me forever want to find some just like them. This was not to be though...

~

Talking of Elvis and shoes reminds me of a pair of blue suede shoes I had once. I had gone shopping with my mother in Grays, and we stopped and looked in the window of a small shoe shop, which I think was called Timpsons. There was a sale on, and there was this darling little shoe in the window. It was flat, with an almond shaped toe – and blue suede!

We went in the shop and asked if they had it in a size three. Yes they did – but the only one they had was in the window. So the assistant went and got that for me, and then went into the back room to get the left one. I loved them, and they were a perfect fit – except – the one in the window, being blue had faded a lot in the sun and so was a completely different shade of blue to the other one.

"That's why they're in the sale", the assistant informed us matter-of-factly.

But no matter about the difference in colour – my mother liked them, they fitted me well, and what's more they were really cheap. So suddenly they were mine. But oh dear, no matter how long I left the left-hand one out in the sun to lighten – it never did. No wonder other girls used to laugh at me...

~

The first day in Brighton, my grandmother would take me to the local Freeman, Hardy & Willis shoe shop, and she would buy me a new pair of shoes every year. They would have to be the kind that would meet with my mother's approval though, because Nanny didn't want to incur her daughter's wrath either. But nevertheless she also let me have a lot of say in what I chose.

I think it is actually quite sweet really, how Nanny would escape to her own world for two weeks every summer. But only two weeks? If only it could have been a new life for her. But no, despite her terrible abuse at my grandfather's hands, she did not want to relinquish being landlady of the Kings Arms.

~

By now, as smart as Nanny Felstead liked to be when she went out, there was something that she had that really *did not* suit her! It was a pair of "butterfly" glasses with emerald green rims, and goodness knows what other decoration! They made her look terribly fierce, which she wasn't, but she loved them.

She really was actually very nice, but would have to kow-tow, so to speak, to her husband and daughter. She got her own back though – with her love of gin – and her boyfriend Fred. Maybe she chose the fierce look deliberately!

Going to Brighton always meant shopping in the "Arcade" which was rather grand in comparison to shopping arcades these days. It was a glass-domed shopping walkway with select little shops on either side. My grandmother's favourite milliner was along there, and she would always go in, spending ages trying on hats, taking advice on style if necessary. Whenever we went to Brighton, Nanny just *had* to get a new hat, even if it had to be made especially for her.

~

Nanny also introduced me to "The Lanes" in Brighton, an area of tiny streets and antique shops. Well that is how it was in those days. Maybe it is something very different now. I hope not though. With my feeling for antiques and their history, even at that age, I loved walking around The Lanes.

The people were nice too and, unlike today, everyone was interested in what the little shops had to offer – and not looking downwards into mobile contraptions all the time. It seems that window shopping now means – shopping on your computer or mobile phone!

Oh dear, I must sound *so old*. But I am from the era when going shopping was just that – not wandering the streets tapping into a mobile phone – and missing everything that was going on around you.

Oh the joys of shopping – as it used to be then! If you could afford it – you would go in the shop. If you couldn't – you didn't. You would then window shop, dreaming about the day that you might actually be able to enter the shop – and not *even* have to ask the price...

My grandmother *could* afford it though. My grandfather may have treated her horribly, both physically and mentally – but he always made sure she was never short of money. As far as I know, she had never had to work in her whole life, going from a fairly well off family to being with my grandfather, and either when they were living together before they were married, or after, he always had a source of funds.

One of his side lines was buying and selling jewellery when it was offered to him during the war, but always giving my grandmother the best items. That was just part of it. But what he knew most of all then was when to buy – and when to sell. It seems that during the war, he was a well-known wheeler-dealer – to those that knew...

~

That week in Brighton each year didn't always bring the best of sunshine. There were usually a few glorious days, but also other days when darkness would descend and the clouds would open.

Nanny used to love sitting in the occasional shelter along the promenade at these times. We would watch people walk by, stoically braving the downpour in their "pac-a-macs". She would do her normal thing of commenting on everyone who walked by – especially the women.

"Look at that old woc – look at her arse". It was the same as being back at home, her favourite pastime of sitting in her armchair in the lounge window looking down at the women below going about their business.

Then she would fall asleep. Always!

It would feel strange when the rain stopped and the sun shone again. The promenade would be wet with rain, and yet there was the steamy smell of those awful pac-a-macs wafting from people as they still strolled by. Then it would be the smell of fish and chips as people bought their tea and sat on the wet seats eating it.

Tea for us, if it wasn't afternoon tea in a little teashop, was sometimes a bag of hot chips, sprinkled with larger-grained salt, and that unique vinegar that it seems can only be found in fish and chip shops! Mmm... It would seep down to the bottom of the little paper bag, and those last remaining chips would be deliciously drenched in it. Such a lovely end to something so heart-warming and comforting!

On one afternoon each week I was there, we would go to the matinée showing at the cinema. It really didn't matter what the film was – because Nanny would always *fall asleep*. She would sit there, all prim and proper, with her hat still in place, butterfly glasses still on her nose, and her hands folded neatly in her lap – and then she would start *snoring*...

Oh dear... Oh dear... No-one ever gave her a nudge though – everyone was far too polite.

Nanny was happy to cook lunch and not go to restaurants. Like my father, she would fry steaks and lamb chops, not being guided by my mother. I think they were more for me though, because she hated her false teeth, and would usually have them out rather than in! But she would cook these foods anyway, probably wanting to treat me, like she secretly did at times at the pub when I couldn't possibly eat what was put before me. So being with her alone, I didn't have to worry about going to bed on an empty stomach.

When my parents were there – like taking us down to Brighton one Saturday then picking me up the next, we would go to a café in the town called "The Black Cat", which had a large black cat shape outside on the wall. There it would be lamb chops again...

One day, a French man was sitting on a nearby table on his own. He was really tucking into his chops, holding them with his fingers and gnawing at the bones with great relish.

"How can he sit there – in public – eating with his fingers?" My mother exclaimed.

"Well – he's *French*" Nanny replied dryly – in a flash.

She could be so funny sometimes. I just hope that her remarks about people were never overheard!

~

Those weeks in Brighton were long before the nudist beach, and I do wonder what my grandmother would have done if it had been there then? Would she have walked across it, getting the odd little glimpse of some proud nudist, spreading his legs and thrusting forward – like some of them do. Yes, I think she might have done. I think Nanny, as ladylike as she appeared on the outside, was a bit of a gal really. She would have done that – got the odd little glimpse – and had a right old chuckle to herself!

Nanny had a friend in Brighton called Johnny. He was a pianist at an underground bar along Brighton sea front called "The Dive", and he was blind. She used to speak in raptures about their friendship, and how she loved going down to The Dive to hear him play. Being such a good pianist herself, she really loved both listening to and playing piano music. Sometimes in the pub Nanny would say "I'll just go and have a tinkle on the old Joanna" – and then sit there playing from sheet music something really lovely.

She seemed to also love Johnny in some sort of way. One evening we went for our normal stroll along Brighton sea front, and we came pretty close to The Dive. We were standing next to a restaurant, and Nanny said she wanted to go down to The Dive to see Johnny – she had something she wanted to say to him. So she told me to stay where I was and wait for her.

By now it was dusk, and the restaurant looked very inviting with couples sitting at little tables enjoying their meal. All the tables were lit with candles, and it all looked so romantic. I had never been to an actual restaurant before, moreover, I had never had my dinner in the evening before! I couldn't help but keep glancing in the window, seeing those people eating, drinking wine, and looking all lovingly at each other. I hoped that one day, I would be able to do something similar – and that some lovely chap would come along – and wine and dine *me* by candlelight...

Maybe Elvis would suddenly materialise – and sweep me off my feet!

~

It was that particular week that Nanny said she was going to buy me my first perfume. I was fifteen years old, and already interested in perfumes, their ingredients, and the way they were made.

It was also that year that I had bought my first ever "Vogue". At 2/6d it was a lot of money in those days – inside it had a pull-out section about the perfumes around at the time, their "personality" and which famous women wore them. I loved that section – I still do – and have it safely tucked away in one of my perfume books. In fact, I still have that Vogue...

I had also read a book from the library about Vogue magazine, which I think was written by the editor at the time, and she said something like – "When you see it in Vogue – then is the time to buy it. When it is all over the high street – then is the time to stop wearing it..." These words inspired me to buy "Vogue" whenever I could afford it. Obviously I couldn't buy any of the clothes shown on those glossy pages, but in subsequent years I was able to recreate some of them with my trusty sewing machine.

~

The advertisements in Vogue also inspired me, as young as I was then. Everything was different to the normal magazines, which advertised Tide and Omo soap powders as being the best and brightest to please your man...

Vogue however, had advertisements for the delight of women, like Max Factor make-up, Revlon nail polishes, and Yardley toiletries. Red Rose soap and April Violets. Once, I secretly indulged myself and with my pocket money, bought one bar of Yardley Red Rose soap, and kept it hidden. I would bring that out of its pretty packaging to inhale the scent of that deep red rose. Then, after a while I felt the time had come to actually *use* it. It still smelled as beautiful, and I would wash with it, and breathe in the deep aroma of those Victorian roses that had been growing in our garden – before the devastation. No-one knew about that little bar of soap, just me, and my conscience, buying and keeping such a little luxury to myself.

Just buying that small bar of Yardley soap though, made me feel that I was a small – *very small* – part of that world out there... Somewhere...

~

One day we went to a lovely little shop that sold perfumes and expensive cosmetics.

"Now which perfume would you like?" Nanny asked as we walked along to the shop.

"May I have Blue Grass please?" I asked, without any hesitation.

"You can have whatever you like duck", Nanny said kindly.

It wasn't an expensive perfume, but it was the *real* perfume that Nanny bought me – women wore *real perfume* essence in those days. Just a little dab behind the ears and the inside of the wrists, anywhere where there was a pulse. It was a little daring to put a dab behind your knees – and also to have a little bit of perfume on cotton wool – tucked inside your bra...

"Put perfume anywhere you want to be kissed" Coco Chanel had advised sensuously...

I still have that little bottle, with its glass stopper, topped with a fake sapphire, summing up the blueness of the perfume notes. I loved it, and that little bottle reminds me of wearing that scent the very first time I ever went to the theatre – incidentally to see Daphne Du Maurier's "Rebecca". Moreover – it reminds me of the time that I was given my very first perfume – one that I had the privilege to choose myself.

If only I had told Nanny all this – and how much I had enjoyed my times with her in Brighton – as we had our own very special "Great Escape".

The Wedding Dress

1963

The dawn of the 1960s had brought a whole new change of attitude towards clothing. Dior's elegant "New Look" after the stark days of wartime clothes rationing had graced many a post-war wedding, but was now being seen as somewhat old-fashioned, even amongst "older" women – like in their thirties and forties!

Amidst all the trendy London influences that were beginning to make their mark, on new television shows such as "Ready Steady Go" (the weekend starts here...!) the shift dress, that had become popular when it was worn by Audrey Hepburn in "Breakfast at Tiffany's" two years earlier, was now becoming quite fashionable. The "Designer" ones were of course very expensive, exquisitely cut and smart, but soon after this simple design – reached Essex!

These copies were just very simple cotton dresses, unlined, and usually with no darts to enhance the figure. They were simple, straight cut, sleeveless, round-necked – and ended, as was still usually the case, just below the knee. It was no frills – just pure simplicity.

I actually had one of these dresses in 1962 and wore it in Jersey. It was that dress, along with having my hair up, and wearing one of my mother's large beaded necklaces, that I imagine got me passed as being eighteen years old and able to go into a pub with my parents – even though my father had pretended I had been ill – but that was what I was wearing, and I certainly looked a lot older than thirteen.

Now it was 1963, and I was still wearing that same shift dress, so I suppose its simple design accommodated any development my thin body may have had during that year.

There was to be a small wedding in Nell's family. Nell was taking me, and we were to initially meet up with just a few other relatives at a terraced cottage in the village where Nell had grown up. I was fourteen and conscious of my appearance and, unfortunately, any new clothing still had to be met with my mother's approval.

I needed a new dress for this wedding. Nothing fancy, I was still a young teenager and didn't need a chiffon suit or a hat. Just something simple, but nice. Something that would make me feel comfortable in company I had never met before, and moreover – confident.

My mother agreed that yes, I needed a new dress to wear to this wedding, and I looked forward to the exciting prospect of going to a nice dress shop or store, such as Chiesmans. I hadn't forgotten that lovely navy blue and white spotted dress that I had been bought from there and made me feel so nice – but which then disappeared... Maybe there would be another one similar to that?

Instead, my mother took me to a certain chain store in Basildon, which was now establishing itself as a shopping centre as well as a new town for housing the huge influx of families who had moved out from bombed London during the war.

I felt a little dubious seeing the racks and racks of clothing which, unlike Marks & Spencer at the time, with its promise of only British made goods, were probably made in China, or wherever else labour was cheap.

This store wasn't as bad as I may be making it seem, but it really wasn't the kind of shop I had hoped to go to for a new smart dress. There were however – shift dresses. This particular chain had picked up on what had been popular during the past year, and I did love the shift dress I was wearing.

My mother picked out one, the smallest size of course, and held it up against me.

"Hmm", she went, with a sound of approval – "we'll have this one..."

Um – no. This dress was the brightest lime green, brighter than any "go" sign on a traffic light, and what's more – it had a pattern of a *huge* daisy, stretching from the neckline right down to the hem...

"But I don't like it..." I quietly protested...

"Well you don't want to look like everyone else do you", my mother answered taking it off to the till...

The wedding day came, and Nell and I took the long journey to that little terraced cottage where we were to meet up with a few of the wedding guests in a tiny front room.

The moment I walked in – I saw my dress... And it wasn't my reflection in the mirror...

Let It Bleed

1963

When I was fourteen I had the confirmation that I really was a girl, and that now I had turned into a woman. My mother had encouraged me to have more boys than girls as friends, saying that girls were horrible, and boys were so much better. So having had Georgie as a playmate when I was little, climbing trees and going on all our adventures across the fields, I had gone on to play cricket and football with him and other boys in the village, down on the "rec" – the local recreation ground.

It wasn't that I was in any way sporty, because as I have said, I always came last in races on Sports Day as I really didn't have the stamina to keep up with all the other children. But being Georgie's friend, I was accepted into the company of all his friends.

But now I was in the third year at Torells – *Torells School For Girls*. Boys were no longer little playmates with which to have innocent adventures. Boys were now *mysterious...* Their voices going from high pitched to *low* – and just in one sentence. Although I expect that they thought girls were even more mysterious than them. Yes indeed – how much did they know about girls bleeding monthly? Did their fathers ever tell them the facts? Somehow – I don't think so.

~

Now I had what I was sure was the beginning of my first period. There wasn't much blood showing on that first day, but enough to show me that that was what was happening.

I told my mother, who was in the kitchen on her own, and she looked quite angry. But *why??* Why was it so bad that I had started my periods – and was therefore turning into a woman? Why was I suddenly being made to feel wholly embarrassed by the whole thing?

"Show me your knickers", she demanded, looking disturbingly disgusted.

So I had to show her and stand there while she inspected them...

"Hmm", she went, peering at them closely.

She confirmed that yes, I had started my "courses", and told me to go into the spare bedroom. That room that was kept back for anyone who wanted to use it – apart from me...

I waited while she went to get what I needed, anticipating a pack of the sanitary towels that we sold in the shop. In those days they came in plain, dark blue paper wrappers, disguising what was hidden inside. She came back into the room with a very old curled up flesh-coloured sanitary belt, two *nappy* pins – and a piece of stained torn up old sheet...

I was horrified. Was this what I was going to have to wear for a week every month? I asked her very quietly, why couldn't I have sanitary towels.

"You don't want those things!" she exclaimed. It was always *"You don't want... You don't want"* with her. But I didn't want these rags and nappy pins...

She laid the torn up bit of old sheet down on the bed and showed me how to fold it over – just like a nappy – and told me to fasten it over the old sanitary belt front and back with the large nappy pins. She said she will give me a few more *"clawthes"*, which she said in a long drawn out tone, if I needed them. But why *clawthes*? I later realised that it was her way of saying "cloths" which I suppose was one step up from saying "rags". She then instructed me to wash them out in the sink at night – then hang them on the washing line to dry. This washing line hung over the pub car park, and anything on there was for all to see.

Sometimes underwear would be stolen – especially knickers. So *someone* was keeping an eye on what was being put onto that line. Could that be the same very creepy man who was telephoning the pub waiting for me to answer – and asking me to take my knickers down? And what would people think seeing inevitably blood-stained pieces of rag drying on the line? They would be like flags flying announcing someone in the household had a period. I had never seen them on the line before, so this would surely have to be *me...*

"By the way" she said as she left the room for me to sort out this contraption "while you're *not very well* – you can't wash your hair…" Oh really??

~

My period suddenly went into full flow. It was awful, and with only bits of rag for "protection", if you can call it that, I was finding it very hard to cope. I had to take these rags to school in my bag, then bring them back, blood soaked, to wash out at night in the sink. I was so worried all the time that the blood would seep through my underwear to my skirt, or run down my legs. I was constantly checking and checking…

Trying to sleep at night next to my grandmother was a nightmare – almost literally. I was forever trying to check that there wasn't any blood seeping out on to the sheet. Sometimes she would give my bottom a little squeeze if she was facing me. "A nice bit of soft" she was apt to say sometimes. I always pretended to be asleep, but now I was terrified that a little squeeze like that might make everything even worse.

This first period went on for three weeks, and I was desperate. Eventually, I plucked up courage to go and tell my mother, because I was finding it so hard to cope. She must have known though, because of all the rags that were put out to dry.

She was in the saloon bar, not doing anything, just standing looking out of the window.

"Mummy" I said nervously, "I have been bleeding heavily for three weeks – and I don't know what to do…"

I'll never forget the look on her face as she turned round and faced me. And then she started laughing…

Little Big Man

August 1963

In the early sixties a mysterious couple moved into a very large house down the lane. They were an odd looking couple, because the man was short and the woman was tall and towered above him. He had dark hair and was quite a snappy dresser, and would come up to the pub sitting on a stool at the counter in the saloon bar, drinking spirits, and puffing away continuously on cigarettes. The woman though, although she did come to the pub once or twice, tended to stay at the house. I think we were all taken aback when we first met her, because she seemed to be more like a man dressed in women's clothes. This was probably an unfair observation, but we all thought the same. As Ray Davies later sang of Lola "she walked like a woman – and talked like a man".

This air of mystery about them sparked a lot of interest amongst customers and people who lived nearby, but the man, although he seemed friendly, only really talked to my grandfather. He was obviously very wealthy, but didn't say much about his life, or where they had come from. He would disappear for a few days at a time sometimes, and my grandfather found out that he went to London, but that was all he said he knew about him.

One hot summer's day, Grandpop and I were walking down the lane, and the woman was in the front garden of the house. Grandpop would always stop and chat to anyone that we met, well, anyone he liked that is, and as we reached the beginning of the drive the woman came out to see us. She was wearing a white skirt and a short-sleeved top in a bright shade of turquoise that made her orange make-up even brighter, and her blonde hair a bit brassy. Having bare arms, I noticed how large her hands were, and standing close to her and chatting, I thought that her hair looked rather like a wig. I felt very confused and also rather disconcerted, especially as her voice, as well as her hands, was also rather masculine.

She was very nice though, and smiled a lot as she talked. I really liked her. Soon she asked us if we would like to go indoors and have a look over the house – oh wow! – would we!

The house was huge, with lots of large ornate rooms and long corridors on all floors. There were rooms everywhere, and as we followed the woman as she led us around, the afternoon sunshine streamed in though the high windows. She was obviously so proud of the house, and smiled all the time as she showed us each room. I seem to remember there being a lot of pale blue along the corridors, either the walls, or powder blue carpets. Maybe both. Whatever it was, there was an air of opulence – and money.

The couple lived there for a while, and then one day they just disappeared – as suddenly as they had first arrived. Nobody knew where they had gone to, just as nobody knew where they had come from. It was all just a mystery.

However, rumours abounded about who this mysterious couple might be... It was even suggested that they might have had something to do with The Great Train Robbery...

Well, he may have been a little man, but to my grandfather he was Mr. Big.

The End Of The Line

Back to earlier childhood

My dentist, when it wasn't my grandfather taking Nazi-type pleasure out of pulling my teeth out in the cook house, was a nice lady in Grays. There were two dentists in the building, a man on the ground floor and a woman upstairs. As far as I know, they were the only dentists in Grays. I hated walking up those stairs whenever my turn came to sit in the black dentist's chair, smelling the chemicals that seemed exclusive to dentistry. So, if I could keep quiet about any toothache I was experiencing, not cry with the pain, and not be seen biting into an apple to loosen the tooth more, then I was able to go to the nice female dentist up the stairs in the surgery.

Before leaving the pub to catch the bus to go to Grays with Nell, I was always given a glass of Advocaat to calm my nerves. I can't help but wonder if the dentist ever smelled alcohol on my breath!

What I remember most of all once sitting on the dentist's chair, was the smell of Fairy household soap with which the dentist washed her hands. Not only did I recognise the smell from Nell rubbing the soap onto my grandfather's shirt collars when she washed them, but it was also on the side of the sink in the surgery. No surgical gloves in those days then! Then, the strong smell of the rubber as the gas mask was placed on my face took over – always a horrible smell of dread to me – and then the gas...

Well, that was so much better than my grandfather yanking out my tooth – "Pain? What pain?" he would say. "*Pain is all in the mind*". He always said that, no matter what sort of pain anyone was enduring.

So, having had my tooth extracted humanely by the dentist, I would then come to, and feel a small plug of cotton wool in the gap where my tooth had been, put there to soak up the blood.

"Swill your mouth with plenty of salt water" the dentist would instruct kindly. "It will heal your gum, and stop any infection getting into the hole". Once home again though, I would straight away be given another glass of Advocaat to calm me down!

~

Time went on, and my adult teeth came through, sometimes pushing out any milk teeth that were teetering on the verge of extraction.

Now, with a full set of adult teeth, which were there to last me a lifetime, this brought with it a different dental experience – the *drill*.

Whether it was totally necessary or not, I had my first fillings. Now, local anaesthetic was administered straight into my gum, and I would then have to go back down the stairs and sit in the waiting room for the injection to take while the dentist was seeing her next patient. Local anaesthetic was very slow in those days!

On one such occasion while I was waiting, a man came in nursing a swollen cheek. He had a woollen scarf wrapped around his neck and was holding it against his cheek. He looked as though he was in a lot of pain. He could hardly speak when he asked the stern and very snotty receptionist if he could see one of the dentists that day.

"Today?" she said in a rather sarcastic tone. "Of course you can't!" she snapped tersely.

The man explained quietly and patiently that he was in agony with a tooth.

"You'll just have to wait for an appointment" she said, looking down at her appointment book, and sucking the end of her pencil.

"Two weeks?" she said, looking over the top of her half-rim glasses. It sounded more like an order than a suggestion.

The man shook his head slightly, still holding his scarf over his cheek, and obviously in a lot of pain.

"Then there is nothing we can do for you", she said, looking down at something on her desk, and trying to look busy.

"Well, I am just going to sit here" he answered quietly, "until someone *can* see me."

~

My turn came, and this was my first filling – with that skull-shattering *slow* drill. I didn't know then that one day dentistry would improve. No wonder my grandmother had had all her teeth taken out!

~

I had just turned fifteen. The weather was awful for springtime, very cold, and with no hint of the summer to follow. I had an excruciating pain in one of my front teeth. It didn't look decayed, well not from the front anyway. But the pain though was hard to cope with.

I remembered that poor man in the dentist surgery those years ago, and how he stoically sat it out, waiting for his tooth to be looked at, and hopefully remedied. I remembered leaving the surgery, and how he was still sitting there – nursing his pain. Had he been able to see one of the dentists that day? I hadn't forgotten him, and just hoped that yes, maybe my nice kind dentist had helped him. So maybe that was what you had to do...

Therefore, I wrapped up warm against the cold, and pulled my woollen scarf across my face – it was the only scarf I had. It was mohair, and although it was very pretty and given to me by my grandmother, I found it hard coping with the itchiness of its fibres. I don't think "allergies" in all their guises had been invented then!

Nevertheless, I got the bus and went off to Grays in order to try to see the dentist. First of all though I would have to get past the dragon on reception...

"Today?" she mocked, with a dismissive tone.. "Ha-ha" – she added, pretending to look at the appointment book.

"No, nothing for... Hmm – three weeks... How does that suit you?"

The man those few years ago had been offered two weeks' wait, I was now being offered three.

"But I need to have my tooth looked at" I said quietly and meekly, struggling to talk.

"No – no – no" she said with feigned authority, as she turned the pages of her appointment book – with its somewhat blank pages.

I was pretty desperate with the terrible pain I was experiencing, but I still remained quiet and very polite.

"Hmm…" she uttered, "you could go to Whitechapel – they will see you there – no appointment necessary…"

I asked her about the hospital she was mentioning. They had a dental school there and would see anyone, even without an appointment. She failed to mention that it would be students working on my painful tooth…

~

When I arrived home, well back at the pub that is, my mother was sitting in the armchair in the kitchen. She had one of the cats on her lap, a more docile one that was happy to be picked up. She was going through his fur with her fingers, looking for nits, which she snapped with her thumbnails. She loved doing that.

"Whitechapel?" she said, now looking up at me.

"Yes", I said, "there is a dental school there – at the hospital."

"Whitechapel" she repeated, as though it was a light bulb moment. "You don't want to go *there…*"

"But I have to" I said, explaining again that I was in great pain with this tooth.

My mother looked down again, back at our little cat, and snapped another nit between her thumbnails.

"No, you don't want to go *there…"* she reiterated.

I explained it all over again, through tears that I never wanted to show.

"Will you come with me Mummy?" I asked, plaintively. I had never been on the Underground before, and to find my way to Whitechapel Hospital was going to be a very tough challenge indeed.

"No I can't" she said, still engrossed in finding nits in the cat's fur.

~

To get to Whitechapel, I would have to get the No.53 bus to Grays, then either pick up the Aldgate bus from there, or get the train to goodness-knows-where in London to catch the underground train to Whitechapel. I took the first option. I knew what I was doing going by bus from Grays to Aldgate. Then I would just have to worry how I got from there to the hospital..

"Mummy – please come with me..." I asked her. She didn't even answer this time.

~

So there I was the next day, full of pain and dosed up to the brim with codeine tablets – aspirin didn't help at all – how was I to know that it was an abscess behind my front teeth?

I left the pub early and caught the hourly bus to Grays, then went along to wherever the Aldgate bus would be. Having boarded that, I eventually ended up in Aldgate, where I knew there was an underground station. No matter how scared I was of doing all this on my own, sometimes pain takes precedence over all and everything – and this was what was happening now.

I knew this little part of outer London. Normally it would be another bus from there to Oxford Circus, but now I was having to find my way to Whitechapel. Anyway, I pondered – what was so bad about going to Whitechapel?

I found the underground, and had worked out how to get to Whitechapel – I could get the underground train to there from Aldgate – it wasn't far away...

But – being dosed up with codeines to try to alleviate the pain – I got on the underground train at Aldgate, and although I was on the right line, I was going northwards – instead of just one or two stops southwards to Whitechapel. I didn't realise this until I reached Baker Street – oh dear – it had to be Baker Street!

So then I had to go back again, southwards to Whitechapel...

By now, the morning was flitting by, and by the time I arrived at Whitechapel it was late morning. I didn't even know exactly where the hospital was either.

Well, eventually, I found it, still in immense pain – and just needing someone to do *something* – *anything* – to alleviate it.

~

It was surprisingly quiet when I reached the reception desk at the hospital.

"We are closing for lunch now" the receptionist told me, just glancing at her watch as if to say that it was fact...

"Come back at one o'clock" she said in a tone of voice that was really saying... *Go away and don't come back **until** one o'clock...*

~

So now I had over an hour to while away before I was allowed back at the hospital. I couldn't help but wonder – this is a hospital – why can't I stay here while I wait? But who was *I* to question this?

I walked around the streets of Whitechapel. They seemed bleak, lots of grey alleyways, and wet pavements from all the rain that we had had those past few days.

"Mummy – why didn't you come with me?" I was crying silently.

I saw a shop amidst all this greyness – the window was bright, displaying lots of bras and knickers, the like of which I had never seen before. They were hanging across the window like bunting in a rather amateur way. Scarlet and black, flamingo pink and purple, knickers, with slits at the bottom where the crotch should be...

I felt uneasy being around this area, and made my way back to the hospital. I went back to the waiting room. I still had ages to wait, the best part of an hour. There was a row of chairs, about twenty I think.

"Take a seat over there" the receptionist said, pointing to one end of the line of chairs. So I sat there and waited – and waited... People were gradually arriving and sitting on the chairs waiting for the afternoon dental school department to open, until all the chairs were taken.

At around one o'clock the door opened, and a nurse appeared...

"Come in" she beckoned to the person sitting at *the other end of the line...*

I was far too timid to go to the receptionist and tell her that I was there first...

And so, I very politely sat and waited until everyone else had been seen.

~

Eventually – after a lot of frustration and *pain* – I was at last taken into the dental school, and had the abscess seen to. After a lot of discussing and messing around with local anaesthesia, it was finally done. Then I had to make the long journey back to Orsett – on my own.

The tutor at the dental school had advised me to see my dentist as soon as possible when I returned home to check my mouth for healing etc. This was more easily said than done though.

"Why did you go to Whitechapel Hospital to have this done?" she asked looking concerned, when I was finally allowed to see her.

"Because I couldn't get an appointment *here*" I explained.

"But my dear", she said kindly – *"I would always see you..."*

My Boy Lollipop

Spring 1964

It was late spring 1964 and Old Woman had had another litter of kittens. This time my grandfather said that I could choose one to have as my very own. One in particular pulled at my heart as I looked at the litter. He was the colour of an Orange Maid lolly. Millie had been in the charts for quite some weeks with "My Boy Lollipop", and so I felt I just had to name this little kitten "Lollipop".

"What a silly name for a cat", my father said when I told him. But never mind he was *my* cat, and nobody else seemed to mind what I had called him. I loved Lollipop, and would cradle him in my arms like a baby. I would gently dance around the room with him in my arms singing along to "My Boy Lollipop" when it was played on the wireless, and I couldn't wait to see him when I was at school. He was just the sweetest little bundle of fluffy ginger fur, and I loved him so much.

Some months later, I was surprised to find out that Mrs. Binns was getting married. She had got to know one of the customers in the pub called Jack. He was relatively new to the area, and was a teacher of shorthand and German Language – coincidentally, he had been giving me shorthand lessons one night a week at the college, and was also now teaching me German, albeit in the taproom! He had found me a German pen friend too – he was called Erich and lived in Düsseldorf and was learning English – Jack helped me to interpret his letters.

Somehow though, I don't think every word may have been interpreted! Then again, maybe Erich had wanted this to be a surprise...

I came home from college one day and, unusually, my mother was waiting for me in the lobby of the pub.

"Quick Yvonne" she said urgently, "there is someone waiting for you in the saloon bar..."

"Who?" I asked her, somewhat weary from my day at college.

"I don't know" she said, "I can't understand a word he's saying – but it sounds a bit German to me."

I opened the door to the saloon bar – and there sat Erich and a friend of his, enjoying a couple of pints, and looking at me expectantly... Their crash helmets were side by side on the table – they had motor-cycled all the way from Düsseldorf!

I couldn't make out whether they had come all that way just to see me, or whether they had just wanted to come to England. Whatever the reason, I hadn't known anything about it! I realised that Erich and his friend couldn't speak any English – and I – without Jack's help and guidance – certainly couldn't speak any German! I could just about get by on paper, but oh dear, actually attempting to speak a language was a far cry from writing it!

So that was the end of a beautiful penfriendship, so to speak. Sometimes things are better left knowing someone from afar – meeting up eventually can be such a disappointment. It wasn't anyone's fault really, although I suppose Erich could have told me that he was coming to see me – but the barriers of language can cause a wide chasm between any friendship. I waved them good-bye as they revved up their motorbikes and went on their way. I couldn't help but think that Erich was rather handsome though...

~

Jack and Mrs. Binns were a strange combination really. He was a short man with heavy rimmed glasses, shorter than she was, and their personalities were very different too. She was outgoing and flamboyant, and he was more introverted and serious. I think it was a surprise to everyone. They lived together for a while in Grays, and then the day came that they were leaving to go and live in Hackney.

They came to the pub to say their goodbyes, and after our fond farewells, I went back indoors as we let Grandpop say his final goodbye on his own. I went up to the kitchen and over to the window that overlooked the car park, and saw my grandfather walking over to the car. He was holding a little ginger bundle – and then I saw him hand my little boy Lollipop over to Mrs. Binns...

Nobody had given me any warning, or indeed spoken to me about it in any way. It was a complete and utter shock. Yet again, something that I cherished and thought was mine was just – given away. This time though, it wasn't my dolls, my teddy bears, my dolls' house or my clothes. This was a little living creature – Lollipop, my beautiful little kitten.

~

We didn't see Mrs. Binns for some time, although she was now Mrs. Matthews – but people still referred to her as Betty Binns. One day I found out that she had telephoned and that my parents were taking me to see her in her house in Hackney. We had been invited to go for tea. I can't say I was terribly pleased to go to see them, because how could Mrs. Binns have let me down yet again? How could she have taken my little kitten, and how could such a respectable man as Jack let her? Well I didn't have any choice in the matter. We were going and, of course, I was looking forward to seeing Lollipop again. So off we went to London in my father's eau-de-nil coloured Ford Cortina.

Our hearts sank as we turned into their road. The terraced Victorian houses that were along each side of the road would have been very nice once, but they were now very run-down and neglected. There was a mosque at the far end of the road, which was something I had never seen before. This caused my mother mild amusement. Oh dear, what had Betty Binns come to? I don't know whether it was seeing what, in those days, was quite an attractive looking car, slowly edging its way along the road as we looked for the house, or more likely that we were *strangers,* but curtains twitched at every window, and every face that we saw was black. My mother muttered something rather detrimental, for she was very prejudiced about any race that wasn't the same colour as us.

Looking back at what the house was like as we entered, I cannot help but think of John Christie's house in the film "10 Rillington Place". That film wasn't released until 1971, but this house had that same general feeling of doom and foreboding, which made it feel as though a murder may have been committed there sometime. I have since seen photos of 10 Rillington Place and, sure enough, it was just like Betty and Jack's house.

Betty and Jack seemed overjoyed to see us though, and welcomed us into their home. The hall was long and dark. A staircase going up to the bedrooms was on the left, and there was another staircase going down to the cellar. There was a sitting room to the right at the front of the house, and behind that a dining room. At the end of the hall there was a small kitchen. The house smelled dank and unloved.

But where was Lollipop? And would he know me? Would he come up to me winding his little body around my feet, purring? Would he nudge his soft little pink nose at my ankles urging me to pick him up for a cuddle?

Well it wasn't long before I found out. This lean and very mean looking ginger Tom soon appeared, probably wondering what all the chattering was about. He took one look at us, then sauntered haughtily out of the room. Each time I saw him he seemed to be looking for the next place to spray. He had a look on his face that seemed to say *"So...?"* Yes, so what? Betty and Jack didn't seem to mind what he was doing.

Betty had prepared a very nice ham salad for tea, and after a while we all sat at the dining room table to eat. Before long we heard a squirting sound coming from under the table... This was followed by a terrible stomach-churning stench that quickly wafted upwards and filled not only our nostrils, but also our taste buds.

My mother and I looked across the table at each other, our knives and forks hovering above our plates. My father just put his knife and fork down, staring silently ahead.

"He always does that", Betty said glibly, as the cat cockily strutted out of the room, his tail in the air, as if to give us an extra whiff.

Betty and Jack just carried on eating, with the pile of cat's mess still fuming under the table.

My father was fuming too. He didn't say a word. He just stared motionless, his face bright red, and his clear pale blue eyes as cold as frosted glass.

That was the last time I ever saw Mrs. Binns.

~

"My mother's cat did that once", my father said as we headed back in the car to Orsett.

Oh?

"I came home from work, just sat down to have my dinner – and the blasted thing crapped on the floor – right next to me."

Oh dear...

"Well he never did it again..."

So what happened...

"I just picked him up by the scruff of his neck – took him outside – and straight to the water butt..."

My mother and I were silent for quite a while. Eventually I plucked up the courage to ask...

"What did Nanny say?" I ventured timidly.

"She was *so* upset", my father said, "and she never did ever forgive me for that."

It was then that I realised that my father was not only very, *very*, cold, but could also be heartless – even to his own mother.

Come Fly With Me

When I was just ten years old I knew exactly what I wanted to do with my life and had it all mapped out. This was 1959 and having spent my early childhood in the fifties, many other girls knew what they were going to do too. For so many girls in the Grays area, the map of life meant leaving school at fifteen, getting a job in the town as a shop assistant, or working at the Thames Board Mills factory. The more intelligent ones would be in the typing pool, the others would be on the factory floor (some for more than one reason maybe).

For me though, my only ambition was to become an air hostess – I was going to "*FLY*"... I was hoping to work for one of the big long haul airlines and fly to far distant and exotic lands... I would be immaculate and proud of my uniform, and would enjoy serving the passengers, some of whom would be rich and famous, which they tended to be in those days on long haul flights. I knew I wouldn't see much of those far distant lands, but the pleasure for me would be in the journey.

Oh yes, that was what I was going to be. That glamorous world was beckoning me. I would fly above the soft downy clouds, and would be near to the stars that only the angels knew... I would look down upon the oceans, the mountain ranges, the barren deserts, and the lush, tropical rainforests.

Then one day, when the time was right, I would marry one of those handsome men, or maybe a dishy pilot. The spark would be there, our eyes meeting and lingering – as I handed him his drink, with my red Estée Lauder lips all a-quiver – as I knew that spark would never end.

We would marry in the lovely old Church of England church, right in the heart of Orsett village, and all my family, my aunts and uncles, cousins, and everyone, would all be there to wish me well. My father would walk me down the aisle, and my mother would be sitting in the front pew, wearing a big hat, and maybe managing a smile... I would be so in love, and my mother would tell me that I had done the right thing – for once in my life…

Well that had been my dream courtship and wedding.

~

I had served my time at Torells, and the plan was that I would then spend two years at Thurrock Technical College, to sort of finish off my education nicely. Oh yes, I was looking forward to that. When I was in the third year of my "sentence" the film "Come Fly With Me" had just been released, and the theme song was always on my mind. The film was about air hostesses, and was a bitter-sweet "romcom" of the day. It didn't matter that the handsome men they fell in love with weren't as handsome in spirit. I just sat back in the cinema seat and enjoyed the flight.

I was wearing my long hair up, neatly twirled around the top of my head, and sometimes in a French pleat, just like an air hostess. I was already looking after my skin by always taking my make-up off before I went to bed, much to my mother's scorn…

"You don't want to use that muck" she said as I poured some Ann French cleansing lotion on to some cotton wool. "You just need soap and water – like me." Oh yes? She didn't use just a light tinted foundation cream on her face like I did. She only used face powder – and that was straight onto bare skin. No wonder she was getting wrinkled prematurely. I must say that it was lovely face powder that she used though. It was by Houbigant, expensive, and it had a beautiful scent. If only she had bought a slightly warmer shade though, rather than the pale chalky pink that she used. Houbigant was known for its "dull finish" face powder, and the red rouge that she used on her cheeks didn't do anything to enhance her looks.

I had bought the cleansing lotion from Woolworths with my pocket money, even though I was only fourteen. I had learned all about skin care in a lovely teenage book I had, which was all about etiquette, skin care, hygiene, being fastidious, and general good behaviour. I loved that book, but unfortunately it had been in my grandmother's fur coat box with all my other things – with which my mother made a bonfire…

One of the pub customers was a very nice man who liked to chat to me, and one day he asked me what I wanted to do when I left school. I told him that I wanted to be an air hostess – and he told me that that was what his daughter was. She was on long-haul flights, and so went all over the world. I was fascinated by this, and especially as he was another source for information for my chosen career.

One day he came in the pub and gave me a stamp album, and also an assortment of stamps. He told me how everywhere his daughter went she would send back a postcard or letter, and he had taken the stamps off for me to stick in the relevant pages. This was the start of a new thing, and whenever he had another stamp he would bring it in for me to stick in my stamp album. I loved doing that, and with each new stamp I was transported to another part of the world. This was all *so* exciting!

Unfortunately, I also kept that stamp album in the fur coat box...

~

I had done very well in French, and I knew that once I left school I could do evening classes in German while I was at the Technical College. Meanwhile, while I was there I could go into the art and design class. I was good at art and drawing, and now I was good at dressmaking. I could combine the two together and have that behind me if it didn't work out for me becoming an air hostess. "Flying the flag" was my ambition – but hey, training as a fashion designer wouldn't be too much of a let-down if it didn't happen! And anyway, it would be a good career to have until I was old enough to apply to the airline.

The rules in those days were much more strict than they are now. You couldn't apply until you were twenty-one, so I had a while to perfect the requirements regarding languages etc. You had to be at least five feet four inches tall, which was because you had to be tall enough to reach the overhead luggage bins. Well I was exactly that height! There were weight restrictions then too. You had to be between seven stone twelve pounds and nine stone eight pounds – I was just seven stone – but I had a few years to grow!

I was working on the requirement to look nice, even though I had no confidence regarding that, but the requirement for a good posture was no problem, because my grandfather had insisted on it throughout my childhood.

"Get those shoulders back girl" he would say if he saw me slouching at all – how could I hold my head high when I was always so unhappy? Then he would come along and push me hard between my shoulders in a particularly painful spot so that I automatically had to put them back. If that didn't work, then he would pull my shoulders back himself. So I had to be aware of my posture at all times when he was around.

Looking back, I can't see why I was made to have no confidence in my looks. Whenever I look through the few old photos that I have of my early teens, I can see that they show how elegant I was trying to be even then. I would think of Grace Kelly and how she had married her prince in 1956 – that was a good thing to keep in mind!

~

"No!" my mother said one awful day when I told her what my plans were... "You are going to be a... *Policewoman*" she informed me.

"What?? A *POLICEWOMAN*??"

"Yes" she said, in a tone of voice that meant that I had no option. "I can't *wait* to see you on point duty..."

This was no joke! Where had this suddenly come from? And why hadn't I heard about this before? What about my Shirley Flight book that I had been awarded, and the excitement that I had shown from that? But my mother was not to be questioned.

Maybe she had got this idea from the fact that her paternal grandfather had been a railway policeman, and that my grandfather had his truncheon and handcuffs hanging on his bedroom wall. Not quite the same as being on point duty, but she seemed to have some fascination with the police force, and I was going to have to do as I was told.

I couldn't think of a worse occupation for me to do. I was small and slim, nervous and timid. And what's more, on a minor note – a policewoman's uniform of the time wasn't the best look!

So now, my mother was telling me to get a book from the school library about police work – and to read it all the way through so that I knew what I had to do. I did that – I *had* to. If my mother told me to do something – then I did it. I actually found it very interesting reading about police work from a career point of view, and not from black and white versions on "Dixon of Dock Green" and "Z Cars". I loved those programmes and others like them, but they were rather sanitised in those days, in comparison to what police men and women really had to deal with. These days everything is shown in such programmes – all the gory details and abuse that goes on behind closed doors...

I knew all about that, through my own experience. So although I had first-hand knowledge of what went on in peoples' homes, there was no way I could have the mental strength at that time of my life to deal with it myself. I did *try* to please my mother regarding this, but as much as I tried, I just couldn't sum up any enthusiasm at all for going into a career where, apart from being on the dreaded "point duty", I might have to hand-cuff and arrest someone. "Going on a raid" was just *not me!*

~

My mother was so disappointed that she was not going to see me in a policewoman's uniform, that she *absolutely refused* to allow me to apply for the art and design course at Thurrock Technical College.

"Well if you're not going to do as I want", she said, "you are jolly well going to have to do shorthand and typing and get a proper trade behind you." And so she put me on to the commercial course, where the main subjects were shorthand and typing, but also *commerce and book keeping* – subjects which were so utterly boring...

My mother may have been right insisting that I had a "proper trade" behind me, but the world of commerce did not fill me with any enthusiasm at all – not one iota.

There was still a chance to follow my dream though – all I had to do now was get through these next two years and all those "office routine" lessons as well, whilst perfecting my French – and *trying* to learn German...

That big wide world was out there waiting for me – and I was going to *FLY*...

The Summer Of '64

It was the summer of 1964 and I was fifteen. I had at long last escaped the perils of Torells and was looking forward to starting at Thurrock Technical College that September. So a whole new world awaited me. I must have been the only leaver at Torells Girls' who wasn't crying on that last day – but not me! I was happy to be leaving those doors for good.

It was also the summer that I found a proper tennis partner, someone I could spend pleasant hours with, playing the game that I loved so much.

A new family had moved into the village, a mile down the road from the pub. They were the Pullingers, a well-spoken and seemingly well off family, and one day they came up to the pub to introduce themselves.

Mr. and Mrs. Pullinger had three sons – David (eighteen), Michael (sixteen) and a younger son Richard, who was about six. Mr. Pullinger had a very good job that had taken them to various parts of the world to live for a while. David had been born in Germany, Michael in America, and Richard in Russia. And now they had come to settle in England – and had chosen Orsett.

Somehow, there was an instant chemistry between Michael and me, and we seemed to be drawn to each other straight away. I was being drawn to a real life boy – and not just some good looking singer on the television.

Michael was *so* good looking. He had blonde hair, that was swept to one side, meltingly expressive eyes, and a demeanour and confidence that comes with Public schooling.

Elvis was still the best looking man in the world, but Michael was the best looking boy in the area. My eyes were opened – and what's more – he was *interested in me...*

We got talking about what we liked to do, and found that as well as the same music and films – we also both loved playing tennis! So I was invited to go down to his house to play tennis. Oh wow – oh wow! I had better not drop the ball – I didn't want *him* calling me butter fingers!

~

It was a lovely detached Victorian house that the Pullingers were living in now, surrounded by a large garden with a tennis court, and situated right on the very edge of Orsett village. Lovely large rugs covered the parquet floors, and what I remember most of all are the cut glass handles on all the doors that sparkled with the sun streaming in through the windows.

I spent many happy times down there playing tennis with Michael – Michael wasn't going anywhere now, was happy in his new home, and his parents seemed to like me, and liked me being there. I think they enjoyed having a girl around the place for a change. I felt so comfortable in their company.

The sun shone a lot in Orsett that summer, with its rays beating down onto the Pullingers' lovely garden. I would sit on the lawn with my head tilted upwards to the sun, feeling such a great sense of contentment, which I had never before experienced at home.

~

Mrs. Pullinger was a lovely lady – blonde like Michael, and nice looking. She was always smiling, was very friendly and kind, and seemed happy and content. She was well travelled, and didn't seem to have the hang-ups that some of the local women seemed to have. She was my kind of woman!

One day, she asked me to go into the sunny kitchen with her and chat, which I thoroughly enjoyed. She stood at the large rectangular kitchen table, preparing the dessert for a dinner party she was giving that evening.

This was a whole pineapple, complete with its long spiky leaves, and I watched her fascinated, as with a small paring knife, she cut into it fairly near the top, in a zigzag pattern all the way round. Then she lifted the top off and set it aside for the lid– and voilà – a very attractive looking pineapple. I thought she was so clever!

Pineapple at the pub came in tins, and cut into uniform squares. We had an ice-cube container on the bar in the shape of a pineapple, but that was the nearest I'd ever got to a real one. The most exotic fruits sold at our shop were grapes and bananas!

Then she carefully cut out all the flesh, cutting it into little wedge shapes, rather than cubes! She then mixed this with other fresh fruits – strawberries and grapes etc. – which she then put back into the pineapple, fitted the lid back on and set it aside for the evening. I had never seen anything like that before!

Then I helped her to lay the ornately-carved table in the dining room for the evening. *I was so happy!*

~

After tennis, Michael and I would sit on the grass under a large spreading apple tree, chatting and enjoying the cloudy lemonade that his mother had made. She would bring it out to us in a tall glass jug, with two tall slim glasses. I thought it was so posh! I had never had home-made lemonade before – it was so different to the bottle of R. Whites that my grandmother kept next to the bed...

One such day, Michael decided to climb the apple tree. He was wearing white tennis shorts, and I watched his tanned athletic legs as he climbed upwards... Then he reached right up to the top – and brought me down a perfect rosy apple. I don't remember him saying anything, but I do remember how I felt receiving such a lovely gesture.

Something within me was awakening, like an early spring flower, peeping up through the ground, and seeing the wonderful world for the first time. A shy little violet, that when you lifted up her timid little head, would be smiling sweetly.

~

I had a very small diary with only a little space to write just a few words each day. It started off with the normal boring things like "school today", "snowed today", "no school today – Orsett cut off", that sort of thing. And then it just petered out.

Now I found myself picking up that little diary again, and writing down "tennis today – sun shining" – which was much more exciting! Today though, I had a new entry, I remember exactly what I said... "Michael

climbed the apple tree today – and picked me a lovely apple from the top."
I am not sure, but I think I may have drawn a tiny heart at the end...

The next time I went to get my diary – it was gone. So where could
it be? No-one had any idea of its whereabouts – although I can't help
but think that a certain person did... My mother obviously went through
everything I had – and probably every day...

~

All too soon the summer was ending, and Michael and I said we would
meet up again sometime. Oh yes – if only...

We both had to take our separate paths to finish our education. Would
those paths ever cross? I hoped so. He had never even kissed me, which I
hadn't expected anyway. But he had climbed to the top of the apple tree
to pick that perfect apple – just for me...

And if only I hadn't had that little diary taken away from me. It would
be so interesting now to read just how many times I played tennis with
Michael that summer – that beautiful summer of '64...

At least I have my memories...

Starting College

The girl who came early...

September 1964

I entered Thurrock Technical College achieving top marks in the entrance exam; in fact I had the highest marks of all the girls who entered that year. Because of that, and the examination certificates I had already attained in the fourth year at Torells – GCEs, RCAs and Pitmans – I was to skip the first year and go straight into the second year. This meant that I had an awful lot to catch up on, but I was happy to do that. I had missed a whole year of shorthand, that strange written language invented by Sir Isaac Pitman in 1837 of lines, dots, dashes and squiggles, that only those who know it can read – so I would practise that over and over again at home, testing myself until I got it right.

This wasn't always easy to do though, because just like when I had been at school and doing homework, my grandfather would very often put a stop to it, by saying that I couldn't sit upstairs doing this, because I was wasting electricity. As I didn't have a bedroom, I would have to do it in the kitchen, where there was only one light bulb anyway. But no, that solitary light bulb was enough to "waste electricity". So he summoned me to do it in the bar, which wasn't a good environment for learning, study and practising my shorthand. There was always too much going on, too much chatter, too much noise, too much smoke – and of course, I was always being roped in to help.

The saloon bar was quieter than the taproom, so I would sit at a table in there until too many people started coming in. Then I would move to the snug end of the taproom, which was roughly partitioned off by a curtain. Even so it was still noisy, and men would have to keep coming past me to go to the toilet. It wasn't easy, but I did the best I could.

The other disadvantage about going straight into the second year at college meant that I was only there for one year, and I really wished that I had been able to do the two years. Sometimes I found myself wishing that I hadn't achieved such high marks in the entrance exam, and could have had two years there. I wasn't ready to leave later that year. I was only fifteen, and needed more time to sort out my career.

Another problem was that Alison, and other girls who were in the first year of college, had to go to an auxiliary one at Ockendon, with the most unusual and amusing name of "Bushey Bit"! I couldn't help but think of that well developed girl who used to show herself off in the showers at Torells...

So as I had been "the girl who came late" at Torells, I was now *the girl who came early!*

~

There were some nice girls at college – they were all from different parts of Essex, and with me being a year younger than them, they were intrigued, so I made some nice friends right from the start. It was good, and refreshing, to be mixing socially with other girls. There was a group of four or five girls who were particularly good friends, and they soon took me into their "clique", so at last I was feeling part of something.

One of these nice girls was German, and she suggested that we went to a German restaurant that she liked in London one evening. None of us knew what to expect, apart from thinking that there might be a lot of oom pah pah going on, like in the film "The Student Prince" that I had seen with Nell when I was five. That was the impression I had had of German eating and drinking establishments – pretty girls waiting on tables swaying huge steins of German beer, and lots of thigh slapping going on – the men that is! We were all too young to go to a bier keller though, but we still thought that this could be rather fun!

So we met in Grays and took the bus to Aldgate, which was in the general area of the restaurant, full of anticipation of this jolly night out we might be about to enjoy.

"Zere it is" the German girl said, as the bus went past it to the next stop. We all turned out heads to see...

What?

The restaurant's bright fluorescent lights were glowing white out of the stark-looking room. This was certainly no bier keller! A few of us looked at each other quizzically. "Is that *it...?*" one of the girls whispered behind her hand.

We got off the bus at the next stop and walked back – it was drizzling with rain and the pavements were wet, but there was that bright light ahead beaming out of the gloom. We were all a bit apprehensive, apart from the German girl who was enthusing...

We sat down at one of the white plastic tables on uncomfortable plastic chairs. I think we were the only people in there. I really don't know what we had exactly but the meat, the sauerkraut and some kind of potato all seemed to merge together in some sort of beigeness. We were all pushing our food around our plates, trying to make out what it was, and none of us enjoyed it – apart from the German girl...

~

I also took part in the trips that were organised by the college. We had a trip to London to see "Becket", a film about King Henry II and his close friend and confidant Thomas à Becket. It had a really good cast starring Richard Burton, Peter O'Toole and Sir John Gielgud. I loved the film, but the problem was – we were all in the front row, which meant we had to keep looking upwards, and couldn't really see the whole screen at one time. Never again!

Another time we went ice-skating in London. This was sure to be fun, even though a little daunting. I loved going to the ice shows in London with Nell around Christmas time – it all looked so easy. First of all we had to be kitted out with the skating boots in our size. I wasn't happy about having to wear boots that someone else had maybe just taken off! But there I was holding onto the wall making my way precariously round to the skating rink.

I was ok at first – as long as I held onto the sides! Then someone decided we would all join up, holding hands as we skated around the rink in a long line...

Guess who fell over?

Well it *had* to be me didn't it! And so I had to travel home on the coach wearing very wet trousers... A bit like when I fell in the pond in Meopham woods all those years ago!

So that was my one and only try at ice-skating – but at least I had a go!

~

As well as the freedom of being at college, things were beginning to get a little more interesting in Grays – a coffee bar had opened next to the Co-op! There you could have espresso coffee – something new in my life – served in wide shallow cups. The frothing of the milk on top of the coffee made drinking it a whole new experience. The lights were bright, so there was no real atmosphere – other than the wonderful aroma of the coffee, and the chatter of friends.

I met up with my friends there a few times on Saturday afternoons, and I was really feeling part of something. After that we would go upstairs to the record department in the Co-op next door. We used to flick through the LPs, and listen to the latest singles in the charts in the only record booth they had.

One day my friends and I all crammed into it listening to part of an LP – I think it might have been The Rolling Stones' second album, but whatever it was it was sure to have been the Stones! I don't know how, but suddenly some other girls joined us – maybe even a boy or two – and I just had to get out. When I counted the people in there I realised that at one point there had been *fourteen* of us crammed into that booth! At least we were all slim – but it didn't do much for my claustrophobia!

~

It hadn't taken me long to make these new friends at college – so very different to when I started at Torells. Having now left school I was able to have more say in what clothes I had too. This was still pre-mini time, well in Grays that is, and skirts and dresses were still being worn "just below the knee". Demure, pastel-coloured twin-sets were still being worn, along with "good" woollen skirts, usually from Marks & Spencer's, ones to last – and be worn over and over again. There was a certain fashion now though for slightly scooped-neck dresses, with round collars. Girls wore very pale make-up and pale-coloured stockings... *Yes – stockings!* This was before the age of tights. Low-heeled shoes with little kitten heels were now fashionable, which suited me fine – I didn't like stilettos! No matter how low the heels though, the little kitten heels still had steel caps – and needed the heel caps at college dances...

It was also good to have more friends to discuss make-up and things with. My favourite lipstick at the time, with the fashion being for pale lips, was one by Miners, which was sold in Woolworths. It had a jade green case, and was called "Shrimp". Once the girls saw that – they all bought one. I was really chuffed!

Our English Language teacher was very arty, and I bravely wore a pale blue pearly nail polish to college one day. She loved that, and wanted to know where I had found it. Again, I was really pleased, and the colour was very pretty.

One of these girls came to college one day looking awful – she had shaved off her eyebrows – and where they had once been was now just bright red, very sore-looking skin. When they started to grow back they came through all spiky and pushing outwards like thick whiskers. So they caused a never ending battle for her. It is funny how these days, dense black eyebrows are very fashionable, with some girls even having them tattooed... Hmm, they're going to have a problem one day too...

The only mascara we had then was a block type made by Max Factor. It was a small rectangular compact containing a rectangular block of mascara and a small eyelash brush. The mascara had to be mixed with a little water to the right consistency and then applied.

One day one of the girls showed us her mascara – it had gone mouldy. So she sent it to Max Factor, complaining about what had happened to it, and awaited their reply. When she heard back from them, they said that they had tested the mould, and had found that it was – cheese mould. They suggested that she had been eating cheese and then *spat* onto the mascara to mix it – consequently, they were not going to replace it. She wasn't at all embarrassed about telling everyone about it – so maybe others did that too? Well, I certainly didn't!

One poor girl had her bag of make-up stolen, and I remember her saying how much it was going to cost to replace everything in it. I can't help but wonder though, if she was one of those girls who spat onto their mascara – the thief might have been in for a little bit of eye trouble!

~

I loved those times chatting to my little group of friends about make-up. It made me feel "part" of something. Lectures had to be attended though, and work had to be done – including the dreaded bookkeeping...

"Turrr-n rroond Yvonne – Yvonne turr-n rroond", Mr. Brown (pronounced Brroon!) our Scottish book keeping tutor would say with some sort of sigh, when boredom overcame me and I would turn round to speak to my equally bored friends behind me. Sometimes, if we all managed to sit at the very back of the class, I would join in with their card games and, like the others, would try to look all innocent when Mr. Brown frowned at us. Well, I was no longer repressed when I was at college. Poor Mr. Brown, he knew there wasn't much hope of trying to teach us girls bookkeeping – especially as the others had been doing it for a year longer than me, and they *still* weren't interested!

He seemed to take in all in good humour though, for at the end of lectures he would chat with us. This was usually about his home town, Troon in Scotland – a small seaside town on the west coast in south Ayrshire, overlooking the Isle of Arran. He showed us photos of a very moody looking sea and landscapes. It made Scotland seem like a rather mysterious and mystical place. Girls would say in mock Scottish accents "Mr. Broon – from Troon!" but he took it all in good heart.

He was really nice, and he smelled nice too, rather like lemons. It always helps having a nice teacher, and one who can understand you, because despite all the boredom during those lectures, the bookkeeping system with its profits and losses, and everything else that was entailed, it actually sunk in, and I had learned quite a lot from Mr. Brown.

However, bookkeeping was never going to be the, er, career for me. There were no computers then, and sitting writing endless lists of debits and credits, and gross profits and net profits etc. etc. did not sit well in my plan...

~

So, I was studying hard with all the commercial stuff I was having to learn, including Commerce in the City, which was so utterly boring, and really would have been of much more interest to boys. At the other end of the scale were such mundane things as being shown how to write cheques and postal orders! At the same time I was still practising my French, only written though, because I didn't know anyone else then who could speak the language. And now, I was learning German. I was determined I was going to get my wings!

~

During the latter weeks at college, we had elocution lessons, or "speech", as the classes were simply called. Maybe this was to try to shorten our Essex vowels somewhat! Not all the girls in the class attended – they weren't going to be told how to talk! I didn't talk badly anyway, and neither did my friends – however, we all went along to the classes anyway. Those of us who did attend, had to stand in a circle behind each other, and although I can't remember the exact spot, we all had to hold the top of the back of the girl in front somewhere, to make sure she was pronouncing words properly. I really don't know how that worked, but that was what we had to do. In a way, I suppose it was like going to "finishing school", but without the expense!

My mother had never let me talk in any kind of sloppy way anyway, so I grew up having to make sure I always pronounced my "Ts" etc. But I remember one day being scolded for pronouncing Brighton incorrectly – according to my mother that is...

"You don't say Brigh-ton" she said, looking down her nose at me, "you say Bri-en". I never did work that one out.

During these speech lessons we also had to learn self assertion, where we had to act out various situations and scenarios that we might encounter and have to deal with, out there in the big world of commerce.

Usually, this was in the form of dealing with problems or aggression in an office environment. I was dreading my turn, but fortunately I was not given the problematical or aggressive role – thank goodness for that! But I was to be the one *taking* the aggression – and trying to deal with it!

I can remember exactly where I was sitting when my turn came. The furniture in the classroom had been turned around in some semblance of an office, and I was sitting there – behind the desk...

The more assertive girls were chosen to "cause the problems", and I was having to confront someone complaining and then becoming aggressive... Oh dear.

"Yvonne – you are far too polite and compliant" my tutor told me raising her eyes. "You have to be more *assertive...*"

Assertiveness was certainly not my forté.

I was trembling with anguish trying to deal with this scenario, even though the girl I was up against was actually very nice – but she played her part well!

~

Commerce – I hated that very word. I hated the whole thing about it. I hated bookkeeping even more, with all its ledgers, and rows and rows of profits and losses, and net profits. Besides, that was a chore I had to do at the pub sometimes with my grandfather. There was nothing more I could learn about it. It was so boring. To my mind it was all such a waste of time.

Air hostesses didn't need to know anything about commerce and bookkeeping – although they might have needed to know a little about *assertiveness.* That didn't occur to me at the time, as I thought that all air passengers were graceful and were much too polite to cause any problems... Well maybe *then...*

If I really couldn't be an air hostess, then I wanted to do something creative and artistic. It was so frustrating knowing that my life was probably going to be in an office environment, and not out there with like-minded people.

However, as my mother told me, I had a *trade* – shorthand and typing, I would always get a job *somewhere* she told me...

Yes, I had this trade behind me. I was good at typing, even on those old Imperial manual typewriters! My speed was good, and I had already attained the relevant certificates whilst still at Torells.

I was working hard at shorthand, especially having missed a year. But I was having evening classes, and practised over and over again in the evenings – when I could that is. It is not easy studying in the pub bar at times when you're not allowed to have a light on upstairs!

"You can do that downstairs", my grandfather would say sometimes when I was sitting in the kitchen practising my shorthand. Then he would walk out the door – turning off the light.

But I did it. I caught up with the other girls, and I *thought* that I might just please my shorthand teacher...

Well no... Mrs. Price, a formidable-looking woman, with a down-turned mouth that depicted years of scowling, had somehow taken a dislike to me. I had done nothing whatsoever to cause all the frowns that she sent my way. What was it that she was thinking? I was always very well behaved and polite, and worked hard.

Although my parents always gave my address as living with them at their bungalow in High Road, I couldn't help but wonder if she knew that I was the girl in the Kings Arms...

Had she heard about all the goings on there? Did she think that I was involved in any way? Well I certainly wasn't! She didn't actually *scold* me for anything, because really there was nothing she could scold me for. But she always made me feel very uncomfortable, with her frowns and uncalled-for jibes.

~

Our class was on the fourth floor, and on the floor above us was the art class. Occasionally I would go up there when I could to be amongst the art students. They were always so laid-back, and were having a thoroughly enjoyable time taking that course. They had a little record player up there, and would play music such as Bob Dylan, Georgie Fame, Booker T & The MGs, people like that. Why "Green Onions" was so called, I really don't know! This was all a far cry from our class, that boring commercial course!

One day I was going to the refectory with my friends to have lunch.

"Have you seen what's on the wall going up to the art room?" one of them asked me.

No, I hadn't.

"Go and have a look", she said.

So I went back to see what she was talking about.

There were some framed drawings, and I could hardly believe what I was seeing. Each drawing was of a naked woman with her legs wide open, showing a close-up drawing of an open vagina...

Actually, I felt a little awkward looking at them, even though they were interesting! I went back down to the refectory again and joined my friends, who were already discussing the drawings.

"I wonder who she is?" one girl pondered...

Yes – who would *do* that?

"It's *my mum...*" said a girl called Susan, without any signs of embarrassment at all...

For once the whole table went suddenly silent.

~

The pictures didn't stay there for long. In fact it was only that one time that I saw them. Our shorthand teacher, Mrs. Price, soon put paid to that!

She came storming into class, absolutely seething, and shrieking words like obscene, disgusting, shocking, outrageous...

Little did she know though that the model was someone I later found out she knew – Susan's mother...

~

Heels...

It wasn't all work and no play though, because when I first started at the college – a certain boy came over to me as soon as he saw me. It was the lad who used to check heels at the college dances – the one that Alison and I used to call "Heels"! What's more – he recognised me! Oh Wow! – he was *nice...*

He was seventeen years old, fair-haired, good looking, wore nice clothes – and the only boy at college with a car! He told me that he was taking the Engineering Course, but also had a lot to do with the Art

Course and photography there. Art was really his love, but he too was doing what his parents had wanted.

Whenever we met in the corridors he would always stop to chat, and we were gradually getting to know each other. Sometimes we would walk to our respective lecture rooms, carrying our books and chatting. He was always making me laugh with his great sense of humour – it was lovely.

"Can I take you home?" he asked me a few weeks later. (*Woww...*)

"Er – I will have to ask my mother first" I replied reluctantly...

Oh dear, why did I have to have my mother's permission before I did *anything.*

But then again, I was fifteen, and I had a while to go yet before I could make up my own mind about what I wanted to do – or not. It was one thing going down to the Pullinger's to play tennis with Michael, but this would be another thing – actually getting into someone's car.

~

"Please say yes – please say yes..." I was saying to myself going home on the bus, with my fingers crossed. Oh the tension!

Why was I so afraid though of asking my mother if I could be given a lift – when she had sent me off in the dead of night when I was only eleven with two awful men – to a "party" that didn't even exist? She always demanded that I was nice to the male customers at the pub, no matter what they said, even things I didn't understand. I had to *smile* at them – even though I hated it, especially with the lecherous ones. All that was fine to her. In fact, she encouraged it. If she heard someone say something untoward to me, she would have a little giggle, whereas any other mother would have had strong words about it. But for me to choose who I saw, that would be another matter.

~

"And what is this boy like?" my mother asked, when I finally plucked up courage to ask her. I told her that he was really nice, and that I had met him before lots of times when he checked girls' heels at the college dances.

"What is his name?" she asked. I told her it was Adam. "Oh – Adam" she said, "that's a nice name – very strong".

Phew! I was getting there...

"And he's got a *car...?*" she said quizzically, but with a look of approval.

Yes, he had, and it was a Ford Anglia with the sloping back window – just like Grandpop's, only a different colour. Just like Grandpop's hey – that was a good move on my part!

"Well – you can tell him that he *can* bring you home", she said thoughtfully, "but tell him to mind how he drives – tell him he has to drive carefully".

The next day I gave Adam the good news – yes, he could take me home that evening... "But my mother said I have to tell you to – *drive carefully...*" I added. Oh dear.

At least he was smiling – "yes, I will *drive carefully*" he said, with an amused twinkle in his eyes.

~

It was a beautiful golden October day, and the trees twinkled in the early evening sunlight. There was a very slight breeze, and I had my long pink chiffon scarf tied loosely around my head, Grace Kelly style. As I wore my hair up it gave the scarf a lift, so it wasn't lying flat on my head, and the ends flowed out behind me. I sat in the car, feeling all-a-butterflies, especially knowing that all the girls fancied Adam, but I was the one he was taking home...

"There's a new Bond film out" Adam said, as he dropped me off at the pub. Yes, I knew that – it was "Goldfinger" – and I loved Bond films. The butterflies were fluttering madly in my stomach now – *was I being asked out on a date?*

"Would you like to go and see it?" he asked me. Ohh... Crikey, *would I!*

"Yes, I would love to", I said politely, with a shy smile, "thank you", even though my heart was crying out *YES YES YES!!*

~

The following Saturday we went to the Ritz cinema in Quarry Hill, that very road where Nanny Mandeville's house stood proudly at the top. I loved the film and was intrigued by how the lovely Shirley Eaton was painted with gold paint, and could still breathe... Well, it was that little bit left bare on her back that helped, but I don't think she would have wanted to do that again!

It was strange going to a cinema with a boy, and not with Nell, Valerie or Alison. Valerie was now married, and Alison had gone to another college, and we didn't see each other much now. We kept in touch though by letters and cards – mainly we would write about the teachers, and their individual quirks.

It was not at all like the stories I had heard about the *back row* – and I was pleased about that – we didn't even sit in the back row. I didn't want any slobbering going on, reminding me of those two awful men...

Adam didn't even kiss me when he took me home. People didn't do that on first dates then. Well, not as far as I was aware.

That first kiss, that very first *romantic* kiss that I had, came a few dates later. It was very sweet, and I felt that I had now got a *boyfriend...*

~

"So when are we going to meet this bloke?" my mother asked, it being more of a command than a question. Yes, I would ask him next time.

Oh dear, what on earth was Adam going to think? He was obviously from a good family, and I didn't want anyone to let me down by saying the wrong things.

Everything went well though. Adam was very likeable, and also very humorous. What a relief – my mother seemed to like him!

~

"He's a bit short" she said after he had left, with a frown and a twitch of her nose. "Why can't you find someone nice and tall?" she added – "like your Dad".

Oh no – oh *no*... What did it matter that he wasn't over six feet tall. He was taller than me, and by quite a few inches, even with my little heels on. He was great – he was lovely – and what's more – he made me feel good.

~

We used to meet for lunch, and would spend a nice hour chatting or, depending on what project he happened to be doing, discussing his posters for forthcoming events, things like that. He liked the way that I was artistic too, and would trust my judgement with the posters, knowing that we both knew exactly what was needed. We used to paint these at his parents' house in Upminster, and I loved doing that. Then I would have the joy of seeing them on the walls of the college.

His parents were really nice, although their house was always so quiet. I don't remember them ever having the television on, well not when I was there. They didn't play any records either. But I liked going to their house, and Adam also took me to meet his sister and his grandmother, both such lovely women, very chatty and making me feel comfortable in their homes.

One day Adam took me to London to show me his father's office. It was an insurance company in the City, and I felt privileged to go there. His father was a real "City Gent", with three-piece suit, bowler hat and rolled umbrella. The City seemed quite exciting really, with lots of hustle and bustle going on. I still didn't want to work in an office though. If I was not to fulfil my ambition and become an air hostess, then I wanted to do something in the art world...

When there was an event coming up at college, I would go to the hall with Adam to see the lighting technicians at work way up high in all the blackness, positioning the lights to be shone down on the stage, in different colours. Sometimes if there was to be a play, the college orchestra would be practising sound effects. Those sound effects always fascinated me, and I could soon tell what each effect denoted, whether it was a romantic scene, danger, a dark and foreboding scene, anything. I remember one time when they were practising some very scary music, and it made me go all cold and shivery. I could almost see the scene, even though I was only hearing the music. I soon realised that each character had their own individual music for when they appeared on stage. Since then I have always noticed this in films.

I loved all this. Anything to do with the Arts, especially actors and musicians.

One day there was something really exciting going on. It was November 1964 and – Adam had managed to book the Moody Blues for a concert! Oh utterly *WOWWW*...

They weren't the enormous stars that they became, but "Go Now" was climbing up the charts, and went on to reach No.1 the following month. So they really were a group to be excited about!

The night of the concert came, and Adam was back stage somewhere while the Moody Blues were playing. This was pre-Justin Hayward, but never mind, I didn't know about him them – I was happy with Ray Thomas!

I was right down the front, swaying to "Go Now", directly in front of Ray. He looked really good in a soft brown leather fitted jacket with a stand-up collar. I was mesmerised as they played "Go Now" – right there – in front of me!

Later on there was to be a raffle – and Ray was going to do the draw. Adam came and got me and asked me to go to the side of the stage as the raffle went on. I had bought a few raffle tickets – and guess what – I won one – then another – then another. It was so embarrassing! But what it meant though was that the band found it so amusing, and cheered each time I went to get my prize – and what's more – I shook hands with Ray Thomas a few times that night.

The only down side though – was that all the prizes were the same – airline multi-packets of cigarettes! At least my father was happy when I got home!

Sadly though – I didn't ask for their autographs... But my memories mean more than that – and I *still* have a line drawing I did of them afterwards...

Signs

March 1965

That half-term holiday is a total blur to me, as I didn't see Adam at all. I don't recall anything, apart from being very unhappy. I missed Adam terribly and was looking forward to seeing him again when we went back to college.

Usually he would be in the reception area chatting while he waited for me. Then we would walk through the corridors together holding our books, chatting away, with Adam making me laugh. I was always so happy when I was with him. Then we would go to our respective lecture rooms until we met up for lunch in the refectory.

I didn't see Adam in reception though, that first morning back after the holiday. I knew he was there because I had seen his car. I walked along the corridor hoping to see him, but he wasn't there. Then – I saw him in the distance. I knew he saw me too, but he didn't wave to me like he usually did, and certainly didn't come over to me. Instead he turned away. I saw him at break time, but he didn't seem to want to chat. It was all very strange.

"Can we talk?" I asked him, sensing his coldness towards me.

"I suppose we must", he said with a sigh.

We went outside and stood just outside the main door.

"It's not *you*" he said, "it's my parents – they think I see too much of you – and I should be going out with other girls..."

Oh. I could understand that. They had nothing to worry about though, because our friendship was purely platonic. He had never touched me inappropriately, nor even tried anything more than just a gentle kiss. Besides I had only just turned sixteen.

That had been a strange birthday for me. I thought it was a special one – to celebrate. I had been looking forward to it – but nothing happened.

Adam had even pretended that he didn't know it was my birthday, then later handed me a card saying "I bet you thought I had forgotten", which was a joke that I didn't appreciate. I had hoped that it would be a nice, maybe even romantic card, but no, it had one of those silly cartoon teddy bears with some sort of joke that I am glad I can't remember. I should have realised then that something was in the air. This wasn't one of his jokes – this was for real.

"So that's what I am going to do" he said.

"But we can still see each other though – can't we?" I asked...

"Well – *I'll see you around...*" he said, shrugging his shoulders, then walked away without even a backward glance.

Well for every door that closes, as they say... But I wish I hadn't gone through the next one that opened...

~

When I went to the refectory for lunch, I sat down at one of the tables on my own, feeling very lost. I had no interest in eating my lunch, and sat there just staring at my plate and pushing my food around with my fork. I kept looking towards the door, waiting for Adam to come in. And then he appeared. I was looking at him expectantly, hoping he would come over, but not knowing what to do. There was no wave, no big smile when he saw me, nothing like he used to be. He walked over in my direction, and then, with just a cursory glance – he walked straight past. I turned my head to see where he was going, and he sat down at another table full of girls. I don't blame him though, he was only doing what his parents had told him to do. *Wasn't he?*

A couple of girls came over and sat at my table. They weren't girls that I went around with, just girls in my class that I liked, but they had their own best friends. Then another girl, Susan, a nice girl, but not one with whom I was particularly friendly, came over to me. She was the daughter of the "model" on the wall going up to the art room.

"Are you alright?" she asked kindly.

At that, the tears started welling in my eyes, and then I was wiping them away from my cheeks.

I could hear Adam laughing, and the girls with him were giggling. Susan sat down beside me, and I confided in her. She knew of course, it was obvious.

That evening when I left college, I saw Adam speeding off in his car. It was full up with girls – all laughing. It was like a scene straight out of the Elvis film – "Girls Girls Girls" – only I wasn't looking at my hero on the cinema screen – this was real life...

~

"There's plenty more fish in the sea", my mother said when I told her I wasn't seeing Adam any more. "There'll be some nice bloke come along – tall – like your Dad."

Oh no – not that height thing again...

Like any teenage girl who has been dumped, I was totally lost. Suddenly everything was bleak again. The pub, sleeping with my grandmother, being tormented by my brothers, abuse in various forms – all that I could see awaiting me was being a little Cinderella again. I had also lost hope of ever being an air hostess. I was still trying to learn German, but I knew that my mother just wanted me to have a "proper job".

"You've got to have a trade in your hands", she had told me. That is why she sent me to college – on the commercial course, learning office routine and book keeping. If only she had allowed me to take the art course or the fashion and design course. It didn't matter to me anymore that out of the whole college – *I* had been chosen to model the bridal gown that had been made by the girls in the dressmaking course. That had been a great honour for anyone, and was usually someone on that course – but they had chosen *me*. As shy as I was, I did all the rehearsals, and learned how to walk like a model, how to turn at the end of the raised walkway. This was my chance to make something of myself. Adam had encouraged me to overcome my shyness at doing that, but now, I wasn't going to have his encouragement any more.

All this – all these thoughts – all these feelings of worthlessness again... And this was just Day One of being dumped...

~

I don't recall anything about going back to college the next day. Well maybe I didn't. All I can remember is my absolute feeling of worthlessness – yet again. My lack of confidence was going to put paid to modelling the bridal gown at the end of term, and all I could see ahead was – well, *nothing*.

Things are so different these days, with young people going out with lots of different people all the time. I wasn't "in love", but I had this wonderful friend who made me laugh and feel good about myself – or *had done*.

I was totally desolate – as always, everything good that I had, or everything that I felt was wonderful, was somehow taken away from me...

~

In the dense fog that I was in, I am not sure whether it was the next evening or the one after, but there was a very fast moving element at work. I was sitting in the taproom with my grandmother, next to the fireplace. It was a large red brick fireplace in the "domino" area of the bar. That very spooky picture of a man and a ghost called "His Master" hung above it. Nanny always sat there in the evenings, whether the fire was lit or not. I hated that ghost picture, and tried not to catch sight of it, especially before going upstairs and along that foreboding landing to my grandmother's bedroom.

This evening though, that foreboding creepy picture kept catching my eye. I was sort of drawn to it. It was probably my very sombre mood at the time. It could have been more though – it was as though I was being *compelled* to look at it.

Could it have been a sign?

~

Someone came into the off-licence which was between the taproom and the saloon bar, and from where Nanny sat, she could always see who was coming into the pub, even if it was just the off-licence. She liked to do that. There was a loud DING! as a hand came down on the heavy metal breast-shaped bell that was there to draw attention.

I noticed a young man standing there, and then he spoke to Nell, who went to the off-licence window to serve him. He didn't seem to be buying anything, and was looking over to me, back at Nell, and back at me.

"Here's a young man to see you" she called across – "someone asking for an Yvonne Mandeville..."

I had never seen him before. Well, I didn't think I had – I was later to find out who he was, and where I had actually seen him. But for now, he was just a stranger who I didn't know – and he didn't know me...

He came over to me and asked me to go into the off-licence with him. I looked at Nanny and she looked at me in a way as if to say "well what are you waiting for?" So I followed him into the off-licence.

Who *was* this stranger? He had a sharp face, dark hair, and thick black rimmed glasses. He certainly was not "my type", but he *was* dressed nicely.

"I am Susan's brother" he said, "she told me that there is a girl in her class who has just split up with her boyfriend – and she's got *long blonde hair* and *lives in a pub* – so I thought, well that can't be bad – so here I am!"

Blinking cheek!

So why did he think that this girl who had long blonde hair *and* lived in a pub – would have anything to do with *him?*

I should have seen the sign...

"Would you like to come to a party with me on Saturday?" he asked.

"What party? Where?" I asked, taken aback by it all.

"It's over on Stifford Clays", he said, "one of my friends' parents are away for the weekend, so he's having a party... So are you coming then?"

Stifford Clays? But that was where I was taken when I was just eleven years old – to the party that never was...

I should have seen the sign...

"Um... I don't know", I said, still perplexed. And anyway, just *why would I* go to a party with him?

Then he spotted my grandmother sitting by the fireplace. An elderly lady, just sitting there minding her own business – but keeping an eye on things – naturally. He went straight over to her, with a sort of Jack the Lad swagger...

I followed him, feeling rather confused and wondering what was going on.

"Er... This is Nanny – my grandmother" I said, not liking this invasion one little bit. She sat there with a sort of half smile, which was saying she didn't know whether she liked this young man – or not...

"Do you want to hear a joke?" he asked her, leaning slightly towards her, in a way that was saying that she was going to hear this joke anyway...

"Oh – go on" she said, not knowing what he was about to come out with. Neither did I.

"Why is a piece of shit tapered?" he said, waiting for her response. Nanny looked at me – and I looked at her – I wanted to curl up like one of those little "cheesy bugs" out in the car park. Those tiny creatures that when you touched them would curl into a ball, and would only unfurl when they felt safe.

"Why is a piece of shit tapered?" he said again... "So your arse doesn't close with a bang!"

Nanny gave a little heh-heh without looking at him, and I can only hope that her hearing was playing her up. I was actually quite shocked that he would tell my grandmother such a crude joke – with no reason at all – and this is the first time I have ever spoken about it since

I should have seen the sign...

Then he beckoned me out into the off-licence. Being used to doing as I was told, I followed him again.

"Phone me" he said, handing me a piece of paper with a phone number on it. "You *will* come, won't you? If you don't phone me – then I will phone *you*..."

Then he left.

Talk about a fast mover!

~

"What's going on?" my grandmother asked when I went back to her...

I told her what he said, including the reference to long blonde hair and living in a pub.

"Well then", she said, "he sounds a bit too cocky for my liking." Yes – and for my liking too!

"But what do I do?" I asked her, "should I go to the party with him?" Really, my instincts were telling me "*No, No No*" – but he *was* that nice girl Susan's brother...

"I can't see why not", Nanny said... "Ask your mother."

I couldn't help but look back up at that awful ghost picture on the wall – and shivered...

~

"Who *is* this bloke then?" my mother asked me the next day when I told her the story.

"He is Susan's brother", I said, trying to convince myself that I ought to try to please her. "She is a girl in my class – and she's really nice..."

"And what's his name?" She used to put a lot of store on what people's names were. "Such a nice name, Adam", she had said, "strong, reliable." Yes, but Adam wasn't around anymore.

"Er, I don't know", I said, realising that I might be about to go out with someone when I didn't even know his name.

"But shall I go to the party with him?"

"Well he sounds a bit too cocky to me" she said grimacing, and echoing my grandmother's words, "but I don't see why not..." *Oh no – why did I always go by what my mother said? Couldn't I ever be allowed have a mind of my own?* "Where exactly is this party anyway?"

"Somewhere in Stifford Clays" I said, knowing there was no bus to Stifford Clays *Ha-ha.*

"So your Dad will have to take you then" she said – "and mind you – he will be there to pick you up at eleven o'clock."

This sort of meant that I was going then.

~

The next day I went back to college, back to Adam averting my eyes, and making the girls laugh. It wasn't easy for me. I could see that he was having a good time. If only his parents knew what kind of girls they might be, and how he might be initiated into a world that neither he nor I had even thought about.

Linda, one of the girls in my class had really fancied a boy. He didn't know, but she fancied him so much that one day she asked me and another girl to help her. She wrote a note saying "Please meet me at (wherever and time) I will be wearing a green dress". The other girl put it on the saddle of his bike, and we all kept our fingers crossed. Sure enough, the lad turned up. He met that girl wearing the green dress, so Linda went out on this date – all at her behest...

The next day she came back to college – with a love bite on her neck. "We did it!" she said. But I still didn't know what sex was all about. I had heard all the noises at the pub, the banging, the grunting, the flushed looks, and the whole feeling that something untoward was going on in my grandfather's bedroom – no matter who the woman happened to be...

He had even once come out of his bedroom and into the kitchen where I was sitting with my mother and grandmother, having bedded Mrs. Binns, saying "It's like the Blackwall Tunnel in there... *Heh-heh.*" Which at the time I thought he meant it was dark in his bedroom!

But why was he chuckling? Why did everyone look so disgusted? Why did my mother give a nervous little giggle? Whatever the "Blackwall Tunnel" was, my grandfather must have liked it, because Mrs. Binns moved in, not only to the pub, but also to what I now saw as the "Blackwall Tunnel" room, and Nell had to move out to the woodworm room – next to theirs. But despite all this – I still didn't know *exactly* what went on.

How did all this grunting and groaning and goodness-knows-whatting – go on? Was this the "it" that Linda spoke of? I was sixteen years old for Heaven's sake, but I still didn't know what "it" was all about and how conception occurred.

So I asked Linda. She was very surprised that at the age of sixteen, I didn't know about what really went on during sex. Between her and the class we had on contraception – albeit embarrassingly quickly skipped through by the tutor – I found out that menstrual blood did not come out of my urethra after all... And that that blood, when it stopped flowing, didn't form the baby either, as my mother had told me. But there were other things that she explained to me as well...

Just how on earth didn't I know? My mother never told me. All she said was "Ask Daddy". All he said was "Ask Nell". Nell just said "You'll find out one day *heh-heh*..." Maybe that was why I had been sent off with those awful men when I was just eleven... There was certainly no readily available pornography in those days – if there had been, I might have had a totally different er, conception, of what it was all about. Despite all that went on at the pub as well – how could I have been that naïve?

(By the way, Linda and her prince married... Such an unlikely beginning – but one that was set to last...)

~

I couldn't help but think of the Blackwall Tunnel whenever my Grandfather was in bed with Mrs. Binns. In fact, no-one really minded what was said in front of me, no matter how sinister it might have been.

Even during the time that the Moors Murders were all in the news, my family would discuss it when we were gathered in the kitchen, my mother being particularly interested. She would talk openly about the poor children being abused, even though at the time the newspapers hadn't gone into minute detail about what had gone on.

"They even used a dog", she said one day. "They found dog hairs on the children's bodies – and the police have now destroyed it..."

I really didn't know, nor had any intimation about, what this vile sadistic couple could have been using a dog for. But all these sort of things were said in my presence.

I have never seen nor read any evidence about what had happened that included the dog, and so I can only guess that my mother was reading far too much into it.

However – one day when my father came home, he was all sort of excited about what he wanted to tell the family. It had been a hot day, and he said he had been to one of the hospitals in the general area. It wasn't for himself, so he may have been visiting someone. He came into the kitchen, and told us the story of what he had seen...

It had been lunchtime, and a matron at the hospital was sitting outside, round the back of the hospital sunning herself. My father said that she was sitting on a chair with her head back, and her legs wide apart... She hadn't any underwear on – and he chuckled as he told us that a large Alsatian dog – was licking her between her legs...

Of course this caused a lot of amusement. No-one was at all bothered that I was in the room, hearing all that was being said, and not understanding at all why any woman would do such a thing. Nor were they bothered about what it might do to my still curious mind.

I suppose that as always – I was invisible...

An Angry Young Man

"My brother said he came to see you last night", Susan said, as she sat down beside me at the refectory table the next day. "So are you going to go out with him?"

"I don't know", I said hesitatingly. Despite my mother giving me permission, I still didn't want to go. I didn't like his Jack the Lad manner – and that awfully crude joke he came out with to my grandmother.

"Oh go on..." she said, smiling at me persuasively.

~

I didn't phone that number, I really didn't want to. Even if I had, I wouldn't have known who to ask for! It hadn't even occurred to me to ask Susan what his name was. I wasn't really that interested.

But *he* phoned *me*. The Kings Arms was easy to find in the phone book. Orsett 219. As simple as that.

~

We had parties at the pub, the sort of parties that pubs have that is, where people do "Knees up Mother Brown" (with, what I felt at the time, were its quite gruesome words), "The Hokey Cokey" (with its instructions being rather like an exercise video!), and the conga, which I used to think was named after the conger eel, as we all held each person's hips in front, and snaked our way all around the bars – and out onto the streets. That was fun, but you never knew quite who was going to grab your hips. I feel sure that by the way that some of the women wiggled their bums at the men, that they were giving the come-on to them to sneak into the line and grab *their* hips!

This though was my first time to a proper party, a grown up party, with teenage boys and girls, well, mainly boys. I don't recall there being many girls. I don't recall any dancing going on either – just people standing around getting drunk. I say boys, but they were all young men, eighteen years and older. These friends were mainly members of the local Young Conservative Association of which "he" was a member, and who held their meetings in the snooker room above the Queen's Hotel in Grays High Street – that very hotel where the boys used to hang out – *watching all the girls go by...*

I have to say, he had made the effort to take me out – dress wise. He was wearing a nice grey suit, white shirt and grey patterned tie. That was nice. I was impressed. So that was a *good* sign – but would there be any other *signs – good or bad...*

I kept listening out, trying to hear what his friends called him. It sounded like "Tony". So should I call him Tony or not? Why couldn't I just ask him? It seemed a bit silly going out with someone, and then asking what his name was, and I was too shy to ask.

But it *was* Tony. Was that a strong name? Would my mother approve? Would I even be seeing him again so that she might even be interested?

I didn't think so.

~

The party was held at the lad's parents' house while they were away. It was probably one of those times when unsuspecting parents trusted their grown up son to look after the house while they were gone – and then returned home to things being somewhat different to when they left...

This impromptu party meant that with everyone bringing a bottle – or a few – there was lots of booze – but no food! So the evening was spent with lads glugging beer from bottles, or tipping back tumblers containing every shade of spirit...

~

"Now, what can I get you to drink?" he asked, turning to choose me something to drink, which was obviously not going to be *my* choice anyway. By now his friends had gathered round. It was obvious he had told them about his date for the night, and how I lived in a pub. They all seemed rather curious, and not only that, a little bit devious I think too.

"As she lives in a pub" he said, with a little glint of mischief behind his glasses, "let's *see* what she can drink..."

"Yeah – go on..." they were urging expectantly.

Well my favourite drinks then were that bottled light ale Double Diamond, sherry, and something like sherry but red – that my grandfather called wine, but it wasn't – Advocaat, Babycham, Cherry B, and Britvic pineapple juice! The last one being much more suitable for my age, but never mind. I had been brought up on a glass of bitter before dinner to make me eat, a glass of egg flip to calm my nerves before going to the dentist, and a glass of the aforesaid "wine" before bedtime, to make me sleep.

And of course there was the gin in my bottle to make me sleep when I was a baby.

Goodness knows what *that* did to me.

~

Egged on by his friends, and obviously wanting to show off, Tony got a half pint glass, poured a drop of every spirit there was there into it (of which there were many) and topped it up with cider.

"I bet you can't drink it" he said – "but let's see..."

I know I shouldn't have drunk it, but always trying to please and not wanting to disappoint (my downfall throughout my life) I started to drink it. I found it most unpleasant. I never chose to drink spirits – I only had them when I was made to have them – but I knew I had to do this. What else could I do with all those chaps standing around wanting to test me?

That awful drink lasted me the whole evening, but somehow I eventually managed to finish it.

~

Sometime during the evening while we were chatting, Tony mentioned to me what he had been doing before working in London.

"Nothing too exciting", he said, "just working at Pollards on Saturdays, selling tea towels and ladies knickers!"

Tea towels and ladies knickers? Hey – *he* was that lad who used to call out to my mother and me on a Saturday afternoon...

"Come and get your knickers ladies!" he would call, holding up various sizes of women's knickers – large – and small... Well as small as they were in those days! He was the boy whose gaze I used to try to avoid. That very one that my mother was always telling me was looking at me – but who I didn't want to know. And here I was – *with him...*

~

So that was my first "proper" teenage party. It was a little like being at the pub – with men guffawing and getting drunk, whilst I remained sober despite being plied with alcohol.

The music was good though. They played Rolling Stones records and The Animals a lot – "Walking the Dog" and "House of the Rising Sun". These were records that I wasn't that familiar with then, but they opened up a new raw sound to me, a rock sound, that was deeper and dirtier than what I was used to – people like Elvis, Ricky Nelson, and Brian Hyland. This rock music has stayed with me all my life though. Little beginnings – hey!

So unlike the so-called party that wasn't, that I had been taken to when I was just eleven years old, this was a proper party – wasn't it? Well it was my first experience of what older teenage parties were like.

I took my father's watch face out of my blue handbag to check the time – it was nudging 11 o'clock. He would be arriving at that time with the pumpkin to take Cinderella home again.

I went upstairs to get my jacket from the pile on the bed in the parents' bedroom – and noticed that a few coats were moving... I didn't realise at the time what must have been going on, but whatever it was, no-one seemed to be bothered about anyone going in there...

~

Tony waved me off as I got in the car, and went back to the party, which he told me the next time I saw him had lasted all night long.

It had turned out to be ok after all. Tony wasn't my prince, well not a prince – full stop. But that party had taken me out of myself, and had brought me into a world of rock music – and, well moreover – a world outside of the pub...

~

"Did you find out his name then?" my mother asked me the next day.

"I think it's Tony", I said with an emphasis, trying to make it sound strong. "Tony!" But why on earth was I trying to make his name sound strong? Were there no limits as to how far I would go to try to please my mother?

Not that it would have mattered anyway. I had had a good night out. I was in the land of the living again.

~

Tony phoned again during the week. Would I go to the pictures with him?

I didn't know, but my instincts were "No!" This was one thing I hoped my mother *would* forbid me to do. If only my grandmother had advised me against going out with him originally, instead of saying "I can't see why not..." The party had been fine though – apart from me having to drink that awful concoction of alcohol – but when I asked Mummy about the pictures she said "Yes". So I was going then.

He said that we would meet outside Congress House, which was the Co-op store by the bus stop, and we agreed on the time. This had to fit in with the hourly No.53 bus from Orsett to Grays, and leave time to get to the cinema ready for the film to start.

I was wearing a blue mock suede jacket at the time, it felt nice on though, and went with my "good" Marks & Spencer check skirt. I was also carrying a navy blue leather handbag, which my father had brought back from the Far East after the war. It had carvings on it depicting Far Eastern scenes, and Daddy had attached a sink plug chain to make it into a shoulder bag. However, it wasn't meant to be used as a shoulder bag...

As I got up to get off the bus, suddenly my bag fell open – absolutely everything in it was on the floor. I felt so awful with people seeing all my bits and pieces flying everywhere. I scrambled around trying to pick everything up, but just couldn't see how that could have happened...

Maybe another sign?

When I got off the bus, Tony's sharp face was like thunder – severe and angry. I could almost feel the dark clouds pushing me downwards, onto the ground. I wanted to be like one of those little cheesy-bugs again, curl myself up into a ball – and roll away..

What had I done? Why was he looking at me that way? His eyes looked like little black dots behind his glasses. I didn't like it.

"You're late!" he said, his deep voice taking on a gravelly, threatening tone. His manner seemed much older than his eighteen years.

"Er – no, I'm not", I said, wondering what this was all about.

"Yes you are – you're an *hour* late", he went on. "I've been waiting here for an hour..."

But I wasn't late. I clearly remembered the time we had agreed on. There was only one bus an hour from Orsett, and I wouldn't have made that mistake. We were well in time for the film, and he hadn't suggested to me that we would do anything beforehand.

With a couple of jolts of his head, he clicked his neck, in a sort of way that was depicting an anger that was about to erupt – but didn't. We walked along to the cinema with him in a huff, and me feeling totally perplexed about the whole thing. He was taking quick steps, making a point, and I had to keep up with him. His head was on one side all the time, and I could detect a vein sticking out of his neck on the right side – throbbing – like something out of a science fiction film.

I shouldn't have tried to keep up with him. I should have just crossed the road, and caught the next bus back to Orsett.

I didn't even like what he was wearing this time. Even though it was a nice evening – weather wise that is – he wore a single-breasted knee-length brown coat, done up to the neck, and with the collar turned up. What was he trying to depict with this mode of clothing?

He looked like someone out of one of the spy films of the time, as though he was about to sit on a park bench next to another spy and say without turning his head – "it's warm for this time of year..."

I should have seen the signs...

~

I felt on edge all the evening, feeling that I had done something wrong. But I hadn't. If only I had just turned around at that bus stop, crossed over the road – and caught the next bus home... But I didn't. I walked with little steps trying to keep up with him, his anger, and his head still on one side all the time – and that awful throbbing vein.

I don't recall what the film was that we saw, all I remember is that it was black and white. That's it – black and white, nothing in between. Angry or happy. Like his moods. The only thing I remember is him suddenly kissing me – and I didn't like it.

He smelled of cigarettes and garlic – the latter being something I had never encountered before. I didn't want to kiss. I had never been kissed like that before anyway. I couldn't help but think about that time that those two awful men, Terry and Trevor, had tried to kiss me when I was only eleven. And that was only the start of what they were intending to do.

His demeanour was somewhat like the characters in the series of "Angry Young Men" films that were around in the sixties. Films like "Saturday Night and Sunday Morning", where Albert Finney was an "angry young man". There were quite a few like that. I actually enjoyed those films, and somehow they confirmed to me what I had grown up knowing all about, and that is that some men can get angry – very angry.

Maybe I should have taken notice of those films...

~

When the film ended, we walked down to the bus stop. We didn't go to the late night chip shop to get a bag of those lovely soft chips steeped in chip shop vinegar, and wrapped in newspaper.

"Chips?" No, we weren't having any chips. The little ritual of enjoying those hot comforting chips whilst walking down the High Street to the bus stop had to go by the wayside.

Was this the first sign of control?

We talked about the film that was being advertised as being on the following week. I can't recall what that film was either, but it might have been another of those black and white kitchen sink type films.

"So we'll see that then", he said, rather assumptively.

Right. So I was going.

~

"Do you like King of the Road?" he asked, as we said goodnight. Roger Miller was in the charts. No, I didn't, I didn't like it at all. I had gone from Elvis Presley to Billy Fury, to The Beatles, The Rolling Stones and The Moody Blues – and still Elvis was in my heart. But "King of the Road"? No, I didn't like it – it seemed to be all about the old boy who used to painstakingly sweep Baker Street with a yard broom... Depressing really.

"Yes, yes I do", I said, trying to please.

Big mistake – the next week he bought it for me.

By saying "Yes" though when I really felt "No" set the precedent somehow.

Oil And Water

1965

Tony started coming to the pub a lot to see me. Being a Public House, with doors open to all (apart from those who my grandfather banned of course!) – there was no escape. Someone would call up to me that he was in the bar, and I would have to go down to see him. We would sit at the long brown wooden seat at the long brown wooden table in the brown taproom, where the smoke hung heavy, even staining the ceiling brown. Everything was too heavy. *He* was heavy.

~

"Not another short arse" my mother scowled the first time she met him. "I don't know what you're doing going around with *short arses...*"

I didn't say anything – what *could* I say? He certainly was no dream boat, and he *was* getting rather obsessive. At that moment I couldn't think of anything that I could say that might please my mother.

"You know the problem with *short arsed men* don't you..." she said. "They have to make up for their lack of height by being far too cocky..."

Mutter – mutter – mutter "short arse" *– mutter – mutter – mutter* "short arse", she went as she walked off.

"Far too cocky..." My grandmother repeated...

Well yes, he had been far too cocky that night he swaggered into the pub, asked me out, and told my grandmother a dirty joke...

But neither he nor Adam was actually *short* – they were both quite a few inches taller than me, but that's how my mother saw any man who was shorter than my father and grandfather. At least he dressed well.

~

One night I had a strange dream about a girl called Kay who was talking to me earnestly – as though she was trying to tell me something. That dream stayed on my mind all day. It really struck a chord with me – this girl called Kay.

The next evening as we sat on that same long brown seat, I told Tony about my dream. All I said was that it was about a girl called Kay. "What!" he exclaimed, being rather taken aback. "Kay! – did you say *Kay?*" I nodded nervously, being surprised by his response. "You must be psychic" he added – "I have been going out with a girl called Gay!"

I only wish I had taken more notice of that profound dream though and what it was trying to tell me.

"She told me she didn't want to see me anymore", he explained, "she said we were like oil and water."

That was us too – *oil and water...* I was the water forever wanting to run away, he was oil, sticking on me and keeping me in place. I was slowly seeping into the earth and turning into mud. Mud, the colour of the taproom. And the colour of his moods. He was morose at times, *so dark brown morose.*

I should have taken notice of the sign... Gay's sign...

~

I so much wanted to be with Michael again, playing tennis and drinking cloudy home-made lemonade under the apple tree. I also wanted to be with Adam – artistic, good humoured Adam, who always made me laugh. I wanted to be with someone who would take me flying, flying out of this darkness and into a lighter place. I wanted to literally fly too, become the air hostess I was never to be. I wanted to be Amelia Earhart. I just wanted to *be...*

The Universal Law Of Attraction

1965

The Universal Law of Attraction is what draws people together, and then the chemistry involved keeps them together. This didn't apply to Tony and me though. Michael Pullinger, and of course Adam – yes! But I wasn't aware of that then, it was only when I didn't see them anymore that I realised what chemistry we had had. The chemistry that kept Michael and me playing tennis together, laughing, and sitting talking earnestly under the apple tree, whilst drinking his mother's home-made lemonade. That to me was *chemistry* – that wonderful feeling of being relaxed with someone – and very happy.

It was a different kind of chemistry with Adam – but it was there... We didn't play tennis, but he did make me laugh and feel happy. I really enjoyed being with him. We had an artistic connection, and he trusted me to paint his posters in my own style, which somehow always matched his. I would be proud seeing our posters on the college walls, advertising whatever dance or play was coming along, knowing I had played a big part in painting them. Art was something I was good at and something I could do well – like playing tennis.

Now though, the only thing I had in common with Tony – was music. So would this be enough? That instant spark of attraction that can be there when you meet someone to whom you are drawn, and want to spend time with, had never been there.

~

Very soon he asked me to go to his house to meet his parents, Eva and Ken. They were wonderful, practically greeting me with open arms, and welcoming me into the family. I recognised Eva – and soon my thoughts about her were confirmed. She was the lady who used to fly by the pub on her motor scooter, with a crash helmet rather too big for her round face – pushing her short fringe down over her eyes – and her kilt flowing, sometimes showing her thighs. This was the woman who Nanny used to comment on, as she sat in the lounge window looking out seeing who she could see.

"Here's that woman on that scooter again…" she used to chuckle. This was Eva.

Without her crash helmet I could see that Eva had short blonde hair, red lipstick, and eyes that held a story or two of her own – and a few stories about the Kings Arms as well – as I later found out…

Eva had told Tony that I lived in a very strange family… She was a home help who used to go to what was known as "The Old Age Pensioners' Bungalows" in High Road – oh dear, I don't think they would be called that now! Well whilst at these bungalows, people would get talking to Eva, and apparently they came out with all manner of speculation about the Kings Arms. Who slept with who? Who was whose father? That sort of thing. Tony told me that it was a general belief that I was my grandfather and Nell's daughter! It seems that it was a great centre for gossip! But what they didn't know though – was *the truth*.

How on earth could they have thought that I was Nell's and my grandfather's daughter? Did I look like either of them? No, I certainly did not! I suppose though that the only times they really saw me, when I wasn't on my own or with my friends, was with Grandpop or Nell. Nell used to take me to school; Grandpop would take me with him walking the dogs… Of course, this was utter nonsense.

This somehow put a query into my mind though – Nell was more of a mother to me than my own mother. This was blatantly clear. Nell never told me off, never ridiculed me, never made me feel worthless, never made me feel that I really wasn't welcome on this planet.. Nell was very odd, very strange, but she was also always kind to me. Yes, she treated me as though I was her own daughter. But there was no way she was my mother. Flora was her only daughter – besides, I was the image of my father.

Then came the next revelation from Eva and the Old Peoples' Bungalows…

"Mum says that they say you are adopted" Tony told me quite bluntly another time.

But why were they saying that?

"It's because you are so different to the rest of the family" he offered.

To be told that you may have been adopted is a terrible thing to have to cope with. Nervous butterflies fluttered around my tummy, and then I felt an overwhelming nausea that seemed to take over my whole body, turning my legs to jelly. It felt as though my whole life, whether good or bad, had been wiped out.

This couldn't possibly be true – could it? How could I deal with this not knowing whether it was or not? After a few days fretting about it, I couldn't stand the thought any more. There was only one thing for it – I would have to broach the notion with my mother...

I very diffidently and quietly spoke to her about what the old people had been saying – the speculation about me being adopted. I didn't want to upset her, I just wanted her to know what was being said – and tell me the truth...

"You are a wicked – wicked girl!" she scolded, her eyes blazing with temper. "How could you tell me that – after that awful – awful birth I had with you..."

She had a penchant for telling me I was wicked, and had mentioned my birth before, comparing it to the "lovely births" she had had with my brothers.

So that was her answer then.

~

I was now having some meals with Tony's family, usually at the weekends. They made me feel that I could stay with them for as long as I liked. Incidentally, having now met Susan's mum, I was also now able to put a face to the "model" on the wall of the art room stairs...

It was then that I tasted garlic for the first time. Eva always used garlic in her cooking, even boiled potatoes. I wondered what this new strange taste was – and I realised that that was the smell that Tony always had wafting around him. I didn't like the smell – but I did like the taste! It was new – and totally different to the rather plain cooking we had at the pub. I liked this new European taste.

Something very odd happened one teatime though. It was a Sunday, and we were all sitting around the table having had a nice salad, and then Eva served jelly and tinned fruit to follow. I started eating the jelly and fruit – then suddenly – horror struck... My mouth was full with fragments of glass. Obviously I was going *"uh – uh – uh"*, as I felt the glass against my tongue and gums, and ran out of the room, straight up to the bathroom. I was ages getting all that glass out of my mouth, and obviously I was very upset.

Everyone had a look at my bowl while I was out of the room – it was all in one piece and not at all broken – and no-one had any idea at all how those fragments of glass had got into it. There was absolutely *no* explanation...

Could it have been another sign?

~

By now Tony had passed his driving test, and I was looking forward to being seventeen and learning to drive myself. On the day of his test, he had arrived at the pub later – driving Ken's car. Ken was more than happy for him to use his car for taking me out, or taking me over to their house.

I loved going to Eva and Ken's house. They also loved music, so usually they would be playing records. Except on Sunday afternoons though, when all the family would sit down to watch the Sunday afternoon film. Somewhat different to being at Adam's parents' house!

It wasn't *only* the family there though at weekends. There was a rather odd-looking man, with a hangdog expression, who tended to sit in the living room – in the corner. No-one spoke to him – except Eva. The first time I saw him there, I didn't say anything at the time, but I did when Tony took me home that night.

"Don't mention him!" he said, with an angry tone.

But I had – and by his response, I was intrigued as to who this odd looking man was.

"It's Guts Ache", he said, "his name is Norman, and he stays at our house every weekend, eating us out of house and home."

"But why?"

"Urghh" he exclaimed through gritted teeth, "he's my mother's er, *friend...*"

"Oh..."

"They go out every Saturday night – sometimes to the pictures, but usually dancing."

He went on to tell me that obviously Ken didn't like this *at all*, and that whenever Norman was there he would usually be down in his shed – keeping away from him. There was apparently nothing Ken could do about Eva's relationship with him. He couldn't make her stay at home on a Saturday night. She did whatever she wanted to do, even if it upset her husband.

None of this shocked me though. I was brought up knowing that people were sleeping with people other than their spouses. This just confirmed to me that all that was normal then! This didn't mean that I wanted to be like that though. I thought it was horrible seeing the hurt that it caused to my family members – and now there was another family affected by this...

"I would murder him if I could" Tony said, staring straight ahead. "I nearly did once... He was sitting in that corner, like he does, with that *look* on his face... We were on our own – and I picked up a chair, held it in the air – and was about to bring it down on him... 'Don't hurt me Tony' he was pleading, 'don't hurt me...' Pathetic!"

I should have taken notice...

~

No matter what was going on in their private lives, Eva and Ken made me feel that *I mattered* and actually that I might be quite special. Their affection for me was tangible. They had welcomed me into their home, and the Universal Law of Attraction had sent its arrow whizzing towards me – drawing me to them.

Well that Law of Attraction may have been drawing me to Tony's parents, but there was still something missing. Something very important in my life – the need to feel *attracted* to someone – physically. It just wasn't there with Tony. And yet, he was still there, in my life, coming over to the pub, and wanting to see me. I think he was actually *obsessed* with me. Yes, that was it. He was being very controlling, and taking over my life.

I should have taken notice of a wonderful song that I loved at the time. It was Lesley Gore's version of "You Don't Own Me"...

"You don't own me
I'm not just one of your many toys
You don't own me
Don't say I can't go with other boys.

And don't tell me what to do
And don't tell me what to say
And please when I go out with you
Don't put me on display..."

Those words still ring in my mind whenever I look back to those days. And with Lesley Gore just being topped in the charts by the Beatles, "I Want To Hold Your Hand" had a strange meaning to me too – Tony was the first chap to hold my hand. It felt strange that first time, but somehow comforting, like a little girl being led safely by her mother.

Being "led" though was the problem. So was being *controlled...*

~

He had some sort of hold over me, in as much as he gave me *affection*. This was something that was never really shown to me at the pub. I don't remember my mother ever holding me or cuddling me, nor tucking me into bed. That was Nell's job. Nor did I ever have a bedtime story read to me. When I heard about children being lulled to sleep by having their favourite little stories read to them, I didn't really know what that meant. In fact, the only people I ever remember reading stories aloud were teachers in the infants school at Orsett. "Milly Molly Mandy" and "Riki Tiki Tavi" were my favourite stories. But if only I could have drifted off to sleep having that read to me – or any story come to that..

So with receiving some kind of affection from Tony, an arm around my shoulder or holding my hand, whenever he wanted to see me – I would see him. I didn't want to incur his wrath anyway. I knew that there was no escape.

Because I was seeing him, I stopped seeing my friends – even Alison. He was taking over my life. Well maybe it might have been a mutual thing with Alison following her own path into the world, but I missed all the girly chats and giggles. I missed talking to her about Elvis, and our mutual sighs over any photos of him we happened to see. I missed going to the cinema with her seeing every Elvis film whenever it was being shown. We would sit there mesmerised in some kind of dream... "Follow that Dream" – *if only I could have...*

Tony wanted my full and total attention, and that's what I gave him. He was possessive and controlling. He seemed to be obsessed with me, and wouldn't leave me alone. Despite me trying not to see him again, he would never take no for an answer. I felt as though I was a possession. Then again, I grew up feeling that I was just a possession. A possession that could be treated however its owner wished. Something that could be taken out, admired maybe and played with – then shut back in the cupboard again...

I was totally dependent on him emotionally. He would come to the pub, and I would go down into the taproom and sit with him on the long wooden seat – the seat where Arthur Kempster used to sit, with his fleas visibly jumping on his tattered jacket. The back of the seat was decorated with an intricate pattern made from holes – not woodworm holes though! These used to get filled with Nell's wax polish, and so I would push the polish through to clear the holes again. I used to get told off for doing that...

Well this particular day I was sitting with Tony on that long wooden seat in the taproom, and he put his arm along the seat behind me. I felt a little apprehensive about it, but I suppose I quite liked this new feeling of affection that it gave me.

My mother came round from the saloon bar, looking daggers at me...

"Don't *ever* let him put your arm around you in here again!" she said angrily later. "It doesn't look right..."

So what was I to think with all the goings-on at the pub? Was a slight show of affection really bad? Was it worse than those two awful men making me dance, and trying to kiss me and probably get me into bed when I was only eleven? My mother had never bothered about that. In fact she had found it quite amusing. So what was right – and what was wrong?

Everyone at the pub "going to bed" with all and sundry – was ok – wasn't it? I had been brought up to accept this all my life as normal goings on amongst adults. But someone putting his arm across the back of the seat behind me was not? Nothing made sense. Nothing ever did.

~

One evening Tony took me to the ten pin bowling alley in Grays. It was fun, although I was quite worried that the bowling balls might have taken my finger and thumb with them! I was sure I had heard of that happening to someone. But no matter – they didn't!

I was enjoying the evening at this new venue and this new "sport". It was yet another challenge for me, trying out my skills at getting those ten pins down in one go!

Suddenly, I was aware of someone over the other side – waving to me. *It was Michael Pullinger...*

He came straight over to me and the nearer he got – the more handsome he looked. Ooh-er – oh crikey... That Universal Law of Attraction was working overtime!

"Hello Yvonne" he said, as I stepped forward to greet him. "how are you?"

Well – I was fine now! I must have been smiling my biggest smile for a long time, not only with my mouth but with my eyes. I could feel it – I was uplifted. Something had put us in that very same place and at that very same time... And what's more, Michael was with another lad – no girl in sight!

Tony wasn't smiling though. I could feel him tensing behind me, and by Michael's look of alarm, I could tell that Tony was seeing him off, his head on one side and that vein in his neck about to explode..

"Great seeing you again Yvonne", Michael said, as he turned to go.

That attraction – physically as well as mentally – had really locked in with me now. My soul was following him like a magnet, and yet reality was holding me back. That was the very last time I ever saw Michael... If only... *If only...* I had had the strength to break away from the controlling situation I had found myself in. If only I had had Gay's courage...

~

Having his father's car at his disposal, Tony then took me to meet all his aunts and uncles. No matter where they lived – from Essex to Sussex, they were all – every single one of them – wonderful. I loved them, and I also loved the way that they responded to *me... They made me feel special...*

In a way, without any words being spoken, and by taking me to meet all his family, was Tony somehow making me feel that he felt I was a little special too? I wasn't sure. His demeanour didn't show it – maybe the mean stance and look was fashionable then? I don't know. But I remember one day Ken saying to me when Tony was in one of his inexplicably strange moods – "He's an angry young man..."

Yes, an angry young man indeed...

~

Although I was no longer seeing my dear friend Alison, at college it was lovely for me to be accepted by new friends, and to feel part of a group. They were all lovely girls in this little clique, and even though I was a whole year younger than they were (it mattered then!) they befriended me straight away.

There was another girl who also befriended me. She was another Linda, and I welcomed her offering of friendship too. Being at college and girls wanting to be friends with me, accepting me as one of their own, was so comforting and warming – and also fun!

Linda was different though. She had short bleached-blonde hair, and lots of really dark eye make-up, with jet-black eyeliner. Like all of us, she wore a very pale lipstick, so her looks were quite stark really. I liked her though, and I also liked the way that she too, had wanted to be friends. So I would hang out with her (as they said in those days) sometimes at lunchtime, as well as being with my other friends. Somehow though, there was a big divide between her and them.

Linda was great fun to be with. She would tell me (what I know now were) really dirty jokes, and I would pretend that I knew it all, and would laugh along with her accordingly. She also talked a lot about her little three year old sister...

~

It was a few weeks away from the end of summer term, and the time when we would all be going our separate ways. We all knew that we would try to keep in touch with each other, no matter where our paths might take us.

I was chatting to Linda outside during a lunch break, and she told me how much she valued my friendship.

"Let's go on holiday together" she suggested. "I fancy going to Bournemouth..."

Oh wow! That sounded fantastic – and I knew that Linda would take charge. She was that kind of girl.

I also knew I would have to ask my mother though. But maybe, just maybe, she might not care what I was doing or where I was going, like when I went to Whitechapel that day. Oh yes, if my mother agreed, this was going to be good.

First of all though, I told Tony about my new friend.

"What did you say her name was?" he asked, frowning.

I told him her name and surname.

"Hmm..." he went, earnestly rubbing his chin. "Does she ever talk about her little sister?"

"Yes!" I exclaimed, "Mandy – she's three..."

"Don't have *anything* to do with her" he instructed, with his head on one side, "and certainly don't go away with her..."

"But she's fun!" I said, beginning to resent being told what to do, or moreover what *not* to do again.

"Fun!" he exclaimed. "That little girl she says is her sister – is actually her *daughter*..."

"What, Mandy?"

"Yes – and Mandy's father is one of my friends..."

Oh dear...

"I'll take you round to see him", he added, "he lives on the Stifford Clays estate – he's a great lad – but very quiet these days..."

~

So, very soon Tony took me round to see his friend, little Mandy's father. He seemed a lovely lad, although very quiet. He looked as though he had the troubles of the world upon his shoulders. I don't know how old he was, but he was probably weighed down with paying maintenance for a little girl he never saw.

What was going on though? First of all it was my friend Elaine who lived in Baker Street, and to whom my mother had given all my cherished baby clothes, purely because she felt sorry for her.

Then there was a girl who lived down in High Road. She was about the same age, and had kept her pregnancy from her family by binding herself so tightly that her baby was born with a club foot.

And now, here was my new friend Linda, who gave birth to a baby girl when she was only thirteen years old...

~

So I did as Tony had told me, and didn't make any plans to go to Bournemouth with Linda. I hadn't even asked my mother. It was one of those times when Fate takes you in the direction you don't really want to go, but you know you have to follow and take that other route.

Leaving College

All this had happened in such a very short space of time. Suddenly, I had become part of this new family – a family that gave me affection, and had welcomed me into their home and arms on just one meeting. So where was all this leading? It didn't matter. I would go back to the pub, back being treated like a skivvy, with no room of my own, and my possessions regularly disappearing – to wherever...

Just weeks into our "relationship", Tony had told me that they were going on holiday in July – down to St. Ives in Cornwall – and *now* he told me that his parents had asked him to ask me if I would like to go? He said they were renting a house for two weeks that overlooked Porthminster beach, Susan was having a twin bedded room – and I could have the other bed...

I had never been to Cornwall, but it held a strong fascination for me. I had always loved it from afar. From photos I had seen, I loved its bleak ruggedness, the tin mines silhouetted against the sun setting over the sea, and the way that the trees on the moors bent in deference to the prevailing winds, creating a bleak, but very alluring landscape that beckoned me on.

Yes! I would love to go! Especially as I had just had to turn down Linda's offer of a week in Bournemouth with her. I had hardly ever had any holidays with my parents – just three: the Isle of Wight when I was seven, Ramsgate when I was nine and my special treat – Jersey when I was thirteen. Other than those three occasions, my holiday was always with my grandmother in Brighton for a week. My parents had either gone on away on their own, or had taken my brothers with them, leaving me behind. I had actually come home one day seeing my father packing the car. I asked him what was going on, and he told me that they were taking my brothers to Wales. Well that was the first I had heard about it. No-one ever told me *anything*...

But now, I was being invited to go on holiday to somewhere I had always wanted to go, and with a lovely family, who were treating me as though I was one of their own.

~

Eva and Ken came over to the pub to discuss this with my parents. They hadn't known me for long, and in fact it was only a matter of weeks or so that Tony and I had been going out together. We would however be going to Cornwall for the last two weeks of term at college, which meant that I would have to leave early.

My parents didn't mind, they seemed happy for me to leave college early and agreed on their monetary share of the accommodation etc. So all was set for me to go. All I had to do now was to inform the college that I was leaving two weeks early – and that sadly my "stand-in" for modelling the bridal gown could take my place. I was also wanting to say good-bye to Adam, but things were happening all too quickly. I hardly ever saw him, he was always with some other girl chatting away and laughing. On my final day I looked for him, but couldn't find him. And so I left on a very down-key note. My lovely time at college came to an end all too abruptly.

If only I had been going back the next term. It had been good, but also somewhat sad for me, that I had been put straight into the second year. I had really enjoyed my time there, and until I had met Tony, I had made new girl friends, all of whom I liked.

My stand-in was thrilled to bits that she was going to model the bridal gown. But was that a lucky sign – or a bad sign – that I never got to be modelling it?

I take it as bad...

St. Ives

July 1965

Travelling down to St. Ives was a new experience for me. I had never been on such a long car journey before. When we had first set off, Ken was at the driver's seat, and Tony sat in the front passenger seat. Eva and Susan sat in the back, which is where I thought I was going to be sitting too.

"Come and sit with us in the front" Ken beckoned, as I was about to get in the back. It was a bench seat in the front, and there were no seatbelts in those days. So there I travelled – sitting between Ken and Tony in the front. Did I feel special? Oh yes indeed!

We stopped off at Jamaica Inn on Exmoor for lunch. It was misty and drizzling with rain at the time. It was also very bleak. I loved it though. Daphne du Maurier, who had written "Jamaica Inn", had summed up its mystery and Exmoor's bleakness exactly, and it was wonderful knowing that she had set that book in that very place.

~

St. Ives sat resplendent in the bay that stretched before us, and as we took that last winding turn, down towards that small harbour town, I was overcome by its beauty. The clear blue sea was twinkling in the late afternoon sunshine, and my heart was already reaching out to those little winding cobbled streets, and the anticipation of enjoying the beaches, the sunshine, and this new way of life that was lying there before me, beckoning me into its arms. The Universal Law of Attraction had now really taken me into its path, and led me to this new and wonderful place.

A new world of folk music also awaited – folk evenings at The Count House, at Botallack, where the sun always set over the sea, silhouetting the tin mine, a sight that I had longed to see and was now experiencing.

At the Count House we would sit on long wooden benches, rather like those in infants school, drinking beer and being enthralled by the folk singers... John the Fish, who I am still in touch with, and Brenda Wootton, who went on to more salubrious venues in her time, but sadly died a few years ago in her cottage on Exmoor. There was also Michael Chapman, and others who would come along to entertain for an evening. But mostly it was John the Fish and Brenda Wootton. John the Fish is still performing, but he has long since given up his bottle of whisky that he used to keep by his side as he strummed his guitar.

All these things brought me closer – and closer – to this lovely family.

~

However, one day, during the second week of our holiday, I was in the house and Tony came in frowning.

"Mum is very upset" he said "she's crying".

Eva was sitting outside in the garden on a bench. "Oh?" I said, wondering from his expression what it might have to do with me.

"She said that you haven't given her any money..."

"What money?" I asked, knowing that my parents had paid his parents whatever they wanted for sharing the accommodation and my keep. This was confusing. I wasn't at work yet, and had only just left college (albeit two weeks earlier than I would have liked). So the only cash I had on me was a few savings from my pocket money which my father gave me, and which I hadn't put into my Post Office Savings book.

"You had better go out and see her" Tony said, nodding towards the door.

So I slowly ventured out to see her, wondering what all this was about, and sat down beside her.

I don't remember exactly what I said to her, but I know I did ask her very kindly why she was upset with me.

"You haven't offered me any money" she said, wiping her tears. Avoiding any confrontation with an adult, as always, and of course respecting their superiority, I didn't explain that I knew that my parents had already paid them however much that they had asked...

So I asked her how much she wanted.

"Four pounds" she answered, now with dry eyes.

This was quite a shock to me. This was another side to Eva that I had never seen before. Where was this kindly smiling woman who I had grown to be very fond of? She had also shown that she was very fond of me. Why else would she and Ken invite me to go on holiday with them?

Thoughts went through my mind as I made my way back to the house. The art work on the wall going up to the art room on the fifth floor of college; Norman, and what I had been told about his rather unwelcome role in Ken's life... This was certainly no business of mine. But where was this lovely woman now? Where was the woman who had welcomed me into her family with open arms. Was I to be wary of her? No, I shouldn't. She was showing me a family life I had never experienced...

~

I went back to the bedroom that I shared with Susan, and took my purse out of my bag. I remember sitting on the bed wondering if I even had four pounds in there. I felt terrible, thinking that Eva thought that I owed her something, but as always respecting my elders, I did not query her, and counted out four pounds, leaving me only a little in change to get me through the rest of the holiday.

I went back outside to where Eva was sitting expectantly, and gave her the money. She took it from me and, clutching it in her hand, without even looking at me, she smiled.

So at least Eva was happy, even though I only had a pittance to get me through the rest of the week...

~

I remember Eva and Ken had taken large tins of white peaches with them that we used to have as dessert in the evenings. I had never had white peaches before, just sliced yellow ones canned in syrup. But these white peaches were something else. It was another culinary experience for me.

Tony later told me that Ken had "acquired" these white peaches from the docks in London where he worked...

Something that I really couldn't even contemplate eating though was the mackerel, freshly caught that very day. Eva and Ken would time it just right so that they could get down to the harbour just as the catch came in. I hated it.

They would buy these mackerel which had been caught early that morning, and take them back to the nice Victorian house that they were renting in Draycott Terrace at the top of Primrose Valley. This wasn't really a valley at all – it was a hill – in the middle of the town... It was as pretty as its name implies though. Ah, but pretty isn't an adjective to use for freshly caught and gutted mackerel...

I really wanted to *try* to eat it – I really did! But these mackerel were sitting in a dish of blood waiting to be soused. Ken had cleaned them – i.e. *disembowelled* them, and put them in the dish – but the blood just didn't stop flowing. I know it is good for you to eat fresh fish – but not *this fresh*...

It was one of those horrific sights that I had seen in the kitchen of the pub all too often, and Tony was turning up his nose in disgust too. Phew! So it wasn't just me!

He suggested that we went out to eat on our own, and from there we explored the little cafés, and always ended up at one of them for a late night hot chocolate, served in a locally made very arty mug. Somehow that hot chocolate, with its frothy topping, always tasted so much better in one of those mugs, made by a local potter.

It was wonderful exploring all the little alleys, and the craft shops that stayed open in the evenings, selling all manner of locally made goods – I particularly liked the necklaces made of little shells, and locally made baskets that we didn't have back at home, and other things like that. I have a black and white photo taken of me that holiday. Being away from home, I could let my hair down – literally, and it is falling down over my shoulders. I was wearing a short-sleeved jumper, crocheted I think, and I remember it was yellow, the colour of the sunshine. With it I was wearing a white skirt. I also had a long string necklace of tiny light grey shells, which was the first thing I had bought in one of those little shops, and was my first nod to the arty way of dressing that was prevalent amongst the locals in St. Ives.

I would see the artists sitting there with their easels and paints, in a world of their own overlooking the sea, but quite happy to discuss their work with passers-by. They were drawn to St. Ives for its wonderful light.

I loved knowing that the sculptor Dame Barbara Hepworth and the writer Virginia Woolf had a connection with St. Ives. I was fascinated with artists and writers like that. The Bloomsbury Group, who lived at that lovely house in Sussex called Charleston, also held a great interest for me, as well as all the regular visitors such as Virginia Woolf and the flamboyant Oscar Wilde. And now, I was walking in the footsteps of Barbara Hepworth and Virginia Woolf, through those narrow cobbled streets.

I loved watching the fishermen mending their nets, and there always seemed to be nets to be mended... They would talk to us, but I could never understand a word they said! Never mind, whatever stories they were telling, they always had someone listening. They just seemed to love telling their stories. I couldn't help but be transported back to Moira and Tom's lovely little cottage in Orsett – and their authentic fishing nets draped across the tiny hallway into their kitchen. These nets though were not dyed purple!

~

There were also groups of young people there called "beats", or beatniks as they later became known, so-called because they were a "subculture" from the Beat generation of the 1950s. I had never seen beatniks before. They were strange, but totally harmless, very quiet, and they just "hung out" on the beach mainly in the evenings – just *being...*

They all basically dressed the same – black polo-neck jumpers and narrow black trousers, and they all had this very serious look that seemed to say – *we are who we are... let us be... man!*

Usually, we would go up to the chapel on the hill and watch the sun set over the sea. There was always a beautiful sunset that holiday, each one of them holding the promise of yet another sunny day.

That evening when the photo was taken when I was wearing that little yellow jumper and a white linen skirt – was the evening that we saw Donovan...

We had planned to go up to the chapel on the hill to watch the sunset again, but heard gentle music down below on Porthminster beach. Donovan was sitting there strumming his guitar and singing his lovely songs. There were a few beats and hippie type people sitting in a circle around him. So we stayed where we were, looking down over the railing and enjoying the whole scene, as the sun set... It was all so beautiful.

"Mellow Yellow" wasn't out yet, but whenever I hear it I remember wearing my yellow jumper while watching Donovan on the beach.

Donovan later wrote "Sunshine Superman" about Porthminster beach...

"We stood on a beach at sunset, do you remember when?
I know a beach where baby, a-it never ends.."

But were we falling in love? No we weren't! But Tony and I had become very good friends, and I had bonded so well with his parents.

~

During those hot and sunny days, we would all go down to that very beach. It was lovely feeling part of a family and doing normal family things. We would sit up by the rocks with a wonderful stretch of sand in front of us which led to the sea. We were all happy and contented. Well, Ken would sit there with his flask of tea and sucking on his pipe. Who knows what was going through his mind? Even when he went in the water – he was still sucking on his pipe! Sometimes he would take photos of the rest of us, doing daft things and generally having fun. We would all hold hands and run into the sea, something I had never done before. Then we would all run back again – all of us laughing. Eva always joined in too. She was a rather plump lady, but was at one with her body, enough so that she wore a red swimsuit. My swimsuit was a navy blue one with white piping that I had bought off a girl in my class!

We always had lunch on the beach too – the most delicious salmon and cucumber sandwiches that we got from a little kiosk next to the beach. I had had cucumber sandwiches, but never *salmon* and cucumber! This was yet another delight I had never known before. Then there were the warm Cornish pasties, straight from the baker's oven in that little town. In those days the seagulls weren't ferocious like they are now, diving down, threatening, and snatching food away. So we could eat our sandwiches in perfect peace, looking out to the Atlantic Ocean with the sun shining down on us, and the sand between our toes.

One of those days we were all sitting there on the beach, just chatting while we looked out to sea, when suddenly Tony stood up – and walked off!

"Look at him – with his head on one side" Eva said in exasperation with him, "he always does that when he's in a mood or doesn't get his own way."

Yes, I had seen that look before – that first time we went to the cinema.

So what was his problem now?

"Leave him be" Eva said, as I wondered whether it was something *I* had said or done. "When he comes back – look at his neck – it will be throbbing..."

Yes, I knew that too.

There was something rather dark about him. It wasn't just his voice, but also the way that he would go into a black mood and make me feel bad, and when he was in one of these moods he would walk around with his head on one side. He did it another time when I was with him in his parents' garden. We never found out what any of us might have done, but he had a "problem" about *something*. So he sulked, and walked around the garden with his head on one side. Silence inevitably followed.

I should have known then really to look out for his dark unfathomable moods.

~

Eventually he came back, still with his head on one side, and yes the vein in his neck was sticking out and throbbing. I did as Eva had suggested – I didn't take any notice. To ask him what his problem was could have caused trouble – massive trouble. I never did find out what had upset him.

Whatever his problem was though, Ken's words had not been in vain. "He's an angry young man" he had exclaimed, and whatever that anger was, it would rear its ugly head from time to time...

Although I had had swimming lessons at Orsett School, when Mr. Simpson used to take us to Grays swimming baths, I was still very afraid of water, and had never learned to swim. Tony knew this.

Porthminster Beach was the first time I had ever really been in the sea. I had had the odd little paddle as a child at Southend, Canvey Island and Ramsgate, but the water had never reached above my ankles. It had been a long time since I had worn a little bathing suit that my grandmother had knitted for me, and the following ruched green and white patterned one that I had worn for those rather frightening swimming lessons when I was eleven. The smell of the chlorine and then walking through the disinfected foot bath, which meant I was about to get into the pool, terrified me.

Now the Atlantic Ocean lapped against my ankles, beckoning me in, and very diffidently I ventured in further – knee height to me was being very adventurous... I was still afraid though of entering those relentless incoming waves higher than that...

Suddenly, I was pushed in... The water rose up to my waist, and the cold water entered the bottom of my swimsuit. Then I was pushed down further... The water was now up to my neck... All I could hear was Tony laughing... But I was gasping...

~

After that I was very nervous about going back into the sea, even though the ocean was calling me. However, Ken bought a blow-up dinghy and it was bobbing around in the sea next to the shore. I was very reluctant to go in it, because I had never been in one before, and didn't trust it. Seeing something that had started off flat, then blown up into something that floated worried me. Balloons started off flat and were blown up – but could easily burst and flop down again... So I was happier staying close to the beach.

How was I ever going to overcome my fear though? I wanted to beat this, swim and have fun like others.

Maybe now was my chance. I could hold onto the side of the dinghy, splash my legs, and try to get used to being in the water. That was the first step. Ken, Eva and Susan were still sitting on the beach, and I was again out there beyond my comfort zone in the sea with Tony.

So there I was – now very bravely up to my neck in water, and holding on to the side of the dinghy. Tony was on the other side. The more I tried, the more I got used to the water. I was able to hold on to the dinghy and reach my legs out into the sea, without touching the bottom, I was feeling good about myself, and actually enjoying it.

Suddenly, the dinghy was thrown upwards – and I *went under...* I was absolutely terrified. I had never had my head under water in that sort of manner before, and the water was going up my nose and down my throat. Now the water was up into my sinuses, which was very painful, and what had gone down in my throat and windpipe was making me choke. Somehow I bobbed up – and Tony was there on the other side of the upturned dinghy – laughing.

I don't remember much about getting to the shore, but the fear of drowning was even more exacerbated now...

Oh – Mr. Porter!

The weekend we came home, my mother didn't show any interest in my holiday at all. All she wanted to know was had Tony's mother worn a swimsuit! Yes she had – and it was bright red.

"Really?" my mother said sarcastically – "What – at *her* size?"

Yes she had. Eva wasn't worried about people looking at her. She was enjoying herself and getting some sunshine on her arms and legs. My mother couldn't understand how *anyone* could wear a swimsuit. She had never worn one in her whole life, not even as a child. The one I had for St. Ives I had bought off a girl in my class at college and it was very plain, navy blue with white straps. It was a little bit loose around my hips, but never mind, the rest fitted!

So anyway, that was the sum total of what my mother wanted to know about my holiday!

~

I had been thinking about what I was going to do about my "career" all the way home. My passion was still to be an air hostess, which might have still been possible – one day – *if* I could get over my fear of drowning! I might not make it to the long haul flights, but there was still the domestic flights – that would be a start. Well that was the plan.

Meanwhile, I would use my shorthand and typing skills, albeit being only sixteen, and take a couple of weeks or so looking for a really nice job, working for someone I would both like and be pleased to work for. A job that I could enjoy, and that would tide me over until I was able to apply to the Airline Recruitment Board. This was my plan – and hopefully it would eventually lead onto my dream...

There wasn't much going on in the local town, just estate agents, building societies, accountants, solicitors, the normal sort of thing.

Nothing arty or interesting! London appealed to me though. I could start off as a shorthand typist in a nice firm, something like Adam's Dad's company. When Adam had taken me to his father's office that day, I felt that I could possibly work for someone like him. He was the lovely sort of man I would have been happy to work for. Yes, someone like him – with his bowler hat and rolled umbrella on the hat stand. If I had to spend all my day taking dictation and sitting at a typewriter, then that was what I would *try* to do.

Moreover though, publishing companies and the press also appealed to me. Mr. Simpson, our headmaster at Orsett School, had taken us on a day trip to Fleet Street once, and I loved that world of reporting, writing, and the sheer buzz of it all. With a lot of hard work, and a little bit of luck, I might just make it one day. Besides, I could do shorthand, so a job as a Fleet Street reporter – wow – that was an idea!

Well, they were my plans. If I couldn't eventually be an air hostess – then I might have a nice little job in Fleet Street!

But plans need good strategies, and strategies don't need spokes in their wheels. Spokes in my wheels were always something that beset me. Someone else's plans always stopping my dreams...

~

On the Monday morning, my mother came up to the pub as usual, looking as though she'd got a problem.

"Right my girl" she commanded sternly as soon as she saw me. "You are going to get on that bus, go down to Grays – and find a job... And don't come home until you've got one!"

Reluctantly doing as I was told, as always, that's exactly what I did. I dressed myself nicely, in my pale aqua blue twin-set (a short-sleeved jumper with matching cardigan), my "good" straight check skirt from Marks & Spencer, my smart little T-strap shoes, and put my hair up in a bun. I could have been going for an interview with British Airways! If only...

Holding a brown A4 envelope with all my certificates, I waited at the bus stop for the No.53 bus to Grays, wondering how on earth I was going to find a job. I hadn't asked my mother for advice on this, she wouldn't have known anyway. She had never had a "job" outside of being behind the bar at the pub, which wasn't really a job anyway, it was something she enjoyed doing. Pulling pints? No, I don't remember her doing any of that. But she did enjoy being "behind the bar", and wearing dresses and jewellery which might at the time be seen as rather attractive.

The No.53 bus came along, and stopped at the bus stop over the road.

So now I was on my way, down to the town. I got off the bus at Congress House, which was basically the Co-op – probably using a different name to make it sound rather more up-market. I really didn't like that bus stop. It was where Tony had accused me unfairly of being an hour late for a date at the cinema, something I really didn't want to think about because it was so wrong. It was also where a woman had waited for a bus with me once, and she had asked me to pick up a sixpence that she had dropped on the floor...

"Put it on here" she had instructed, stretching out her arm, which had some kind of huge wobbly pudding shaped ball in place of a hand. She grinned menacingly as I dutifully picked up the coin and placed it on whatever that piece of human flesh purported to be. I will never forget that look on her face...

~

With these negative thoughts and memories shooting their way into my soul, I looked around me.

I had never been in this position before. To me that area of Grays had always before been shop fronts, for shops selling knitting patterns, embroidery silks, baby clothes, my mother and Nell's favourite little jumpers. Now though I was suddenly in this new world of estate agents, building societies, solicitors, accountants – all the sort of offices I had never encountered before.

I had no idea where to go with regards to "getting a job". I thought that there must be some sort of job agency around, but where?

I desolately walked around the town looking for any shop or office front that could have been classed as a "job agency". I eventually found an office window covered in white postcards, all of which were offering various "jobs". I couldn't see anything that would suit me. Office cleaner? No, I did enough of that at the pub. Barmaid? Uh-oh – no way.

Nevertheless I ventured in. I told the rather stern looking woman at the desk a little about myself, my education, and really just repeated my mother's instructions of what she had wanted for me...

At her request, I showed her my certificates, and she nodded, actually venturing some semblance of a smile. Then she said she wanted to do a typing speed test...

"I can hear how good you are" she said, before I had even typed a few words. Then she told me that there was a vacancy – ready and waiting immediately for a shorthand-typist. Within minutes of walking back down the High Street, I was at the interview...

"What qualifications do you have?" the rather plump man behind the desk asked me.

"Well..." I replied, shyly listing what I had attained at school, and at college, but not of course, mentioning what I really wanted...

How could it be that here I was being pressured by my mother into getting an office job – when all I wanted to do was to – fly the skies. Did air hostesses really need to be qualified in shorthand and typing? I didn't think so.

So I did yet another shorthand/typing test. I found this quite terrifying, what with the man dictating being the very person that I might possibly work for. I took the test with an unfamiliar fairly blunt pencil and shorthand notebook. Then I typed it up.

"I need you to start tomorrow" he said, seemingly pleased with what I had done.

~

The position was for a shorthand typist, and very low paid, but which turned out to be with duties that were more befitting of an experienced secretary than a sixteen year old. I was indeed to be working for the rather plump man – a Mr. Porter – this was going to be very challenging indeed.

The company was in fact called Porters, an estate agent situated right next to the bus stop where I would catch the bus home from the cinema. So I knew where it was, but it was a foreboding-looking place. Goodness knows how so many people would step through that door to buy the house of their dreams (or not)...

~

Porters was a crummy little office, and Mr. Porter with his rather portly figure and thick rimmed glasses reminded me of Billy Bunter. In fact I found out that quite a few people thought that! Indeed, to my mind he looked like an overgrown schoolboy. All he needed was a little cap, a blazer, and knee-length shorts. He certainly wasn't like Adam's father, in his smart three-piece pinstriped suit and bowler hat. Where had my plan of working in London gone to? Or was I just being unfair to this man who had straight away offered me a job? My heart was telling me that my dreams were rapidly melting away – right there before me.

As Oscar Wilde once said "We are all in the gutter – but some of us are looking at the stars..." Yes, I felt as though I was in a gutter with my very soul being drained away. But, like Oscar, I was still looking at the stars. I knew I could do better than this – but would that time ever come?

But I respected him. Like all adults were respected then, especially when one was one's boss.

My salary was just £6 a week, out of which I had to pay my mother £2 a week, and then I had my fares to pay.

At the end of that first (horrible) week, on the Friday evening as I was leaving one of the girls said "see you tomorrow".

Er, no... Tomorrow was Saturday...

What I hadn't been told at the interview was that my £6 a week would include every other Saturday – and that I was to be working in the building society attached to Porters!

So this was something new, something not mentioned to me whatsoever at the interview. This wasn't doing secretarial work, this involved bookkeeping, ledgers and accounts. This was *not* what I wanted to do! I had had enough of ledgers and things at college, and knew that I didn't want anything whatsoever to do with that sort of thing. Moreover – I hadn't been told I had to work every other Saturday – all day – and just for £6 a week!

~

One evening after work, I was waiting at that very bus stop for my No.53 bus to go home, when I saw someone who brought back memories from when I was in the infants at Orsett School.

I was five or six at the time, and I was in the playground at the front of the school. Then I realised that I was on my own – where had everyone gone? A girl came running down the side of the school and grabbed my hand...

"Come on Yvonne" she said excitedly, "we're all round the back – come and see what Amber is doing..."

I don't really remember her name, but I am referring to her as Amber because of the colour of her hair. She was such a pretty little girl, with golden hair, dark eyebrows and long black eyelashes. I saw her as the prettiest girl in the school, and I felt that one day she would be a very beautiful film star.

So I ran along with the other girl who was holding my hand, wondering what was going on. The whole of the infants school was gathered at the back – all looking in the same direction. There was Amber standing against the wall – her navy blue knickers down around her ankles and holding her skirt up to her waist. I think we were all silently fascinated, looking at Amber...

Looking back, I can't help but wonder what made her do it. Was it normal for her to do that? Was she enjoying what she was doing and having so much attention? I can't remember whether she was smiling or not – we were all looking elsewhere...

When I went back to Orsett School again at the age of nine, having been away for two years, Amber was no longer there. Maybe someone had found out what she had been doing, I really don't know.

~

So there I was, sixteen years old and waiting at the bus stop outside Porters. There was a pretty looking girl with a baby in a pram. She had golden blonde hair, dark eyebrows, and long black eyelashes. I immediately recognised her as being Amber. There was no mistaking her looks, although her face was much older now, her once pretty eyes were now just dark and blank looking, and her little cherub mouth was now down turned and hard.

My immediate thought was to say hello to her, and tell her I remembered her from Orsett School. I hoped she would remember me too. She was talking to another young woman though, so I was holding back to when the other woman would go, rather than butt in on their conversation.

The baby was young, but old enough to be sitting up in the pram, so he would have been about four to six months old. He was screaming loudly, but Amber took no notice. Everyone at the bus stop seemed to be shuffling a little, seemingly uncomfortable with this poor baby screaming. Surely Amber could do something to find out what was causing him such distress?

Suddenly, still in mid conversation, Amber swung her arm round straight across the baby's head. The poor little mite was so stunned, he just stopped screaming and went silent. Meanwhile Amber just carried on with her conversation.

All I wanted to do was comfort the baby, but no-one could step in like that, not even in those days. Amber was only sixteen, but now she was a mother, and it was very evident that she couldn't cope. That is no excuse to hit a baby so badly like that though.

So what did I do? There was nothing I *could* do. Like everyone else standing at the bus stop we just stood still. The only person who could have stepped in and said something was the young woman she was talking to. But she just carried on with the conversation as though nothing had happened.

Well, Amber never became a beautiful film star. And I can't help but wonder what happened to her poor baby...

~

I hated it at Porters – just *hated* it! There was one very nice woman though who I liked. She was called Enid, and had welcomed me with a genuine smile. It was one of those smiles upon first meeting, when you *know* that you are going to get on. We just seemed to gel.

She was recently married, and I remember her telling me about how she was decorating their house. Not standing precariously on a stepladder painting and wallpapering, no that was her husband's job! She told me how she had Black Watch tartan carpets throughout, and everything else was in the colours of the tartan – namely dark blue and green. I thought she was very brave doing that, and she reminded me a lot of Moira and Tom who lived up the little alley near the pub. So I think that talking about home decoration – and our mutual love of perfumes etc., brought us together. What she was doing working in an office like that, I do not know. But then again – what was *I* doing there?

However, I very soon realised that the other girls didn't seem to like me. I don't know what their problem was. Maybe though it was because at just sixteen I had gone straight in as the boss's secretary (hmm), but I really don't know. It was like being back at Torells all over again.

~

That dark brown dingy office, with its creaky narrow stairs that led up to it, made me feel that I was shut in some attic room. The mottled grey and very dusty Lever Arch files, which had been stacked on every shelf for donkey's years, and the croaky Gestetner copying machine, that spilled out hundreds of copies of my neatly typed house particulars along with copious amounts of leaking black ink, did nothing but depress me.

Typing the Contracts of Sale was a nightmare. I could not make one single mistake. This was the most stressful part of my job. It was awful – just one typing error and the whole contract would be void. At sixteen years old I was far too young to have all this stress on my shoulders, and worry day in day out about what the next day was going to be like.

Apart from Enid, the other women were pretty offish. One in particular was Maureen, who was just a general office run-around, but she acted as though she ran the show. She took an instant dislike to me the moment she saw me. I knew that because she had a really smarmy grin on her face that was sort of saying *"Oh yeah... So we have a new girl – and she's the boss' secretary – we'll soon see about that"*.

I knew she was going to be trouble.

During the winter months Enid and I would take a tin of soup each in for our lunch. Next to the toilet was a little stove, a bit like a Primus stove, on which we could heat our soup. So that is what we did, and we would spend our lunchtimes in the office chatting and enjoying our soup, while the others went out shopping or whatever. This was nice. I liked Enid – she was a lot older than me, and reminded me a little of Gina.

They must have been about the same age, and were similar in looks with their short dark hair.

One day, in February 1966, Maureen was in the office at lunchtime. Enid and I heated up our respective tins of soup, and sat down to enjoy them while we chatted. Maureen had that awful smirk on her face again, and as I took a couple of spoonfuls of my tomato soup – I was horrified to find that something green-coloured was rising to the top of mine – it was neat washing up liquid... Enid felt the same as me – horrified. It could only have been Maureen who had squirted that washing up liquid into my bowl – especially as she was sitting there like the proverbial Cheshire cat. I'll never forget that smirking face.

Another time, Enid told me that Maureen had reported that I had stolen a £5 note from the till in the building society section. What?? I would never – *ever* – steal *anything*... I had never even taken so much as a packet of crisps from the bar, or a sweet from the shop without permission. To be accused of stealing money, was probably the worst thing I could have been accused of. As it happened, Enid told Mr. Porter that I would never do such a thing, and so officially the blame was taken off of me – but that awful feeling of being blamed for something that not only had I not done, but where I had also been "set up", never left me.

~

I somehow managed to hold back my tears going home on the bus that day, but I could contain myself no longer once I went indoors.

Without any sympathy, I spent that evening crying. I cried and cried and cried.

"That's what women are like" my mother retorted, on this rare occasion that I told her about it, and showing me no sympathy at all... "Now, what did I tell you".

"You need to get down to that doctor's and get a tonic", my mother said, when I couldn't stop crying.

So doing as I was told, as always, that's what I did the next morning. Being a village, the doctor's surgery was in his house. You didn't need an appointment. You just sat in the small waiting room and waited your turn. He also had his own pharmacy in his surgery, so prescriptions weren't needed.

He listened to what I had to say, and I told him what was going on at work. Although I tried hard not to, I suddenly found I was crying, I couldn't help it. He wrote on my notes that I was tensed up and weepy, and not happy with my colleagues at work. The moment I mentioned how I was having problems with my mother as well, he totally dismissed that.

"Every girl falls out with their mother" he said abruptly, and didn't want to hear anything about it. I really wanted to tell him something in confidence about how unhappy I was at home as well, but he really didn't want to know.

He counted out a number of Stelazine tablets, an anti-anxiety medication, using a triangular shaped metal object and put them into a jar. So even though I was only sixteen years old, I was already on this type of drug.

Of course, taking something like this meant that I had to avoid alcohol.

One evening Tony took me to a pub called "The Olde Dog" at Bulphan. This was a very old pub, small inside, and full of character, in a very rustic way. I stepped down into the little bar, and sat at an old oak table. Tony asked me what I would like to drink, and being sensible I asked for a pineapple juice.

He came back to the table with a Pernod for me. When I asked him why, he said that the bar man had thought he asked for a Pernod, so as he had it – I might as well drink it...

I hate Pernod – I always have done. But as usual, I did as I was told – and drank it...

Tony knew about the pills I was taking, but that didn't seem to bother him. Maybe he had other ideas... But that is another story...

~

Springtime 1966

The sweet scent of springtime pervading the woods and the senses, as the late afternoon sun shines its glowing rays through the trees, highlighting the most beautiful hue of the bluebells, which had multiplied happily over the years – this fragrant carpet of blue was an experience not to be missed. Soft bright green moss nestling around the tree trunks added to this glorious profusion of colour and scent.

Strolling through Langdon Hills in springtime was always a joy, and a place where local families would wander sometimes on Sunday afternoons. It was never crowded though. The woods were extensive, and the only evidence of other people being there was the distant sound of the happiness of children as they ran through the trees, free to roam, but knowing that their parents were nearby, strolling arm in arm along the natural paths, trodden by many families before them.

The only visual evidence of people being there were the sometimes discarded bunches of bluebells that children had picked and then dropped to the ground, as they made their way back to their parents' car. These pretty flowers had been left forlorn, when their petals had hung their heads in despair at being plucked from their natural home. The joy had been in the picking though. It was natural for children to do this, and learn about nature, smelling the sweetness of flowers, and then realising how quickly they can wither...

As I child I had had what I called my "plant hospital". As silly as it may sound, I would pick up any flowers that had been carelessly dropped to the ground, buttercups, daisies, campion, that sort of thing. I would take them home, put them in jam jars of water, and hope that I could make them well again. Daisies were always the best to perk up, but usually these wild flowers had a little struggle... I did my best though!

~

"Let's go to Langdon Hills" I suggested enthusiastically to Tony one Sunday afternoon, when he pondered about what we might do. My parents rarely took me anywhere with them now, and I needed to experience the feeling of walking through the bluebell woods again.

Tony looked at me quizzically.

"Oh *please...*" I said, "it is so beautiful there..."

After a frown, and a look that said 'do I really want to do this?' he agreed – as long as we later went to a pub...

~

The woods were a delight as always, and I felt happy strolling through them, with the late afternoon sun glinting through the trees. The bluebells were still glistening with the previous day's rain, but this only added to their fragrance. I don't know whether Tony enjoyed it like I did, but I was in my element – at one with nature...

He was wearing a brown corduroy jacket reminiscent of a stern school teacher, who would look at you over the top of his glasses. Maybe that depicted how he felt – having command over me?

"Time to go" he said, suggesting that we went to "The Oak" pub at Socketts Heath. Feeling a slight chill from the dampness, we turned to go back to the car. Outside of the woods, I knew it would be a lovely evening, the sort of evening where you could sit outside until the sun went down.

I turned to walk back along the natural pathway, which was comparatively dry to the rest of the woods.

"No, we'll take a short cut" Tony commanded, pointing over towards a bank. I didn't even know if it was in the right direction. Dutifully, I followed, carefully walking through the bluebells so as not to crush any of them.

"I can't get up there" I exclaimed, looking at the steep soaking wet bank that rose up from a pool of mud.

"Of course you can" he said. "I'll carry you up".

He was certainly no Sir Galahad or Sir Walter Rayleigh coming to a "damsel in distress" and I didn't believe at all that he would be able to carry me up that slippery slope, in fact I felt rather afraid of ending up in the mud.

"But you'll drop me!" I exclaimed again, just wanting to get back to the path.

"*Rubbish!*" he answered, picking me up, probably now more than ever wanting to prove something...

Just one step up that slope, he slipped... And down I went, straight down into the mud...

~

I felt very uncomfortable as we made our way back to the car, via the well-trodden route that I knew so well. Sitting in the car with a soaking wet skirt and underwear was not the sort of thing I had ever had to experience before.

"Can I *please* go home first to change?" I asked him, knowing that the Kings Arms was on our route.

"No!" he said firmly, "we are going to The Oak..." so that is what I had to do.

~

I was so embarrassed walking into that pub with a large brown wet patch on my skirt. I was always very concerned about the way I looked anyway. The memories of being goaded at Torells for the way I was dressed sometimes, and the girls who didn't know me laughing at me, always made me feel conscious of how I looked. To have a large wet brown stain on the back of my skirt – in public – was unthinkable. I also hated the feeling of mud against my skin, and just wanted to wash it off. But there was nothing I could do – again, I just did as I was told.

We sat on a bench next to each other just looking across the dim bar. I so much needed to get home, get washed and changed.

Why was sitting in a gloomy pub, when the sun was still shining outside, so preferable to taking me home and allowing me to get cleaned up and changed?

It wasn't as though he was enjoying it – he just sat there – staring towards the door, unflinchingly silently knowing he was having his way – again...

I should have seen the signs...

A Different Side Of London

As young as I was, I knew London well. Going to Oxford Street shopping with my mother and grandmother, had shown me which buses and trains to take – the No.53 bus from Orsett to Grays, then the Green Line bus from Grays to Aldgate. That was where we would wait for the red London bus to take us to Oxford Street. Now that I was travelling on my own, I knew that I could get the train from Aldgate station to Oxford Circus. So all in all, what with wandering around finding places I had never been before – and of course the fateful day going to Whitechapel to have my tooth abscess seen to – I got to know London pretty well.

Now though, I was to experience a different side of London. Tony and I would go there sometimes on a Saturday, and he would take me round back streets where vegetable trimmings and all manner of rubbish were strewn along the paths. We would go to a little Italian restaurant in Brewer Street, Soho. That is where I had my first steak cooked in red wine with mushrooms. Such a small place, but such wonderful food. I had never been to a restaurant before, let alone an Italian one. I had never actually drunk wine with my meal either – I had usually been given beer.

One time we went to The Marquee club. It was all very dark in there, and whilst standing there listening to the live music, I noticed two women laying on a bench, kissing and fondling each other's breasts... Ah, so that was what lesbians did! This is what my mother had referred to when she had said in front of me sometime that my grandfather had called Gina a "*lesbian*" – because she refused to go to bed with him...

I couldn't help but be intrigued by these two young women though. I had never seen anything like it before – women kissing and fondling breasts? I must say though that it was all very interesting, and they didn't mind being looked at – at all...

~

I absolutely loved Carnaby Street, with all its quirky shops, bringing a whole new concept and lightness to what had been for some years a rather post-war austerity. Most of all though, I favoured a small shop in Kensington called Biba, which offered all the beautiful things that I loved. It was dark and wonderful, with huge feathers adorning the displays, and I just adored everything in there. It was the whole concept of it – artistic, brave, inviting, meaningful images – that I loved, and really the Biba style has stayed with me for years.

One evening we ventured into a bar in this same sort of area. There was a lot of chatter and noise going on, but the moment we went through the door – it all went silent. It was then that we realised that everyone in there was male, and they were all the sort of male that would rather "be with" another male...

At that time no-one talked about "gays". I still thought that gay meant being happy, and dancing in the daisies. But this was a different sort of *gay*...

Red warning stares with twitched noses and wrinkled brows were beaming towards me... Oh dear... I had already seen lesbians writhing with each other, and no-one had batted an eyelid, but now – a quick exit beckoned...

~

The Kings Road was new to me as well. I had been used to shopping in Oxford Street, or rather window shopping that is. Well, more than that – display shopping... I had once bought myself a rather lovely two strand jet necklace though, which I still treasure, and I have even worn around my waist at an evening occasion once! I also bought a chunky brown necklace that looked rather like amber – but probably wasn't. I still have that too.

But back to the Kings Road though – this was another experience for me. Walking along behind a young chap with a circular hole cut out of the back of his jeans – just where his rear opening was – was another thing I had never experienced. This sort of thing never went on in Orsett or Grays!

So there I was, drawn into another world of London back streets, red lights, lesbians, gays, and "inviting" exposed anuses peeping through little round holes cut into jeans...

~

Throughout my childhood I had been told by my mother that I had to save any money that I was given. My aunts would give me money occasionally for my birthday by way of a postal order for five shillings – 25p in today's money – and little things like half a crown for example for sewing my uncle Cecil's button back onto his jacket. I also had National Savings Stamps that I would stick into a savings book. When it was full, this would then be transferred to my Post Office Savings Account.

I always saved as much as I could, even when I was only earning £6 a week at Porters. Urging me on to save was the dream I had about buying myself a little Mini when I passed my driving test. This of course never happened with Ralf having jumped out in front of me on one of my lessons. However, all in all, by the summer of 1966 I had accrued over £110 – that accounted for an awful lot of savings!

I always had to pay my way with Tony though, no matter where we went. At times he even took me to a post office to withdraw some of the money I had been saving. Tony would tell me how much he wanted me to withdraw, and waited in the car while I did it. As always – I did as I was told. I didn't exactly feel that I was being treated...

My Post Office account shows that in just one week during that summer I had withdrawn £45...

Controlled And Confused

I am not a promiscuous person – I never have been. I had been on Stelazine since February for anxiety and for what had been going on at Porters. The following month, at the end of March, I told Tony I really didn't want to see him again. I wanted to break away, find myself, *be* myself. We had been quarrelling a lot, and what with what was going on at the pub, the total control over me was overwhelming, and I really couldn't cope any more. He then wrote to me professing his *"love"* for me – no-one had ever said that to me before. So yet again, I was taken in by this written outpouring of *"affection"*.

He was still so controlling though, and from my upbringing, as always, I felt that I had to please. Like when he said he wanted me to have my long hair cut short, I did it. It was October 1966 and Peter and Gordon were in the charts with Lady Godiva. As I sat in the chair having my hair cut, as chance would have it Lady Godiva was playing...

"Her long blonde hair
Lyin' on the barber's floor
Doesn't need it long anymore..."

And there was my long blonde hair – lying on the hairdresser's floor. But I *did* still want it long.

I sat looking down at the floor, my long hair lying in clumps, and gathering in volume by the second.. I hadn't until then realised just how much hair I had – "The girl with the crowning glory" Mr. Simpson had once said to me – and now it was gone...

A junior with short black hair and an over clipped fringe, came along with a wide broom – and with a blank look of nothingness, swept my hair into a dustpan – and took it away. I remember thinking that is *my* hair – that *I* had grown. How could something that was part of me be taken away so quickly, so briefly, and without a care for my feelings or desires...

When I left the hairdresser's, I was so despondent, I put my head scarf over my head and tied it tightly under my chin, as I didn't want anyone at the bus stop to see me looking like that...

~

I clearly remember losing my virginity. I remember when it happened, and where it happened. We had been going out for some months, and so I suppose it was inevitable, if not in my mind, in Tony's. It hadn't occurred to me that it might happen – although we had had some good times together, and had become quite close, I didn't envisage this major step in my life being inevitable with *him*...

Considering everything that was going on at the pub, I was incredibly naïve. When I was sixteen and had asked my college friend Linda what went on, she had told me in her own way what happened, but I still hadn't really understood the birth control diagrams on the blackboard shortly before we left college.

When it was to eventually happen, I thought I would be all dewy-eyed and *in love* – how Doris Day and Grace Kelly were depicted in the films. Being in love, getting engaged, and then married. The wedding night would then be something else – something wonderful. That is how it was in those days. Or maybe that is just how *I* saw it.

I was fully aware of what my grandfather was getting up to with other women, once I had seen the diagrams of the mechanics that is. But like my parents, my aunts and uncles, and all the other married people in my life, I felt sure that even they must have at some time fallen in love, courted, got engaged, and then got married. The reality may have been very different. But that was my dream. *That* was how I would one day lose my virginity – on my wedding night – in the arms of my husband.

~

It was a dark, cold winter's evening, and the rain was pouring down relentlessly. We were in the car, in the pub car park, and I was feeling really rather cold and uncomfortable. There was no heating in cars in those days. Well not in that car anyway. It was fairly late in the evening, but before eleven o'clock, because I had to be home by that time. I remember watching the rivulets of rain, cascading down the windscreen side by side, watching them as they carried on like this, and then suddenly merging into one another... Little did I know that this was maybe rather symbolic of what was to come...

It was really just an extension of a goodnight kiss, and a bit of a fumble. To be fair, I wasn't exactly protesting. I think that maybe I was enjoying the physical affection, that affection that I had longed for throughout my childhood; the cuddles that I had needed so desperately, when I had been so badly treated that I just sobbed alone. But there was no way that I had it in my mind that anything more would happen.

Being the days before tights had even been invented, well, where I lived anyway, I was wearing stockings, like all women and girls of my age did in those days – "American Tan" was *de rigueur* at the time – even in the depths of winter. So, with wearing stockings and a stretchy waist high "girdle", which was totally unnecessary with my slight, six to seven stone build, it wasn't difficult.

Nothing had been planned, and really, it all took me rather by surprise. I was still in the front seat of the car – his father's with the long bench seat – and had made no indication that I wanted to go further, but suddenly – he was on top of me...

I remember feeling a burning stinging pain, a pain that I had never felt before – and then a very strange feeling – of something being somewhere where nothing had ever been before...

There was no huffing and puffing, no *passion*. Nothing. Just *silence*. All I remember is thinking that he must have "done it" before, because he seemed so matter of fact. We didn't even talk about it. He didn't even acknowledge that he had just taken my virginity.

It was still pouring with rain when I ran indoors, holding my scarf over my head. I went into the cold stark lobby, steeling myself to face everyone, when all I wanted to do was to hide. Everything in the pub was still as normal. The clinking of glasses being gathered, Nell wiping down the counter tops, and my grandmother knocking back the gin. Nobody took much notice of me, which was just as well really.

I went upstairs into the bathroom, and found that I was bleeding. It wasn't like this in the films. Grace Kelly and Doris Day were always in a misty haze, and a dewy-eyed glaze of joy. I was just sore and bleeding.

Then I went to bed. Later, my grandmother joined me.
To everyone else, it was just another night.

The Bond That Ties

I had never wanted this to happen. I regretted it so much. Maybe it was the drugs mixed with alcohol, I really don't know. Maybe it was just *me* – forever trying to please, and not saying NO! I didn't even enjoy it. To me it was just the pain of something tearing inside me and allowing something in, an invasion into my body.

The next day I went to work. I was crying in the toilet with the stinging and soreness. Enid was looking at me quizzically when I came out, but she didn't say anything. All I could do was just carry on as usual.

Other people were courting, getting engaged, getting married with all the family wishing them joy and happiness in their new lives to follow. It would be on the wedding night that the couple would make love, and find the true joy of physical love... Wouldn't it? Well that's what they implied on the films...

I still longed for the love of my life, that irresistible person that I wanted to fall in love with and marry. But, having lost my virginity – *who would want me now?*

~

One day I came home from work and my mother was waiting for me in the kitchen. She was angry – *very angry...*

She stood in front of me with her dark eyes threatening. Her hair was all sort of standing on end, as though she had been pushing her fingers through it all day in anger.

"How *DARE* you tell anyone what goes on in this pub!" she scolded. "Haven't I drummed it into you enough – YOU DO NOT TELL *ANYONE* WHAT GOES ON HERE... *Do you hear me?*"

Yes, I did hear her, especially as by now she had taken another step towards me, holding her right hand in the air. I was frozen like a timid rabbit in headlights. I knew I that had done something very wrong, but she didn't know about that, and that obviously wasn't what she was referring to. The threat of her striking me across my face was nothing compared to the fear of her wrath.

So what had I said?

Well, having this new found bond with Tony, I had confided in him about something in particular that had gone on at the pub, something very upsetting. I hadn't told him all the nitty-gritty, but had confided in him something that had recently happened, and had blurted it out to him. I can't remember what that particular thing was, but probably I could no longer contain my silence – I know I was crying, but whatever it was about, enough was enough...

"*YOU* my girl should know better" my mother scolded again, this time lowering her hand. "Don't you realise that Grandpop could lose his licence if this got out – and we would all be thrown out of here..."

A frightened rabbit indeed. I didn't know that something I had said in confidence had been passed on.

Unbeknown to me, Tony had phoned my father and had a right go at him, telling him that he shouldn't allow these things to go on.

"He's a cocky little bugger" my mother said. "How could he have the gumption to phone your dad and say all those things to him?" But *what things?*

"He's no good" she said, ignoring my question. "He's no good – you mark my words – do you hear?" she added. "These short arses are always the same – always got something to prove. He can't stand up to your dad – so he phones him..."

"I didn't know..." I was saying... "I really didn't know... He didn't tell me..."

"He's no good" she repeated as she turned away from me. "Now – get out of my sight – and don't let me see your face any more..."

There was more to come though. My father had immediately phoned Ken after Tony's abusive phone call, and complained to him about his son. Having a go at an elder was something beyond my notion of respect. You respected your elders, no matter what.

My mother never did tell me exactly what had been said, and neither did Tony. He just admitted that he told my father that he should not allow me to be treated like that – and to do something about it. Quite right. But there are ways of saying things, and he should never have put his point across in the apparently abusive manner that he did.

I didn't even have any inkling at all that he was going to do this. However, at least I now knew that the life I was living at the pub wasn't really as normal as I had been led to believe...

Strangely, I felt a little bit sorry for my father, and ashamed at what Tony had done. Even more, I felt ashamed of myself – for having confided in him. I had *never* told *anyone* anything about what went on at the pub before.

It also confirmed to me that there was something very dark and deep about Tony. The way that he walked with his head on one side sometimes, showing an unspoken anger, a gesture that meant that it was best not to speak to him.

He was like that when I asked him why he had betrayed my confidence in him, and had phoned my father without my knowledge – but in a way, I was also grateful for his concern for my welfare.

The next time I went to his parents' house, Ken took me to one side.

"I know what's going on at the pub" he said gravely, even though he only knew about that little bit I had confided in Tony. "But you just have to keep it to yourself – *deal with it yourself* – and *don't* tell Tony any more about what goes on..."

So that was it. Someone else was telling me to keep quiet – and I always have done – until now...

~

I tried many times not to see him again. I would make excuses when he phoned that I wouldn't be going out with him. He was so manipulative though, and would not take "no" for an answer.

One time I told him I had a cold, and he sent me a letter wishing me well and writing the most obscure jokes, saying he hoped they cheered me up. Political correctness was not his scene! Despite the jokes though, he was also telling me how much he wanted to see me. So before long there was another trip to the pictures.

I was still not happy seeing him though. There was something about him that I really didn't like. He would find fault with me, even though all I was trying to do was please, and as ever, if I ever said what he thought was the wrong thing, his head would go on one side and his neck would be throbbing again.

The next time he phoned I told him that I really didn't want to see him again. But he was insistent. I was trying to tell him quite firmly that I wouldn't be going out with him again – then I saw Nell standing at the end of the landing. She didn't say anything, she was just looking at me. I told him then that I was going to have to say bye-bye and that I was putting the phone down.

Soon I received another letter. He was telling me how much he missed me – and *loved me*. What could I do? No-one had ever told me they loved me before. Not even my father, who I loved very much.

This was in a letter though – he didn't seem to be able to actually *say* the words. But then again, I wasn't used to people being demonstrative in a loving sort of way anyway...

~

Valentine's Day had always been a horrible day for me. Girls at school had come into class showing off their cards, and also at college. I wasn't the only girl who didn't receive one, far from it, but had so much wished that I could have a Valentine's card too. Traditionally, they were always anonymous, but the girls seemed to know who they were from, and there would be a lot of giggling and flushed faces...

Well, one day I did receive a Valentine's card. I wanted the writing of the address to be unfamiliar to me, but I could see it was Tony's writing. I have to say it was a lovely card, but he had put "love from..." followed by an awful black mess where he had scratched out his name. That awful black mess might have foretold what another murky mess my life was going to turn into...

~

So – was that *it?* What were these written so-called words of love all about? Why didn't my eyes go all misty when he wanted to kiss me, like Doris Day's and Grace Kelly's? It was because I didn't love him – I knew that. How could I love someone who bristled every time I said something that he misconstrued, said *"rrrrubbish"* if I said something he didn't agree with. He also made it very clear to me that he wanted to make me look like someone else. That's not love. That is possession – and control.

I wish my mother had *forbidden* me to see him. That would have been easier to convince him. But she didn't. Maybe she was happy just getting me out of the house and "out of her sight", as she often told me. She made it very clear that she didn't like him though.

"But you can't be... Um – *in love* with him..." she said one day.

"No – I'm *not!*" I answered quickly – I had no need to ponder on that!

"He's a cocky little bugger", emphasising what she had said before. And I thought she was going to go off into another rant about short people...

If only I had had the presence of mind to tell her that I didn't *want* to see him – I had tried... But he wasn't going to let me go...

When you are controlled by someone who is so obsessive it is very hard to break those chains and flee.

I wished I could have been in love – seeing someone's smiling face whenever we met. But Tony was not like that. His face was usually down-turned with some kind of feigned criticism or disapproval. He didn't like my lovely long hair – so he made me have it cut... He needed me to fulfil his fantasy of Mia Farrow, Petula Clark and Katie Boyle. For Heaven's sake – Petula Clark and Katie Boyle were old enough to be my mother!

"It Was The Best Of Times –
It Was The Worst Of Times"

"It was the best of times – it was the worst of times" as Charles Dickens wrote as the first line of "A Tale of Two Cities". That could almost read as "A Tale of Two Sixties", being the best of times and the worst of times...

The sixties were certainly the best of times for many of my generation. We had been born just after the war, many of us knowing the hardships of rationing that still went on into the fifties, but the sixties were a breath of fresh air, literally with no more gas masks, and mentally with the threat of war gone, and the brightness of this new free era that was taking place.

There was Twiggy, Mary Quant, Biba and her wonderful shop, the Kings Road, Vidal Sassoon, not to mention all the wonderful music of the era.

I enjoyed the fashions, the make-up and the lovely little shoes of the time. I had left Freeman Hardy & Willis and Timpsons behind for Lily & Skinner, Manfield, and ultimately Ravel. I still have the first ever eye shadow I bought. It was in stick form like a lipstick, the make was Lenthéric, and was in a silver case. It was called "Charcoal". Sometimes I look at it, and remember the innocence, and the time I would spend with my eye shadow creating the perfect look, well, for me anyway. I could have enjoyed that wonderful era more... If only...

Somehow though, for me, the worst of times overshadowed the best of times. It was a time of hope – but in my case – hopelessness. So what the Dickens did the worst of times have to do with me?

Well, there had been worse times during my childhood, with what I now know was serious abuse. I didn't know then though that the things that had been going on at the pub were so wrong. Instinctively I felt that the goings on weren't right, but adults were *always* right... *Weren't they?*

I knew I couldn't tell *anyone* what went on at the pub – but I didn't know exactly *why*. The threat had always been there, that if I uttered one word to anyone, I could be taken away to a "home". What was this "home" then? That place for naughty little girls who spoke out about what was troubling them, and what the adults were getting up to.

There were songs from the fairly recent past, and in the charts, that made everything seem so normal – but they were also confusing. Like Johnny Burnette's "You're Sixteen" which suggested to me that at sixteen you could belong to a man – and no-one else. These days that sounds so far-fetched, but back then I was very vulnerable to what male/female relationships were all about. The goings on at the pub were telling me something – but my heart was telling me something else.

Even the lovely Jack Jones had sung "Lollipops and Roses". I really liked Jack Jones, and in fact in recent years have met him, which was wonderful, but the implication of the words of that particular song was very confusing – especially as one of the accompanying films of the song at the time showed him singing to a little girl.

Then there was Neil Sedaka's "Happy Birthday Sweet Sixteen" – what had he waited for, and what was he going to do to her when she turned sixteen? The lyrics to that song made me feel that at sixteen years old there would be *something* that I ought to be *doing...*

~

These were part of the worst of times. I didn't like feeling that I must be a "prude" not to take part in the awakening to "rude" things. All the things that I thought were "rude" were becoming normal life in that big world out there.

Were the things that went on at home really as rude as I thought? Were they in fact "normal" behaviour? I didn't know. Then when I met Tony's parents – and his mum's boyfriend who she used to go out with and who would stay at weekends – I thought that it really must be "normal". I was still confused as to what was the "best" thing to do – and what was the "worst"?

Still I followed my instincts. I valued my body. Men staying behind at the pub had watched me undress as an innocent little girl, just getting ready for bed in front of the fire. Yet I was able to go with my instincts when I was eleven and see off the men who wanted to get me into bed – with both of them...

If I had seen an erection though as a child, then I have forgotten about it. I still have it in my mind what happened when I was just two or three years old, and being sat astride my grandfather's body, facing away from him – but wondering what those things were growing out of his tummy lower down... And the way that he guided my little hands on to these "things"...

I don't remember anything about what happened next. All I remember is Nell coming into the bedroom, and just standing there – looking. I suppose I must have thought that it was some kind of a game...

~

The sixties, and the films that were also around at the time, especially those being shown in London, opened my eyes to things that went on. They weren't pornographic, but they were much more than I had ever seen before. I enjoyed seeing them with Tony – the nudity, the dangly bits, and the whole naughtiness of what was happening on the screen.

~

As Charles Dickens went on to say in that first paragraph of "A Tale of Two Cities"...

"It was the age of wisdom, it was the age of foolishness..."

So yes, it was the age of wisdom for me too – beginning to realise that what was going on at the pub really wasn't normal. Husbands and wives – yes. That was romantic love that can last a lifetime, and what "making love" is all about. I still wanted to be like Grace Kelly and Doris Day in their films, falling in love – and making love – with the man of my dreams. Of course, like my friend Linda at college, Grace Kelly went on to marry her real life prince!

So the age of wisdom was with me. I knew what I wanted. It would be wise to follow my instincts and dreams, and one day find that man that I fell in love with, and married...

Somehow though, the age of foolishness and this whole new world took over...

~

The following March it was my seventeenth birthday. It was tradition at work that the birthday girl would go out and buy fresh cream cakes for everyone in the office. Not the men – just the women – people were rather sexist in those days! So that is what I did. I went to that lovely little bakers at the bottom of Grays High Street that sold such wonderful home-made pastries etc., and bought a fresh cream cake for everyone in the office.

"Happy birthday to you..." Maureen said – as she pushed my cream cake into my face... It was in my eyes – all over my face.

The humiliation was far worse than the mess on my face and the waste of the cake, and really, because of the evil grin on her face, that was the final straw...

That afternoon I made a typing error. Mr. Porter in his buffoon-like rage was shouting at me like no-one's business. This wouldn't happen today. But there he was, because of this little error shouting at me in front of everyone. It wasn't as though it was a contract, so goodness knows what he would have been like if it had been. It was just a simple typing error that anyone can make.

Going against all my principles of doing the right thing, enough was enough. I found myself walking out of that door onto the street, and as coincidence would happen – the No.53 bus was waiting there – ready to take me home...

I didn't go to work the next day – nor the next – nor the next.

No-one phoned to ask me where I was, nor did anyone ask me where I had been when I returned to work three days later. I think everyone knew about the abuse I was getting there, and no-one wanted to get involved – not even Mr. Porter.

By now, I knew that I was never going to fly the skies as an air hostess to those far distant lands. I was never going to marry that rich man on my travels who looked like Elvis Presley... Hmm, that was just a childhood dream – as it had been with so many other young girls at the time. To me he was always the "most handsomest man in the whole world"...

Well Elvis may have been singing "Crying in the Chapel" at the time, but I was crying in my sleep. In the bed that, even at my age, I was still forced to share with my grandmother.

It had always been difficult for me sleeping with my grandmother. Even when I did manage to get to bed before her and fall asleep, she would usually come to bed reeking of the gin that she had gulped down straight from the optic, and the drunken outbursts of song when I needed to be up early the next morning for work didn't help me face the next day at all.

To my mind Porters was the pits. And so was that blasted Gestetner machine that spilled out black ink whenever I was printing my carefully typed out house particulars. But as downhearted as I was, all was not lost. I had to believe in Hope.

I could use a typewriter proficiently, I could do shorthand, and above all – I could write. I would search the job vacancy page in the local newspaper every week, and this I did diligently.

One day, I saw an advertisement in the Thurrock Gazette. It was for the post of a Junior Reporter. Those black printed letters were jumping out at me! This could be it! This could be what would give me some kind of fulfilment! I loved the thought of being a reporter, even though it was just a junior – well at the start that was.

A Junior *REPORTER?* Hey – *that* was for me!

I telephoned straight away. Well, as soon as I was able to get to the privacy of the telephone box over the road from the pub. I couldn't do anything at home without someone knowing about it.

"What are you doing old girl?" my grandmother would call out. She may have been a little bit deaf, but she could always hear the click of the old telephone if ever I lifted the receiver! "Nothing like a nice bit of ear-wigging" she would say, as she listened out to whatever anyone was saying on the phone.

Then there was Nell. She had been standing at the end of the landing listening to me when I was telling Tony that I really didn't want to go out with him anymore. So any calls that I didn't want anyone to know about I had to do over the road in the telephone kiosk.

The Editor sounded really nice on the phone, and he asked me to go along to the Thurrock Gazette offices for an interview. To my amazement and total joy – I was offered the position!

"Junior Reporter" – that sat very nicely in my map of life. A map that was no longer the map of the world – but one that was now leading me on to a career in – journalism!

"You will have to go to Court with me" the Editor informed me, but with more of a question than an actual assumption. "Do you think you can cope with that?"

"Yes – yes, *of course!*" I answered, putting the potential challenges to the back of my mind.

"There will be rather, well, delicate, cases you will have to deal with – like domestic violence – child abuse – things like that. Can you cope with that sort of thing?"

"*Yes...*" I answered slowly, on a rather down turned note. I could deal with it...

"Well then" he said, believing in me. "You will have to take down notes, and then write them up for publication in the Gazette..."

"Yes – YES!" Writing for the Gazette – wow! – what a dream! I was over the moon! It was like standing on the first step of Jacob's Ladder! And what's more the Editor believed in me – he knew I could do it!

~

I was to give the necessary one week's notice to Porters (yippee!) and then I could start. A whole new world was opening up to me. The shorthand notebook and finely sharpened pencil was now taking on so much more of a significance to what it had ever been taking dictation from Mr. Porter.

With my heart full of joy and excitement at what lay ahead for me, I returned home and told my family all about it.

"You don't want to do that" my mother said, as she always did about anything that – yes – I *did* want to do... But I was so excited that I didn't pay much heed to what she was saying. My father didn't say anything. He never had a voice, all the time my mother spoke first.

Mentally, I made my plans to give in my notice the very next day.

~

Later, my grandfather beckoned me to sit down at the kitchen table. This was where any necessary serious "discussions" would take place. Although, in my family, the so-called "discussions" were always one-sided.

"This is no job for a young girl like you" he told me dismissively. "You will be cycling around to all of the pubs in the area asking for stories". But no, I wouldn't – I would be going to Court, reporting on cases and writing them up for the Gazette – the Editor had told me that.

"Tell him you don't want the job" my grandfather commanded, frowning over the top of his round tortoiseshell glasses...

Protesting against his decision was *not* an option.

I would have thought that my family would have been proud of me, writing for the local weekly newspaper, perhaps even seeing my name in print... But no... And no meant NO!

And so, with my heart heavily sinking, and with a great deal of reluctance and disappointment, I *had* to make that call. Somehow, I summoned up the courage to do it. Choking back tears, I picked up the handset of that old black telephone, and dialled the Gazette's number, knowing that I had to convince the Editor that I really had to turn down his offer of the job that I *really* wanted and *really* felt sure I could do.

So there I was, straight back down in the gutter.

As the old song says:

"Oh! Mr. Porter, what shall I do?
I want to go to Birmingham
And they're taking me on to Crewe..."

Well – I wanted to go to... *THE WORLD*...

But here I was at – *well, Porters...*

Trying To Cope At Cope's Taverns

Enough was enough. I really couldn't stand working at Porters any longer. It was hard for me scouring the "Situations Vacant" section of the Thurrock Gazette, knowing that I could have been working on that very paper. But it had to be done.

"I've found you the very job" my mother told me, in a rare burst of excitement. "They want a shorthand-typist at Ockendon police station!"

How did she know about this? My grandfather was well in with the local police, so I expect he found out from them.

"Now – you go and get that job" she instructed, "and with your foot in the door – you can then go on to be a police woman!"

Oh – no... Not all that again about wanting to see me on point duty!

"And then – one day you'll be at Scotland Yard!" she added, looking pleased with herself.

"Now – here's the phone number" she said, ushering me a piece of paper – "go and ring them *now*".

Oh dear, what could I do? I could never go against my mother, especially if my grandfather might be involved. My grandfather had cruelly made me turn down my job offer as a junior reporter at the Thurrock Gazette, but was he agreeing with my mother that I should go into the police force?

I didn't know. I wasn't allowed to question the whys or wherefores of anything. Even if I did, I knew I didn't always get an honest answer.

So I dutifully went along the landing to the telephone and, having nervously answered a few questions, I was given a date for an interview at Ockendon police station the following week.

~

The next day, my prayers were answered. The latest edition of the Thurrock Gazette arrived and standing out from all the mundane jobs that were on offer was one for a shorthand typist/secretary at Cope's Taverns, at the top of Grays High Street. This was a branch of Charrington's Brewery, and as with Porters, it was only one bus ride away. I plucked up courage, and told my mother. Besides, working for a subsidiary of a brewery could only be good!

"Cope's Taverns!" she exclaimed – "that's where Gina Binns used to work when she lived in Grays – she was a comptometer operator you know", she added with some pride.

"Yes!" she said "phone them."

I managed to get an interview straight away, and it was still some days before my interview at the police station. I really wanted this job, it sounded interesting, typing letters and reports about London pubs.

I proudly went off to the interview, wearing a lovely jade green bouclé suit. It had a knee length skirt and a little boxy jacket, the sort of suit I had seen Grace Kelly wearing, and like her, I also wore cream coloured gloves.

The Managing Director at Cope's Taverns was a really nice man, and he seemed to like me straight away. He asked me to take a shorthand test, and read it back to him, and handed me a shorthand notebook and pencil. Suddenly my gloves felt tight, and I remember tugging at them to get them off!

He asked me how much I was earning at Porters, and I told him £6 a week including every other Saturday.

"Well I can offer you more than that!" he said, "how does £7/10' a week sound?"

Well yes, that sounded very good. A whole pound and ten shillings (50p) a week more than I was earning at Porters – and no Saturdays!

He said I could start whenever I wanted to, but – I had to give Porters a week's notice. Oh what joy!

Mr. Porter just grunted when I handed my notice in, but Enid wished me well. All I had to do now was telephone the police station and cancel my interview. Joy upon joy! And at least my mother and grandfather were happy that I was now going to be working for a brewery!

~

I was walking on air my first day at Cope's Taverns. I reported to the Managing Director's office, where he introduced me to the manager for whom I would be working directly. He was really nice too, and he reeled off a list of London pubs that was his domain. He was also involved in dealing with Phonographic Performance Limited, a company formed by EMI and Decca Records, sorting out music licences for the various pubs. This was *so* exciting!

He introduced me to the office manager, Mrs. Price... *OH NO*. She had short grey hair and a face that looked as though she hadn't smiled for years. Yes, it was Mrs. Price, my shorthand teacher at College...

Oh dear. My heart sank a little. Well actually – it sank a lot. How was it that if ever I was happy about something, which wasn't that often really, it would all be wiped away from me – in an instant.

In total silence she took me across the yard to where my office was to be. She was silent all the time...

"This is Miss Mandeville" she said, introducing me to the girl on reception. I recognised her too, as one of the girls in a lower stream at Torells who used to torment me. She was another Maureen.

Maureen looked me up and down a bit. I was no longer that waif-like little girl, sent to school in the wrong clothes, toes cut out of my shoes with a Stanley knife when they got too small, a raincoat that had to fit me for four years, and all the other awful things that my mother made me wear to Torells. Now I was dressed so smartly in a skirt suit and gloves, wearing make-up and my hair just so.

"*Eee-von...*" she said with a little smirk.

Mrs. Price told me that she was the post girl, and that I would have to get all the letters signed, stamped and to her on time every day. That was ok, I would do that. Then she told me that each day when I arrived I would have to sign in – and that Maureen would draw a line on the signing in pad at 9am sharp. Anyone signing in after the line was drawn – would be LATE!

"We expect good work, good behaviour – and PUNCTUALITY" she emphasised, sounding like a headmistress.

She then showed me into what was to be my office, and told me that I would be sharing with one other person. Joy upon more joy! The young woman sitting there was Pearl, who used to live in Orsett. I knew her well as she was one of Valerie's friends. She was a few years older than me, like Valerie, and was married now, but we had often chatted. She was lovely.

I really enjoyed my work. It was interesting finding out the various things that went on in the pubs, and also the work regarding the music industry, dealing with applications for licensing etc. I loved working with Pearl too. With Pearl having lived in Orsett, and with Valerie being a mutual friend, we had a lot in common.

So at seventeen years old I had grown up. I had a job that I loved, and worked with a lovely young woman who I was happy to be with.

And then the rot set in...

~

I was always at work on time. If my bus was late, I would run up the High Street and make sure that my name was not after the line.

One day I got to the office and Maureen looked at me – her tongue sticking out the side of her mouth, and a smirk in her eyes... And just as I was going through the door – she drew the line across the page.

"But it's not nine o'clock yet" I said. But she took no notice. She just pointed at the line with a horrible wicked pout of her lips.

This started happening more and more. She would see me walking across the yard from the High Street – and would draw the line...

"Miss Mandeville" Mrs. Price said to me one morning, with her mouth down turned in an awful condescending look. "It has come to my notice that you are continually being late – and as you know – we do not suffer lateness here..."

I protested as politely as I could, but she was having none of it. "Maureen draws that line every morning at precisely nine o'clock – and your name is continually under that line..."

Maureen was sitting chewing on her chewing gum, her mouth open as she did so. I almost felt that she was about to blow a big bubble out of her mouth at me in satisfaction of what she had done. She carried on chewing, her mouth still open, mocking me.

When the rot sets in, there is no escaping. When a poor frightened animal is injured, unless it is saved, it will surely die. The crows, Maureen and her ilk, will pick it to bits, and then the dung beetles will take over, dragging the victim's remaining flesh underground...

This is what it felt like to me. I was being accused now of always being late. That look on Maureen's face when she saw me approaching – her tongue sticking out of the corner of her mouth, and that never ending smirk whenever she looked at me.

She was up to something – I could tell. But why? Was her job so boring that by trying to get me into trouble she was brightening her day? Maybe her whole life? Yet again, something that I loved was slowly being drawn away from me.

~

Then came the day that the ground opened beneath me, and I completely sank under... It was one of the most awful days of my seventeen years of life...

Mrs. Price came into the office that I shared with Pearl. Her eyes were glaring red at me, and her down turned mouth was shouting at me...

"Come with me" she glowered, beckoning me to follow her up the stairs to a room that I had never been in before, and where there was a bed against a wall. "Now look under there!" she hissed, pointing to the bed.

I did as I was asked and looked under the bed.

"So what's that?" she said pointing to a large plastic bag. Well that's what it was – a large plastic bag. It looked as though it was full up with something, but I didn't know what.

"Well take it out" she hissed again, which I did. "Now look inside..."

I slowly opened the bag not knowing what it might contain. It didn't smell very nice. In fact it smelled absolutely awful.

"Open it!" she commanded...

I peeped inside, trying not to breathe in the stench. It was full up with well-used sanitary towels.

"You are such a disgusting girl!" she growled. "How could you do this?"

"But... I didn't" I told her, horrified at having been accused of doing such a vile thing...

"Oh yes you did!" she shouted – "Maureen told me you did!"

WHAT??

"And what are you going to do about them?" she glared with more of a command than a question.

Well *I was doing nothing.* I didn't put them there.

She stormed off, leaving the bag in the room, expecting me to take them away. But of course I didn't.

Distraught, I went downstairs back to my office, and told Pearl what had just happened.

"I know it wasn't you", she said, "you would never do anything like that... Anyway, it's not me either – I don't use them."

"Nor do I", I said. Of course I didn't – I was still having to use the rags that my mother had deemed suitable for me to use. If I didn't have those rags hanging out on the car park washing line in some erratic periodic way, then I worried that I might be questioned about it.

This hanging out of the flags was a total embarrassment to me. Hanging out the bunting was something I thought was in celebration, something joyous. Something to dance and sing beneath, to show your happiness with others at what was going on...

But no. Difficult to remove by hand, copiously blood-stained pieces of roughly torn sheets were nothing to celebrate. I felt ashamed – so ashamed that I had to hang these relics up on the pub washing line – for all to see...

Why, oh why, had I never been allowed to use those discreetly hidden "things" that we sold in the shop? Those "things" hidden in plain dark blue bags, which disguised their contents, and were always kept on the top shelf.

~

Pearl looked at me with a knowing look – "it's her..." she whispered discreetly, turning towards the reception desk.

Maureen sat there, with that evil look in her eyes, and that horrible nasty smirk – that said it all.

~

I gave in my notice straight away. My boss said he was very sorry to lose me, but he didn't question me why. If I hadn't been accused of something so disgusting and personal I would have mentioned to him how unhappy I was, but I just had to leave it at that, and to try somehow to get through my notice.

Maureen had a permanent smirk on her face all the time, and Mrs. Price didn't even speak to me. I felt mentally exhausted and weepy all the time. Pearl did her best to console me and tell me what a terrible thing Maureen had done, but I couldn't bear having such a terrible accusation against me.

I really couldn't cope, and went back to see the doctor. This time he put me on Librium, and I showed my mother what I was taking. The green and black capsules were larger than anything I had had before. I thought she might have been alarmed by the size of the capsules. Something to draw her attention to what I was going through. I was trying to get her sympathy and for her to ask me what was troubling me. But she never did.

I told Tony the next time I saw him that I was leaving Cope's Taverns because, along with the post girl, Mrs. Price had accused me of something terrible.

"I know" he said, "Mum knows her – and she's been slagging you off. Don't worry, she doesn't believe a word of it".

"Come and work with me in London" Tony suggested. "We can go up on the train together. They're a good crowd I travel with – you'll have fun with them."

That sounded good. I loved London, and knew it well. I had regularly gone shopping with my mother and grandmother in Oxford Street and Kensington, and was looking forward to late night shopping there on a Thursday evening. Yes, this would be fun – as long as I found a job!

~

"Why are you leaving that nice little job?" my mother asked me scornfully when I told her I was going to London to find a job. "You don't want to work in London!" she exclaimed. It was always "you don't want – you don't want". How many times had she said *that* to me?

"It's *him* isn't it" she said, "turning your head to different things, taking you to these *foreign* restaurants, making you eat all that muck".

Well until I went out with Tony I had never eaten Italian, Chinese or Indian food, but I found I developed a liking for it. I had never had garlic before either until I had a meal at Ken and Eva's house, and the only spaghetti I knew about came out of a tin in an orange coloured sauce. I had been very worried about trying my first Chinese and Indian meals, because once again the only rice I knew was round rice that was baked in the oven in milk with sugar and nutmeg on the top. All this so called "muck" I was having was far more enjoyable than pig's trotter stew!

I couldn't tell my mother what I had been accused of. I wouldn't have actually been able to get the words out to her. I told her that I loved my job, and that I liked working with Pearl, but that Mrs. Price and the post girl were making my life a misery.

"They're just jealous of you" she said, which was something she said a lot. "It's because you live *here...*"

But why? Why would anyone be jealous of me living at the Kings Arms?

"See – I've told you all along – you can never trust a woman" she said, twitching her nose.

Well I knew different to that. There were lots of nice women who I knew, but I couldn't help but wonder though – what was it about the Kings Arms that had an effect on some people's opinions?

Going To London

The first time I went to London to find work it was great. Tony's pals were fun, like he had said. They made me feel comfortable with them straight away. I loved travelling by train, and being part of the normal morning rush. With Tony and his pals joking around, it made early morning feel much more tolerable!

That first day I went to Fenchurch Street, Tony and his travelling pals left me while I went to find a job agency. It was the usual thing, a typing test and looking at my certificates. Then the woman told me that there was a vacancy for a shorthand-typist just around the back of Fenchurch Street station. So I went for the interview wearing my nice suit, and of course, my cream gloves, and was interviewed by the Managing Director.

The job seemed a bit boring being a shipping company, and would involve taking dictation for letters, and typing up Bills of Lading and Manifests for goods being shipped all over the world. Tony had already versed me in what sort of salary to expect.

"Ask for £13 a week he said, because whatever you ask for – they will lower it.

"I am looking at £13 a week" I said shyly when the MD asked me what sort of salary I was looking for.

"Mmm..." he went, clicking his tongue. "That's rather a lot to start with... How does £11 sound?"

Yes! That would be great! The fares were going to cost a lot, and I would still be giving my mother £2 a week out of that, but that sounded very good to me.

I was able to start as soon as I wanted to, and my direct boss was again very nice. He was a really kind man, and would praise me for my accurate work. He also told me that my style of presentation was "inimitable". I liked that, and felt that even though it was only typing, my artistic side was being recognised.

The girls were nice too. I wasn't in the typing pool, but in a smaller office with a few girls who were comptometer operators and shorthand-typists for other bosses. I couldn't help but feel I had the best of the bosses though. The girls in my office were all Londoners – they were great. Everything seemed very relaxed and on my very first day they took me to a coffee shop nearby for our morning coffee break. That was the usual thing to do there, and it gave us a little time to chat and get to know each other. I was surprised to see that when they had finished their work, they would sit and knit until they were given some more! That would never have happened in Grays!

I remember one of the girls who was from Penge telling me one day how she had got on the train and there was a French couple on there.

"Oh... *Parnge!*" one of them had exclaimed when they saw the sign. She said that Penge had never sounded so posh!

~

I was thrilled to bits with my first week's wages, which were given to me in a little square brown envelope in cash. I went late night shopping the next Thursday evening in Oxford Street, and found the most wonderful coat I had ever seen. I had loved "Doctor Zhivago", in fact at the time it was the best film I had ever seen. Julie Christie was gorgeous, as was Omar Sharif. I loved the whole staging of it, and especially the clothes...

I was in D.H. Evans, walking around the clothing department, and a certain coat stood out – it was Russian style. I was drawn to it immediately, and just had to try it on. The colour was a rich shade of plum, with black fur collar and cuffs, and black "frog" fastenings going down the front. It was quite long, the waist was nipped in and, and the skirt flared out. With my high black boots, wow... I felt wonderful! I could just about afford it with my new wage packet as well! I just had to have it. Then I found a matching plum felt hat. I may have been just a little bit young for a hat like that – but it made me feel good!

By the time I got home that evening it was too late to show everyone what I had bought. The next day though I proudly put on my coat and went into the kitchen to show everyone.

"What are you doing!" my mother scorned, "buying a coat without me!"

Oh dear. I wanted everyone to tell me how lovely it was, but no-one said anything. At seventeen years old and working, did my mother really think that I should wait until she was with me before buying myself a coat?

And so it went on. I couldn't do anything right, as far as my mother was concerned. I proudly went to work though wearing my Russian style coat, my hat, and my long black boots. I also bought another suit. It was a pink tweedy type, again with a knee-length skirt and a jacket a little like the Chanel style. I had found it at the right price though! So I felt really smart wearing this to work, and my other suit, straight skirts and twin sets.

However, October 1966 and I was back on Librium again, and still being plied with alcohol. Living at the pub was still as tough as always. I didn't have to work as hard as I had done when I was at school, because I was now getting home much later. But it was all still there... Staying up late at night, clearing the tables, washing up glasses in one bowl and rinsing them in the other. Drying with tea-towels that really needed to be boiled, and helping Nell with the usual supper of cheese on toast.

I was also still sleeping with my grandmother, which the older I got, and the older she got, the more unpleasant I found it to be. She was still waking me up all night, even though I had to be up so early the next morning to get to work in London. As I have said before, I also hated the way she would sometimes squeeze my bottom and say "a nice bit of soft". I don't suppose she meant anything by it, but one day I heard her saying to my mother "I had a nice bit of soft last night". Well she hadn't, not in the way she was implying. I don't think she ever did anything more than squeezing my bottom, but my mother's giggles upon hearing that made me feel that the intention might have been more.

I had hardly anywhere to put my things, and was always afraid that something I loved would be taken away from me and given to some other girl who I would then see wearing it along the street.

This was October though, and my new Russian coat stayed with me. I wore it every time I left the pub. It was safe on my back. And I was safe in the arms of Librium, which somehow got me through the evenings and night time.

~

I enjoyed working in London. Nell would wake me up in the mornings with a cup of tea, at goodness knows what time, and I would get ready for work. She was always up at six, washing the bar floors and cleaning the toilets.

Nanny would be oblivious to all this. She would still be in bed snoring away and farting.

~

Hmm – farting... The passing of gas from the digestive system out of the bowel through the anus... Not that I have ever used the word before now, but in this instance it describes the situation perfectly. I have always found the smell very difficult to deal with, as well as the thought of breathing in of someone else's obnoxious gasses. Which reminds me of custard creams...

They were always one of my favourite biscuits... The smooth taste of the custard "cream", sandwiched between the two layers of crumbly biscuits – simply heavenly! But custard creams, as tempting as they may have been all my life, have been tainted with a long distant memory...

Tastes and smells merge together, and can stay in our memories forever. Usually they are good memories, our olfactory senses taking us back to those times – but whenever I see a packet of custard creams, as much as I used to enjoy them, I am immediately taken back to a certain time sitting at the kitchen table at the pub, with a cup of tea – and a custard cream...

I opened my mouth to take a bite, and at that instant, with my mouth open, my grandmother, who was sitting next to me, let out a very long and heavy waft of intestinal gasses... i.e. a most horrible *fart*...

♪♪ *"doh re mi fa so la ti doh...*
what makes me fart I do not know... ♪♪

she would sing...

"The soft ones are always the best..." she used to say at times like this.

But this one was certainly not *soft*... *This* one hung heavy in the air – and in my taste buds. I have never been able to eat a custard cream since without being transported back to that day.

Hence – they will never be seen in my shopping basket!

~

So, whether being kept awake at night through my grandmother's chatting, singing, snoring – or farting, I would still have to be up early in the mornings to be ready to go to work.

As usual, I would stand in the lounge at the window, which looked out over High Road as far as the bend at Hill House Farm – well Reynolds Farm as we knew it. Then, when the bus came into view, just around the bend, I knew I had enough time to run down the stairs (as long as there was no food on there from my grandfather's rages...), out of the pub, over the road, and just in time for the bus to reach the bus stop.

8.30am, and the bus would arrive at Congress House in Grays, i.e. The Co-op, or "Carp" as my father called it! I really did think it was called The Carp when it was first built! My father had this funny way of pronouncing words sometimes. Integral garages were just making an appearance in new-build houses, which were often being built on the old sites of some of the pre-fabs that had been quickly erected just after the war. Well my father called them *"interegal"* garages, and I still call them that to this day – in a little nod to him! Likewise, he liked to have a *"nice bit of concrate"* in the garden somewhere – he thought every garden should have some *concrate...* I really don't know where he got these strange pronunciations from!

~

So there I would be, having got off the bus at the "Carp", it would then be a quick jaunt up Grays High Street, to catch the 8.45 train to London, and hoping that the level crossing hadn't closed. Usually though – it had.

So then it was a run up the steps and across the bridge in the dense mist of the steam coming from the train. Then down the other side – showing my season ticket to the ticket collector, then another quick dash onto the train. No time to check where Tony and his friends were – I just had to hop on board just before the whistle was blown.

Sometimes, especially during the winter months, the train would be late. It would be freezing cold on the platform. I would be stamping up and down on the spot, like a Royal Guard in my black leather boots, trying to get some warmth to my feet.

Having arrived at Fenchurch Street station, travelling past the back yards of rows and rows of old back-to-back terraced houses, which must have all rattled at the close proximity of the railway line, it was then a quick sprint round to the other side of the station – and then to my office. Luckily the start time was 9.15 – so I usually made it... Phew!

~

I didn't see Tony at lunchtimes, even though we would usually travel together. Sometimes I would go late night shopping in Oxford Street on a Thursday evening on my own, and travel home basically on an empty train. I remember waiting at Oxford Circus waiting for a tube to go to Fenchurch Street where I would catch the train back to Grays. One night I was totally on my own. It felt rather eerie down there, and goodness knows what danger I could have been in. No-one at home was bothered though.

One day the Managing Director's secretary was due to go on holiday for two weeks. She was pregnant and would be leaving in a few months' time. I was delighted when the Managing Director asked me to stand in for her while she was on holiday! I enjoyed those two weeks working for him, and he mentioned that he was looking for someone to take his secretary's place when she left to have her baby. He said this in such a way that I thought he was thinking that it might be me. I was only seventeen, but he seemed very happy with my work. And what a job that would have been for me!

And so I was working happily in London and travelling there on the train with people I had got to know. Tony's family were giving me the affection I so badly longed for at home, and I really needed their comfort when my life at the pub was so upsetting. Of course, I couldn't confide in Tony any more about what was going on, but he seemed to have an idea, remarking one day that the song "House of the Rising Sun" reminded him of the Kings Arms – especially the bit about ruining a poor girl...

Yes, my unusual and unconventional childhood living at the pub did ruin me. As Flora recently told me, when I went to that awful "party" which wasn't when I was eleven years old, I was probably being groomed for child prostitution. Although I was very shy, and didn't really know what was going on, I had the strength and presence of mind to say "stop it! I'm only eleven!" If only I had had that strength of mind on that fateful occasion when I was seventeen...

~

He said it was safe.

I said it wasn't.

He insisted it was.

But it wasn't...

PART 3

CONSEQUENCES

Options

To have options is normally a good thing, to be able to think about what you *want* to do most of all. I never did have any real options – I always did as I was told – and was *always told what to do...*

"To be or not to be", as Shakespeare once wrote – "that is the question."

Unlike Hamlet though I wasn't pondering on whether to live or commit suicide, although I do remember a time when I told my mother that I wished I had never been born... I must have been in a terrible state to say that, and I was just a child at the time. She scolded me by telling me what a wicked – wicked – girl I was saying that, and I know I was wrong. But I felt so bereft and unhappy at the time that I really did think like Hamlet.

To say I used to cry a lot is an understatement. I would sob my heart out sometimes.

I don't know whether anyone knew or not. Probably not, but I did not have any privacy – anywhere. I didn't have my own bedroom, and my grandmother's bedroom wasn't exactly *private...* My brothers had carte blanche to treat me however they liked, to do whatever amused them – and especially at my expense.

Trying to get dressed or undressed in that bedroom was always a problem. I was always in fear of my brothers bursting into the room and ridiculing me in whatever state of undress I was in at the time. It didn't matter even if I shouted at them to go away – they knew they could do whatever they liked...

Sobbing my heart out was something that I could not control. The feeling came from deep down in my stomach as well as my head. That feeling of nausea that can hit your brain and your senses, when there is nothing else that you can do.

I remember physically collapsing on the landing, whether it was once or more times I don't know. But I was standing there holding on to the bannisters looking down at the stairs that led down to the bars, and I just slowly slid down onto the floor, sobbing and sobbing.

No-one ever heard. Or maybe – no-one ever *cared*... Was there anyone putting their arms around me, consoling me, and making me feel loved? No. I cried alone.

But *why??* Why didn't anyone ever try to help me? *Why* didn't anyone care about how I was being treated? *Why* didn't my father ever step in and try to put a stop to it? Were his feelings for me really as cold as his ice blue eyes? I don't think so, because I did love him, and I respected him not only for being my father, but also for all that he had done in the war fighting the Japanese, way out there in that other universe...

~

"Look at your face" my mother scolded sometime. "You can't go down into the bar with red eyes and those bags..."

Bags? What bags? Those soft sacks under my eyes where unspilt tears would gather?

But that didn't mean that I was let off of that duty. Standing there behind the bar pulling pints and dealing with money was so very difficult when I felt like that.

I longed so much for the privacy of having my own bedroom, with posters of my favourite stars pinned on the wall. And most of all, somewhere that I could grieve for whatever my awful situation was at the time.

But I couldn't have it – and sleeping with my grandmother was so difficult, especially when I was trying to keep my distress so quiet that I was almost choking holding back my tears.

Well what would my grandmother have done about it? Would she have cuddled me and tried to make me feel better? She was normally too drunk to even notice, and as always I have done a pretty good job of covering up my sadness. Moreover, I didn't want her cuddling me in bed. I didn't like the times that she would squeeze my bottom and say in a drunken breath – "a nice bit of soft".

No, I didn't want any touching and squeezing, especially during a period when I had old fraying rags fastened with nappy pins inadequately covering my dignity.

~

So what were my options to be – what was *I to be?* Well, I was not to be a policewoman – that was for sure. I couldn't imagine arresting someone, or going into a home where there was a murder or child abuse. I have never been able to bear seeing a child crying in anguish, and would have found it very difficult to cope with. Besides, I was certainly not strong enough to be a policewoman. I couldn't go chasing after someone – and arrest them! To my mother it was the be all and end all of what she wanted me to be. But, uh-uh, no way... Not for me, anyway.

The other option that I was being forced to go along with, was to be a shorthand-typist/secretary – having a "trade". Failing that, then I would just have to be a barmaid, and pull pints for the rest of my working life. Well, according to my mother that is.

Why didn't my father ever take a hand in it? Why didn't he ever speak to me about what I *really* wanted to do? Wouldn't he have been so proud of me if I was an air hostess? Failing that, would he have appreciated me being a fashion designer, a dressmaker, or even a hairdresser. Anything creative would have been wonderful for me if I hadn't made it through the selection board to "fly the flag".

They were the good options that unfortunately I never had. And now I had the bad options... Which really boiled down to – *no option at all...*

~

I was now beginning to feel more and more unwell. It was dreadful travelling to London every day on the train, then doing a day's work, and travelling back again.

It was also quite a task trying to keep this sickness away from everyone else. But as Nell always got me up in the mornings, she knew that I was finding it hard to drink my tea, that I would dash to the bathroom, and she would hear me retching over that awful brown stained toilet, that no amount of Vim powder would actually totally clean.

I was feeling very, very ill. I was also quite unsteady on my feet at times, and remember stumbling as I was about to cross a busy road in London. I didn't actually fall into the gutter – but that is where I felt I was.

~

"Could you be pregnant?" was the first thing my doctor asked when I plucked up courage to go and see him.

"I don't think so", I said honestly. How could I be *pregnant?* How could I possibly be pregnant when Tony had told me it was safe? Somehow, the strangest thing is, that I remember that time so clearly – I know when and where it occurred, and that I was saying that it wasn't safe.

I had been right.

I went back to see the doctor again when I was feeling physically more ill than I had ever done in my life. I had had all the childhood illnesses, which had me laid up on the lounge settee when my previous doctor, Dr. Headon, came to call. He had probably wondered why I wasn't in bed, but I suppose that was because no-one wanted anyone to know where I slept. I had even been sent to school as a young teenager with what I have now found out was German Measles. I look dreadful in the school photo that was taken at the time. But as my grandfather had said I wasn't ill enough to be off school – so he wouldn't write me an excuse of absence note – then I had to go. I still have that photo, and in it I look so very unwell. But no, I was well enough to go to school – and nobody questioned my grandfather about that.

So here I was – just four years later. Had I really grown up so much in so few years?

What was all this retching sickness about now?

The doctor didn't take "I don't think so" kindly when I answered him again as to whether I could be pregnant...

"I need to examine you" he explained, "but as you are under 18 – I will have to have your mother with you..."

"My mother with me"???

"Well, in that case you will have to do a urine sample" he said, handing me a small clear jar. "Take it to the hospital and go from there..."

This was something totally new to me – and awkward... I had never had to stand astride a small jar over the toilet before! I felt so embarrassed handing it in at reception. Not as embarrassed as some other people though, who had handed in jars of faeces. Oh, what on earth would have led them to having to do *that?*

I was so naïve at the time.

~

I waited the specified length of time, then went to the telephone box over the road to call the hospital to ask about the result. It was the only place I had some privacy to make a call, even though there might be someone outside waiting.

Not many people had telephones then, well not where we lived. And mobiles hadn't even been thought of! If you wanted to speak to someone – you would go and knock on their door! So I needed to make this call before anyone else turned up waiting outside the telephone box – also timing it for when my grandmother wasn't looking out of the window...

"My name is Yvonne Mandeville" I said, trying to sound confident, "do you have the result of my water sample?"

"Your *what*??" the woman asked.

It was so hard saying the word "urine" – I had never said that word before. I was sinking to the floor as I waited on the end of the line with my handful of coins for Button "A".

The woman came back to the phone. "It's positive" she said in a very matter-of-fact voice. It meant nothing to her. Taking these sort of calls was all in a day's work. But to me, it was my *life*, and I stood there holding the phone just staring ahead, until Button "A" ran out.

~

"The – er – water test has come back positive" I told Tony when I phoned him after standing there for a while, contemplating what my life was turning into. I may have pushed button 'A', but the 'A's in my life were rapidly falling through the earth, into a deep dark dankness that had no end. What good would my little collection of qualification certificates do me now? Where was God? Where was Jesus? Where were the angels?

No – better not mention any of those entities, I had had to put them to the back of my mind and never speak about them – Tony was an atheist... With a *capital 'A'*...

I didn't know what I expected him to say. 'I'm sorry' would have been a good start. I can't remember what he actually said, but it was very short and to the point. I felt that, although having gone along with our relationship and what he wanted to do to that point, I *had* said "no" at that particular time and that it *wasn't safe...*

~

Why had I yet again got into the back of that car? It wasn't the only time that this had happened – stopping in some pull-in off the A13. There would be other cars parked in that curved bit of road that had once been part of the main road to Southend before the "new" A13 had been built. Those cars contained what were at the time called "courting couples". But *I* wasn't going courting – *was I?*

"Going courting" was something out of 1950's musicals, something that I aspired to, romantic and sweet. Stopping off like that in a cold, soulless pull-in was not romantic nor at all sweet. This was stopping for what he called a "proper kiss" before we went home... A "proper kiss" – what was that anyway?

Actually, a "proper kiss" meant that I was going to have some affection – which is something I never had at home. To my mind though, I felt that a kiss and a cuddle giving me that affection should have been enough.

"NO!" I said firmly, knowing that I really must *not do this... I knew it wasn't safe.*

Not only had I scoured magazines and books, trying to find out the truth about physical relationships, and conception, but I knew deep in my heart, my very soul, that it – *was not safe...*

But what could I do – apart from saying "NO"? I had been brought up at the pub to believe that I was just a nobody in this world. I clung on to affection, in its many guises, and this was what I needed so badly. It didn't occur to me that being on the back seat of a car – meant that apart from a few somewhat reluctant kisses, I may be consenting to *anything...*

"No" I had said... "No..."

~

Tony wasn't at the station as he usually was the next time I went to work. I looked and I waited, but I had to board the train when it arrived – without him. I had heard nothing from him, no phone calls – nothing.

The same thing happened the next few days. I didn't want to telephone his parents, because I didn't want them to know what was going on. Surely he was still going home at night though...

We had never met up for lunch, because we were working in different areas of London, but I had found a little café where I would go and have a really good "sausage, egg, chips and peas". I would eat there on my own. Sometimes, if there was a birthday or anything else to celebrate I would go with the other girls to "The Tower", a pub near Tower Bridge that did a lovely cottage pie. Normally though, I would go to lunch on my own. I loved browsing around Petticoat Lane market having been to that little café. How is it that an hour can last so long when you are young? One of the mysteries of the ageing process I guess.

Now though, I didn't feel strong enough to walk along to Petticoat Lane any more, and it was very hard to eat anything... Certainly not anything in a café that did anything you wanted – as long as it was fried... Uggghhh...

One day I found a place called "Toc H" down the bottom of some steps. There were strange looking people in there, but I just joined the queue. Their meals were very cheap, and they did things like some kind of meat with potatoes and cabbage, which I found I could eat better than anything fried. Even if I only ate the cabbage it was something. What I didn't know then though was that it was some kind of Christian benevolent place for "down and outs", or whatever people of ill means were called then.

So there I would be, dressed up in my London office clothes, and going down into Toc H to get my dinner!

~

Trying to keep my terrible morning sickness from Nell and my grandmother was a nightmare. My grandmother was usually still asleep when I got up really early for work, but Nell was already up, cleaning the bars, and coming to wake me. Strangely, I didn't even know at the time that this sickness was due to my pregnancy. I had never known my mother to have morning sickness, but then again I had rarely seen her in the mornings.

I made my excuses in the evenings about not having my dinner that had been kept in the airing cupboard all day. I said I was eating at lunchtime at work now. Meanwhile, I was getting weaker and weaker.

~

It was winter, and one lunchtime I was trudging along one of the streets in the City, with men in bowler hats, three-piece suits, and rolled umbrellas walking past in their usual confident gait. They were so much like Adam's father.

I wondered what Adam was doing now? Would he have followed his father into Insurance, and joined one of these many men wearing their City uniforms? No, of course not – he would be doing something in art and design, and his clothes would depict his artistic personality... Or maybe not.

I was dressed in my plum Russian style coat, with my matching plum coloured hat, my black leather boots, and the black leather gloves that my grandmother had bought me.

My life could have been so different. What if I had been an air hostess and met a dishy pilot? What if I could have gone into the world of art and design? Well, my mother had deemed it to be a secretary's life for me, as I wouldn't go into the police force. But there was this opening though – the vague possibility that I could be the Managing Director's secretary. That would have been a very good alternative...

So what now? What options *were there?*

The men were striding past me in a sea of black; black bowlers, black suits, black umbrellas which they used like walking sticks. I really was slap bang in the centre of the City.

I saw someone walking along the pavement in my direction... It was that same familiar gait – yes – it was Tony...

As soon as he spotted me, he quickly turned – and walked back in the other direction. There was nothing for it – despite how ill I was feeling, I found myself hurrying towards him. He looked back at me with his usual disapproving frown from behind his black rimmed glasses, and carried on walking quickly away. I carried on hurrying too...

"We have to talk" I said, plaintively, when I somehow managed to catch him up. I really can't remember what was said next, it is all a total blur... All I remember is that I quietly and politely reminded him I was *going to have a baby...*

"*Hmmm...*" he frowned, looking down at me, stroking his chin with his thumb and forefinger. That was something he did a lot whenever he wanted me to feel that I had displeased him.

Displeased him? But hadn't I always tried to *please* – no matter what?

I didn't remind him that I had said it *wasn't safe...* To have done so might have caused quite a showdown on the very public streets of the City...

But that evening we travelled home together on the train.

~

"Have you had intercourse with short arse?" my mother asked me the following Saturday when I was so ill I was staying in bed. My grandmother had got up, and so I was alone with my thoughts and my worries – when she had suddenly burst into the bedroom..

"Er no..." I lied.

"Good!" my mother said, and promptly walked out the door.

She had never mentioned that word to me before, but she said it in such a forceful way that she seemed to know that I knew what it meant.

What would have happened if I had said "yes"? It doesn't bear thinking about. I was lying in my grandmother's bed, sick and vulnerable. Why had she asked me anyway?

Maybe Nell had told her about my morning sickness? Maybe everyone could see how ill I was and not thinking it could possibly be anything else. Did anyone care about what it was if it wasn't pregnancy? I doubt it.

I saw the doctor again, and he put me on anti-sickness pills. He didn't offer me any advice at all about what to do as a pregnant seventeen year old. He knew my family, and I suppose he didn't want to get involved.

~

I told Tony that our parents really needed to be told – and he agreed with me.

He came with me when we told mine. Again, the words that were spoken are a total blur.

Life at the pub from then onwards is something I wish I could put into the darkest depths of my memories... Suffice to say – it was very, *very difficult...*

~

Tony also told his parents, although I don't know what their initial reaction was. I knew they liked me, and somehow they didn't blame us for what had happened. The same thing had happened to them...

~

No-one was talking to me at the pub – apart from my mother when it was to put me in disgrace...

"Hussy..." she would hiss under her breath sometimes when she walked past me...

"I wish I had seen you!" my mother said with the most evil look on her face... "I would have thrown a bucket of water over you..."

Ok, I knew I had done such a terrible thing, but what did I *really* know about what was the right thing to do – and the wrong thing? I had been sent off to that awful party-which-wasn't when I was just eleven years old. It seemed that even though I didn't know about such things at the time, everyone had expected me to go to bed with the two men...

Here I was now – *pregnant* – and all I really wanted was the affection that I had never had from my family. To have an arm around me meant the world to me...

~

"You should have told me" my mother said another day, still with that total look of utter disgust on her face. "I would have – washed you out – *washed you out...*" she emphasised *"DO YOU HEAR ME?"* her voice verging on a scream. Then her voice went quiet and sinister, as she looked at me with piercing dark eyes... "I would have washed you out..."

The thought of my mother spreading my legs and getting a douche or whatever it was that people might have been "washed out" with at the time, is something I hate even to think about. Would she really have done that? Is that what would have happened if I had gone along with all their weird fantasies at the pub, and had succumbed to some man I didn't even know – or even two? Is that what really went on?

~

My grandfather summoned me to the kitchen, so I knew there was something very serious that he had to say.

He had arranged for an abortion for me, which would have been "back street", as this procedure was referred to then. This seemed to be the general wish of everyone at the pub. Abortions at that time were still illegal, although the Abortion Act was passed later that year – and came into effect in April 1968.

Tony had no comment on the matter. As I have said before, he was an atheist anyway which, with my Church of England education, I couldn't really understand. Apart from my feelings and beliefs though, he had his own life to think about. I don't think it even occurred to him that I might keep the baby.

If this had been just a year later, and carried out without delay by a competent doctor in a hospital or clinic, then I *might* have considered it. I say *might* because I would have had to challenge my faith, my feelings about the morality of it, and also my love of babies...

But this was early 1967 – and it was going to be "back street". A year earlier, in the spring of 1966, I had seen the film "Alfie", starring Michael Caine. This included an illegal abortion – it was sordid, seedy, done without any anaesthesia, and carried out, rather later than advisable, by a dirty, male abortionist. When the normally immoral Alfie looked at the aborted foetus, lying in the sink, with its perfectly formed little body, he cried – and then he sobbed... *What had they done?*

Despite the awful pressure from my family, I couldn't go ahead with this. I couldn't contemplate having that little baby that was growing inside me being so brutally taken away from me.

~

I have recently been told that my grandfather was himself an abortionist during the war, for local women – so could he have been planning to do the abortion *himself*? I will never know – because I would have none of it.

So does that then explain the bottles marked "poison" in the loft, and the bag of women's clothing with the totally blood-stained knickers?

~

"What are the customers going to think!" my mother scolded day after day. Is that all she could think about – *what would the customers think?* "You are a total disgrace!"

But what about what the customers *knew* anyway? What about the "customers" who used to watch me get undressed – why wasn't the whole caboodle of what was going on at the pub a total disgrace?

What about Elaine who lived up the road? She was younger than I was when she became pregnant, and my mother felt so sorry for her she gave her all of my baby clothes. She went away, and I didn't ever see her with a baby – but I didn't have any of my baby clothes given back. So why wasn't *she* a disgrace? Well *she* didn't live in the pub.

~

"As you insist on going ahead with this... er... pregnancy", my father informed me in a fairly embarrassed way, "then yes, I will go along with you... But..."

He then told me that he would make the loft in the bungalow into a "room" for me, and I could live up there throughout my pregnancy.

"No-one will ever know" he said. "And then, when you give birth – well, we'll think about what will happen then..."

It seemed that everyone was going along with this idea, as cruel as it was. What *would* happen to my little baby after I had given birth – which would of course have been entirely on my own. It really doesn't bear thinking about. I had no idea what they had planned for me after the birth.

~

"Well we have suggested all we can for you", my mother said when I declined both options. "So there's nothing for it my girl – you are going to have to go to the unmarried mothers' home..."

This was a home in Essex run by nuns, and I feared those nuns so much. I have mentioned here many chapters ago how when walking along Grays High Street, if a couple of nuns were coming towards us along the pavement – we would always cross over to the other side of the street. I had heard so many accounts of what had gone on at the home. I had always been threatened with going to a home anyway if I had ever "told" anyone about what was going on at the pub. And now, this was a very real likelihood.

"My God" my mother said, when she told me that that was what was going to happen to me. "You will be made to work my girl – scrubbing floors on your hands and knees – and goodness knows what else you will be put through. Those nuns are vicious – *vicious – hear me?*"

Well I could put up with hard work. But "home for unmarried mothers?" No, it was more like "home for pregnant girls..."

"Then – you can have the baby adopted", she said, abruptly walking away, with a nod of her head that meant she had made up her mind...

~

There was no way I was going to have my baby adopted. Throughout my young life everything I treasured had been taken away from me, or destroyed. No-one – absolutely *no-one* – was going to take my baby from me...

The Solution?

I didn't tell any of my friends about my shameful secret. Well, circumstances, and the way that life tends to twist and turn without any warning sometimes, had distanced us all from each other.

Georgie, Michael, Valerie, Emma, Alison – our paths just didn't seem to cross any more. Fate had led us in many different directions, even though none of us had ever gone away.

Long gone were the climbing of apple trees and adventures roaming the fields with Georgie; playing tennis with handsome Michael; walking the lanes and going on all sorts of journeys with Valerie; sharing the sweetest of times with Emma and her family, talking about Jesus, and what his presence meant in our young lives; and then my years spent with Alison, going through puberty together, noticing boys, and going all a-flutter over Elvis.

They were now all growing up with new friends, and Valerie was married, which I had only found out long after the event – something that had upset me greatly at the time. But it was quite usual for me not to be told about these kind of things – until well after they had happened, and sometimes not even then...

~

Tony had taken over my life in the most forceful of ways. His possessiveness and control suffocated me. But his family were showing me the love and affection that I had so longed for all my life

If only I could have confided about my situation with my close female friends. But I couldn't. I couldn't tell anyone *anything*... That was how I had been brought up. Such shame upon my family had to be kept secret – no matter what they had been getting up to throughout their lives.

I was "in trouble", "in the family way" – such derogatory phrases thrown at me hurt me tremendously. I was a total disgrace – and as always, utterly worthless...

I remembered the postcard in Nell's handbag that she used to show me sometimes years ago – the one of the young woman being banished out into the snow...

"GO!" her father had demanded, as she trudged through the snow that led nowhere, holding her baby wrapped in a blanket...

~

I know it must have been so hard for my parents having a pregnant daughter, especially for my father. It hadn't been that long since I had found out how babies were conceived – literally just days before I even met Tony. We had been going out for eighteen months, and in that time I had found out a lot...

"I am keeping the baby" I choked amidst many heart-felt tears to my parents. "But don't worry – I know I can't stay here – but I will find *somewhere* to go..."

"Well you have a few months grace" my father said, not showing any feelings whatsoever. His plan was still that I would stay in the loft of the bungalow. He had said that he would make it into a room for me, but there was no window up there, and I would have to get up and down a basic ladder whenever I needed to go to the bathroom. How on earth would I cope with the ladder, especially later on when I was in late pregnancy? How on earth would I be able to cope being shut away like that?

I have always been terribly claustrophobic, and the thought of having to live like that appalled me. Well having ensconced me in the loft, they would then think about what to do about my baby when it was born – also in the loft. Yes, I wonder what they *would* have done with baby – having kept my pregnancy secret...

My mother's words "*what will the customers think?*" kept going through my mind. What did the customers think of this den of iniquity I was living in anyway?

~

I had it in my mind that I would contact Mrs. Binns, who was now Mrs. Matthews, and ask her and Jack if I could stay with them for a while. They were now living in rural Norfolk, so a long, long way away from Orsett. They would understand – wouldn't they? I didn't know, but they were the only people I knew who I could turn to.

Well, Mrs. Binns was hardly of a high moral standard, especially with the way she was behaving on the bed with those two horrible men that night, when I was eleven. She was totally immoral, and had nearly got me raped at such a young age, so I hardly felt that she would take the moral high ground with me.

I couldn't ask Gina, because she was now remarried, and there was no way I wanted to intrude upon her new life. But Betty Binns though? Yes, I felt pretty sure she and Jack would understand...

If they agreed, I would have to somehow make my way to Norfolk. I worked out the possible route. I would take the bus to Grays, then the train from Grays to London, where hopefully I might find a north-bound train to Norwich, or wherever it may lead... I had so few things to my name to take with me, with so many possessions having being taken away from me all my young life.

That might just be the solution – could it? I knew I would be able to explain everything to Mrs. Binns – er, Matthews – and I felt sure that they would let me stay with them – if only for a little while. If I gave birth whilst living in Norfolk, then I would work out some way of working and living there – and my little baby would grow up in that lovely unspoilt area of Britain. Would this work out? I didn't know. All I knew was that I was cosseting this new life that was growing inside me, and I would do my best to give that little one the best life that I could.

~

Before calling Mrs. Binns though, I had to phone Tony.

"I am keeping the baby" I told him rather diffidently, in much the same distressed state of mind as I told my parents. "I am *not* letting anyone take my baby away from me". I went on to tell him that not to worry – I knew someone who I thought I might be able to stay with for a short time – and I would go from there...

I could be thought presumptuous, thinking that Betty and Jack might take me in for a while. But I knew them both very well, and I felt that they really would have taken pity on my plight.

I didn't tell Tony what my plans were. I didn't even know what his thoughts were at the time. I was pregnant – he was the father – but what to do next? It seemed that the problem was *all mine...*

~

"Mum and Dad said they want you to come round and see them..." Tony told me when we next spoke.

Yes, I would do that, I agreed nervously, as embarrassing as it may turn out to be.

~

Eva and Ken were as nice as they always were.

I sat on their Ercol settee next to Tony, looking ahead at Eva's self-portrait above the blocked up fireplace taking centre stage in the room. This was the very place where I had had many happy times with them, watching the Sunday afternoon films, playing cards, and generally just feeling the warmth of a real family.

"Tony's told us that you are keeping the baby" Ken said, with a smile. "We are really pleased about that – but where are you going to live?"

"I'll find somewhere" I said, hoping that I really would... "I am going away..."

"Yes, Tony said", Ken replied, "but where are you thinking of going?"

"I don't know..." I answered diffidently. "I'll find *somewhere...*"

Eva was still sitting quietly on her armchair, her hands placed on her lap as she stared at me intently. Despite her dalliances and the way she treated her husband, she had always made me feel that I was family. There was something very manipulative about her though. She would always get her way, no matter how obscure her plans could be, and everyone would just accept what she wanted.

"But I can't live – knowing that I have a grandchild *somewhere* – who I am never going to see..." Eva pleaded...

I hadn't thought about that. My parents hadn't shown any interest in having a grandchild, nor where I would be living with my baby. So why would Tony's parents care?

Eva sat there still looking at me. Her eyes were pleading, but more in a persuasive way, knowing that she would always get what she wanted.

"We would like you both to get married..." Ken said, with a smile and a look of hopefulness...

Then he agreed with Eva, that they didn't want to know that they had a grandchild somewhere that they would never see.

But weren't they being a little bit selfish I wonder? I didn't think that at the time, nor did I realise that I was being coerced into a life that I didn't really want to enter into. I didn't say anything, I just sat there – listening to what they had to say.

"We love you" Ken said, "you are like another daughter to us..."

~

My parents had never told me they loved me. Yet there were these two lovely people who were going to be grandparents of my baby – they loved me – and they wanted to be part of their grandchild's life too...

The thought of marrying Tony had never entered my head before then, and we certainly hadn't spoken about it. He and I looked at each other, as we sat there together on that settee. I don't think our eyes were saying much, but we both nodded.

"Yes" I said, yet again doing as I was told. Then I burst into tears.

~

"Well that's it" my mother said, looking like the proverbial lemon sucker, when I told her I was getting married. "You've ruined your life – you've made your bed... *Now lie on it...*"

But wasn't my life ruined the day I was born? Wasn't she so unhappy with me when I was just a tiny baby that she let Nell take me away to live with her and my grandparents at the pub?

"You don't want to do that... You don't want to do that..." she would say, whenever I really wanted to do something. How did she know what I wanted to do – or didn't want to do? She stopped me from doing so many things that I wanted to do – but made me do even more things that *I didn't want to do...*

Why did I have to get undressed when I was a little girl, in the saloon bar, and in front of men I didn't know? Why was I sent to a "party" that wasn't a party, when I was only eleven, and had to fend for myself with the two men who were trying to get me to bed? Why did she just laugh the next morning when I told her about my ordeal? Why did she turn away from me and just laugh when I told her I had been bleeding with one of my first periods for three weeks and couldn't cope with just using the rags anymore? Why, oh why, oh *why* – did I always take notice of her and do as I was told? The biggest question is though – why didn't she try to help me? Surely she must have known how unhappy I had been throughout my childhood whilst living at the pub. I was only really happy when I was out with my friends.

And now the biggest question of all – why did I just go along with Tony – when I told him it wasn't safe – but he insisted it was? Because I have always done what I am told, and I have always been told what to do...

Whatever Love Means

"**D**on't you *ever* come crying to me" my mother scolded with more venom added to the "you've made your bed – now lie in it" lecture. "You know you can never come back to this pub..." Then she muttered words like "disgrace" – "customers", even though so many customers and locals knew what was going on behind the scenes at the pub.

"No, I won't..." I assured her quietly, knowing that whatever my life was to be, I didn't want to go back to the Kings Arms – ever again... I didn't know what lay in store for me. All I knew was that I was not going to abort my baby, nor have the little love adopted. I was already feeling my overpowering love for that little boy or girl who was alive and growing inside me...

It wasn't only my life that was going to be changed forever – it was Tony's too. Once I had stopped work, and our baby was born, he would have a very young wife and child needing his assistance – and maybe some love and care...

~

It was so bad still living at the pub whilst plans were being made – sometimes unbearable. Other than my mother's rants from time to time, no-one was talking to me – absolutely no-one.

I was still having to sleep with my grandmother, which was so awkward – she never said a word to me, and I felt each night that I was getting into bed with a complete stranger.

No longer did she wake me up standing at the foot of the bed singing songs to me. She didn't even ask me to pass her the lemonade any more. I had never liked her cuddling up to me, but now the coldness towards me was tangible – and the feeling that I didn't want to be lying beside her was more prevalent than ever.

~

My pregnancy and pending marriage were being kept secret, and even my brothers didn't know that I was about to get married. Eva and Ken though were totally different, they were pleased about our predicament, and were already treating me like a daughter-in-law – or even, as they said "another daughter". So I would stay with them sometimes when it got too much, and they understood. The only difference between being married or not, was that I would sleep in Tony's bed, and he would sleep on the settee. Whenever I went back to the pub it just got worse. It was as though I didn't exist. Well I have always thought that anyway. It was difficult though walking into the only home I knew, and being ostracised – so very difficult...

~

"You can't be *in love* with – er – *him...*" my mother queried one day, during one of her rants. "I thought he was just a friend..."

Well yes, he was a friend, but no, my heart didn't go all a-flutter when I was with him. I think I could have been *"in love"* one day with Michael Pullinger – if I had been given the chance! As would every girl in the village! I wonder what would have happened if I had gone down to their house – put my head over the wall – and said "anyone for tennis?" If only!

I could have been *"in love"* with Elvis – if I had been given the chance! As would every girl in the world!

My close relationship with Tony had developed over eighteen months, as had my relationship with his lovely family. They all gave me something that I never had at home – when I was at their house I felt *enveloped* in their affection...

~

One day my mother mellowed a little and said "it's nice girls like you who get caught out – other girls go with lots of boys – but *they* know what to do..."

For that brief moment, and for once in my life, I was a "nice girl" after all – so why, oh why, hadn't I ever been treated like one?

~

My grandfather may, or may not, have been an abortionist during the war, but from what I have been told – *he was* – and all the signs were there. He wanted me to have an abortion, but it would have been "back street", so he knew who to ask, but again, he could very well have planned to do it himself...

What on earth would have happened either way? If Grandpop had carried it out – would it have been up there in that dirty loft at the pub where he kept his chemistry bottles and poison? Would I have managed to get back down the ladder again? Would my mother, grandmother or Nell have helped me? What would have happened if I was bleeding to death? What would they have done with the foetus? Where would I have recovered? Would it still have been in bed with my grandmother?

Likewise, what would life have been like if I had spent my pregnancy and given birth in my parents' loft at the bungalow? Who would have helped me give birth? What would have happened to my baby?

I can't help but think that having taken one of those options I could have died or been maimed for life – and goodness knows what would have happened to my baby...

~

Maybe my grandfather had my best interests at heart, even though an illegal abortion could have killed me, or at the very least made me infertile for life. To him, and the rest of my family at the pub, everything was so matter-of-fact. Feelings didn't come into it. Did he ever think about what he was doing to my grandmother when he used to abuse her the way he did? At least she responded in her own way by having her boyfriend. It seemed to me that maybe they were once "*in love*", and that is why my grandmother married him. "He was always so nice to me..." she had explained to my mother one time, when she asked her why she ever married him.

"I'm surprised she's still alive", my mother said to me one day when my grandfather had been particularly violent to my grandmother. "But she has a strong constitution" she added, as though well, that was alright then – "but I know there's going to be a murder in this house one day..."

I had this strange notion about marriage. My father always treated my mother very well. Well if he hadn't, he would have had my grandfather to answer to. But he was not a cruel or violent man. I think my mother might have liked him to be more like her father though. She always seemed as though she was looking for a little more excitement. If he had stood up to her more, then perhaps they both might have been happier.

So my notion was that if a husband had a mind to, he could treat his wife how he liked. Could the time have come when my grandfather had murdered my grandmother? This wasn't some kind of fantasy – this was a real danger. So I saw that violence and male adultery was all part of being married.

Besides, those films I had seen in my youth – "Dial M for Murder" starring Grace Kelly – what had she done for her husband to plan her murder? And then "Midnight Lace" starring Doris Day – it was the same kind of story. So if Tony was showing signs of aggression – wasn't that just normal?

Ivy Cottage

There was a different side to my grandfather though, one that showed itself when we used to go down the lanes walking the dogs, and he would point out to me all the different flowers and birds. I used to love those times. Then when we got back to the pub, he would go into his "Landlord and Master" mode...

One day he summoned me to the kitchen again where, as always on these occasions, he would be sitting at the table and looking very serious.

Uh-oh – was he going to have another go at trying to persuade me to have an abortion?

"Of course, you'll need somewhere to live, my dear" he said kindly. Yes, I did indeed. Then he told me that he had paid his tenants in No.1 Ivy Cottage – an offer they couldn't refuse – to move out, so that Tony and I could live there.

"You'll have to pay me £2 a week rent" he said, as I stood there trying to take it all in. Well that was what I was paying my mother anyway.

"And I'll give you and young Tony £100 to do it up", he added. "How does that sound?"

Oh! That was unbelievable... I was suddenly to have a home of my own – and the money to do it up!

I was *so* – *so* grateful – and suddenly, the world seemed a little brighter.

~

Ivy Cottage did indeed need doing up. The previous tenants hadn't seemed to care for it, and they had even taken my grandfather's large collection of Toby jugs that he had hung from the beams in the living room when they left. The back door, which led into the kitchen, didn't quite reach the floor, so draughts – and mice – were coming in through there. There was no bathroom, so stand-up washes at the kitchen sink, and baths at the pub were in order, usually in the afternoons, when my grandfather was either out or asleep. Also, the toilet was outside – so lots of trudging out there in the dark!

None of that mattered too much though. I loved that cottage. It had a garden at the back, which I could plant and tend, and this led to the fields, and the view of the dilapidated windmill which looked wonderful in the sunset.

I loved the whole history of the cottage. As I have mentioned before, my grandfather once showed me the title deeds, which went back to when the cottages were first built. They were on yellowed parchment and written in meticulous calligraphy, and with a wavy line down the side that he explained had to be matched with the other side if anyone else took ownership of the property.

It was all so interesting, especially knowing that I was going to be living in a property of great historical interest – well to that area of Essex anyway. It had once been a landmark, being the "bakers" of Baker Street – and the original oven was still in No.2 Ivy Cottages. Even Grays Library had shown interest in the property as being an "important" property.

I was a little uneasy about my neighbour-to-be though. She was Mrs. Jobson, Celia's mother. Celia was the girl to whom my grandfather had given my dolls' house that my father had just finished making for me. Celia had now left home, but it was deep set in my heart that Mrs. Jobson had accepted that dolls' house for Celia. Didn't she even ask my grandfather why?

Neither did I ask him though.

As always, I was never to question *why* about anything...

~

I didn't know what my mother thought about me living in Baker Street, because I would still be in Orsett, and the customers and locals would see me as my pregnancy progressed. However, she did tell me that I wouldn't be going out shopping with her any more, as it would be too embarrassing for her with people staring at me, such a young girl being pregnant.

I can see her reasoning, but why did she feel so sorry for other girls in the area who got pregnant whilst still teenagers? She hadn't seen anything wrong with Elaine, the girl who she gave all my baby clothes to...

"When are you going to get yourself a bloke", she used to say to me when I was still at school. She seemed to think – and made me feel – that there was something wrong me with me that I didn't have a boyfriend like other girls.

Well now I had – and look what happened to me...

~

With £100 in cash in my purse, Tony and I went to the decorating shop in Grays. It was the same shop where eight years earlier, when I was nine years old, I had chosen the wallpaper and paint for what I thought was to be my bedroom. Now I was choosing wallpaper and paint again.

I knew straight away that the wallpaper I was gazing at and touching was the right one... It was a raised design of white broderie anglaise on a pale pink background. It was so pretty, and the illusion of fabric would give a warm look to the bedroom. Tony agreed with my choice, he didn't have an opinion on bedroom wallpaper anyway.

The cottage was furnished, albeit basically, but what was in there was "antique" furniture, which I have since found out had belonged to Uncle George, one of my grandfather's brothers.

I loved it. I felt so "at home" doing up that little cottage. Tony was wallpapering, and we were both painting most evenings, so as to have it finished before we got married.

~

"You don't know what you're in for" my mother informed me, when I spoke to her about setting the wedding date – and she didn't mean married life...

"You will have that long brown rubber tube put up your bottom – filled with soapy water which will go right into your bowel – that is called an enema... And that is just the start..."

So that was what the long brown tube was all about.

"And then you're going to have the worst pain you have ever experienced" she added, "and don't forget – they don't treat unmarried mothers kindly you know..."

But I wasn't to be an unmarried mother though – I was going to be married. I just hoped that they would believe me.

I went down to Woolworths in Grays, which I knew was a good source of fake jewellery – I was looking for a replica wedding ring to tide me over until I was actually married. To my surprise they had lots of fake wedding rings for sale, and I can't help but think that they sold a lot at the time! Even so, I still felt rather awkward buying it. At least it would only have to last for a few weeks until I was married.

I still have that ring – and it is as bright as the day I bought it.

~

The day of my first ante-natal examination arrived, and I walked the mile down to Orsett hospital on my own. I had never had an internal examination before, and I was very – very – nervous. I kept telling myself it was just a doctor and maybe a nurse – and it was all in a day's work.

To my absolute horror there were three or four male students in there standing next to the examination couch – and they were all so young, not much older than me. Unlike these days, I wasn't asked my permission to have students in attendance, so I had no option.

The nurse told me quite abruptly to take off my knickers – and lay down on the couch. This was *so* embarrassing – why couldn't I have been given a gown, and somewhere to get undressed? Taking off my knickers in front of four male students was really not on.

Memories of getting undressed in the saloon bar after time, in front of men who I didn't know, came flooding back. This was beginning to be unbearable – but as always, I was doing what I was being told to do...

I lay back on the examination couch wondering what was going to happen. The nurse wasn't impressed by my fake gold wedding ring. I was beginning to think that my mother was right in how an unmarried mother could be treated – and this was only the first appointment.

She pulled my skirt and petticoat up to my waist, and I noticed that the students were all looking at each other with knowing smiles...

"Now draw your legs right up" the nurse instructed – "and then just let them fall open..."

Well I drew my legs up, but by now I was trembling and shaking so much that I couldn't open my legs. All these people were about to peer at the part of my body that I held most private. In fact, despite being pregnant, I hadn't even been looked at there before, apart from Nell when she used to rub that awful cream on...

I was so aware that the students were looking at my bottom half – and in anticipation of what was about to happen... I felt sure this was their first viewing of an internal examination...

"Open your legs... Open your legs..." the nurse was shouting at me...

The doctor was getting very impatient with me, as he stood with his right hand at the ready. By now I was crying and I had no control over the shaking of my legs.

Suddenly, the nurse got hold of my knees – then thrust them apart. She was holding them tightly so I couldn't move. My legs were still shaking, despite the firmness of her grip. I felt so exposed and open as she held my legs firmly apart like that.

I tried not to look at the grinning students, but they were now all taking a closer look as the doctor put his hand inside me...

This was just the beginning...

The Dawning

I was willing to make a go of our marriage for the sake of that little baby that was growing inside me, and Tony's parents were being very supportive. I never did make that call to Mrs. Binns (Matthews), although looking back, if she and Jack had been kind enough to take me in, I might have got on alright as an unmarried mother. I could have gone on to find somewhere else to live and maybe taken in home typing work. They could have said no, but it would have been worth a go. They had always shown a lot of affection to me, and as I have said, I felt pretty sure that they might take me in, if only for the next few months.

What would happen after that, I really didn't know. Where would I have given birth? Where would I have lived alone with my baby? Whatever lay ahead of me, no matter how destitute I may have turned out to be, I was *not going to give up my baby...*

~

But now – I was getting married.

"We'll do whatever we can to help you" Ken said, and I believed him. He was a lovely, and very genuine man. He was also actually normal – and I hadn't met many normal men in my life.

Eva wasn't quite as "normal" as a wife, having her boyfriend Norman, but that was only what I had come to accept from the goings on at the pub, and besides, it was none of my business. That was between her and Ken. The main thing is, they had welcomed me into their home, their family – and their hearts.

~

One day I came home to the pub from work in London feeling absolutely wretched. I had had a hard day, still nauseous, unable to eat, and travelling on the bus and train. I knew that my hopes of ever being the Managing Director's secretary were now completely dashed, as very soon everyone would know that I was about to get married – and the reason why would be showing...

I went into my grandmother's bedroom where I still slept with her, and my mother was in there – going through all my things...

Everything I had was out on the bed, well everything that she had found was. I felt awful, it was such an invasion of privacy, although I had never had the normality of privacy in my life.

She held up a portrait photo of Adam that he had given me, which I secretly treasured, even though I knew I would never see him again.

"You won't be wanting *this* anymore..." she said, with a horrible black stare, as she tore it right down the middle...

Poor, good-looking Adam – I hated seeing his face torn in half like that... And then she tore the photo up into little bits in front of me, letting them all fall to the floor...

~

My mother looked at me with a look of disgrace, and her usual lemon sucking disgust, when I went into the kitchen at the pub and told her I was about to go to the Registry Office with Tony to confirm our wedding date.

"Mind you tell him to change your date of birth" she instructed, adding that she didn't want it to be known that her daughter was married when she was only seventeen.

Of course, as difficult as it was, I went along with what she had told me to do. It was indoctrinated into me to *always* do whatever she told me to do – no matter how embarrassing or bad it was.

"My mother said can you change my date of birth to 1948 please?" I obeyed quietly, asking the Registrar, knowing that "my" request was futile. It was one of those terrible moments when I knew that I would be put down doing as my mother told me, but nevertheless I *had to – I was doing as I was told...*

The Registrar remained solemn, as he answered with a very strong "No". His female assistant turned to him with some strange sort of grin that made me feel I was a little girl back in the infants, not someone about to get married. The date was set for Thursday 23rd March.

~

I was standing in the pub kitchen on my own, just gazing out of the window towards the wet grey car park which had once been our garden. The green lawn where I had played with my friends, and the Victorian roses that would fill my senses with their deep perfume, had all long gone – that terrible day when I came home from school to find all these beautiful wonders of my little world churned up and ready to be taken away forever. All I could see was greyness; the sky was still heavy from a thunderous storm, and the car park merged into a watercolour wash of nothingness.

Someone opened the door and came into the kitchen. It was my father. He stood there just looking at me as I turned to face him.

"I am giving you my blessing" he said quietly and looking very sad.

I smiled shyly. "Thank you Daddy" I whispered.

~

"Don't you get anything *white!*" my mother instructed when I told her that I was going to Oxford Street to find my wedding outfit. "No, I won't" I assured her.

Where had all my hopes and dreams gone of having a wedding like other people, taking my vows in Orsett Church with Reverend Godwin, with whom I had grown up, and my family there wishing me well, and showering me with pastel-coloured confetti? That was never to be.

I just do not understand all the pomp and glory these days. The bride has to have her "day". Some may say I am just jealous. But I am not. I would have loved to have worn a simple white silk dress, but most of all – I had always wanted to take my wedding vows in Church.

~

The outfit that I chose was lovely though. It was a cream lace sleeveless dress, just on the knee, and a matching cream lace coat. To go with it I went to Manfield shoe shop in Oxford Street, and bought a pair of leather, light-gold shoes with a little shaped heel, and a matching tiny leather handbag.

I still have these things, stowed away somewhere, along with the peachy pink Yardley lipstick that I wore on the day. It may not have that same distinctive smell that Yardley lipsticks used to have, but it has never lost its colour, and nor has its gold coloured, star-patterned case tainted in any way.

But why do I keep all these items? I really don't know. Do I have to be reminded about all these things? No, I don't have to – but in some strange sort of way – I *need to keep them...*

~

22*nd* March – around midnight

"I'm getting married tomorrow" I reminded everyone, as they stood around the counter in the saloon bar having late night drinks. Everyone suddenly went silent. I think they had all forgotten, because no-one had said a word about it. I wanted them to acknowledge what I was just about to embark upon the next day, to perhaps hopefully toast me, and to drink to my future happiness – but of course they didn't.

"I hope you've got your fur trimmed night-dress" my father suddenly exclaimed with a laugh.

"Why?" I asked him, innocently.

"To keep your neck warm..." he laughed – and so did everyone else.

This was all so utterly embarrassing, and I didn't say a word.

"Right – you've made your bed now – so lie on it", my mother scorned again, her eyes now glaring. "And when it all goes wrong – don't come crying to me... And don't you *ever think you can come back here...*"

"No, I won't" I very quietly agreed.

~

23*rd* March 9am

I was at the hairdresser's in Grays having my hair done. Although it was growing again, I had had my long hair cut really short, as Tony had wanted me to look like Petula Clark! Petula Clark? Had he really thought he could transform me just on a whim to look like someone else? But, as usual, I had gone along with it.

It had grown to an acceptable length, but it wasn't as manageable as having it long.

I sat in the chair having my hair put in rollers, and then I was put under the dryer for a while – one of those dryers with the big pink hood. I so much wanted to tell the hairdresser that I was *getting married* today, and that was what this hairdo was for. But I didn't. I didn't have all that fuss of sitting there with my bridesmaids, all having our hair done together, with pretty fabric flowers woven into the curls, or being fitted with a rhinestone tiara.

No, to the hairdresser, this was just another day. She tried to make small talk, as all hairdressers do.

"Are you going anywhere special tonight?" she asked.

I hesitated. Tonight I would be moving full-time into Ivy Cottage – *that* was pretty special. But I didn't say anything at all...

If she had asked me about my day, then yes, I might have said I was – *getting married...* But she didn't...

There was no fuss. My hair was done – and then I caught the No.53 bus and went back to the pub to get ready.

~

No-one said a word as I got ready in my wedding outfit. My grandmother was up and sitting at the breakfast table in the kitchen, so I was able to get dressed in her bedroom without disturbing her in bed.

There were no bridesmaids fussing around, primping and preening, zipping me up and twiddling with my hair. There was no mother looking at me proudly with dewy eyes remembering her wedding day, and wishing me a lifetime of happiness. No, nothing like that. To everyone else – this was just another day.

~

So there I was, all dressed up, and about to cross over the road to the telephone box on the corner. This was around the time that the burglars had broken in, poisoned poor Butch, and had cut all the telephone lines, so we didn't have a working phone in the pub.

I was on the edge of the kerb and about to cross the road, when my father appeared. It was a Thursday – shouldn't he have been at work?

"What are you doing?" he asked me, as I teetered on the edge of that high kerb.

"I'm going to call for a taxi" I answered.

"But why?" he queried.

"Because I'm going to get married" I said.

"Get in the car" he beckoned – "I'll take you down..."

Oh!

So I got into the front passenger seat of the car, which he had just driven out of the garage and parked in the pub car park. Perhaps he had been getting the car out of the garage to take my mother to Tesco's shopping – I don't know – but there it was...

Then he disappeared, but not long later he came back to the car – wearing his best grey double-breasted suit – and matching grey trilby hat, that he always kept in the fourth bedroom at the pub. I must say, he did look rather dapper.

"I am sorry Daddy" I whispered, looking down at my lap, as he sat next to me in the driver's seat. Long moments of silence followed. If only he could have said that he was sorry too – sorry for not sheltering me from the danger and vice that I had to encounter living at the pub. Sorry for papering and painting my pretty bedroom at the bungalow blue for my brothers to take over. Sorry for not being a proper father to me, and for letting my mother treat me as though I was worthless. Sorry for the whole rotten life I had to put up with at the pub. But no, he stayed silent, just looking straight ahead, as though he didn't want to start the car. I still sat looking down at my lap.

~

My cream lace dress looked beautiful as its scalloped hem rose slightly above my small knees. I followed the edge of that pretty lace, as it wrapped around my thin legs. I felt so demure, so very Grace Kelly. But unlike the lovely Princess Grace – I was not going off to marry my prince...

~

Suddenly – my mother appeared.

"What are you doing?" she asked, frowning as always.

"I'm taking Yvonne to get married" Daddy said.

"Oh – I'll come then" she uttered, going indoors. She came out a short while later, wearing her beige coat and very plain little blue hat that she always wore to Tesco's.

Then my grandmother appeared...

"What are you doing?" she asked too, standing there, not seeming to know what was going on.

"We're taking Yvonne down to get married" my father answered.

"Just a minute" Nanny said – and she went back into the pub.

A few minutes later she appeared again, wearing her nice cream spring coat and her pink hat – so it just might have been a special day after all. Well, other than the fact that she was wearing her normal day clothes and cardigan underneath...

So there we were – four of us now in the car – and the time was ticking round – tick tock – tick tock – it was almost wedding time...

We left the car park, and turned into Baker Street.

"So where are we going?" my father asked...

~

We arrived at the Registry Office, my father's pale green Cortina unadorned with any wedding paraphernalia, and saw that Tony was waiting there, with Eva and Ken, and Susan and her boyfriend. Ken's car was festooned with white ribbons, showing that they were obviously very proud taking their son to get married. I didn't have any flowers, but Susan handed me a white satin horseshoe with a silver coloured "Good Luck" token attached. I think I needed that!

We all went into the office, and Tony and I walked up to the desk where we were to take our vows... I can't remember exactly what they were, but they were pretty much like a Church wedding service, but without the religious part.

I felt a long way away from Orsett Church and Reverend Godwin. Where were my senses? Was God with me that day? Were the angels with me? Would someone step forward when the Registrar asked if there was anyone who had any just reason for this marriage not to go ahead?

No, nothing happened...

And so I very quietly took my vows, not knowing if Tony really wanted this marriage either. Why had he disappeared when I became pregnant? Would he have been happier forgetting about me and the child I was carrying? I didn't know...

But my mother's words were solidly in my brain – *"Don't come crying to me... Don't you ever think you can come back here..."*

~

But what was there to go back to? *Nothing...*

I made an extra silent vow to myself – I would never treat my child or children as I had been treated... And I never did.

I turned around to face my parents, who were standing behind Tony's. My mother had her normal disapproving scowl on her face, which was to be expected. And then I looked at my father – tears were streaming from his blue eyes down his cheeks. Why hadn't he ever shown me this kind of emotion before?

Maybe my childhood was rushing through his mind – the times that I was hurt, both physically and mentally, and the times that I sobbed all through the night. But he didn't know that though – because he wasn't there...

Maybe – he blamed himself – or maybe he blamed my mother. Maybe he blamed my grandfather, and the whole dirty saga in which I grew up at the pub. But that I will never know, because he never talked to me about it.

Maybe – ultimately – from what he knew about Tony – he was guessing what I was about to be in for...

~

If only I could have married Elvis... Then I really would have been

"The Girl in the King's Arms"